Cognitive Semiotics

Bloomsbury Advances in Semiotics

Semiotics has complemented linguistics by expanding its scope beyond the phoneme and the sentence to include texts and discourse, and their rhetorical, performative, and ideological functions. It has brought into focus the multimodality of human communication. *Advances in Semiotics* publishes original works in the field demonstrating robust scholarship, intellectual creativity, and clarity of exposition. These works apply semiotic approaches to linguistics and nonverbal productions, social institutions and discourses, embodied cognition and communication, and the new virtual realities that have been ushered in by the Internet. It also is inclusive of publications in relevant domains such as socio-semiotics, evolutionary semiotics, game theory, cultural and literary studies, human-computer interactions, and the challenging new dimensions of human networking afforded by social websites.

Series Editor: Paul Bouissac is Professor Emeritus at the University of Toronto (Victoria College), Canada. He is a world renowned figure in semiotics and a pioneer of circus studies. He runs the SemiotiX Bulletin [www.semioticon.com/semiotix] which has a global readership.

Titles in the series include:

Computable Bodies, Josh Berson
Critical Semiotics, Gary Genosko
Music as Multimodal Discourse, edited by Lyndon C. S. Way and Simon McKerrell
Peirce's Twenty-Eight Classes of Signs and the Philosophy of Representation, Tony Jappy
Semiotics and Pragmatics of Stage Improvisation, Domenico Pietropaolo
Semiotics of Happiness, Ashley Frawley
The Languages of Humor, edited by Arie Sover
The Semiotics of Caesar Augustus, Elina Pyy
The Semiotics of Clowns and Clowning, Paul Bouissac
The Semiotics of Che Guevara, Maria-Carolina Cambre
The Semiotics of Emoji, Marcel Danesi
The Semiotics of Light and Shadows, Piotr Sadowski
The Semiotics of X, Jamin Pelkey
The Social Semiotics of Tattoos, Chris William Martin

Cognitive Semiotics

Signs, Mind and Meaning

Per Aage Brandt

BLOOMSBURY ACADEMIC
LONDON • NEW YORK • OXFORD • NEW DELHI • SYDNEY

BLOOMSBURY ACADEMIC
Bloomsbury Publishing Plc
50 Bedford Square, London, WC1B 3DP, UK
1385 Broadway, New York, NY 10018, USA
29 Earlsfort Terrace, Dublin 2, Ireland

BLOOMSBURY, BLOOMSBURY ACADEMIC and the Diana logo
are trademarks of Bloomsbury Publishing Plc

First published in Great Britain 2020
This paperback edition published in 2021

Copyright © Per Aage Brandt, 2020
Per Aage Brandt has asserted his right under the Copyright,
Designs and Patents Act, 1988, to be identified as Author of this work.

For legal purposes the Acknowledgments on p. viii constitute
an extension of this copyright page.

Cover image: © Neil Setchfield / Hiroshi Watanabe /
The Image Bank / Getty Images

All rights reserved. No part of this publication may be reproduced or transmitted
in any form or by any means, electronic or mechanical, including photocopying,
recording, or any information storage or retrieval system, without prior
permission in writing from the publishers.

Bloomsbury Publishing Plc does not have any control over, or responsibility for,
any third-party websites referred to or in this book. All internet addresses given
in this book were correct at the time of going to press. The author and publisher
regret any inconvenience caused if addresses have changed or sites have ceased
to exist, but can accept no responsibility for any such changes.

A catalogue record for this book is available from the British Library.

A catalog record for this book is available from the Library of Congress.

ISBN: HB: 978-1-3501-4330-2
PB: 978-1-3501-8966-9
ePDF: 978-1-3501-4331-9
eBook: 978-1-3501-4332-6

Series: Bloomsbury Advances in Semiotics

Typeset by Integra Software Services Pvt. Ltd.

To find out more about our authors and books visit www.bloomsbury.com
and sign up for our newsletters.

Contents

List of Figures — vi
Acknowledgments — viii

1 Introduction — 1
2 On the Mind of the Body: Spinoza, Descartes, and the Philosophy of Cognition — 15
3 The Architecture of the Embodied Mind — 31
4 On Consciousness and Semiosis — 41
5 The Dia-logic of Discourse — 57
6 Mental Spaces and Discourse — 65
7 More on Mental Architecture, Spaces, and Blending — 83
8 Blending in the Poetics of Songs: Leonard Cohen's *Hallelujah* — 103
9 Forces and Spaces—Maupassant, Borges, Hemingway — 117
10 The Meaning of Translation — 147
11 Elements in Poetic Imagination — 161
12 Words in Language and Thought — 175
13 Numbers Are Things in Time — 187
14 The Meaning and Madness of Money — 203
15 Postscript — 231

Index — 238

Figures

1.1	The circularity of research	10
2.1	Spinoza's view of the constitution of meaning as truth	18
3.1	Five levels of integration in meaning production	32
3.2	Symbols in mental architecture	35
3.3	Icons in mental architecture	37
4.1	Subject "intending" Object. Subject surrounded by space	41
4.2	Subject situated and intending	42
4.3	Subject and Relevant Others of salient categories in the immediate surrounding space	42
4.4	Five levels of consciousness	51
5.1	Arguments in dialogue	59
5.2	A construction model of discourse	59
5.3	A mental space network for conditionality	60
5.4	Dialogue with the Lord	61
6.1	Thermometer as a material anchor	77
6.2	Probe barrier schema	77
6.3	Double network in painting	79
7.1	Mental space building. "In 1929, the president was a baby."	83
7.2	The space delegation cusp	85
7.3	Space delegation types	85
7.4	The mental architecture of perceptive integrations	88
7.5	The mental architecture of agentive integrations	89
7.6	*If I were you ...*	90
7.7	XYZ. Louis Armstrong is the king of jazz!	91
7.8	Metaphor. *Snake in the grass* blending	92
7.9	Hypothesis. What on earth is going on here? Could it be ... X? Or Y? ... Or ...	94
7.10	Agency as a blending network	95
8.1	The semiotic blending model	107
8.2	The first blend	108
8.3	The resulting blend	110
9.1	Narrative forces	119

9.2	Narrative world variations	121
9.3	Diegesis of "The Diamond Necklace."	124
9.4	Diegesis of "A Piece of String."	127
9.5	Diegesis of "Emma Zunz."	129
9.6	Diegesis of "La otra muerte."	131
9.7	Diegesis of "A Very Short Story."	132
9.8	The force-barrier schema	133
9.9	Semiotic square of *making* and *letting*	136
9.10	Force-barrier schema of *letting* and *not letting*	137
9.11	*Letting* versus *making*	137
10.1	The semiotic formula of translation	147
10.2	Formula of the untranslatable expression and its semiotic loop	149
10.3	Six semiotic instances and their interaction	151
10.4	Genres of translation	153
10.5	Greimas' model of actant structure	154
10.6	The actant dynamics of writing	155
10.7	The actant dynamics of translating	155
11.1	The strata of the bio-imaginary space	163
11.2	The strata of the socio-imaginary space	163
11.3	The strata of the phantasmatic imaginary	164
12.1	Language, seen from the *word*	176
12.2	Enunciation as a deictic structure	178
12.3	Stemmatic representation of (1)	180
12.4	Unstable exchange	181
13.1	The Aztec calendar. A (originally colored) rendition of the Sun Stone, or the Stone of Axayacatl. Museo de Antropología, México DF	189
13.2	Cave painting: Kondusi stick dance. The painting may date 25,000 years BP. This reproduction is in the Nairobi National Museum	193
13.3	A blending network of exchange and value	196
13.4	Borneo, Gua Tewet, The tree of life. From Luc-Henri Fage, *Borneo, Memory of the Caves*, Kalimanthrope, 2010	197
13.5	The synesthetic cascade	198
14.1	A negentropic loop	204
14.2	The organic, the technical, and the symbolic loops on the entropic flow	206
14.3	Three strata and six stasis categories in the formation of social reality	208
14.4	The three forms of monetary capital (in grey on the graph): reproductive, productive, and financial	210
15.1	A socio-ecological topology	233

Acknowledgments

Every effort has been made to trace copyright holders and to obtain their permission for the use of copyright material in this book. The author is grateful for the permission to republish the following articles:

"On the Mind of the Body. Spinoza, Descartes, and the Philosophy of Cognition"
> An earlier version was published in the journal *Language and Semiotic Studies*, Vol. 2, 1, 2016. Soochow University.

"The Architecture of the Embodied Mind"
> An earlier version was published in the net journal *TECCOGS, Revista Digital de Tecnologias Cognitivas*, #4, 2010, PUC-São Paulo.

"On Consciousness and Semiosis"
> An earlier version was published in the journal *Cognitive Semiotics*, #1, 2007. Peter Lang Verlag.

"Mental Spaces and Discourse"
> An earlier version appeared in *Journal of Pragmatics*, Vol. 37, 10, 2005. Elsevier.

"More on Mental Architecture, Spaces, and Blending"
> An earlier version was published in (Ed.) Douglas Niño, *Ensayos semioticos II: Semiotica e integracion conceptual*. Universidad de Bogota Jorge Tadeo Lozano, Col. Humanidades, 2013.

"The Meaning of Translation"
> An earlier version was published in (Ed.) Peter Hanenberg, *A New Visibility: On Culture, Translation, and Cognition*. Universidade Catolica Editora, 2015.

"Elements in Poetic Imagination"
> An earlier version was published in the journal *Cognitive Semiotics*, #2, 2008. Peter Lang Verlag.

"Words in Language and Thought"
> An extended version was published in *Acta Linguistica Hafniensia*, Vol. 50, 1. Taylor & Francis Eds. 2018.

"Numbers Are Things in Time"
> A reduced version of this text was published in (Eds.) Bockarova, Danesi, Nuñez, *Semiotic and Cognitive Science Essays on the Nature of Mathematics*. Fields Cognitive Science Network: Empirical Study of Mathematics and How It Is Learned, LINCOM GmbH, 2012.

"The Meaning and Madness of Money"
> Earlier versions were published in the journal *Language and Semiotic Studies*, Vol. 3, 3, Soochow University, 2017, and in the journal *Cognitive Semiotics*, Vol. 10, 2, De Gruyter, 2017.

1

Introduction

The essays in this book originated from my work at the Center for Semiotics, University of Aarhus, at the Center for Advanced Study in the Behavioral Sciences, Stanford, and finally at Case Western Reserve University, all written since the turn of the century and most of them after my latest volume of essays, *Spaces, Domains, and Meaning* (2004). I want, first and foremost, to thank my editors Paul Bouissac and Andrew Wardell for opening their series *Advances in Semiotics* to my book and for their insightful suggestions as to the difficult selection of texts from the much larger inventory of recent papers in cognitive semiotics I proposed.

Where This Comes From

The direction in research on meaning represented in this book draws both on cognitive science, including linguistics, semantics, poetics, and on general semiotics, including the often competing schools of Ferdinand de Saussure and Charles S. Peirce. It emerged in the 1980s, when the interest in force dynamics in cognitive semantics—as proposed by Ronald Langacker, Leonard Talmy, Eve Sweetser—met the semiotic interest in dynamic phenomena in structural semantics as understood in Algirdas-Julien Greimas' Paris school. In my own history, this happened early in the 1980s, while I prepared my Thèse d'Etat at the Sorbonne with Professor Greimas, on the modalities, and discussed with my own generation of scholars, in particular philosopher Jean Petitot and linguist Wolfgang Wildgen. Both had direct contacts with the mathematician-philosopher René Thom, who had developed a "qualitative mathematics" for purposes of morphological, biological, and linguistic analyses. Thom's "morpho-genetics" appeared to be compatible with Greimas' structural semantics, especially via the reanalysis of dynamical schemas that allowed us to account for and rewrite many semantic formalizations in the more logical style used by Greimasian semioticians. Talmy's model of force dynamics and his work on causation, as well as Sweetser's work on the modalities, fitted well in this emergent framework, and Scandinavian semiotics of the 1990s now became a laboratory of the new, dynamical, cognitive semiotics, in particular at the Center for Semiotics at the University of Aarhus—an institution of which the glossematic, structural linguist Louis Hjelmslev had been one of the founding fathers. Then the cognitive literary scholar Mark Turner and the logician Gilles Fauconnier came into the picture with their mental space theory (MST) and its prolongation, the conceptual blending analysis, which we had the opportunity to discuss in San Diego, at Stanford, in Aarhus, and later in Cleveland. In my Danish context, it became clear rather early that a semiotic elaboration of this theory was possible, and that it was even needed in order to take its potential insights out of the rather nominalistic analytic framework and place it in a viable phenomenological environment. We thus developed an "Aarhus model" of semiotic blending, described at length by Line Brandt (2013), who contributed substantially. We created a journal, *Cognitive Semiotics*, in 2007 and, later, a supporting association. My role in the latter is now marginal; after finishing my teaching career, I have returned to my former research milieu in France.

Semiotics was often conceived as the more or less intuitive study of signs in society and of their direct and indirect messages, the latter to discover and criticize, as in Roland Barthes' *Mythologies*, or as a social extension of logic, devoted to the study of inferences in informal thinking in communication, fiction, and discourse, as in Umberto Eco's *The Absent Structure*. There were hardly any semiotic attempts to philosophically ground the research on communication in a *phenomenology of meaning*, despite the impact of Maurice Merleau-Ponty's *Signs*, or in a study of *human cognition*, despite Jean Piaget's *Structuralism*, that is, of the role of the *mind's own configurations* in the configurations of signs and language. In short, signs and signification were one thing, and minds and cognition were seen as something totally different. Semiotics, in the humanities, was too distant from any idea of "hard science" to approach the underlying questions.

The classical cognitive sciences, psychology and linguistics, are experimental disciplines that often prefer to avoid theoretical commitments, apart from evolutionary hypotheses, and although it is generally accepted that cognition is in a sense both individual and collective, there are few theoretical suggestions as to how the "collectivization" of cognition happens. In view of the fact that human beings spend most of their lives exchanging signs of all kinds with conspecifics and animals, and that these exchanges manifestly determine much of the mind's properties, it is also the fact that these cognitive disciplines have long missed the opportunity to develop a noticeable interest in semiotics (despite David McNeill's gesture studies).

Cognitive studies need to become (more) semiotic, as much as semiotics needs to become (more) cognitive, if a more fully developed research into mind, meaning, and signs is to be achieved. This is the general claim of this book. The essays offered in this book suggest some basic principles and models that typically address both the cognitive and the semiotic side of meaning. The stratifying model I call *mental architecture* describes a fundamental dimension in meaning formation, one that language follows rather closely. The *mental space* model describes the elementary principles of more complex meaning formation via conceptual blending, a process rooted in communication. The model of *semantic domains* shows how complex meanings, on higher levels of the architecture, naturally unfold, across cultures, as different modes of experience and imagination. My last essay in this book, inspired by the difficult question of the semiotic status of money—is it a sign?—explores the social and ecological grounds of meaning formation and finds, among other surprising things, that these meaning modes give rise to a canonical series of *expressive modes* that might explain both the sign classes and the basic ecological structure of human societies. This finding changes our view of how society and subjectivity are related.

What Happens in This Book?

Chapter 2 offers an episode of my inquiry into the *metaphysics of meaning* as springing from classical rationalism and in particular, opposing within the framework of rationalist thinking, the "dualism" of Descartes and the "monism" of Spinoza. Grosso modo it can be said that works of cognitive science prefer references to Spinoza and Spinozist patterns of reasoning, hence the influence of logical empiricism in these works, whereas semiotics is "continental" in the sense of walking in Descartes' footsteps. Spinoza is to Descartes as cognition to semiotics. The contrast between these two lines in modern rationalism is striking. I try to pinpoint the essential questions involved, such as the understanding of the relations holding between mind and body, Descartes' *res cogitans* and *res extensa*—the immaterial meanings and the material things, which in Spinoza are aspects, attributes, viewpoints, or facets of the very same entities. Descartes posits possible causal relations in both directions between mind and body, since they are different but connected substances or realities, while his critic, Spinoza, rejects such relations, given that for him, minds and bodies, or concepts and material referents of concepts, are ontologically the same. Spinoza therefore rejects the possibility of an autonomous semantics, which for Descartes is an obvious possibility. This philosophical debate of course concerns a cognitive semiotics directly. My conclusion recommends a mostly Cartesian but more explicitly embodied and Spinoza-friendly phenomenological ontology more generously inviting empirical research on signified meaning. My particular use of the terms *body, bodily, embodied, embodiment* is due to this preliminary philosophical inquiry.

Chapter 3 explores the *mental architecture* of perceived meanings that integrate to form the levels of mental content that attention can fixate: *qualia* integrate into *objects* that integrate into *scenarios*, scenarios integrate into *concepts*, and concepts eventually inform our *affective* states. Five levels are distinguished and compared to the possible levels of signifiers in language. Mental contents span from perception to concepts that make our affects meaningful. Affective states in turn influence our somatic states, so we may think of the afferent, integrative processes of consciousness as extending from the somatic sensory realm to the equally somatic realm beyond consciousness. "Mind" runs from perceptive soma to affective soma. Contents are furthermore signified by efferent processes linking lower-level signifiers to higher-level signifieds. Since the linked items can be stabilized in social exchange, signs can be read as they are expressed, in afference as in efference. Signs work both ways. I show that iconicity is a particularly clear case.

Chapter 4 presents a *narrative* model of situational and actantial meaning in animal and human *consciousness*, compatible with the architecture just shown. On the level of scenario representation, a dynamic constellation of narrative "actants" emerges. The subject is intentionally attracted to a value object but has to confront an antagonist and seek help from an adjuvant, who also may be determined by the same attractor.

The resulting intersubjective interactions involve mimetic fights with antagonists and symbolic exchanges with adjuvants, that is, semiotic acts delaying the access to the object and thereby dramatizing the scenario. Immediate situational awareness thus implies a narrative default setting of intersubjective phenomenology, and the essay shows how this leads to affective perspectives determining both an ethical condition (based on helping versus harming) and an aesthetic perspective. The affective investment of the object may singularize it as the unique target of desire and inscribe it in a logic of love that ends in self-consciousness and something like the momentary disappearance of the self in higher-order instants of impersonal "pure thought." None of this could happen without the narrative grounds of immediate situational consciousness. However, it takes many cognitive-semiotic steps to reach such a final level of meaning.

Chapter 5 takes us further in the direction of otherness in language, namely toward a view of *coherence in discourse as built on dialogue*, a view and a model that explain the linking of arguments in coherent discourse as based on presupposed, implicit, virtual interpersonal exchange set in terms of the pragmatic and semantic relation between speaker and hearer, writer and reader, in discourse. I first offer a pragmatic text example, then an application of the analysis to the understanding of *conditionality* as an implicit interpersonal and dialogical relation. My second pragmatic example is somewhat poetic, a simulated prayer found in the media of American political and religious communication. It shows us a remarkable negotiation with God. Finally, I present and comment on three stanzas by the renowned American poet Rosmarie Waldrop, whose contemporary "language poetry" would be unreadable without the dialogical approach here recommended. Language is thoroughly structured by and for dialogue, from internal sentence grammar to coherent social discourse.

Chapter 6 presents the theory of *mental spaces* and the technical development of conceptual *blending* theory. It applies the philosophical criticism (discussed in Chapter 2) to the problematic aspects of these theories or models, in view of a new version of MST that depends less on analytic (Spinozan) views of meaning, and which makes possible and even necessary a semiotic explicitation of the grounds of blending in semiosis and particularly in discourse. The discourse-grounded model presents the advantage of being able to take over the cognitive, conceptual metaphor modeling and to avoid some of its weaknesses. It offers clearer accounts of the blending process in textbook cases discussed as examples of the former version, such as the "material anchors" that combine symbolic and indexical signification, and it lets us venture into the study of pictorial meaning formation, that is, blending theory applied to visual art, here a famous painting by Henri Matisse.

Chapter 7 further develops the *semantic* account given above on stratified mental architecture, especially the elementary but still complex question of determining the types of links we establish from space to space, by what I call "space delegation," in time and space but also in terms of other mental modes of existence. And it applies this stratifying model to a series of semantic problems calling for clarification, such as counterfactual conditionality (*If I were you…*), evaluative projection (*X is the Y of Z*), metaphor, hypothesis (similar to C. S. Peirce's abduction), and, finally, intentional agency (involving the semantics of motivated action). This chapter is a laboratory of what I consider to be wonderful problems.

Chapter 8, on blending in songs, and a detailed analysis of a masterpiece, *Hallelujah*, coauthored by the Swedish semiotician and rock music specialist Ulf Cronquist, explores the legendary song by Leonard Cohen (who was also a great poet). After some obligatory philology, we first discuss the important general difference between a *song* and a *poem*, pragmatically and semantically. Then we describe this song and its musical structure and the role of lyrical metrics in relation to the music. The semiotic blending network, once more explained, lets us see how the schematizing musical pattern affects the text's two predominant themes, the love relation and the religious relation of the subject. Since the mental space network is modeled as a process based on articulated performance, its meaning production runs and completes a cycle from verse to verse, with the refrain each time stabilizing the thematic blend. The sacredness and the bitterness of both relations blend into a "broken hallelujah" that keeps moving the soul of listeners, because the network (or what corresponds to it) lives in their cognitive architecture, and the poignant music carries it into our hearts.

Chapter 9, on *narrative discourse*, that is, coherent fictional prose, offers a theory and a model of narrativity in stories of sufficient length to display the supposedly obligatory series of *narrative spaces* necessary to shape the dynamic framework of story logic on the level of events, agents, situations, and causal coherence (not on the level of narrators). Firstly, I discuss the problem of narrative *worlds* and narrative *genres*, distinguished by the dynamic consistency of these worlds, in terms of narrative *forces*. The narrative forces are tentatively classified, and it is shown that the genres can be categorized according to the types of forces that their respective worlds admit. Within each story, there is furthermore a specific inventory of active forces in each of its spatial settings, and the coherence from space to space, or setting to setting, is the result of a change of these forces and the variable unfolding of causal effects from space to space. Even a temporal backfiring of forces is possible, and as shown in stories by Guy de Maupassant, Jorge Luis Borges, and Ernest Hemingway, such effects—forward or backward in time—are as essential to the intelligibility of stories as the transfer of agents from space to space. The explicitation of the dynamic networks built by these connections constitutes the story-logical analysis of each narrative on this basic level of "what happens," without which no general interpretation could work objectively. If this approach is tenable in the narrative scale of "stories," I believe it to be useful to the analysis of larger narrative entities, novels and multi-novel prose, or corresponding narrative unfoldings by other media, either by stipulating concatenations of the basic series or by embedding these into more complex forms of *diegesis*.

Chapter 10 discusses *translation*.[1] To translate is to transfer meaning from one semiology to another. I thus mention Roman Jakobson's distinctions between interlingual, intralingual, and intersemiotic translation. In the interlingual version, to translate is ideally to make the content of a text in one language become the content of a text in another language. This is possible, when the translator finds approximations to the source sentences in target sentences, one by one, approximations comprising lexical, phrasal, and clausal parts of sentences. Moreover, semantic and pragmatic properties of discourse are to be reproduced, simulated, as closely as possible. I discuss cases where the process is in principle blocked by semiotic situations that make such transfer impossible; they typically involve figurative word and phrase meanings becoming literal, as in certain jokes, reverse metaphor, or other similar thematizations of the signifier in its own signified. Such humor laughs at language itself, we could say. I further show that there are significant differences between the *norms* of literary translation, commercial translation, and philosophical translation. Literal semantics is more important in literary translation than in the commercial genre, where pragmatics is of course primordial; in philosophical translation, a compromise between both is often sought. After having suggested a semiotic model of the complex semiosis network of language in use, I describe the dynamics of forces in conflict determining both the writing of a text and the rewriting implied in translating it. A narrative format allows me to point out how the scriptural dynamics involves the subjectivity of the translator. Finally, I discuss an example, the translation of a great poem by Edith Södergran.

Chapter 11, coauthored by literature professor John Hobbs, Oberlin College, further studies the subjectivity of the *poetic imaginary*, with a special focus on the semiotic function and meaning, in poetry, of the natural *elements*—air, water, soil, fire, the unbounded matter of our perceptible world—and the dynamics of their polarized values as experienced by the embodied subject.[2] It applies to two well-known examples of poetry, the findings by the Danish poet and scholar Hans-Erik Larsen, that the embodied subjectivity present in poetry is inscribed in a dynamical, "thymic" relation to the surrounding elements, in such a way that in a basic bio-imaginary register, *proximity* is euphoric, whereas *distal* sensory experiences are dysphoric; in a superimposed socio-imaginary space, thymic values are inverted: the distal becomes euphoric and the proximal dysphoric; finally, in a further superimposed, phantasmatic-imaginary register, proximal relations are again euphoric and distal relations dysphoric. The first and the third register share thymic orientation and therefore show a tendency to merge. The idea of superimposed registers of the embodied subjective imaginary has a counterpart in the theory of experiential, semantic domains. We here apply the model to poetry by W. Wordsworth and W.B. Yeats, plus Tu Fu, and it seems to work pretty well, given that biographical and intra-textual subjectivity are closely connected instances in poetry.

Chapter 12 continues the reflection on *language as text*, this time in a usage-based linguistic framework. Strictly speaking, a language is not a "system" or a unified "structure" but rather a constellation of separate and more or less coordinated components that cooperate in production and reception. I propose an account of this constellation of components, taking my point of departure in the multiple structural properties of the *word*. The word is an under-researched entity in language and thought. Not only has any word a complex sensible expression and a richly varied intelligible content, but it has a set of "word class" properties that inscribe its meaning in the encyclopedic semantics of discourse and always also a set of possible semio-syntactic functions in grammar. Additionally, it has *enunciational* properties (as discussed by Emile Benveniste), indicating the speaker's viewpoint, the hearer's status, or the referent's epistemic mode, and the genre of discourse. In this essay, I unfold my version of a theory of enunciation and also, shortly, my version of a *stemmatic* syntax (inspired by Lucien Tesnière). These models allow me to bring to the table a literary example, namely a very short literary text by the French writer Félix Fénéon, so short that I get the opportunity to unfold it in the five directions corresponding to the structural constellation presented around its words.

Chapter 13 discusses another grounding property of human cognition (present, as we have seen, in poetic meters), and no doubt the most prominent symbolic ingredient in the world's current digital culture, namely *numbers* and counting. Numbers appear to be some sort of signs, so where is the semiotics of numbers? Numerals are names of concepts whose origin is not clear and not well elucidated by current references to visual space and explanations by conceptual metaphor from source perception of spatial content. I argue that numbers instead appear in our *temporal* cognition, and that rhythmic body experiences may be their real cognitive base. Singing and dancing presuppose rhythm, especially when bodies coordinate their movements, and music delivers such temporal grounds when organized by beats grouped into stable measures ("bars") that again form parts of larger groups, or cycles. Beats have to be named in order to be shared and taught. The cyclic and multicyclic structure of human perception of regular beats, by *gestalts* based on named beats, therefore gives rise to the sort of names that numbers carry. The elementary semiotic circumstance, ignored by current cognitive theory of numbers (Lakoff and Nuñez), is that musical counting straight-forwardly creates the idea of the signifieds of one-two-three-four …, that is, the beats, in French *les temps*, that must exist in the bodily world of shared dance steps, syllables of songs, tones of instruments, hand-claps, which then become larger socio-temporal units, days, weeks, months, years. *Calendars* as organizers of social life have always been the main endeavor of the priests, who consequently developed mathematics, for example in the Aztec or the Mayan cultures; and calendars of course still rule the ritual routines in modern religious cultures. Calendars always regulate cults, as they subsequently came to regulate social life altogether. Their multicyclic principle, which matches the scales of arithmetic notation, for example the decimal scale, is identical with that of the metrical patterns that regulate bodily rhythms and music in human cultures. I add a consideration concerning the difference between the basic counting of discrete things and the measuring of continuous masses (by extended things used as yardsticks). The practice of exchange, as discussed by Marx and others, implies a conceptual blending of counting and measure, creating the more abstract "quantity" that mathematics proper further develops. The priests also invented money, as I explain in the last essay here; counting became a predominant sacred cognitive endeavor. It is unbelievable that numericity should have escaped the attention of research inquiring into the roots of meaning in human civilization; the humanities have had nothing to say about it.

Chapter 14 has a double focus: one on a general social *ecology* in a cognitive-semiotic perspective and the other on the ontology of *money*, as a sign and a thing of a very peculiar kind. Ecology: human societies and activities extract, consume, and expel matter, and clearly different *types* of matter, from nature, and they all do this on exactly three levels, first on the level of simple subsistence, then on the level of urbanization, specialized production, and institutional activities, and finally on the level of *symbolic*, transcendent, sacred, ritually violent activity serving the creation of authority. On each of the three levels, we find, across cultures, on the one hand, the reproductive collective endeavors, which contribute to the relative *closedness* of a society, and on the other the distributive and commercial enterprises that tendentially *open* the societies to one another: in modern terms, a "state" and a "market." The third level is that of transcendent and transgressive sacredness and violence, universally characterizing "Power" and sovereignty. It is the third level that primarily, in early human history, gives rise to the emergence of the very phenomenon of money. This decorative metallic substance adorns the divinities of the temples and is therefore used by the priests as divinely impregnated "payments" for work. Temples become banks, when armed priests manage to lend and get their loans redeemed. Money first, in the eyes of believers, magically contains and then semantically *means* divine "protection," which is an efficient *force* of resistance and a resource everyone will want, so it easily spreads throughout societies and thereby gives rise to their "economy." Barter and prostitution at the bottom (first level), wages and taxes at the urban (second) level, and weapon, drugs, and religious pomp on the level of transcendent power and authority. Ethical corruption on all levels, manifesting the *madness of money*, as it becomes capital—financial, productive, or simply exchange-bound. Surprisingly, the three levels here identified furthermore show strong analogies to the levels of meaning in language: performative semantics (symbolic, speech act, force-driven, power-oriented), informative semantics (institutional, truth-oriented), and existential semantics (affective, connotative, love-oriented), and this fact is finally interpreted as an isomorphism between socio-ecological stratification and the semiotic structure of subjectivity as such! Subjective and intersubjective embodiment in fact include the same types of sense-making: manifestation of authority (symbolic), informative communication (imaginary), and basic affective exchange. Due to the isomorphism, *money and language* deeply influence the human mind; therefore, the *ethics* of communicative, philosophical, poetic, and artistic language use may counteract the disturbing effect of money on the human character, and eventually tame the capital, before its global destruction gets irreversible. Words *can* be stronger than money; they just need to be used. I end the essay—and the book—on such a note of hope and mitigated trust.

The Postscript further elaborates on the overall consequences of the ecological model of the sociosphere. It introduces a dynamic, topological version of the model and shows some conceptual advantages of this view for the understanding of power and authority and the relation of these to subjectivity. This is research in the making, so the book could continue instead of leaving the reader with this open-ended and interrogative discussion based on cascades of models and analyses. But I believe to have treated and sometimes elucidated elementary aspects of a relatively young trans-discipline that may have a chance to contribute to the understanding of the metaphysics and physics of meaning.

So What Is the Question?

The basic question preceding and underlying the research and the reflections giving rise to the studies in this book is the following rather ambitious one: Is it possible to apply the idea of a scientific approach to the reality of which human imagination and experience is made? Can things in that realm of reality be *known*, not only as we factually "know" our own history, our friends and family, our work, and our material surroundings but as a matter of structured *meaning* common to imagination and experience? Is it possible to find the patterns of structured meaning shared by our conspecifics, which form the human reality studied by the disciplines of the humanities—can there be a "hard science" of the human world, based on the ways in which meaning is conveyed by language, art, thinking, social practices, and grounded in the ways in which the human mind and the human means of communication work?

What Do I Mean by Meaning *Here?*

The straightforward answer is precisely what justifies the connection between *cognitive* studies and *semiotic* studies announced in my book title: the internal *cognitive* structure of a *thought*, the way we construe a story, an argument, a description, an evaluation, a complex emotion, *and* the way we arrange the external *expression* of such a construal, which has its own *semiotic* communicative logic. Meaning is thus the ontological basis of the project; it refers to contents of the human mind (and to what may be known about its hosting brain); *and* it refers, through semiosis,[3] to the existence of a sphere of communicative networks in the world of intersubjective exchange and sociocultural discourse in a broad sense. In that sense, meaning is the necessary object of a cognitive semiotics—an ambitious new project to develop as a scientific discipline of disciplines.

Ontology, however, is not methodology, but it must underlie a project's methodological approaches. The "object" of research is not entirely determined by its methodology—otherwise research would be tautological—and it should keep its ontology under variations of methodology. Multiple methodologies are normally relevant within the scope of one same ontology. In our case, the ontology consists in assuming that there are events in the communicative mind that can be experienced as meaningful and that this experience is due to some sort of principled organization that can be described and understood in terms of the description. We could call this primary instance a first level of the project's research. A second, methodological level would then consist in elaborating *models* for specific aspects of meaning to look for, such as dynamic models of processes and morpho-dynamic conflicts, mental space models, dependency schemas, and other formal devices characterizing such "small meaning-production machines" and applying them to clear and exemplary cases of manifested meaning. A third level is evidently that of a larger empirical study and description of the targeted sociocultural phenomena, be it a poem, a story, a piece of political, religious, or gastronomic discourse, or the structure of a city or a society, testing the relevance and descriptive force of the models. The fourth level would be the concluding and generalizing *redescription* of the phenomena in terms of the models applied, a redescription allowing us to evaluate the extension of a possible new understanding obtained. For example, if, suitably described, narrative phenomena can be redescribed in terms of forces and barriers, and poetic phenomena in terms of "thymic" (evaluative) topologies, as I will suggest in this book, then how far will this new understanding reach? Will it also shed new light on historical (narrative) discourse or on emotional experiences in general? Will it offer new explanations of poorly understood things? The fourth level of the "strategy" eventually leads to new cycles, possibly changing the technical content of level two and importantly that of level three.

To summarize (Figure 1.1):

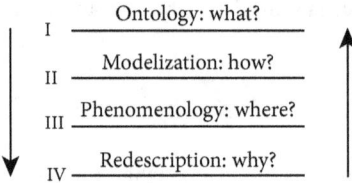

Figure 1.1 The circularity of research.

Between the first and the last level, there exists a close connection, since the redescription can show affinity or even causal connections to other results of research in related areas, thus contributing to a modification or an enlargement of the initial ontological assumptions, motivating new inquiries. Results bearing on the dynamics of modality, for example, may shed some light on conditionality and causation. The same "little machines" might be doing more work than hitherto assumed.

The mind's inner workings can of course not be accessed directly by mentally "seeing" them, so therefore we have to describe what we experience and then redescribe that through a modelization. In that sense, meaning is not very different from any other region of reality that we can study. The main difference is, clearly, that here we are looking at and comparing *two versions of the same item, both existing in our mind*: the immediate and the modelized version, meaning described and then redescribed. Do they match? Sufficiently? Deciding on that question is also how we evaluate former analyses or alternative renderings in similar research projects, namely by comparing to the pre-modelized versions that an immediate phenomenology of meaning offers us. *We are data* ourselves, in this specific sense.

Linguistics is a prominent part of cognitive semiotics, and a syntactic *model* makes a huge difference in a grammatical analysis, which always relies on the analyst's understanding of what a given construction "means." A change of syntactic model therefore affects the way the meaning, that is, the semantic import, of the syntactic construction appears to the linguist. A simple example of alternative models is as follows:

(1) Peter loves Mary = loves (Peter, Mary)
versus (2) Peter loves Mary = tr {loves (Peter), Mary}

In the first case, the implied agents are on the same level, whereas in the latter they are not. The analyst may be able to decide, by comparing to phrases like (3) "John plays Beethoven," (4) "Eve reads Shakespeare," and many more, with different types of transitive verbs; is (1) or (2) the better analysis? (2) seems more appropriate, if the analysis includes constructions that use transitivized intransitives ("Bob works two jobs").

The four-leveled trajectory presented above is of course really a collective enterprise. No individual researcher is supposed to perform excellently on all levels, so collaboration is as called for here as in other fields of knowledge. This book testifies to that both directly and indirectly—only philosophy seems to be possible as a strictly individual endeavor, and although some semioticians are mostly or wholly philosophers, like C. S. Peirce, my own philosophical effort here is mainly devoted to getting the ontological presuppositions clarified.

So I should add some words on the philosophical problems involved. The relation between meaning and matter was put on the agenda at a time—in the seventeenth century—when the scientific pressure on thinking produced new attempts to formulate a conception of being that would not be grounded on a scriptural divinity but on observations and argument-based representations of the world. Bruno, Galilei. The scholastic discourse gave way to modern rationalism. Descartes, Spinoza. Then Newton, Leibniz. The rationalistic views had to include accounts of the relation between meaning and matter, that is, a metaphysics of meaning. The scholastics, from Aquinas to early Kant (!), revered a distinction between two aspects of the sign, the *sensibilis* and the *intelligibilis* side, those that I reinterpret in the model of mental architecture, but if everything is not a sign, this distinction does not amount to a metaphysics. The *intelligibilis* aspect of something is of course its meaning to someone, but what about the *sensibilis* aspect? Is it the materiality of the sensed or the sensedness of a piece of matter, be it sign or thing? If our senses are still material, at some point the sensed becomes intelligibilis, namely when we remember a sensation. This is where the distinction between Descartes' *res cogitans* and *res extensa* starts. The "understandability" of something is its potential meaning; it is made of stuff that does not reside in physical space and time. Thoughts do exist, since we use them while interpreting things, whether general meanings of signs or particular meanings of things to someone. Meanings exist but not as material things. They can be in more than one time and place, in many minds at once. They don't have sizes and weight. Hence their existence in thought shows that thought is a place where something can exist, immaterially but really. That is Cartesian *dualism*: meaning is immaterial reality, different from material reality, or matter. Spinoza was first an enthusiastic student of Cartesianism but eventually found that the duality should be ascribed to matter, which would carry its own conceptual thought in itself. God is nature, and God's logical thought is therefore matter; the intelligible aspect of material things is their own "thinking" of themselves. This peculiar *monist* mysticism gave rise to modern empiricism, or logical positivism (the Vienna School and Wittgenstein). The dualist form of modern rationalism is found today in all scholarly and scientific disciplines, the humanities, the social sciences, medical science, the "hard sciences," and even mathematics, but curiously enough not in predominant philosophical trends. However, phenomenology (Husserl, Merleau-Ponty) remains, somewhat hesitantly, Cartesian, since it has to distinguish the reality of experience itself from the reality of what it is experience *of*. It is in this sense that phenomenology appears in the "strategic" plan mentioned above. Cognitive research as well as semiotic studies may be characterized as halfway philosophical and halfway empirical, or scientific in a broad sense; this is why these two disciplines or rather traditions, which I argue should collaborate in order to obtain more and better knowledge of meaning, often sound monistic in theory and dualistic in practice. Dualistic, because meaning in signs and thought has to be acknowledged in its own right—certainly not as events of a "soul" in the religious sense but as a reality different from that of material events and states. Just as the solution of a mathematical equation can "exist," the solution of a narrative conflict can "exist" in a text.

Cognitive semiotics is a research project that cares for the semantics of expressions and for the phenomenology of cognition, and which, comparing this semantics to that phenomenology, studies the structures they share. Those structures may be the constitutive properties of the communicative mind.

Is This a Sort of Structuralism?

I would say, almost the contrary. Structuralism, according to my favorite caricature, told you that *the structures* express themselves through you without your knowledge. When you speak, the structures use you as their mouthpiece; *you* don't know what you are saying, the thinking is in the structures that you unconsciously transmit. Consciousness is a cover-up; by contrast, the unconscious is speaking through you, from the structural discourse of society to the deepest level of yourself. This was an anti-consciousness philosophy. On the contrary, I would claim, we do know in principle what we say and what we think; we do know more or less why we say and think what we do (otherwise we could not correct ourselves "online," as we do)—only we do not know *how* thinking itself works and precisely *how* our use of language or other semiotic means of expression depends on underlying mechanisms of attunement to different semantic or pragmatic routines of the communicative mind. And the infinity of human history is there to further determine our limited understandings. Meaning occurs automatically, and its mechanisms are not accessible to voluntary introspection. We have to reconstruct the inner workings of these automatic mental devices while using their manifestations in mental life or communication as empirical starting-points. This distinction may be hard to grasp; we can indeed access meaning but still need research to access the way meaning *works*. That is what I have been trying to do in the following studies.

Notes

1. The author is a translator of Bataille, Borges, Calderon, Koltès, Lorca, Merleau-Ponty, Molière, Roubaud, Sade, Serres et al.
2. Just for the record: In 2018, the author published a four-volume work of poetry called *Weather reports* (in Danish, Vejrmeldinger).

3   Minds "communicate" (transfer) meaning to each other, but that is not all: they create new meaning by using semiosis experimentally. This is clearly the case in art, poetry, music, and aesthetic practices in general. It is also, I claim, the case in fundamental research in the sciences. "Using semiosis experimentally" means letting meanings that do not already "know" each other interact, in order to discover truths through new meanings. We might call this a principle of natural surrealism. Einstein riding on a beam of light …

2

On the Mind of the Body: Spinoza, Descartes, and the Philosophy of Cognition

Introduction

For some time, modern neuro-cognitive research has been facing a curious theoretical problem: it is philosophically inconsistent. It cannot be *hermeneutic*, in the sense of "continental" historicism, since it has to acknowledge the importance of evolutionary properties of the human mind and its hosting brain. *Meaning*, that is, mental content, intended to be remembered or communicated, can therefore not be seen exclusively as created by human history alone. History must have been created by minds. Nor can neuro-cognitive research overtly endorse *analytic* or *language* philosophy, since it cannot limit itself to the critical study of language and linguistically manifested concepts or in practical terms, of propositions and propositional logic. *Meaning* cannot be reduced to inter-propositional consistency and truth conditions. Neuro-cognitive science cannot subscribe to classical *phenomenology*, whether existential or formal, because this approach would rule out any empirically specialized research, from semiotics to neuroscience, since in such research, the phenomenological reduction would not work. In the actual panorama, there is no consensus to adopt any coherent "cognitive philosophy," or "neuro-philosophy," or "naturalized philosophy of meaning," and the realism of ordinary philosophy of natural science does not suffice for the study of the human world, including human intentional structures of meaning, narrative meaning, emotional meaning, and aesthetic meaning.[1]

The cognitive sciences emerged in a late twentieth-century atmosphere of anti-hermeneutic thinking and computational scientism. Occasionally, cognitive strains of thought and research alluded to phenomenological or phenomenalistic motives,[2] encouraged by the fact that the study of cognition is inherently connected to studies of

---

An earlier version of this chapter was part of a trilogy of essays under the title *The World Seen From Within,* published in *Language and Semiotic Studies*, Vol. 2, 1, 2016. The third of these essays, "On Mind and Matter, and the Founders of Rationalism," is a patiently commented reading of Descartes' six Meditations, the ontological part of Spinoza's Ethics, and Leibniz's Monadology. They are unquestionably the founding fathers of modern rationalism before the Enlightenment. One could argue that Kant is a follower of Descartes, and Hegel a dialectical version of Spinoza. C. S. Peirce has been called the American Leibniz.

perception and consciousness; but in the last instance, in the absence of alternatives, the cognitive sciences often gave in to an all-pervasive *analytic* philosophy that had determined much of the academic life and the style of thinking in the disciplines affected by this research.[3] They stayed inhabited and inhibited by the meaning skepticism and the logical dogmatism of a long analytic century. In this chapter, I will address the problem of cognitive Spinozism and discuss some possible ways to rethink it.

The Divide

It can in fact be claimed that in essential respects, analytic philosophy is not soundly connected to the study of "mind and brain" and in particular not compatible with the study of cognitive semantics, which has to rely on introspection and interpretation of meaning in communication and therefore cannot use only a truth-conditional semantics. However, it should also be acknowledged that analytic philosophy is organically linked to the history of the cognitive disciplines, in particular to Anglo-Saxon neuro-behaviorism and neuropsychology. It is not inclined to stray from the discourse of these areas of research, unless new and very strong arguments enter the debate.

By contrast, the sort of structural research (including structural research in anthropology, linguistics, literary criticism, and psychology) which in Europe has been associated with studies of cognition—since Jean Piaget—is often philosophically anchored more or less explicitly in variants of *formal* Husserlian or Merleau-Pontyan *phenomenology*. In such a framework, semantics is free to distinguish signified meaning from referential (veri-conditional) meaning and to localize the former in the human mind, not in the archive or protocol of truths of the outer world. The actual[4] project of elaborating a "cognitive semiotics," in which the overall study of *meaning* and the *mind*, and of *culture* and *communication*, that is, of *signs and semiosis*, still in the perspective of *cognition* and *consciousness*, is approached both from the angle of the neurosciences and from that of a structural and cognitive semantics, in a sense, *both* from the neural "outside" *and* from the mental "inside", thus admitting a form of practical methodological dualism, is therefore presently both an inspiringly productive laboratory and yet still a philosophical battlefield opposing both reductive analytic and anti-reductionist phenomenological motives; hermeneutics has already left the field, since History is not considered a sufficient structural cause in itself.

My claim here is that such battles can be viewed as basically opposing Baruch Spinoza's and René Descartes' heirs. *Spinoza is*, I propose to think, *the father of analytic philosophy*, as *Descartes is the father of phenomenology*. This historical state of affairs is by no means evident, so I shall try to sketch out some of my reasons for suggesting this genealogy. Descartes the "dualist" distinguishes categorically meaning and matter: thought and extension, *res cogitans* and *res extensa*. Ideas and spatiotemporal things. Ideas have no extension, and things with extension are not ideas, though some things with extension do have ideas, namely ourselves. Spinoza the "monist"—and the critical student of Descartes' work—decides that these two sorts of *res* are properties, or attributes, of one and the same substantial *res*, because God, or God's *logic*, is in the nature of this *res*. So for Spinoza, things and ideas of things are indeed the same, and ideas of things are attributes of the things of which they are attributes; the meaning of an idea is *its* thing itself, which is its inherent *truth*, as in modern truth-conditional semantics. But since for both thinkers, meaning and the mind are *res cogitans*, not definable by space and time, whereas brains, bodies, and behaviors are *res extensa*, given in space and time, which are thus either the same or different *res* (substances), the metaphysical differences between these rationalist masters directly concern our contemporary and cognitive research and debate on minds, bodies, and embodiment and particularly our research on meaning and semiosis.

The historical divide that disconnects analytic and "continental" thinking thus separates substance monism and substance dualism. Monists believe that meaning is part of the material world, while dualists believe that it resides in immaterial contents of minds. In semantics, dualists therefore distinguish meaning and reference, whereas monists insist that meaning *is* reference, things referring to other things by themselves. Dualists understand meaning in terms of mental representations; monists are by contrast (often) ready to reject the notion of mental representations and "inner life" in general. Dualists are more prepared than monists to accept that meaning is shared by signs, because they accept that there are representations by which minds or people let some things "stand for" other things.[5]

Realities

Historically, it may thus be argued that contemporary phenomenological philosophy is rooted in René Descartes' experiential rationalism, allowing and inviting both introspection and extrospection and comparing these; and that the analytic, or logico-empiricist, movement in contemporary philosophy stems from the "geometric" axiomatic style and the epistemological doctrine developed by Descartes' first popularizer and then critic, Baruch Spinoza. Descartes had founded a science-oriented philosophy where intentionality and mental events could be acknowledged as *real* in a key distinct from the reality of physical space-time and where these two reality variants could be examined in their connections. There were, as the philosophical mathematician René Thom would say, distinct "regions" in reality, some immaterial and others material, and there were certain causal paths between them, in both directions. Thus, thought and extended matter, though ontologically or regionally distinct, were contingent and could *causally affect* each other.[6] Descartes' experiential rationalism admitted *causal interaction between mind and body* and even initiated the technical study of this interaction (in Le Traité des passions, 1649, his last published work); strictly speaking, his philosophy is therefore a *causal monism*.[7] His Dutch-Jewish critic, however, felt that thought and extension must be aspects or attributes of one and the same substance, which consequentially had to be *dual* itself, namely immediately both material and spiritual, both ideational (conceptual, in today's terms) and physical, idea and thing in one. Spinoza's famous "monism" substantially identified mind and body and so had to rule out all such causal relations between mind and body, stating[8] instead that a mind *is* nothing but the idea (or essence) *of* (or: in) a body, it is the idea that this body *has* of itself, in the same way that any other object must contain its own idea, or mind, as a natural and divine part of itself, as a being.[9] Since things must also contain ideas, and ideas in themselves are not things, Spinoza's thinking is, strictly—substantially—speaking, in fact an ontological and causal *dualism*. His ideas must be caused exclusively by other ideas and his things by other things.[10]

In the *causal* respect—and which other respect could matter more to ontology?—we would have to say that *Descartes is the monist, and Spinoza the dualist*. This may look and sound confusing, but it does not dissolve the divide, on the contrary. Either ideas presuppose minds and brains, or they do not. In the first case, cognitive and semiotic research can make sense.

In terms of epistemology, Spinoza further tried to prove that while minds *think of* the bodies whose minds they are, they can think of objects different from their own bodies in so far as they, being bodies, are *affected by* other bodies (things) that they encounter physically, through sensory *perception*. But such thoughts, he says, in his *Ethics*, are originally nothing but vague, chaotic, and meaningless impressions: imaginations (*imaginationes* versus *rationes*). In order to overcome this imaginary condition and become real and meaningful ideas, or *thoughts*, these impressions are further to be ordered formally, logically, or "geometrically," today we could say "analytically," in terms of a formal and propositional demonstration, a logical proof. Only in this way can they become real ideas (of these other things), ideas whose *meaning* consists in the *truth* they are part of in the world they are about. Without such an ordering, they will just stay *imaginations* and vague images, idle noises from the sensory organs, and will have no cognitive value, no meaning, no truth.[11] We might summarize this view in Figure 2.1.

Imaginations are still meaningless. Ideas are truths that the body produces out of sensory impressions, *if* it applies to them its *logical* capacity, which it somehow inherits from Nature (God). Unclear imaginations can thus be transformed into clear

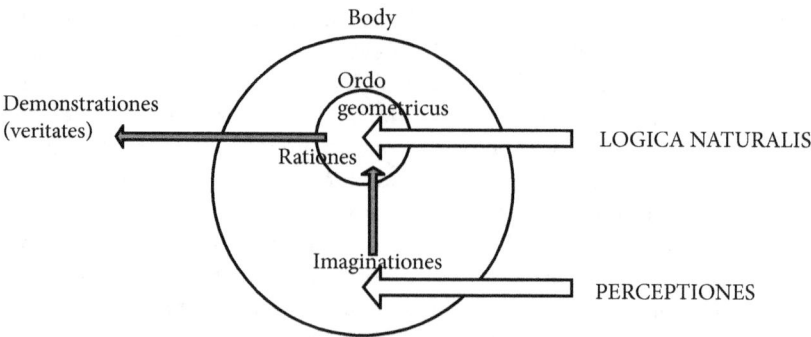

Figure 2.1 Spinoza's view of the constitution of meaning as truth.

ideas, if they can be ordered logically. Logic is the language of God, *Deus sive natura*, it is in the things and is therefore acquired by our bodies through their contact with the natural world. Nature thinks, reasons, and humans "pick up" the principles of this reasoning while also perceiving things and their inherent ideas (conceptual attributes).

Spinoza's epistemology was therefore to become a "meaning skepticism," since meanings are imaginations, but not a science skepticism: natural science was to him an all-important moral enterprise and a means of achieving happiness and, in a sense, eternity of the soul (active participation in Divine Nature, *Deus sive Natura*) being part of truth by finding it, through "empirical" reasoning based on observation and demonstration only.[12] The feeling of discovering a truth was for him a mystical experience of beatitude, divine grace, since the idea filling one's truthful thought was God's natural presence. False thoughts, which would be clear and logical ideas of nothing, of no real existing things, by definition do not exist; they may seem to be false but are only meaningless. For there are no false things in nature. Such apparent meanings are just instances of noisy mechanical imagery: unstable and dreamlike nonsense. Therefore, there are no stable and clear but purely hypothetical representations in the mind, no stable and meaningful mental pictures of real possibilities that could be false: just *possible* and still fallible ideas are not meaningful, because what is (and is true), *is so by necessity*. Spinoza's explicit *necessitarianism* does not admit arbitrary, hypothetical meanings, or uncertain reasoning, let alone counterfactual thinking.[13] Thinking, if ordered logically, axiomatically, is literally identical to a bodily state of being, divinely inhabited by the things thought of. Representation is nothing in itself and cannot be distinguished from perception, which is "picking up" from the world. Phenomenology is therefore impossible in Spinoza's perspective.[14] In Descartes' philosophy, by contrast, free and hypothetical imagination is an evident and prominent part of human reality; otherwise, systematic doubt would be impossible. The relation of correspondence between thought and extension is as solidly established as later the relation of reference underlying the Saussurean linguistic sign relation between the *signified* (a concept or meaning) supported by its *signifier* (a concept of an expressive event), on the one hand, and the acoustic sounds used in communication and the worldly states of affairs *referred* to in communication, on the other hand.[15] Language can indeed be meaningful and still express thoughts turning out to be wrong, untrue, or "false." Cartesian and, later, Saussurian "semiology" therefore finds no difficulty in distinguishing the *signified* (conceptual) meaning (*le sens*) from the *referential* (veridical) import of signs (*la signification*); here, meaning is the signified aspect of the sign, *le signifié*, a mental concept, whereas *the truth of the meaning* is an independent matter of correspondence between signified concepts and referential "things" in an immaterial or material world. In terms of truth theory, this is an opposition of Cartesian "correspondence" versus Spinozist "coherence" epistemology.

Simply put, for Descartes, meaning is not necessarily truth, while for Spinoza it is. More strictly speaking, for Spinoza, untrue meaning is not even meaning but just a noisy chunk of the mind of the world.

So What?

Spinoza's line of philosophizing is, in this view, the real historical origin of the immensely influential positivist, empiricist, and analytic movement in modern philosophy. This line of thinking is inherently at odds with elementary phenomenological observation (of the human imaginary) and also with the neuroscientific project (exploring the correlations between mental content and brain states). It is reluctant to admitting and supporting the study of meaning as such, meaning in itself, the cognitive structures of signified content, that is, the objective field of the humanities and the social sciences, from cultural or political studies to linguistics and semiotics.[16]

Descartes' line of thought, ontologically monistic in the sense that thought and extended things such as our bodies are predicted to causally affect each other, has stimulated research into the interaction of mind and brain, for example, in *agency* and in *emotional states*. Still it is Spinoza's "monism," which is, ontologically speaking, dualistic and mystically ascribes thought to extended things[17] and rejects the principle of an *interaction* of mind and brain (since the brain *is* the mind), that has become predominant in modern behavioral thinking and research, even in the humanistic and social domains, where, for example, literary criticism is then reduced to the biographical, or to "reader response" studies, and sociology to the statistics of poll responses.

Curiously but characteristically, there is no reference in Spinoza to the nervous system, only to the body, although Descartes had discussed nerves and "animal spirits": ideas in principle need no nerves, not even heads, since they emanate from the substance of natural things and bodies. All existing things, or modes of substance, have—as the German idealists would say—a *für sich* embedded in their *an sich*, so there is no need to look for special devices like neural processes in order to follow any neuro-mental or psychosomatic paths of correlation and interaction between subjectivity and objecthood.

The Spinozan inspiration is clearly present in the physicalist Vienna Circle and in early—as well as late—Wittgenstein, whose *Tractatus Logico-Philosophicus* (1921), named (apparently on G. Moore's suggestion) after Spinoza's *Tractatus Teologico-Politicus* (1670), contended,[18] also in its very numerical composition "ordine geometrico," that the propositional structure of language, if organized axiomatically, and as a "language" in the sense of formal logic, would directly reveal the structure of reality, or the world. This is a view that gained considerable influence within the Circle and would continue to do so in the subsequent spreading and development of logical positivism. Projects like R. Carnap's *Logical Construction of the World* (*Der logische Aufbau der Welt*) are characteristic. The line starting in Spinoza's mysticism—and, I would therefore venture to say, Spinoza's early *logical empiricism*—leads through the hard-core empiricist Bishop Berkeley and the idealists of the nineteenth century, including F.H. Bradley and J. Ward, through the all-important psychologist W. James, to Russell, Moore, Ayer, and others. The militant behaviorism of J.B. Watson and B.F. Skinner and their followers in "behavioral science" is another direct consequence of the rejection of the epistemic autonomy of meaning. Behaviorism is necessarily a *meaning skepticism*. We might, by the way, add C. S. Peirce to the list of Spinozist and "dualistically monist" thinkers led toward basically the same religiously motivated cult of a logic-of-the-world.[19] Characteristics of this line are the truth-conditional conception of semantics, the rejection of representations and of imagistic models of meaning or of their relevance to the study of meaning, the principle of a behavioral *embodiment* of meaning (note that the general theme of embodiment[20] in the cognitive sciences is a Spinozist motive, rather than a phenomenological product), and in particular this strange and stubbornly absolute belief in formal logic as the "language" or expression of reality, and therefore, implicitly the idiom of the Divinity itself,[21] an idea forcefully professed by G. Frege, whose *Begriffsschrift* (concept-notation, 1879) was—after Peirce's diagrams—a direct modern translation of Spinoza's "geometrical order" and who believed that formal logic was a real *language* (though unspoken), not a metaphor but really a language in which formal laws would be laws of empirical truth. Philosophy therefore could have direct access to profound knowledge of the world through logic alone, just by using it, and it would not need any academic disciplines (such as anthropology, sociology, psychology, let alone linguistics) in order to produce valid statements on language, meaning, and concepts and even on political, ethical, or cultural issues. The Spinozan conviction is that for the human body to organize perceptions logically in terms of formal axiomatic systems of propositions is per se to understand the world, since the order of a formal logic supposedly *is* the world order. Frege influentially redefined "analytic" (after Kant) to mean "provable from logical laws and definitions," which was further believed to mean: true about the world, and E. Kant would say: synthetically true. So in this philosophy, analytic and synthetic are merged, or rather, the Kantian synthetic is absorbed by the analytic condition.

Now What?

To summarize again: in Spinoza's epistemology, perception gives rise to two distinct forms of mental activity, *imagination* ("imaginatio") and *reasoning* ("ratio"). The former consists of blurred superpositions of perceptions, forming images of no order or value, thus of no meaning (i.e., of no truth), despite the fact that people confusedly think they are indeed meaningful. By contrast, the latter mental activity, real thinking, consists of imageless ideas—expressed by symbols—by which we participate in the (mentally equipped) things of nature.[22] Ideas (if clear) are meaningful because they are *in*, or are *part of*, the substance of their objects. Truth is of course not correspondence (between a statement and the state it states) in this perspective: it is essential *identity*. This explains the ontological importance of logic here; the natural order of ideas is formal logic, not people's vernacular tongues, their miserably confused colloquial and chaotic pseudo-languages, which must be corrected. Logic therefore becomes the language of truth and a source of truth in itself. No philological grammar is needed in order to understand *language* in this sense. Occurring mental contents, life-related experiences, and generally all modes of phenomenological presence,[23] presence-to-the-mind, are radically dissociated from meaning, that is, they are meaningless, since "meaningful" now exclusively means "logical," which in turn means "real," belonging to the natural, physical world. This strong turn of *naturalization* (and referentialization) of meaning, as mentioned, had to wipe out of its horizon all representational philosophies[24] and correspondingly to isolate itself from the (Husserlian, Cassirerian, or otherwise theorized) lifeworld-oriented phenomenological philosophies and claims to the semiotic autonomy of meaning in the human imaginary—as those held by the modern and in a sense neo-Cartesian, continental anthropological structuralists. Modern Jakobsonian or Lévi-Straussian structuralism would evidently admit the principle of possible causal connections between mind and body. Freudian and Lacanian views also most certainly do, albeit in the framework of a peculiar methodological solipsism. Structuralism was regularly rejected by anti-representationalist naturalizers of many kinds.

The recent robotic elucubrations on "symbol grounding"—S. Harnad, L. Steels—tend to argue that meaning has none of the iconic, representational properties of human consciousness but is a question of anchoring "internal" symbolic signs in "external" things by a learning process of naming, as if the "external" things categorized themselves beforehand. In a different key, Andy Clark's "extended mind" thinks that the world we experience *is* in itself our representation of it; we don't need a "Cartesian theater" in the mind, since the outer world is its own divine Spinozan theater. In fact, we wouldn't need to have individual minds at all, since the world is its own mind in which we simply participate. By contrast, the neuropsychologist and philosopher Merlin Donald, who emphasizes the evolutionary importance of external techniques of symbolization, the materialization of symbols, for example in libraries, argues that these techniques allow our minds to build both external and internal semiotic supports for the enlarged realms of reference that culture presupposes; but in this view, individual consciousness is where the meaning of these references has to unfold, giving rise to the *sharing of meaning* we call communication. He is a cognitive semiotician.

Artificial intelligence—A. Newell and H. Simon's project—led to the zombie antinomy: if something looks like intelligence, it *is* intelligence, even if this cannot be true, but who cares?[25] We may acknowledge that "intelligent" behavior comes with an epiphenomenal supplement called consciousness in the human case, but this needs not be significant, since all things can think anyway, according to the underlying Spinoza (some just a little more than others).

As mentioned, Spinoza's radically and drastically mono-dualistic view of the mind–body relation as a strict two-in-one identity has turned out to be not only acceptable but positively attractive to some, perhaps a majority of, cognitive scholars. In most cases, I think, it is just tacitly assumed, because it is part of modern education in the analytic and anglophone culture. As also mentioned, this is due to one essential motive, namely that its principle of *embodiment* of thought seems to suit the need for explaining thought and representation away by reference to an "embodied mind" in the sense of the mind's being identical with the physiological body of the biological organism having or hosting it. The mind *is* this body, according to the Spinozio-cognitive claim. Rather than an embodied mind, which would be a Cartesian concept, we have an *enminded body* here. Where the phenomenological notion of body—cf. Merleau-Ponty's use of the term "flesh" (*la chair*)—sharply distinguishes the experiencing-experienced body (my experiencing body as experienced by me and my "other"), that is, the experiential, *phenomenological body*, from the physiologically given body, the Spinozan notion of body instead directly *identifies experience and physiology* (cf. in this respect the Spinozan cognitive linguist G. Lakoff's so-called neuro-linguistic program and its use of the embodiment principle: here, image schemas simply *are* motor programs, not derived from them but identical with them).[26]

Contemporary cognitive understandings of mental "embodiment" are nevertheless often challenged by this extremely strong claim of "enmindment" of the body and its radical referentialization or naturalization of meaning. For instance, the conceptual entities we call *metaphors* are reluctant to such claims, since the metaphor's source (imagery) and target (reference) differ as to their *semantic domain* and apparently have to contradict each other's ideational reference, truth, and meaning. They therefore ought to be generically meaningless, as analytic philosophy originally thought and declared they were, and no doubt basically still suspect they are. However, the meaningfulness of metaphors in natural language was thought to perhaps be saved, analytically speaking, if it were shown that they have a *logical*, propositional format which is predicative (A IS B), yielding a logical *inference*, thereby assisting the mind in building a *true idea* out of the imagistic magma of imagination, that is, if it were shown that metaphor lets the mind connect a concrete and bodily source (B) to the abstract ideational target (A), establishing by inference from B to A a truth which would still indeed be "of the body," by B, since the body is a body of mind. This is mainly, but implicitly, what the Spinozan cognitive theory of conceptual metaphor, initiated by Lakoff and Johnson, have tried to do. The Fauconnier-Turner theory of mapping and conceptual integration (blending) is in the same case, I suspect.[27] These follow-ups on Lakoff's conceptual embodiments still want to show that abstract notions can be derived from concrete ideas that our bodies have. That said, there is little doubt that procedural motor schemas are involved in the development of schematic concepts of spatial and temporal relations, but metaphor is a completely different affair.

Semiotic and semantic analysis[28] show that metaphors are not simple factories of concepts, but that they instead, through their nonrealistic imagery, express judgments, evaluations, emotions, and speech acts that are *about* the ideas or states of affairs they refer to. Metaphors therefore can never be reduced to an inferential B → A relation in A IS B but must be seen as meaningfully structured imaginations that express thinking *about* their deictic content, instead of just constituting or construing that content.[29] This "aboutness"—Searle's term—is a major problem in analytic cognitivism, because it is representational. It is nevertheless a basic fact of the human imaginary, which prefers to "see" and say—represent—same affairs in many different ways (cf. Aristotle's *to einai pollakos legomenon*).

Conclusion

I think it is necessary to realize that truth-conditional semantics does not serve the analysis of the human imaginary.[30] It is not a fruitful assumption that ideas are or consists in the real things they are the truths of. Ideas are often of non-existing things-in-the-world and still these ideas exist. Ideas are indeed often "about" each other (this is their critical dimension). Ideas can exist as such, because they are made of immaterial, *representational reality*—and this expression does not have to be an oxymoron. In the mental life of humans there is a neutral medium that makes it possible to seamlessly combine imagined, dreamt, remembered, expected, perceived, and communicated contents in one and the same representation and representational *format*. The human mind can even simulate all these content sources in a pure imaginary form as a narrative or theatrical *fiction* that has all the features of ordinary belief-related (remembered, expected, perceived, or communicated) contents but still has no ontological grounds other than that of being imagined in this format.[31] How does this seamless integration of heterogeneous elements happen? The only rational answer to this question is that these heterogeneous elements are all representationally structured and thus obey the same structural principles that are principles of the human representational, theatrical, imagining *mind*.[32] The simple point I want to make is that this mental format of imagination, neither true nor false but just heuristic, and given as a result of our semiotic evolution, can be explained by the existence of an autonomous structural capacity of this human mind, and that a rational philosophy is needed that could acknowledge this possibility in order to invite us to explore it, instead of anathematizing it.

Such a philosophy could start from some simple assumptions. Firstly, that the content of *inner experience* is as ontologically (though not materially) real as the communally observable and measurable outer world—even if we still do not know technically how inner experience comes about and is staged in consciousness by our brains. Secondly, that the experiential systems and processes of meaning production are capable, at least in certain respects, of being *structurally stable* in human minds, and that such structural stability of meaning implies a representational format, an internal semiosis, so to speak.[33] If internal and external semiotic processes (i.e., thinking and communication) cooperate, these dual semiotic processes may further become culturally stabilized through inter-mental attunement and communication using conventionalized external *semioses*, from gesture to music—written, drawn, played, enacted—that allow an ongoing *semantization* of the experienced outer macro-physical (pheno-physical) world in terms of inner schemas so that it can be experienced as a multiple cultural and potentially shared human reality.

A philosophy of this form might be termed a semiotic phenomenology, a cognitive semiotics, or something else. And as Ferdinand de Saussure ventured, referring to semiology: *puisqu'elle n'existe pas encore, on ne peut dire ce qu'elle sera; mais elle a droit à l'existence, sa place est déterminée d'avance* (CLG III, §3).

Notes

1   What about the philosophy of mind? For an overview, I recommend Lyons (1995), whose inventory runs from James and Watson, through Carnap, Wittgenstein, Putnam to Dennett, Churchland, Fodor. The main concept is that of *behavior*.

Behavior replaces meaning. Mind is behavior. This is comfortable, since ordinary language describes behavior. But it cuts out meaning in texts, in discourse, in signs in general, and in particular in art. Only pragmatics will work.

2   Shaun Gallagher is an exception. See Gallagher and Zahavi (2012).
3   For a critical approach to this philosophical situation in cognitive science, see Line Brandt (2013).
4   As in Zlatev et al. (2016).
5   *How can anything exist outside of the material world?* As a spiritual being? No. Descartes was a mathematician. If an equation has a solution, where does the solution exist? In the mathematical universe, of which the materially physical universe is only a part (since a lot of good math does not have physical counterparts). In the heads of the mathematicians, if they are lucky, but math is a science, and that science is not psychology. The mathematical universe is immaterial and its properties can be studied through *res cogitans*. Ideas are immaterial things just like numbers; they do not need material counterparts in order to exist, as Spinoza thought (they just need minds), but Spinoza was a logician, not a mathematician.
6   Antonio Damasio opposes Descartes and Spinoza in his book titles and comments in ways that do not contribute to clarification, see Geir Kirkebøen (2001) on Damasio's Descartes. Heidi M. Ravven criticizes Antonio Damasio in "Spinoza and the Education of Desire," *Neuro-Psychoanalysis*, 2003, 5 (2), for not being sufficiently Spinozan in his new book *Looking for Spinoza* (2003); he still separates mind and body. Damasio replies: "Ravven takes Spinoza's identity of body and mind quite literally. My view, however, is that Spinoza would have liked to know how that single natural substance managed to produce within itself what we call mind. The Spinozan 'identity' of mind and body to which Ravven refers is no more a scientific fact than my saying that emotion plays out in the theater of the body and feeling in the theater of the mind. In both instances, these are modes of expression. They are meant to dramatize a certain historical moment in the understanding of a complicated problem given the knowledge of the time. Three-and-a-half centuries later, I believe Spinoza would have wanted to know, chapter and verse, how that 'idea of the body which constitutes the human mind' comes about in neurobiological terms."—The centuries would thus clearly have turned Spinoza back into Descartes! Rather, Damasio is showing us that his view is in fact Cartesian: the body *produces* the mind, as a causal fact of neurobiology; Spinoza couldn't care less and would even strongly disagree, since for him, the body, *any* body and thing, already *is* or *has* mind. Geir Kirkebøen (2000) offers a masterful account of Descartes' mind-body thinking in his article "Descartes's Regulae, Mathematics, and Modern Psychology: 'The Noblest Example of All' in Light of Turing's (1936) *On Computable Numbers*."
7   Again: *substantial* dualism or monism is one thing, *causal* dualism or monism quite another. Two substances can be causally connected, two attributes of one substance cannot.
8   As M.D. Wilson says in Garrett (1996): "[Spinoza's] proposition [is] that the mind is 'the idea of' the body (or the body 'the object of' the mind)" (pp. 100–101).
9   Again: bodies must have minds, in Spinoza's view, because bodies are part of nature, which is God; so God is in every body, or existing thing, giving it a mind. This mind is not due to any cause; so, nervous systems, neurons, brains, or whatever may be causally involved have nothing to do with there being a mind in a thing. The human body in particular is supposed to host a vivid and migratory mind, a soul; by the

way, this supposition was already stated in the Torah. Jews express gratitude to God every morning for renewal of both body and soul: "I offer thanks to You, living and everlasting King, for having returned to me my soul with compassion and great faithfulness" (the *Modeh Ani* prayer).

10 Leibniz saw this difficulty and proposed as a solution to let God assure that the causal line of ideas and the causal line of extended things are running nicely in parallel; otherwise, nature would be a total chaos: its laws would not know where and when to apply.

11 One of the remarkable consequences of this view is that representations cannot be false, but only meaningless, that is, fuzzy, unclear. This was to become the great call of analytic philosophy: to raise a campaign against meaningless ideas expressed by *only apparently* meaningful language.

12 This is of course the central and rather direct link from Spinoza to the scientistic Vienna Circle inspired by the results of Max Planck and animated by Schlick, Neurath, and others—Wittgenstein, after Russell, is no doubt the culmination of this trend of modern mysticism. Russell's famous attempt, with Whitehead, to unify logic and mathematics expresses the notion that the logic of thinking and the mathematics of nature *must be one*. Still, mathematics is a science, and logic is not; they remain ontologically distinct.

13 Negation in the sense of "not true" is not admissible here, strictly speaking; Spinoza would say: "no" must mean "not clear, ergo nonsense."

14 Spinoza makes it attractive both to believe in natural science and in God, but not to believe in the cultural and social autonomy of a human mind and a lifeworld of meanings built up and maintained by consciousness and communication. Analytic philosophers consequently do not understand how semiotics could be meaningful.

15 In language, there are words and sentences. Words only have signifieds, whereas sentences have reference. Sentences are inherently deictic, in that they refer through speaker's time, space, and "personhood." Noun phrases in sentences can be made deictic by the use of demonstratives and other "shifters" (Jakobson). Isolated words do not have deictic semantics, only conceptual semantics, as Saussure insisted.

16 Why does it matter whether the notion of falsehood is maintained or not? Well, if a hypothesis is thought to be wrong, that is, false, arguments can and should be presented against it. If it is considered to be meaningless, it does not even make sense to argue against it. Analytic spinozism therefore does not discuss theoretical hypotheses; it just silences them and cuts the bridges of discourse. In contemporary terms, "fake news" are likewise treated as meaningless, discretely silenced instead of being countered by arguments.

17 The French philosopher Gilles Deleuze thus famously ascribed "desire" and "intensities" to machines and saw "streams" of meaning flowing through networks of machinery and people; he scorned the Freudians for being too Cartesian. Deleuze and Guattari (1972).

18 Cf. J. Heil in Audi (1995).

19 There is even a contemporary Danish strand of radical world-logicists, including Peter Øhrstrøm (1995) and Carsten Hvidtfelt Nielsen (2003); Hvidtfelt Nielsen understands that consistent meaning skepticism cannot be stated without being self-defeating, so he suggests, in his doctoral thesis, a logical calculus, a "formal theory" to do the job, thus hoping to avoid self-defeating *language*.

20 In conceptual metaphor theory, it is thus plainly believed that the human body contains an idea of itself, namely the *container*, which becomes an image schema that

can serve as a source structure in ontological metaphors (Lakoff and Johnson 1980, p. 29): "Each of us is a container." Our body knows what it is, because it knows itself. The container schema is the idea *of* the container body. The body schematizes.

21 Behind Spinoza's logicism there is probably a kabbalistic mysticism; this mysticism is in harmony with modern forms of religious sensitivity, in which the divinity is identified with the physical world, and experimental science therefore is a form of religious ceremony—natural science, that is, but certainly not the humanities, which are built on human knowledge of human, signified, meanings, so-called scholarship. Strictly speaking, scholarship is meaningless; therefore, institutions of truth should skip it.

22 Hofstadter, in *I Am a Strange Loop* (p. 294), lets his avatar #641 explain his view of consciousness: "The basic idea is that the dance of symbols in a brain is itself perceived by symbols, and that step extends the dance, and so round and round it goes. That, in a nutshell, is what consciousness is." And since symbols are made of nonsymbolic neural activity, there is no way that there can be a self, a conscious agent deciding what a person should do—no room left for "downward activity," that is, determination "downwards" from mind to body. There goes the free will, and this is Hofstadter's alternative: neural determinism versus (other) religious beliefs. It does not occur to him that the alternative to this trivial opposition is the view that *meaning* is what the consciousness debate must address. His substantialist monism does not account for the existence of immaterial realia such as ideas, poems, melodies, equations, things that can travel from person to person and be shared, whereas neurons cannot; those things are what cognition is about and of course also what personal identity, hence also ethics, aesthetics, politics, and philosophy are made of.

23 Jacques Derrida's anti-presence philosophy was of course as well received in the Spinozan tradition as his meaning skepticism.

24 By contrast, J.A. Fodor, in his recent defense of a representationalist, Cartesian view and his vivid critique of monist reductionism, writes: "I think we're overdue for a counterrevolution both in cognitive science and in the philosophy of mind. It's a Cartesian truism that minds are for thinking, and... that concepts are for thinking with. For all sorts of bad reasons... the twentieth century came to flout these truisms; indeed, to think that flouting them is a condition for responsible theorizing about the mind. So, by and large, the twentieth century thought that mental states are dispositions, typically the kinds of dispositions that get manifested by behavior." However, he continues (p. 48), "Mental states have causal power." Fodor's position calls for reconsideration; he was no doubt among the most lucid cognitive philosophers of the contemporary panorama.

25 Well, J.R. Searle certainly does care: this is what his famous Chinese Room imaginary experiment was all about. Meaning and sense-making do make a difference. See, for instance, one of his Chinese Rooms and the critique of Simon and Newell in the chapter "Can Computers Think?" in *Minds, Brains and Science*. I suspect that Searle is at least hesitantly a Cartesian.

26 I am referring to Lakoff and Johnson (1999). The "challenge to the Western thought" mentioned in the title of this monumental volume is in fact a Spinozan challenge to the Cartesian thought.

27 Fauconnier's "mappings" look representational but are still just logical operations, and the meaning emerging in conceptual blends is supposed to be some sort of truth, not representational meaning. Fauconnier (1997) and Fauconnier and Turner (2002).

28 Cf. Brandt (2004). Brandt and Brandt (2005). Line Brandt (2013).
29 Instead of Lakoff's A IS B, we would have to say, at least, that B IS ABOUT A—and that what B has to say about A is C, different from A itself.
30 In Fauconnier and Turner, *The Way We Think* (2002), truth-conditional semantics is explicitly rejected but implicitly reinstated. The models of conceptual blending offered seem to extract ideas directly out of the external world, disregarding their semiotic status as communicated meanings.
31 Fictions are representations of representations: they represent a narrator representing some "world." Human minds are deeply in love with fictions, since these mental creations offer us lively as-if experiences, allowing us to imagine without imposing the burden of perception.
32 This format may be diagrammatic; the diagrams we spontaneously draw for all sorts of purposes may reveal a thought-constitutive graphic-symbolic talent of our mind that urgently calls for study. In *LoT2*, Fodor insists on the representational character of mind; it is noticeable, though hardly surprising, to see how his overtly Cartesian stance, rather carefully argued and revised to include all sorts of formats, is received by the cognitive community: visceral rejection.
33 It is likely that the format of inner representations is *diagrammatic*—halfway between symbols and images (icons)—and that linguistic semantics, utterance meanings, and meaning in discourse are connected to this diagrammatic format and its extremely variable but still stabilizable patterns, thereby constituting a continuity between language and thought.

References

Audi, R. (Ed.), 1995. *The Cambridge Dictionary of Philosophy*. Cambridge: Cambridge University Press.

Brandt, L., 2013. *The Communicative Mind. A Linguistic Exploration of Conceptual Integration and Meaning Construction*. Newcastle upon Tyne: Cambridge Scholars.

Brandt, L. and P. A. Brandt, 2005. "Making Sense of a Blend. A Cognitive-Semiotic Approach to Metaphor." *Annual Review of Cognitive Linguistics*, 3, 216–249.

Brandt, P. A., 2004. *Spaces, Domains, and Meaning*. European Semiotics Series, No. 4. Bern: Peter Lang Verlag.

Deleuze, G. and F. Guattari, 1972. *L'Anti-OEdipe*. Paris: Ed. de Minuit.

Fauconnier, G., 1997. *Mappings in Thought and Language*. Cambridge: Cambridge University Press.

Fauconnier, G. and M. Turner, 2002. *The Way We Think. Conceptual Blending and the Mind's Hidden Complexities*. New York: Basic Books.

Gallagher, S. and D. Zahavi, 2012. *The Phenomenological Mind*. Abingdon-on-Thames: Routledge.

Garrett, D. (Ed.), 1996. *The Cambridge Companion to Spinoza*. Cambridge: Cambridge University Press.

Hvidtfelt Nielsen, K., 2003. *Interpreting Spinoza's Arguments: Toward a Formal Theory of Consistent Language Scepticism: Imitating Ethica*. Lewinston: The Edwin Mellen Press.

Kirkebøen, G., 2000. "Descartes' Regulae, Mathematics, and Modern Psychology: 'The Noblest Example of All' in Light of Turing's (1936) On Computable Numbers." *History of Psychology*, 3 (4), 299–325.

Kirkebøen, G., 2001. "Descartes' Embodied Psychology: Descartes' or Damasio's Error?" *Journal of the History of the Neurosciences*, 10 (2), 173–191.
Lakoff, G. and M. Johnson, 1980. *Metaphors We Live By*. Chicago: University of Chicago Press.
Lakoff, G. and M. Johnson, 1999. *Philosophy in the Flesh. The Embodied Mind and Its Challenge to Western Thought*. New York: Basic Books.
Lyons, W. (Ed.), 1995. *Modern Philosophy of Mind*. London: Everyman.
Øhrstrøm, P. and P. Hasle, 1995. *Temporal Logic—From Ancient Ideas to Artificial Intelligence. (Studies in Linguistics and Philosophy, Vol. 57)*. Dordrecht, Boston and London: Kluwer Academic Publishers.
Zlatev, J., G. Sonesson, and P. Konderak (Eds.), 2016. *Meaning, Mind and Communication. Explorations in Cognitive Semiotics*. Berne: Peter Lang.

3

The Architecture of the Embodied Mind

The Basic Architecture

The contents of our consciousness, or conscious awareness, that is, "the things we can be aware of," are accessible in a variety of levels of complexity. Whether in sensory perception or in mental recall, we access items by directing our attention to specific versions of their appearance. The mono-modal forms such as colors, visual shapes, sound shapes, odors are either foregrounded as they are, as aesthetic *qualia*, or absorbed in higher-order entities, normally multimodal, such as *objects, acts, or events* of which they are aspects. It is worth noticing, for example, that our attention freely can go from the occurring tonal sound of a musical instrument to the act of its being played and then back again to the "pure" tonal event. Furthermore, objects, acts, and events can be, and normally are, experienced as situated in some space and a certain time frame forming their *situated scenarios*, caused or motivated by certain forces, including personal intentions. Again, we are free to focus on the "pure" gesture of an act or the "pure" process of an event or on the entire situation and context in which it occurs. This freedom is essential in situations of learning, where a skill is to be acquired and then "lifted out" of the situation where it was studied. We are able to "understand" situations as conditioned by a contextual history and as likely to bear consequences in their contexts—even if we are not able to perceive such conditions or consequences directly but only to imagine them as based on our encyclopedic knowledge. "Understanding," in this sense, contextualizes situations on a more comprehensive and, in so far, a more complex level of consciousness; here is where language will distinguish perceiving and conceiving or "seeing" and "thinking." Finally, the result of the experience of understanding, typically a narrative integration, may give rise to comparative evaluations of the "case" in a framework of so-called values or criteria: degrees of justice, truth, elegance, utility, wisdom, or "evil," "ugliness," "horror," and so on. This ultimate level of mental activity leads to, or is directly linked to, *affective* reactions, such as personal emotions (pride, shame), general moods (elation, gloom, boredom), passionate feelings (love, hate).

What we have described through this series of steps is a structure of *integrations*, from qualia into things, from things into situations, from situations into states of affairs (cases), and from states of affairs into affective motives. The processes underlying the appearing of qualia are evidently the physical and physiological

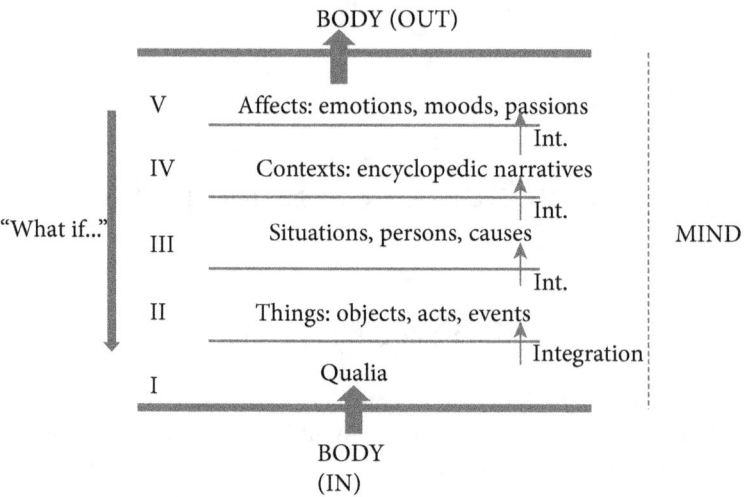

Figure 3.1 Five levels of integration in meaning production.

processes of perception and memory. What further happens to our affective states of mind is related to their affecting our body and triggering motor reactions. Our mental associations then change our mental work from its ascending cascades of integration to a descent through the same levels into plans of possible action. The details of such plans can trigger every sort of imaginary productions downwards, from multimodal scenarios, concepts, or emotions back to mono-modal qualia, this time as representations. Whereas the ascending integrations are in principle passively reflective, the descending imaginary constructions, productions, representational "fantasies" are oriented toward action. A hypothetical action plan will be mentally examined by ascending integration before the emotional evaluation we call a decision "stamps" it as good for execution.

The mental architecture summarized above, as in Brandt (2006), is shown in Figure 3.1.

The mind, we could say, is a small opening in the neural tissue surrounded by the bodily functions of external perception (BODY IN) and internal physiological reactions (BODY OUT) and internally served by memory at all or at least several levels. Our strong, and maybe overly strong, claim is that there are exactly these five phenomenological layers or levels, as shown, and that they are ordered by integrative processes ("upwards") that allow imaginative retro-processing ("downwards": "what if…"), especially to prepare expressive response acts.

Language and Culture in Mental Architecture

If the mental architecture is in itself transculturally and transhistorically stable, which is our actual hypothesis, the question of cultural and historical specification of meaning must be addressed. In order to do so, we need to relate an architecture of meaning to the semantics of human language. In fact, the grammatical language of our species, across idioms of all kinds, does make it possible to grossly label and refer to certain qualia (Level I: certain *adjectives*) and to certain affective experiences (Level V: certain *adverbs*), but mostly to the price of massive use of metaphors; it appears to be a preference of human language reference to literally operate on the intermediate levels (II–IV). Category-naming lexemes and phrases operate on Level II: *nouns and nominal phrases. Sentence* meanings on Level III: *verbs* and their constructions. Higher-order discourse-creative concatenations, including dialogue, on Level IV: *text*. These three levels—II, III, IV—are also, interestingly, the mental locations of all cultural creations, whether they be artifacts (II), institutions (III), or narratives (IV). It has not been found that qualia or affects as such are culturally (or ethnically) variable—at least to any important extent, despite the evident variations in terminology. By contrast, phenomena of Levels I and V are differently integrated and thus found in widely different cultural settings; comparable cultural "things" of course have variable sensory and emotional properties and aspects. This is what the comparative studies in the humanities are essentially about.

The core of human consciousness, or conscious awareness—Levels II, III, and IV—is thus culturally variable as to its actual content. It is not variable as to the *sorts* of integration that articulates it but certainly regarding the actual objects, situations, and knowledge forms that it contains. Transcultural communication, including interlingual *translation*, is possible because the elementary *format* of entities stays stable under all variations: acts are still formatted as acts, events as events, objects as objects, situations as situations (not as objects, for instance), and narratives as narratives. Translation works from sentence to sentence. This might seem evident but is less so in the perspective, for instance, of interspecies communication.

The peripheral instances, the all-important afferent first (I) and efferent last (V) levels, are the most physiologically dependent and therefore the least culturally malleable. They assure the very "embodiment" of the mind, its functional continuity with our hormonal and neuromuscular body, a relation that has to be less constraining on the internal levels (II–IV), where consequently our "intellectual" creativity unfolds. Inversely, our body is "en-minded" in the sense that the conscious mind and its architecture are inserted between two neurophysiological "faces," one organizing our multimodal perception and the other interpreting our affective states in nonmental terms of organic, psychosomatic reactions. Our conscious mind is, as in other animals, a tiny displacement in the cerebral *soma*, an opening that produces our mental theater.

Signs and Communication

This view of mental architecture makes it straightforward to describe the semiotic function—the phenomenon called sign—as distinct from contents and entities in general. All semiotic theories, from Antiquity to Modernity, distinguish the two aspects of any "significantly" signifying phenomenon: it can be perceived, and it can call our attention to some idea; it thus has a "sensibilis" side and an "intelligibilis" side; it has a "signifier" and a "signified," a form and a meaning, a "representamen" and an "object," and so on. It is of course the case that any phenomenon we can experience can be perceived or conceived as having such aspects. Any artifact "signifies" its function. A chair has a characteristic configuration as a multimodal object, and it has situational and social uses and cultural meanings.[1] However, it is obvious that in signs, the two aspects, one being of lower level in the architecture and the other of a higher level, are *separated* by lacking intermediate integrations. There is and there has to be a *semantic gap* between the signifier and the signified, so to speak. A sign calls for splitting our attention toward the two separated aspects.[2]

Traffic sign posts are objects whose graphic qualia are readable as instructions for specific narrative behaviors that have generic descriptions addressing pedestrians, car drivers, and others. Such signs are typical *symbolic* signs. Their expressions are entities of Level II, *signifiers (sa II)*, and their meanings are entities of Level IV, *signifieds (sé IV)*; they do not integrate on the intermediate Level III (the street can do without the parking sign post). The signifier is bound to the signified by the sign function, as a perception to a specific understanding *without* the normal integration. Following the instruction is, for the driver, to perceive the *sa (II)*, to understand the *sé (IV)*, and then to perform the content of the instruction in his situation *act (III)*.[3] Obeying the symbol is filling in, or supplying, the lacking integration. The sign *post* as "support" is the necessary *deictic* mediator that points to *where* the symbolic instruction is supposed to be followed.

To read a musical score, and then to "play it," would accordingly imply a similar process: *sa (II)* → *sé (IV)* → *act (III)*. This formula summarizes the meaning involved in symbolic communication. Symbols are therefore essential to all cultural formations and creations. Whether the behavior "intended" by the instructional meaning be physical (traffic) or mental (calculus), or both, as in music, the dynamic process is one and the same: filling the gap that makes something a sign is "interpreting" it.[4] The immense advantage of written language over spoken is precisely this gap constituted by the absence of situation, when the "author" replaces the "speaker." Texts, written, have (and need) intellective interpretations; spoken utterances, by contrast, are often integrated immediately in the pragmatics of their situations of use.

In Figure 3.2, I propose a simple representation of this view of the symbolic form of semiosis. In general, symbolic signs are, as mentioned, instructions to be performed in the present. The semantic content would correspondingly refer to possible *present* states of affairs. However, monuments and similar memorial setups are symbolic signs referring to *past* states of affairs while inducing present behaviors of respect, remembrance, awe, and so forth; and it may be said that writing—whether linguistic, musical, or mathematical—refers to states of affairs that will be real at the time of their being understood, interpreted, read, performed, or "executed," thus in the *future* of its formulation. The latter circumstance is then particularly productive in cultural contexts, where such "realizations" of the writ are often collective endeavors.

Symbolic signs are said to be conventional, or arbitrary, or coded. They are of course historically intended, conceived, and worked out by human beings in certain situations, just as proper names are ceremoniously *given* by someone

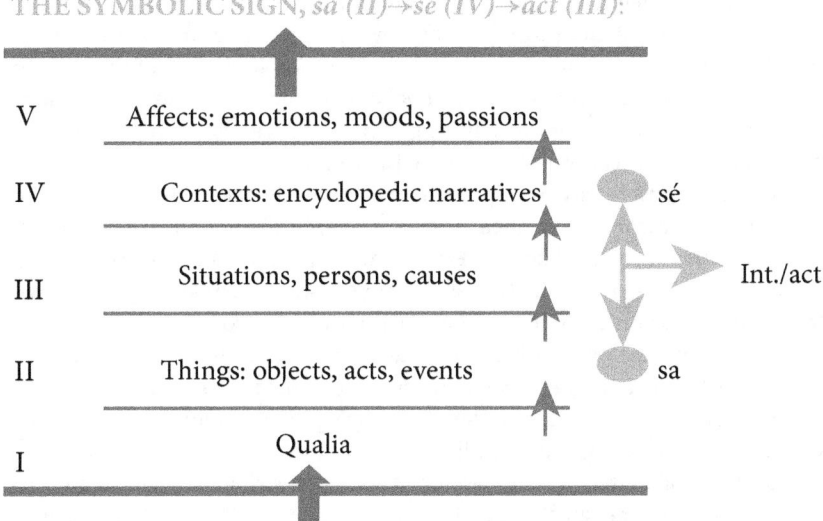

Figure 3.2 Symbols in mental architecture.

to someone through so-called speech acts; we could call the instituting acts of symbolization *symbolic acts* (such acts would include speech acts).[5]

A necessary comment: digital, graphic "signs"—letters, numbers, notes, and so on—must be integrated into sequences manifested on surfaces that are objects of some specified sort; in themselves they are qualia, short curved lines and line combinations that do not signify symbolically. The spaces of their composition define their meaning potential—so, for example, due to the character of its space of manifestation, a telephone "number" is not really a number.

Iconicity

Many digital symbols share graphic properties with drawn figures that we would call images. The A of the alphabet (and alpha) seems to be a descendent of an archaic ploughshare. So, what is an image, an iconic sign, in this perspective?

If we ask a visual artist, we will learn that it consists of intentionally reproduced qualia observed in objects, events, and acts in space-time. These qualia are typically maintained in the artist's attention during moments of observation and then imitated in some material different from their original place of appearance (the color of an apple will be painted, not on an apple but on a canvas).[6] They then naturally induce the idea of the original place of appearance, an object, and so on—of which they are images. Such an image can furthermore become a symbol, since it is an object, and even more easily than other objects, because its materiality has no default functional place and context. It *denotes* what it looks like, while it *connotes* ideas to which the denoted content may be or is often related; such connotation will easily assume symbolic force.[7] The entire image, framed and possibly signed by an artist, or cut out of a magazine, additionally connotes social information about the person in control of the space of exposition; this sort of meaning is again symbolic (in so far as it invites an attitude on behalf of the viewer) and also, ultimately, simply causal: it is a symptom of its "owner" and in this capacity, a so-called *index*, a causal indication.

Images are signs by *iconicity*. They point back and forth in deictic time (now; before now; after now). So, iconic signs include portraits, typically oriented toward a *past* (here is what someone looked like at a certain time); maps, particularly useful if they offer information valid in the *present* situation of the viewer; and models, typically used for planning of *future* or hypothetical constructions of some kind. Icons are natural signs in the sense that the way in which their qualia integrate in the object they present in perception naturally guides the way they integrate in the representation they form on the non-objectal support. The painting of an apple presents colors and contours of the depicted or imagined apple in a similar disposition, seen from some angle, on the new support that makes the result a representation. The distributed qualia of an apple are presented in a similar disposition in the image of an apple. The way an apple offers its qualia is not in any important way dependent on culture; it is natural (even if its perception will edit the way it is culturally experienced, especially if it is symbolically significant by connotation). The sensory material is naturally integrated as qualia of its material source in the pheno-physical world. This is why icons allow immediate communication across cultures, while symbols do not.

Art demonstrates another remarkable property of icons, one that is all-important in so-called *design*: qualia can be stopped in perception and withheld from integrating on the next level of meaning, that is, they can be experienced on their own level (I) as colors, lines, sounds, and so on—as "form" and "forms." Forms can have names, like musical beats, tones, and scales, and like certain colors and shapes; this testifies to the fact that there are important circumstances where they are perceived as only integrated in the framework of a secondary support, without necessarily being selected from an original object (event, act) that they will now represent. These circumstances constitute what we call *aesthetics*. Humans possess a faculty of *aesthetic perception*, whose basic characteristic is to allow the experience of "free qualia," forms disintegrated from former integrations or manifested without any other integration than the present manifestation; we call this phenomenon *composition*. Basically, composition requires mono-modal perception: music is perceived mainly in the auditive realm, painting mainly in the visual realm.[8]

Compositions of "free qualia" are maybe still iconic signs, even when their components or constellations do not represent anything on the next level of meaning. Anyway, it turns out that aesthetic perception universally entails feelings, states of mind appearing on the emotional level (V). Such aesthetic feelings are variably described, but there is little doubt that they occur by cognitive necessity. All "pure" qualia presentations evoke affective reactions of the mind; different "styles" of qualia are then developed as expressions of "styles" of affect. *Style* in general can be seen as the result of this differentiable connection; styles in language, architecture, music, pictorial art, dance, arts-and-crafts, and even industrial design, are always somewhat emotionally effective. The factor that drives human interest in form, "pure" or "free" qualia, probably is precisely this immediate and direct mental connection it establishes to affect. Form–affect constitutes a proto-iconic sign relation: *sa (I)* → *sé (V)* that opens an immense semantic gap: *II–III–IV*, to fill in the contexts of communication where this proto-icon appears.[9] When a representational disposition of form—*sa (I)* → *sé (II)*—fulfills the iconic sign, the aesthetic form–affect connection remains effective, unless it is neutralized by some functional pragmatics of the image (for instance, in the case of robot portraits in criminal investigation), and the gap essentially consists of imaginative concepts (of Level IV) that can be triggered as a "narrative affect" by the semantic schemas inherent in affects—*sé (V)* → *sé (IV)*—inspiring possible behaviors (III). Icons represent only *possible* states of affairs,[10] not actual instructions, or injunctions, as symbols do; this important distinction is simply due to the fact that the iconic signifier is a *sa (I)*, not a *sa (II)*.[11] The signifier is a constellation or arrangement of qualia, a form, not the actual object carrying this constellation (the iconic sign is the "text," so to speak, not the book!—an essential distinction, as we know from religion).[12] Figure 3.3 shows the mental structure of iconicity, as this analysis proposes to describe it.

Proto-iconic and iconic communication is cross-cultural; in fact, communicating (proto-)iconically is, for humans, the main or only way to transcend cultural constraints on meaning in communication and thought. As individual persons, we are of course capable of naturally understanding images as such, and we are capable of experiencing form as expressions of human affect, with its narrative implicatures (sorrow and grief implying loss, anger implying offense, etc.). Cross-cultural

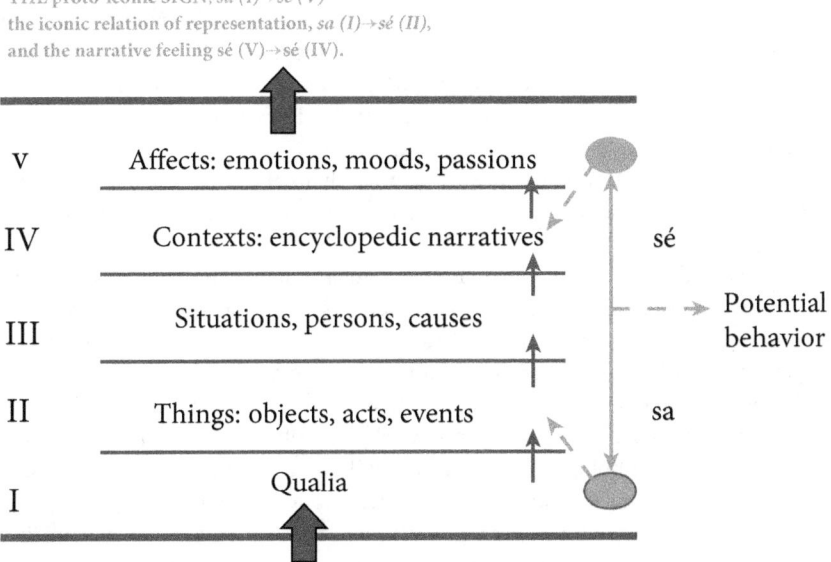

Figure 3.3 Icons in mental architecture.

communication is primarily affective, as art demonstrates, to the extent that it is displayed internationally and travels across cultural boundaries. Art is crucial to human freedom and to critical thinking, because it is based on this semiotic property of the mind that allows us to *not* adhere entirely to any culturally specific community.[13]

In terms of modality, we could say that the core part of mental meaning architecture, II–III–IV, is dominated by displays of cultural instructions, that is, of a social ontology of things we *must* have (or not have), *must* do (or not do), and *must* know (or ignore). This central mass of meaning, which could be termed the *deontic core* of human consciousness, is negotiated through symbols, symbolic communication. The peripheral part of the architecture of meaning, I and V, embeds the former and consists of our most embodied contents: sensations and feelings, and their extensions: images (II), imaginations (III), and intuitions (IV) that inform and guide our experience of the lifeworld—a reality made of possibilities, of things that *may* exist, that we *may* do, that *may* be the case, a reality semiotically offered by the mechanisms of *iconicity*. The world of the (socially or physically) necessary is given as a part of the world of the possible.

Conclusion

In human evolution, the semiotic chapter begins when iconicity disintegrates from a former state of compact meaning integration that only consists of functional behaviors. *Theatrical* behavior, as we know it from technical teaching-by-showing, may be an important transitional form.[14] Then some theatrical gestural routines expressing *extreme states*—ecstasy, panic, sexual arousal, passionate love, and subsequent grief—lead to the invention of new collective forms, which become entrenched as *inducing* affect, not only expressing it.[15] Once affect can be induced intentionally, it can drive symbolization—which needs to be grounded in shared affect. Shared feelings develop shared stories that subjects will feel they are part of. Participation drives identification and grounds the entire deontic core of culturalization.

A contrario, affective disturbances—from individual psychosis to collective "hysteria"—can cause deregulation of the symbolic routines of individuals and groups. Neologistic and altered speech in schizophrenia manifests a certain dissolution of the binding between first-language phonetics and affect, namely the emotional charge of its sounds. The semiotics of psychosis sometimes manifests correspondingly an extension of the deontic core to the entire domain of consciousness, potentially erasing the "free qualia" altogether or submitting them to a deontic occupation.

The view of the mental architecture of meaning we have sketched out here may shed some light on mental pathologies and thereby contribute to the general cognitive psychology of our "symbolic" species. Immediately, I would like to just emphasize one single point: the aesthetic and the functional modes of perception are distinct processes within the same mental architecture; their difference gives rise to iconicity, which drives symbolization but stays distinct from it. We might as well call humans *the iconic species*.[16]

However, the underlying point of all such semiotic points is the cognitive fact that the embodied mind indeed has an architecture of integrations by stable levels of complexity—not just of increasing complexity but rather of different sorts of complexity—which is what makes the semiotic evolution of our species possible and allows subjects of our species to think and to communicate and—mirabile dictu—even to share thoughts.

Notes

1. Cf. Umberto Eco's discussion of chairs in *La struttura assente*, 1968. Eco argues that the co-presence of these aspects in fact lets chairs be signs. Then all functional things would be signs, whether artifacts or not. Their meaning would be their function. Eco misses the point I am making here. (I forgive him.)
2. So, again, a piece of furniture, in a museum or in a picture, can be an icon of a historical style or epoch; a urinal can be a work of art, as we know, if we create the semantic gap I am considering here, by changing the context and thereby removing the intermediate integrations. Duchamp's urinal can no longer be in a toilet.
3. This account could explain in general what it means to "follow a rule." Wittgenstein should read this.
4. The term "interpretation" therefore seems polysemic: the musician "interprets" the written music by playing it. The actor "interprets" a role. The critic commenting a poem "interprets" it. The online translator "interprets" from language to language.
5. Symbolic acts would thus consist in producing some object intended to mean some instruction and to carry this meaning for some specific reason—the simplest version being the pure decision: A means B "because I say so" (the Humpty Dumpty version). The decision itself is a historical reason motivating the symbol—"arbitrarily." Many symbolic acts have more detailed historical motivations, as we know from proper names.
6. As a matter of fact, I know of no artist having painted an apple on an apple. My point seems overly obvious; but in concept art, an artist—in casu William Anastasi—can take an accurate picture of a wall and then cover that same wall with that picture (*Untitled*, Dwan Gallery, New York 1966; this work is called "the wall on the wall").
7. This is why Roland Barthes, in his *Mythologies* (1957), critically studied connotations as ideological mechanisms.
8. The mono-modality of elementary aesthetic perception may account for the frequent forms of synesthesia found in art (and the myriads of "synesthesic" metaphors describing experiences of art).
9. In my essay "The Semiotics of Diagrams" (Brandt 2004), the proto-iconic binding discussed here is explained as a diagrammatic and topological phenomenon. The objectless forms are graphics of diagrams that mean conceptual, schematic mental spaces of spontaneously imagined geometries, topologies of imaginable but invisible states of affairs (still on Level III); abstract paintings would go into that category.
10. The great philosophical semiotician C. S. Peirce saw icons as signs of "possibility"; however, he did never try to explain this modal phenomenon.
11. The author happens to have a non-parking sign in his garage; it is now only an *image of* a non-parking sign, since it has lost its indication of relevance; and the idea of

prohibiting "parking" in the space reserved for parked cars is now just what we call a "joke." Symbols degenerate into icons; thus, in clothing fashion, military uniform caps are used as ironic and coquettish icons of what they "have been."

12 People swear on books, not on texts. They therefore characteristically lay their hands on the book-object while doing so; forms cannot be touched in this ritual way.

13 On the other hand, the pressure from culture is massive in perception, especially in the auditive domain: tonal pitch and timbre in music and phonemic fine-tuning in first language are unavoidable, as Aniruddh Patel (2008) stresses. But this is precisely why foreign music and languages are often experienced as more aesthetically pleasing or interesting than the sounds of one's "own" culture. In order to experience the homely sounds as aesthetically significant, we have to modify them intentionally and thus to be "creative"—something which we can only or mainly be in our "own" acquired music and language, the idiomatic forms we grow up with.

14 It corresponds to the mimetic phase in Merlin Donald's (2001) account of cultural evolution.

15 Drug-induced ecstasy is found in many religious practices; extreme states of mind (and body) are regularly related to artistic activity and aesthetic sensibility; such states have been (and are) creative in so far as they involve the unfolding of proto-iconic connections.

16 In Terrence Deacon's *The Symbolic Species* (1997), it is rather evident that the blind spot is iconicity.

References

Brandt, P. A., 2006. "Form and Meaning in Art." In: (Ed.) M. Turner, *The Artful Mind. Cognitive Science and the Riddle of Human Creativity*. New York: Oxford University Press.

Brandt, P. A., 2004. *Spaces, Domains, and Meaning. Essays in Cognitive Semiotics*. Berne: Peter Lang.

Deacon, T., 1997. *The Symbolic Species. The Co-evolution of Language and the Brain*. New York: W. W. Norton.

Donald, M., 2001. *A Mind So Rare. The Evolution of Human Consciousness*. New York/London: W. W. Norton.

Eco, U., 1968. *La struttura assente*. Milano: Bompiani.

Patel, A., 2008. *Music, Language, and the Brain*. Oxford: Oxford University Press.

4

On Consciousness and Semiosis

The Dynamics of Basic Consciousness

In our present experience, that is, in the integrated perception of here-and-now states of affairs in the outside world, offered to our consciousness when awake, we find ourselves inscribed in two distinct forms of spatial organization, namely a frontal angle of opening and orientation spanning from our sensing body and fanning out toward possible objects of sensory attention—a spatial schema evidently based on the scope of vision—and a "surround" space in which we are situated as a mobile entity in the middle of a stationary place—a spatial schema most likely based on auditive perception, a soundscape. In this sense, the "presence of presence" is a representation of the following components (allowing the surround to be represented by a square) (Figure 4.1).

In general, these components are superimposed by a basic format in consciousness, according to which we will have a paradoxical double formation that is both "Olympian" ("observing from above") and "Subjective" ("observing from the position of the body of the subject"). The angle (or vantage) space and the surround space are correlated, so that we can sense our own "present presence" as a superposition, a dual installation, typically with the angle as a *foreground* and the surround space as a *background* (Figure 4.2).

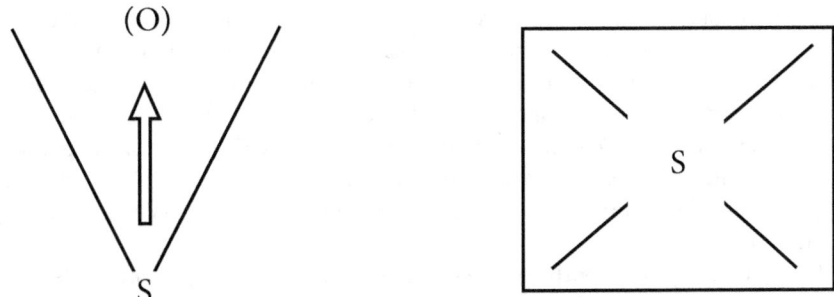

Figure 4.1 Subject "intending" Object. Subject surrounded by space.

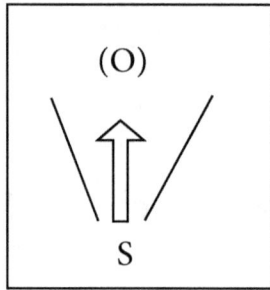

Figure 4.2 Subject situated and intending.

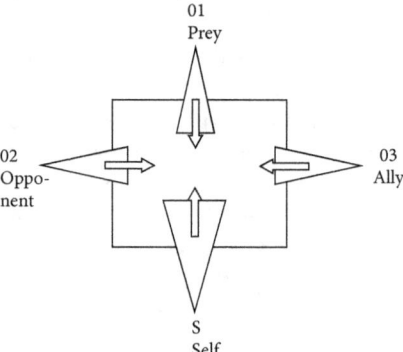

Figure 4.3 Subject and Relevant Others of salient categories in the immediate surrounding space.

The surround component does not, of course, just "contain" stationary and uniform Objects; the individuals and categories of different possible Objects in an elementary presence representation—let us term it "animal consciousness"—will most often be detected and perceived as only partly manifested, only "signified," by their traces or indices, visual, olfactory, auditive. Such Objects especially include what we can call Relevant Others: mobile, animated, conscious, subjective beings, engaging in interactive contact and exchange with the Subject of consciousness we are modeling. Relevant Other categories in animal consciousness, in this sense, will typically include *preys* (O1), dangerous *opponents*, competitors or predators (O2), and *allies* (O3). These categories are in turn conceptualized as conscious, perceiving, and intending, that is, as co-Subjects. We may specify them by letting the Object horizon appear in terms of semiotic "windows" in the present surround space, through which these categories manifest significant parts of their embodied and perceptually active beings (Figure 4.3).

This primary dynamic portrait of elementary consciousness[1] represents subjectivity as embodied and situated, immediately involved—inscribed, so to speak—in a pluri-subjective drama, where the identification of an object of a certain category will imply a corresponding type of response behavior, that is, of interaction. In order for the Subject to take control of an attractive O1, for example, it has to counter the action of an antagonistic O2 (targeting and attempting to control either O1, O3, or the Subject) and to interpret the attitude of an ally O3 toward O1, O2, and the Subject. Situations are thus already rather complicated on this basic level.[2]

Metaphorically speaking, the surrounding space has "walls" and "windows." Instead of making visual contact with a prey, for instance, the Subject most often has to follow traces of O1 that are causally produced *indices* of a proximal or distal being (e.g., an animal hiding). The subjective attitude of intending is thus technically a matter of *attending* to such causal markers. The relation from Subject to Object opens a semiotic window in the wall of presence-space. The typical *action schema* of the relation Subject–Object (S–O1) would be one of accessing/"taking"/incorporating and then of "holding." A possible generalization may consist in associating this schema with a Subject's interpretation of percepts via *attractive indexicality* as such, or rather, indexicality plus "desire": an object relation program for detecting, accessing, and "getting hold of" ("taking" and "having").

The relation that the Subject must establish with an antagonistic O2 may be characterized as iconic, in that the emergence of the antagonistic Other in S's space prompts for two inverted images of the Subject's desire: a serial image of (S–O1) (= "I want to eat this one"), in which S maps onto O2 and O1 now maps onto S (yielding the chiasmus S:O1:: O2:S = "I want to eat this one, but [::] an antagonist-predator wants to eat me"), and a parallel image in which S maps onto O2 and O1 onto itself (S:O1:: O2:O1 = "I want to eat this one, but so does my competitor"). The expected aggressive attitude of O2 toward S may therefore iconically—that is, perceived in the scope of an intentional exchange of the same schema variably invested, oriented serially (O2 → S → O1) or in parallel (O2 → O1 ← S)—signify the "same" desire. In this dimension, such object relations are thus again semiotic, albeit by force of a different semiotic mechanism, something we could call *antagonistic iconicity*.[3] The ambiguous orientation of the iconic mapping is an essential aspect of the triangular drama S–O1–O2. The Subject may mimic O2's attitude, for example by staging a mock attack to scare O2 away; or else, S may mimic O1's attitude by pretending to flee.[4]

We may envisage yet another semiotic drama as a standard condition, when it happens that an ally, O3, that is, normally, a being recognized as conspecific, meets and greets the Subject. O3 engages in an interaction with S and conceptualizes the situation in which S is found. Likewise, but inversely, S conceptualizes some ways in which O3 will interpret S's situation. The interaction between S and O3 typically includes the behavior we call "politeness." S will gesturally (by yielding) signify to O3: "Please have a bite of O1, I can wait": "Your turn first." Or S will (by calling) produce a political invitation: "Please help me fight O2." A conditional coupling of these initiatives will be straightforward: "IF you help me fight O2, THEN you can have a bite of O1." A *conditional* idea like this one, combining "helping" and "sharing," creates a relation of complicity. It binds the first and the second person in an exchange: "If you X, then I Y," where X is a change in S's situation and Y a change in O3's situation. We are encountering here a basic intentional phenomenon, namely shared intentionality (I want X, you are supposed to want Y). Interrogative checkup gestures ("Do you at all want Y?") followed by an affirmative or negative response are the elementary modes of this type of interaction. *If X, then Y*: give me X, and I will give you Y; X is the code that opens Y to you. *X/Y, signifier over signified, is a symbolic, conventional sign*. Polite-political and negotiation-oriented behavior and gesturing are thus primordial expressions of *symbolicity* in the intersubjective framework of basic consciousness.

The above analysis gives us a dynamic-schematic picture of basic *consciousness as semiosis* in the simplest classical semiotic terms: indexical, iconic, and symbolic. There are many possible implications and consequences of this view; we will briefly develop a series of effects, highlighting those that seem to be the most immediate and immediately important.

The Dimensions of Memory in Experience

Perception has to be periodical, rhythmical. It cannot constantly process the same sensory flow but has to rhythmically scan and "update" previously processed percepts, in terms of both surround space changes and Object-related states of affairs. Even if the rhythm is as fast as, or faster than, a sequence of E. Pöppel's basic temporal "windows" (Pöppel 1997) of fully conscious presence, approximately three seconds long, it has to connect percepts already processed and new percepts that "update" the former, and in this sense, it has to constitute both a remembering and a "remembered present" (Edelman 1989). How would this view of perception as a process of immediate, spontaneous, automatic revision[5] of our "memories of here-and-now," so to speak, translate into functions of consciousness as semiosis?

Categorization of Objects and Relevant Others—such as a prey or an otherwise attractive entity (O1) that the Subject intends to "take"; or of the danger (O2) it seeks to avoid or eliminate; or of the ally (O3) it wishes to negotiate with—is a form of recognition: seeing something *as* a specified individual allows the Subject to retrieve it under a distinct, specifying category, recalled as attached to a location to where the Subject should then direct attention and response. Object constancy, a fundamental property of perception, is of course not only a gift of the "given" but has to be mentally achieved as re-cognition of some cognized entity under a constant (and spatially localized) category: sameness of an individual as "belonging to" a category remembered to appear at some location in the Subject's surround space.[6] Categories are, in this view, localizers; they help the mind retrieve individual Objects and understand them as "same" during the process of perception and, subsequently, from one scene of perception to the next or another. Human beings later superimpose language-based naming on categorization and eventually manage to share categorical paradigms, which leads to an expansion of the mental capacity of identifying and holding knowledge of individuals in experience. However, when categorical knowledge is nominalized and held as purely "semantic," it loses its inherent spatial meaning; spatiality must then be added syntactically to the de-spatialized category, whether generic or deictically identified ("the cat *on the mat*").

If the Subject's interaction with O1 is maintained over time intervals longer than those allowing automatic categorical recall, the Subject will appeal to experiences of scenes involving {O1}, that is, objects of O1's category, experiences of dealing with "this *kind* of things."[7] The *episodic* recollections coming to mind will typically be supplemented by notions of formerly experienced {O1} properties—*semantic* attributes, we would call them—and by proprioceptive traces, bodily markers, of the Subject's own actual reactions to {O1}—*procedural* recall.[8] The result is optimally but not necessarily a combined episodic (i.e., localized, procedural, and semantic) attitude of the Subject: a certain locally oriented bodily disposition and a corresponding mental (conceptual) orientation. In the O1 window, O1 is now a sign (token) of this semantico-procedural meaning of {O1} (as its type).

O2 may be categorized and subcategorized as well; here, recall includes the experience of the animated Object's own view of the Subject, in so far as it is accessible to the Subject: in the case of human beings, a view of the situation as seen from this Other and empathically "theorized" by the Subject.[9] We remember what we believe that Others—and especially antagonistic Others—experience when they encounter ourselves in a situation of intending. {O2}, let us say, the category of a given sort of opponents, will be able to perceive and "objectify" both S and O1, and the relation S–O1, as parts of a dramatic situation. At least in principle, the Subject will register this external view of the situation and be able to integrate it in the memorized *narrative* (thus including an external "narrator": the opponent) of the constellation S–O1–O2. The Subject, human or animal, has to cognize the fact of *being seen* (being perceived by the Other) in order to grasp and evaluate the danger of a situation. This rudimentary reflexivity, self-awareness, acquired through the iconic interaction S–O2, is of course essential to human narratives in which the dimension called veridiction[10] is important, namely when truth and falsehood are explicitly on the dramatic agenda.

Seeing oneself through Others seeing oneself, and remembering this allo-scopic vision, is essential to consciousness on higher levels. The interaction with O3 is particularly significant in this respect. This Other is invited to decide if and to what extent S is in danger; if so, all things being equal, it will itself be implied in the scenario as a "helper," or in narratological terms, an "adjuvant" actant.[11] For the Subject to enter in contact with the "helper" is to imagine itself *being* the helper (of someone like the Subject). If the Subject's signal toward O3 means "help me!," and if the interaction is human, it iconically also means "… as I would of course help you, if you were in my shoes."[12] This reversibility is, I suggest to think, primordially built into the empathic and theoretical mental contact competence of the Subject. The call for help involves a commitment. It entails an implicit promise. Calling for help means asking the Other for a gratuitous act of *giving*.[13] In the notion of "generosity," giving and helping merge into a normative phenomenon: doing "good" to Others by acting on a situation in such a way that these Others are truly less in danger (of dying, in prototypical cases) after the act than before. Calling for help is inviting for giving. Giving binds the giver and the receiver to each other, creating lasting representations of "owing" in the receiver (cf. the phenomenon of "gratitude") and "status" in the giver. *Not giving* is, correspondingly, being "bad" or even "evil"; the person who refuses to give refuses to establish "bonds." Politeness can be understood as behavior that signifies a disposition to be "good" and accept "goodness" of Others, in this sense. In this communication, the self of the Subject thus acquires yet another aspect: an ethical dimension.

To summarize, so far: the situational Subject is first *narrativized* (by O2) and then ethically *normativized* (by O3). The distinctive feature of the ethical self, resulting from recognizing one's situation from O3's position, is that a Subject is seen as being in danger, in a "critical" situation, and that this *crisis* is a reason for acting generously, politely, "responsibly."

The Subject can mentally leave its initial position and identify with its Others, O2 or O3. It will then be able to recall situations in the past where it was de facto an O2 (opponent) or an O3 (adjuvant) of Other Subjects. The Subject will in particular have to remember what it "owes" to Others, the help they may need in the future. Here is a major source of *representational* and therefore *temporal* consciousness, as thinking beyond the present. Human "on-line" perception itself is colored by representational imagination, that is, by "off-line" versions of intersubjective spaces introduced iconically, through O2, or symbolically, through O3, in that we partly escape, so to speak, into past, future, or *uchronic* spaces, through their windows in our presence space. Similarity (iconicity) and contiguity (here: temporal linking of acts, symbolic doings, signs exchanged) are, as Roman Jakobson suggested, semiotically basic connectors. They are, I wish to add, windows through which our consciousness can reach *more reality* than meets the eyes and ears of present experience. Such reality is offered by—and therefore dependent on—the Subject's memory, which adds depth and resonance to the present contents, by virtue of these vital actantial connections. We think through Objects and Others. Therefore, we think through signs.

The semiotic dimensions of consciousness are responsible for its basic determinations: a narrative self, born in conflicts; an ethical self, born as binding to Others. These basically spatiotemporal dimensions characterize what we apperceive as a constitutive feature of a Subject's "inner life," namely *feeling*. To feel "responsible" is to "feel," tout court, in the sense of more or less knowingly having "feelings," or affects, including (proprioceptive) pain, emotions, moods, and passions.[14] In our view, to acquire a certain capacity to "decode" Others' feelings in the present is to begin, in infancy, to have the extra-present "inner life" that is characteristic of higher "selves."[15]

Singularity, Metonymy, and Art

We now have to leave the ground shared by higher animal and basic human consciousness and to study some aspects of human "higher cognition." Human Subjects equipped with an "inner life" develop the concept of a *critical* condition of self and Other as a matter of *personal* being or "personhood": we attend to the *singularity* of the vulnerable Other; the singular, particular, individual One-ness of the Other as a self-identical entity, in so far as this Person is One and only One, exposed to dangers in unique situations that we may happen to witness. Persons as unique beings have proper names that signify their uniqueness. This symbolic phenomenon is strong enough to allow inversion: nonhuman entities that are given proper names are also treated as unique persons.[16]

Phenomenologically, consciousness is—as I hope to have shown—primarily *situational*, secondarily *narrative*, and tertiarily *ethical*. These three "laps" follow from the actantial and semiotic logic of the Subject's (Relevant Other) object relations. Based on the cognitive singularity effect of ethical personhood, the fourth lap in the semiotics of consciousness will further unfold *affectivity*, a characteristic of human minds that cognitive research has so far only studied in its most elementary emotional aspects.

The transformation of O1—namely as Object of the Subject's *desire*, as psychoanalysts say, or *love*, or *admiration*, or other forms of liking and "wanting-to-be-with"—into a singular individual, a unique being beyond classification or categorization, occurs, in the case of persons, typically when this Object has already been experienced by the Subject as an O3, an adjuvant. The singular Object of passionate interest, on behalf of the Subject, is typically believed to be a highly responsible, ethical person. If the passional O1 is not a person, it is instead typically an aspect of a person, a part, a product, a trace, a sign, a metonymical representative of the person. Metonymy[17] is essentially the cognitive logic of personhood; this well-known rhetorical trope is really a cognitive process that is as deeply rooted in the human mind as the concept of Person: a self, understood as a Person, transcends any bodily reference (you are not "just" your body), because it is determined metonymically as the abstract or ideal referent of all accessible indices of the activity and existence of the individual. This metonymic referent is, I hypothesize, the source of singularity. We think *pragmatically* in terms of social status, professional identity, ethnic affiliation, and so on, all related to metonymy; we spend our own lives trying to leave traces that can be read in some specific direction, as indications of our "essence"—this is what existentialists have referred to as "creating your self" and the Sartrean principle according to which "existence precedes essence" (Sartre 1946). But metonymy can flow backwards from the referent to its signs, so that these, the "relics," inherit the value or force attributed to their source; this is probably what is happening in *aesthetics*.[18] Our appreciation of the formal "beauty" of artistic expressions is determined by inverse metonymy, letting the signs and the referent enter a loop of inter-reference between "form" and "meaning" (the latter in the sense of "someone who *means to* do or express something by forms"). Works of art are metonymic expressions of something (inherently valuable[19]) characterizing their creators, but once these creators have obtained acknowledgment from a group of human Subjects, the artistic expressions themselves—and sometimes even trivial life details—can become Objects of intense perception, close to worship, in their own right; these expressions, the works of art, receive proper names (titles) and are experienced as singular, unique, and lovable. They are recognized and "loved," as manifestations of great art—or at least as fetishes, "relics," marked by an aura of genuine sacredness. We can then forget about the creators and stop idealizing them.

Human *love*, the lap (level 4) of the unfolding of consciousness that we have to situate as superordinate in relation to the ethical lap (level 3), may well be of exactly this sort: a long-term feeling that flows from signs toward their author, the beloved person, but also backwards, from the person to its signs. The "beauty" of the beloved is of the same semiotic kind as the "beauty" of the work of art; so, the vocabulary of art is the same as that of love. Beauty is the inverse-metonymic energy flowing from the objectivated person toward her acts, gestures, properties, traces, communicated ideas, belongings, characteristics in general.

Art is historical for a reason having to do with the metonymic logic of the singular works. Since the appearances of a beloved person or work of art are appreciated as forms, they are of course iconically efficient: forms are copied into other forms that refer to the former (persons and works of art are imitated, admiration produces epigonism), but the copies will then "banalize" the original and neutralize its singularity, that is, its aesthetic core characteristic. Therefore, singularity has to be restored by invention: history of art may be driven by this dynamic *dialectic of singularity*: de-singularization, followed by re-singularization, new creativity. Iconicity is still agonistic, in a sense.

Originally, O1 is the prey of the subject. But in the realm of *eroticism*, it becomes the position of the desired entity! In the framework of aesthetics and desire, that is, in the *erotic* mode of meaning, *O1 is the valued position*, so some agents of the category {O2}, opponents of the S–O1 relation, will now want to occupy that position, in front of some S. Such an O2 can be trying to be the passional O1 of some passional Subject by copying O1's style. The copier may be an artistic agent who thus tries to "steal" love or desiredness from someone else, an established O1, by imitating it and thus weakening its singularity. The copier may, as well as the original was, be an artist[20]— the psychology of artists often literally consolidates them in this general determination, the presence of a disposition to paradoxically be "more original than some original" in order to attract some preexisting "love" (attention, interest, recognition, a certain aura of sacredness pertaining to "desiredness"). The artistic form of consciousness thus has traits of "evil," we might say.[21] The field of love as a mode of consciousness thus leads us from ethics to aesthetics and from "good" to intentionally "bad" or "evil" intentions and deeds. Art, as rivalry, from this perspective, can be a form of aggressive, unethical behavior.[22]

Levels of Consciousness. Consciousness in Language

A semiotics of consciousness naturally builds on the sign status of objects of conscious attention. The levels or aspects or dimensions of consciousness and selfhood we identify on phenomenological grounds can be directly derived from the structural dynamic properties of the basic semiotic design of conscious scenarios. These aspects are thus not really of a "higher order" of cognition but may instead be understood as *aspects* of certain intentional processes that are *inherent* in the basic design.

The Objectal syntax—O1, O2, O3 in the space of the Subject—is actantial in the dynamic sense we have briefly explored.[23] In a Subject's perspective, O1 is an attractor, O2 is an antagonist, O3 is an adjuvant: a lateral attractor, and these instances meet in one and the same space. But the Subject interacts with its Object-Others and also *remembers* itself as seen from their point of view—as cognized in their perspective, *by their conscious attention*. Subjects interact in so far as they participate in *each other's conscious scenarios*. If these scenarios share the same *format*, intersubjective interaction does not have to be chaotic, even if it can be highly conflictive and driven by significant misunderstandings. Subjects may inherently "know" that they are the actants of one another. They can and do categorize each other as specified actants, and they even can and do, occasionally or regularly, agree to a shared status of Subjects, {S}, in a common story or project.[24]

The first levels of consciousness follow from such intersubjective and actantial identifications: "If you are my O2/O3 now, then I 'am' you in my immediate and perceptive imagination, so I can see myself as I still am as Subject, as if it were you…"—This curious mental "I am you" ("in your shoes") operation in the human mind has been amply commented in mental space and blending theory,[25] and there is little doubt that it plays a major role in human thinking and communication. Here, I am only adding two aspects: it is crucial to basic consciousness, and it is crucial to the function of memory in perception, imagination, and consciousness in general; and it allows the Subject to remember other people's experiences and to "mesh" them into perception.[26]

However, in order to produce a minimal model of the stratified structure of elementary human consciousness, built on a primordial model of animal consciousness, as we have seen, we need to explore the possibility of identifying a slightly more complex, fifth level or stratum: a *linguistic* region of consciousness.[27]

The use of language presupposes the ethical, loving, aesthetic, and either generous or malignant attitude to forms in conscious content. Language tells stories that serve the urge to imitate, simulate, steal beauty, or redirect love: slander, gossip,[28] is apparently a grounding function of language use in all cultures, but these stories can also serve the "law," the restoration of truth, the project of justice, the maintenance of respect, and so forth—all against the presupposed malignant tendency. Language creates opposing semantic representations of versions of states of affairs; it does not directly represent a Subject's monistic perspective. It is inscribed in a dialogical "discourse," a diatribe, an unending polemic debate between versions and evaluations of "what happens" that constantly imply differing and conflicting actantial voices.[29] Linguistic *enunciation*,[30] the structure of persons, voices, viewpoints, modes, emotional speech temperatures, and so on, in the grammatical organization of human language in sentences as utterances, is a result of this underlying linguistic polyphony, not only in its use but in the core of its constructionality.[31]

The most striking fact of enunciation is probably the "Olympian" phenomenon: the fact that we can talk "objectively" and state *what is the case* about a state of affairs without having to specify our own actantial involvement as interactively cognizing speakers.[32] We most often use this neutral mode of what I would like to call *linguistic consciousness*: "The truth is that…" It is a totally disembodied mode of stating positive or negative facts; from nobody's point of view in particular, something just is the case, "objectively." Here, the primordial, objective surround space itself apparently acquires a voice and speaks, in some languages using the core copula verb (Latin: ESSE) meaning *to be*.[33] Language is apparently coextensive with the very *space of unlimited presence*. It can therefore speak, describe, predicate, evaluate, without having to signify or specify a speaker. Or rather, the impersonal *thought* of the space in which contents (states, events, acts) take place becomes language that affirms its "objective" content—and the actual speaker appears as an appendix that gives voice to this "spatial truth," the unembodied truth of "what is."

We may ask how it is possible that language can express the existence, state, and essence of things without referring to a subjective anchoring of such expressions. In other words, how did humans happen to develop such an impersonal form of consciousness—paradoxically, the expression of a *disembodied consciousness*, to be experienced through language as a "voice of truth"? As the voice of things themselves ...

The answer, I think, lies in an experience of shared time. What time *is it*? (ESSE again). It is this or that time for all subjects copresent. Time fills the social space of presence as a shared atmosphere. In human evolution, time eventually acquires this generic status in so far as it is *symbolized* in a musical and/or calendaric metric, based on numerical and personalized names of beats, units, and slots in time.[34] The shared *now* is a metrically determined moment in an either musical or chronological sense. It is highly probable that music and chronology were directly and constitutionally interconnected in the mind-set of our early ancestors. Time was sung and played; watchmen's hour songs still give us an idea of the "music of nights and days" as an early temporal symbolization, whose micro-format is music and whose macro-format would be the calendaric expansions of the concept of universal time slots into named entities such as hours, days, weeks, months, years, or cycles. *Truth and time* still coincide in sentence grammar: many epistemic adverbs or adverbials are universally used to specify both (examples: always, sometimes, never; seldom, often; once, twice; one fine day, *ad calendas grecas*).

The mode of consciousness that allows us to speak "olympically," and thus to describe, judge, evaluate things, states, events, acts, from nobody's point of view, is a creation of language or is inherent in the cognitive mode that creates language. This mode can of course be personalized emphatically, but simple sentences are most often still as neutral as they are simple: "It is raining." The linguistic creation has to be *performed* and in such a way as to show that the "sayer" is not the speaker (in the sense of the subjective source of an expressed stance); it has to be embodied "impersonally," through shared rhythmic symbolization, possibly music and (ritual) dance. In music and dance, time and space become animated and in real time create a collective, impersonal, trans-personal subjectivity. Otherwise, "It is raining" could not mean "It now rains (here)," instead of "I see rain." We still use ritualized prosody in the performance of administrative and media-borne prose, the institutional triumph of impersonal language. Notice the use of "background" music in news programs, for example.

This ultimate mode or level of consciousness, allowing us to communicate thoughts without an author, as impersonal statements, has had explosive impact on the communal life of our species. It has allowed us to develop technologies, deontologies, historiographies, philosophies, and, lately, sciences. Religions, by contrast, can be seen as attempts to re-personalize the impersonal ("It is raining" → "Tlaloc[35] rains").

A vertical architecture of forms of consciousness and corresponding versions of selves and others, as presented here, would look like Figure 4.4, representing the five distinct stages and five semiotic instances that may have made possible the cognitive transitions from a lower to a higher stage:

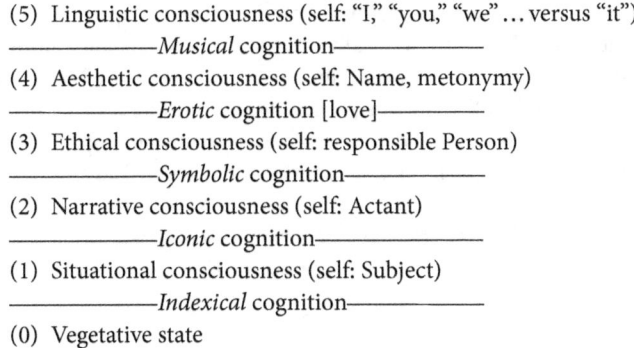

(5) Linguistic consciousness (self: "I," "you," "we" ... versus "it")
———————*Musical* cognition———————
(4) Aesthetic consciousness (self: Name, metonymy)
———————*Erotic* cognition [love]———————
(3) Ethical consciousness (self: responsible Person)
———————*Symbolic* cognition———————
(2) Narrative consciousness (self: Actant)
———————*Iconic* cognition———————
(1) Situational consciousness (self: Subject)
———————*Indexical* cognition———————
(0) Vegetative state

Figure 4.4 Five levels of consciousness.

Once the linguistic form of consciousness is achieved, through the semiotic, intersubjective, and affective evolution of our species, this particularly lightweight (impersonal, disembodied) mode is immediately applied to the underlying, heavier modes (of embodied consciousness). So, we could, and did, invent (4) an *art* based on language (poetry, literature); we develop (3) normative *discourses*; we (2) tell *stories*, anecdotes, create myths; and (1) we simply *chat* and twitter about everyday events and situations. We could easily, and did, get the (wrong) idea that all this is instead due to language and that therefore language and consciousness are coextensive or even somehow identical. We then need to remember that *it* still cannot rain on level (1).

Concluding Remarks

Consciousness, "the mind's display layer," according to Francis Steen (2007), is presentation—through the semiotic "windows" in the directly perceived present scenario—of states of affairs existing mainly outside of this scenario; the space of presence is just the limited "office" of consciousness, where things that happen deliver laconic "reports." These things and states of affairs are thus construed contents that consciousness has to *represent* during the presentation of their "representatives." Representation functions as the background of presentation. Representation—the offline mode of consciousness, so to speak, backing up its online mode—is, as we have seen, based on intersubjectivity, which is itself a complex cascade of interactions that leads to shared meaning stabilized culturally through symbolization and, particularly, through language. Thinking may be the very process that articulates, interrelates, what is presented and what is represented, in consciousness. What is *presented*, Descartes' *res extensa*, and what is *represented*, that is, given by consciousness as *res cogitans*, as taking place on the stage of the "theater of the mind"—a problematic metaphor that still however may be useful[36]—are semiotically connected as two sides of the same reality. This reality is of course cognized in terms of an "external world," which has a *sensibilis* and an *intelligibilis* aspect. We do not cognize represented states of affairs *as* internal to our mind:

consciousness does not represent itself, so conscious contents have to be experienced as linked to the real by relevance, that is, to be "really" relevant at least in some domain of reality.[37] Consciousness basically knows and handles reality in terms of accessible (sensible) things that are signs of their own (intelligible) hidden, inaccessible, "underlying" existence, including their non-materialized and only just hypothetical and potential properties. The immaterial is cognized as the reverse, the far side, of the material.

Therefore, the semiotic functions of consciousness may be considered the keys to the study of its architecture.[38]

Notes

1. The most elementary, semantically empty, meditative or vegetative state of consciousness that in principle precedes this actantial drama is transformed into such a deictic and situational stage by the perceptive identification and "gestalting" of Objects, especially Others, physically present or semi-present. Object detection makes use of causal schemas interpreting "things" that move and possibly perceive and possibly move because they perceive; I assume that such schemas are active in states of being awake and "focused." Categorization of objects, others, and situations is therefore directly involved in consciousness as attentively focused perception.
2. This dramatic topology was inspired by my cats and summarizes the result of careful observation of their behavior and sense of situations.
3. What I am essentially implying here is that emulation, mutual threats, and even chase are exchanges of iconic signs.
4. Pretense is iconic behavior. A more radical idea may be to also consider any direct intentional behavior as an iconic sign of itself, in so far as the act is consciously performed and *shows* what it is while performed. Demonstrative performance of a functional act is then still semiotic: *auto-iconic*, so to speak.
5. Short-term memory would correspond to such an involuntary, automatic updating, whereas long-term memory would phenomenologically correspond to (non-rhythmic) voluntary recall, intentional recollection.
6. Categorization is directly related to localization and thus to J. Piaget's (1953) "object permanence." See also Ballard et al. (1997). The authors argue that "at time scales of approximately one-third of a second, orienting movements of the body play a crucial role in cognition and form a useful computational level, termed the embodiment level." The time scale targeted happens to correspond to categorization time (200–400 msec). Nevertheless, literature on deixis and object constancy still does not link *location* of object and *category* of object.
7. I write {X} to refer to sets of elements *of the category X*.
8. Tulving (1984) suggested the distinction between three memory systems in long-term memory: episodic, semantic, and procedural. This list has become a standard reference in memory literature.
9. Mammals, and especially primates, that distinguish mechanically physical and intentional, voluntary movements, that is, movements caused by Others and movements caused by inanimate Objects, do attribute at least a rudiment of mind to such causing Others. In inter-animal mind-reading, in this sense, basic action plans (simple "narrative schemas") are of importance to survival.

10 French: *véridiction* (Greimas 1979), the semantic variations occurring in the combinations of being (*être*) and appearing (*paraître*), such as simulation (lying) and dissimulation (secrecy).
11 A.-J. Greimas' canonical actant model, in Greimas (1966), has six functions: Subject, Object, Addressor, Addressee, Opponent, Adjuvant.
12 Several philosophers have seen this generic inter-adjuvancy, including Emmanuel Lévinas (Lévinas 1982) and the great Danish thinker K.E. Løgstrup (Løgstrup 1956): "Den enkelte har aldrig med et andet menneske at gøre, uden at han holder noget af dets liv i sin hånd." [An individual never deals with another human being without holding a part of the life of this being in his hand.]
13 Cf. Marcel Mauss (2001). This author sees *giving* as a symbolic act, in that it entails (and means) a (due) response from the receiver, in the form of further giving, either reciprocal, as giving back, or transitive, as giving to a third part. Speaking is arguably a form of giving; language then presupposes "symbolic" exchange in this sense. "Giving signs" is a primordial mode of giving; inversely, the gift is necessarily a sign—of goodness or gratitude—and the sign is *symbolic* to the extent that its specific social meaning is conventional, that is, arbitrarily motivated by the historical and pragmatic context in which it is given.
14 I distinguish moods, emotions, and passions in the following way: short-term, minute-long, feelings that have anecdotal motives and, correspondingly, have marked onsets and gestural or face expressions are emotions; daylong background feelings are moods; and potentially lifelong feelings about persons or activities are passions.
15 Developmental psychologists discuss the temporal unfolding of this panorama of "feelings" in infants and their relation to occurring interactions (Trevarthen 1979, Stern 1985, Tomasello 1999).
16 This is the case of pet animals. They become uneatable for the same reason. Naming is also symbolic in Mauss' sense; the giver and the receiver must have some sort of names (name tags) in order to bond "responsibly" over time.
17 By metonymy, I understand plain simple formulae like "Shakespeare is on the shelf," meaning a volume containing his plays—works referring to their author. Shakespeare is of course "more" himself in his art than in his body. Metonymy defies bodily death. Deceased people are still people.
18 If value is attributed to the referent, for example Picasso, of a set of metonymic expressions, for example paintings, then other metonymic expressions will typically inherit the value of the referent. The paintings will each be a "Picasso." All metonymic expressions carry the connotation of awe, veneration, or fear and trembling. Positive or negative respect.
19 Artistic creation is of course *giving*, which may explain the basic value effect. Works of art have to be "good," skilled, crafted, and the artist therefore has to be gifted.
20 This may sound confusing: the artist is here described as "jealous" of an Object of desire, and so, imitating it to emulate and replace it. We know that art is based on mimesis; this is an extreme case: intra-aesthetic mimesis.
21 Cf. Bataille (1957), discussing relations between literature and evil, in particular with reference to Marquis de Sade and Baudelaire.
22 The standard view or claim is the opposite: art is the didactics of ethics—but a cognitive aesthetics has to empirically look at the human beings involved, and the biographical results are not very supportive of such a claim.
23 There may be many other Object categories in a Subject's basic conscious space, but the ones foregrounded here as dynamic and actantial appear to be doing elementary

and indispensable work for a semantics of thinking and feeling, so there are reasons to believe that they are indeed fundamental.
24 This view is in agreement with Gallagher and Hutto (2008), who claim that narrative attunement is a fundamental aspect of human intersubjectivity. Of course, agreement is primarily on who is the Subject (protagonist) in each drama.
25 Turner (1996) has a particularly significant early manifestation of this study of the counterfactual, conditional, highly complex but intuitively simple operation as an indispensable cognitive phenomenon.
26 This would be my modest addition to Glenberg's view of memory in perception (Glenberg 1997).
27 Is language already constitutively involved in earlier processes, starting from the narrative mode? I see no reason to think it is and thus disagree with Gallagher and Hutto (2008); however, it strengthens and re-elaborates all areas it inherits.
28 See, for example, Jaworski and Coupland (2005) on "othering."
29 Cf. Chapter 5, on the dia-logic of discourse.
30 French term (*énonciation*, "*uttering," versus *énoncé*, "utterance") introduced by Benveniste (1966), hitherto not used in anglophone linguistics, designating the realm of signified subjectivity in language: morphological indicators of personhood, first-person, second-person pronouns, determiners, demonstratives, shifter adverbs, modal adverbs, tense, mode, aspect, speaker-addressee relation markers, and the semantic variations thus expressed to manifest the presence of "l'homme dans la langue" (man in language). *Enunciation* can be determined as the structural properties of a sentence that prepares it for being integrated into a form or genre of discourse. Of course, many literary, philosophical, and linguistic scholars have otherwise treated aspects of "man in language."
31 Embedding of clauses in clauses thus reflects the uptake of things said in things said about them.
32 Cf. Brandt (2004).
33 Even if the first utterances of infants are quite "egocentric," they clearly can do the trick: "Juice—gone" (meaning "give me more").
34 The *symbolization of time* in terms of cyclically appearing periods—by calendars—is in fact a cognitive feat that can hardly be overestimated as a culturally constitutive factor. The origin of mathematics is to be found in the counting of temporal units.
35 Aztec rain god.
36 Dennett (1991). The notion of representation leads naturally to the idea of a "theater," but the plays offered on the stage of this theater are seen as taking place somewhere *in the world*—however, not "in the head."
37 Nothing we can think of can be experienced as appearing *in the mind*: consciousness does not seem to have such a place. The Subject experiences itself as existing "out there"; even counterfactual and false scenarios appearing to consciousness are experienced as external! This paradox is a serious challenge to any philosophy of mind. Negativity—*not* being the case—is cognized as some sort of potentiality: real but unrealized or unrealizable possibility. Consciousness is radically externalistic (cf. Freeman 2006).
38 There are now quite a few researchers, and not only in cognitive semantics and poetics, who find it appropriate to argue for a "semiotic turn" in cognitive science altogether, including Sonesson (2006), who finds support in Deacon (1997) and Zlatev (2002). The views debated under this heading are different in many respects; however, a common ground may be identified in the claim that *signified meaning* is data.

References

Ballard, D. H., M. M. Hayhoe, P. K. Pook, and Rajesh P. N. Rao, 1997. "Deictic Codes for the Embodiment of Cognition." *Behavioural and Brain Sciences*, 20 (4).
Bataille, G., 1957. *La littérature et le mal*. Paris: Gallimard.
Benveniste, E., 1966. *Problémes de linguistique générale*. Paris: Gallimard.
Brandt, P. A., 2004. "Evidentiality and Enunciation. A Cognitive and Semiotic Approach." In: (Ed.) J. Marín Arrese, *Perspectives on Evidentiality and Modality*. Madrid: Editorial Complutense.
Deacon, T., 1997. *The Symbolic Species. The Co-evolution of Language and the Brain*. New York: Norton.
Dennett, D. C., 1991. *Consciousness Explained*. New York: Little, Brown & Co.
Edelman, G. M., 1989. *The Remembered Present. A Biological Theory of Consciousness*. New York: Basic Books.
Freeman, A. (Ed.), 2006. *Radical Externalism: Honderich's Theory of Consciousness Discussed*. Imprint Academic.
Gallagher, S. (Ed.), 2010. *Handbook of Phenomenology and Cognitive Science*. Berlin: Springer.
Gallagher, S., and D. Hutto, 2008. "Primary Interaction and Narrative Practice." In: (Eds). J. Zlatev, T. P. Racine, C. Sinha, and E. Itkonen, *The Shared Mind: Perspectives on Intersubjectivity*. Amsterdam: John Benjamins
Glenberg, A. M., 1997. "What Memory Is For." *Behavioral and Brain Sciences*, 20 (1).
Greimas, A. J., 1966. *Sémantique structurale. Recherche de méthode*. Paris: Larousse, "Langue et langage."
Greimas, A. J. and J. Courtés, 1979. *Sémiotique. Dictionnaire raisonné de la théorie du langage*. Paris: Hachette.
Jaworski, A. and J. Coupland, 2005. "Othering in Gossip: "You Go Out You Have a Laugh and You Can Pull Yeah Okay but Like ...." *Language in Society*, 34. Cambridge: Cambridge University Press.
Lévinas, E., 1982. *Ethique et infini*. Paris: Fayard.
Løgstrup, K. E., 1956. *Den etiske fordring* [The Ethical Requirement]. Copenhagen: Gyldendal.
Mauss, M., 2001. (1923–1924). *The Gift. The Form and Reason for Exchange in Archaic Societies*. London: Routledge.
Piaget, J., 1953. *The Origin of Intelligence in the Child*. London: Routledge and Kegan Paul.
Pöppel, E., 1997. "Consciousness versus States of Being Conscious." *Behavioral and Brain Sciences*, 20 (1).
Sartre, J. P., 1946. *L'existentialisme est un humanisme*. Paris: Editions Nagel.
Sonesson, G., 2006. "The Meaning of Meaning in Biology and Cognitive Science. A Semiotic Reconstruction." *Trudy po znakyvym sistemam—Sign Systems Studies*, 34 (1).
Steen, F., 2007. "Integrating Consciousness." Manuscript presented in the Colloquium of the Department of Cognitive Science, Case Western Reserve University.
Stern, D. N., 1985. *The Interpersonal World of the Infant*. New York: Basic Books.
Tomasello, M., 1999. *The Cultural Origins of Human Cognition*. Cambridge: Harvard University Press.
Trevarthen, C., 1979. "Instincts for Human Understanding and for Cultural Cooperation: Their Development in Infancy." In: (Eds.) M. von Cranach, K. Foppa, W. Lepenies,

and D. Ploog. *Human Ethology: Claims and Limits of a New Discipline*. Cambridge: Cambridge University Press.

Tulving, E., 1984. "How Many Memory Systems Are There?" *American Psychologist*, 40 (4), 385–398.

Turner, M., 1996. *The Literary Mind. The Origins of Thought and Language*. Oxford: Oxford University Press.

Zlatev, J., 2002. "Mimesis: The 'Missing Link' between Signals and Symbols in Phylogeny and Ontogeny." In: (Ed.) , A. Pajunen, *Mimesis, Sign, and the Evolution of Language*. Turku: University of Turku.

5

The Dia-logic of Discourse

This chapter intends to show how even written monological discourse is driven by implicit dialogue to the extent that its semantic coherence depends on this underlying "dia-logic." Three very different examples are discussed—taken from the genres of invoice, prayer, and poetry.

The Invoice. The Dia-logic of Functional Prose

The following letter is what I take to be a rather coherent text. It is a clearly functional message, a comment accompanying an invoice. It is safe to say it belongs to the pragmatic genre of texts and also safe to add that it constitutes some sort of request[1]:

Dear PAaB,
[1] We understand how easy it is to overlook a small invoice.
[2a] But the fact is, the above invoice remains unpaid.
[2b] And although we know you intend to pay it, I'm sure you can understand that we can't keep sending you our magazine on faith.
[3a] So please use the enclosed envelope to return this duplicate invoice with your remittance.
[3b] Do it today!
[4] That way, we can both be sure The New Yorker will continue to illuminate your world each week.
Sincerely,
P. W., Circulation Department[2]

In the context of a subscription and the actuality of an unpaid invoice, the coherence of the sequence [1–4] may be established as a replay of an implicit or underlying dialogue as the following stipulated, imaginary exchange between sender (A) and receiver (B):

Reconstruction.

Implicit, A (the subscription manager): **You haven't paid our invoice for your subscription on our magazine.**
Implicit, B (the subscriber): **Oh, haven't I? Well, I must have overlooked it, I guess. I am so sorry.**
Now A says: [**1 above**]

Implicit, interpolated, B: **Yes, isn't it?**
A: [**2a**]!
Implicit, interpolated, B: **Of course, I intend to pay it, so there should be no problem. Please have faith in my fidelity. And have a nice day.**
A: [**2b**]!
Implicit, B: **No, I understand perfectly. So what do you expect me to do?**
A: [**3a**].
Implicit, B: **When do you want me to do this? I haven't got too much time, you see.**
A: [**3b**].
Implicit, B: **Ok then, if I must. But can I be sure this would help?**
A: [**4**].
Implicit, B: **What a bombastic way to put it: "Illuminate my world ..." Do you believe I am otherwise immersed in obscurantism?**

Seen through this creative reconstruction, the semantic coherence of the text [1–4] appears to be a dialogical[3] phenomenon; the utterer (A) anticipates the responses of the relevant reader (B), given that both utterer and addressee define each other and the actual situation in terms of a (here, literally) preexisting contract (a subscription). Theory of mind, the anticipation of the other's thinking, and empathy, the feeling of the other's emotional state, should therefore be implied in the active cognitive instances of meaning production responsible for its coherence.

In this sense, discursive coherence might be a matter of "distributed cognition"—another word for communication. Let's see how that view affects the analysis of *transphrastic semantics*.

The core of the argument is the information given in [2a]. [1] and [2b] contain concessive statements, the former followed by a concessive conjunction, *but*, the latter initiated by another concessive conjunction, *although*. The agent, "we," (A), understands...(namely, my (B) forgetting) and knows...(namely, my intention); however, this does not entail that he will overlook my missing payment. *Concessivity* is apparently, and really, an important contributor to discursive coherence but so is *consequentiality* (something is the case, *therefore* something else is the case), and concessive formulas presuppose the consequential relation they apparently protect against counteractive arguments (Figure 5.1).

It would be difficult, perhaps impossible, to account for the dynamics of this argumentative process without referring to the underlying dialogical stances of communication (staging speakers A and B), the dialogical deep structure of the monological surface text, so to speak, motivating the *connectives*: the post-concessive *but* occurring after an empathic act and before an act of insistence; the *so* occurring after the *but*-initiated act of insistence and before a statement of consequence; the pre-concessive *although* occurring before the empathic concession and the restatement of consequence.

$X \rightarrow Y \ldots$ although $Z \rightarrow negY \ldots$ but $negZ$—so still Y.

If we think of textual expressions in terms of form-meaning[4] pairings, also called Saussurean sign structures (i.e., signifiant-signifié relations), we may obtain a viable model by elaborating on R. Langacker's stratification[5] (Figure 5.2).

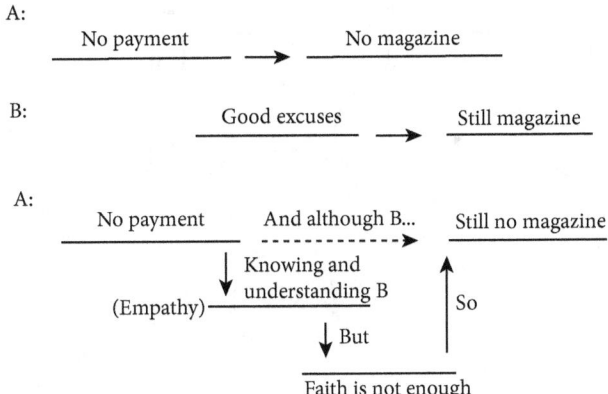

Figure 5.1 Arguments in dialogue.

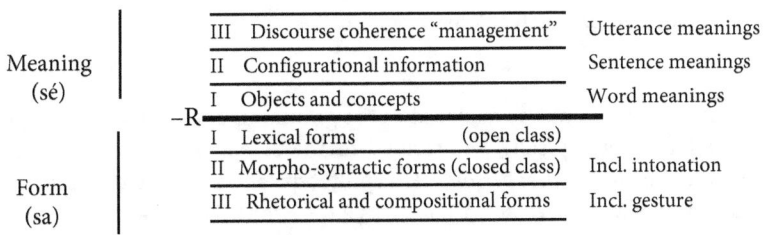

Figure 5.2 A construction model of discourse.

The symphonic (totally harmonic) architecture of linguistic signs existing according to this view would then let dialogical, *enunciation*-related mechanisms of argumentation operate at the overarching (and "deep") Level III, while more local processes of semantic organization would configure situational scenarios, episodes, state-of-affairs information on Level II, and the phonologically segmental lexical surface would appear as hyper-embedded on Level I.

Instead of analyzing current structures of natural logic such as *conditionality* only in terms of truth conditions or validity spaces shared by protasis and apodosis in a closed propositional framework, we might thus inscribe these *operators of natural logic* in the dialogical perspective of *enunciation*. Let us briefly consider an example. In many languages, as in French, the *if* form is also an interrogative conjunction (of yes/no questions):

Je ne sais pas *si* tu es d'accord // Mais *si* tu es d'accord, alors ...
[I don't know *if* you agree // But *if* you agree, then ...]

The epistemic openness of the protasis would be due to the underlying question: Est-ce que tu es d'accord? [Do you agree?] I don't know *if* you do, but in that case (*if* so), then ...

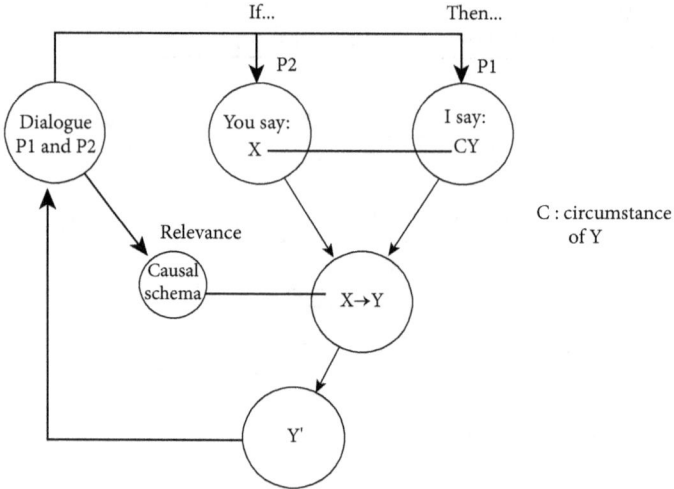

Figure 5.3 A mental space network for conditionality.

So, interrogativity could be analyzed as the ground of conditionality. The protasis meaning would prototypically be ascribed to the *second person*, P2, whereas the apodosis would be in the *first person*, P1, as prototypically manifested by the formulas of promise (**if you ... X, then I ... Y**). P1 asks a question, and while P2 is considering possible answers and responses, P1 calculates the contextual meanings of either answer (if yes [that is, X, by you, P2], then Y [to be presented by me, P1]; if no [non-X by you, P2], then maybe non-Y [by me, P1]).[6]

The semantic structure of this principle of semantic coherence between representations may be modeled by a mental space network[7] (Figure 5.3).

Example:

If it is snowing tomorrow, I may have to cancel my journey.

P1 already has a reason for thinking of the weather forecast and talking to P2 about it; maybe P2 knows what is to be expected of the upcoming weather. But then there has to be a *causal* relevance motive linking the protasis content (X) to a circumstance (C) of the apodosis content (Y)—here, for example, the way in which snow can block roads and take-off lanes or make traffic too[8] difficult, so that the consequence (Y) will follow.

Mental space networks of this sort are seen, in the framework of this constructional stratification, as formats of the structural contents of Level III. They are dialogically construed coherence-making meanings.

The Dia-logic of a Prayer

I would like to offer a curious example from American political culture, as it is spread through the internet. One day I received the following anonymous email; American academic colleagues confirmed that it was a seriously meant message from a Republican group.

The Dia-logic of Discourse

Hi Lord, it's me!
We are getting older and things are getting bad here.
Gas prices are too high, no jobs, food and heating costs too high.
I know some have taken you out of our schools, government and even Christmas, but Lord I'm asking you to come back and re-bless America.
We Really Need You!
There are more of us who want you than those who don't!
Thank You Lord,
I Love You.

Figure 5.4 Dialogue with the Lord.

It is straightforward to reconstruct the implied dialogue in this prayer: *Picture of little girl praying.*

Girl: Hi Lord, It's me.
[The Lord: Hi, how are you today down there?]
Girl: We are getting older and things are getting bad here. Gas prices are too high, no jobs, food and heating costs too high.
[The Lord: Well, you know, I abandoned you and punished you (as you know from my book, I usually do that in such cases), because you have ignored me grossly. I am extremely angry at you!]
Girl [concessive response]: I know some have taken you out of our schools, government and even Christmas (post-concessive clause) *but* Lord I'm asking you to come back and re-bless America. We Really Need You!
[The Lord: We…!? Most of you don't even want me at all. So: no!]
Girl: There are more of us who want you than those who don't!
[The Lord: O.k. I didn't know that. *If* you are right about the statistics, I will think about it [conditional]. You will hear from me.]
Girl: Thank You Lord, I Love You [consequential].

Prayers belong to a pragmatic genre where the second person is categorically silent, and yet analysis of its discourse readily shows the massive semiotic presence of this addressee, particularly in the shape of coherence-making *consequentials*, *concessives*, and *conditionals* as those we have already seen. Notice that the implicature that the Lord has made things go badly because he is angry at the population that no longer wants him is an "explicature" in the reconstructed dialogue.

The Dia-logic of Poetic Discourse

In poetry, the expectation of similar coherence-makers often appears to be actively and strategically opposed by the author. Here is a series of poems by American "language poet" Rosmarie Waldrop[9]:

[A]
I'm looking out the window at other windows. Though the pane masquerades as transparent I know it is impenetrable just as too great a show of frankness gives you a mere paper draft on revelations. As if words were passports, or arrows that point to the application we might make of them without considering the difference of biography and life. Still, depth of field allows the mind to drift beyond its negative pole to sun catching on a maple leaf already red in August, already thinner, more translucent, preparing to strip off all that separates it from its smooth skeleton. Beautiful, flamboyant phrase that trails off without predicate, intending disappearance by approaching it, a toss in the air.
(2)

[B]
All roads lead, but how does a sentence do it? Nothing seems hidden, but it goes by so fast when I should like to see it laid open to view whether the engine resembles combustion so that form becomes its own explanation. We've been taught to apply solar principles, but must find on our own where to look for Rome the way words rally to the blanks between them and thus augment the volume of their resonance.
(6)

[C]
My love was deep and therefore lasted only the space of one second, unable to expand in more than one dimension at a time. The same way deeper meaning may constrict a sentence right out of the language into an uneasiness with lakes and ponds. In language nothing is hidden or our own, its light indifferent to

holes in the present or postulates beginning with ourselves.
Still, you may travel alone and yet be accompanied by my
good wishes.
(22)

This contemporary poetic style of writing, or "écriture," a sort of pseudo-prose, relies entirely on the use of adverbial or conjunctional coherence-makers, as, say, *negotiators*. In [A], note the concessives *though*, *still*, and the two comparatives, one factual, *just as*, the other counterfactual, *as if*. In [B], note the three instances of post-concessive *but* and a consequential *so that*. In [C], we find a *therefore*, a comparative *the same way*, and the two concessives *still* and *yet*.

[A] discusses transparency versus impenetrability, and the text slides semantically between referring to perception and to language: words. [B] uses the saying that "all roads lead to Rome" and continues the discussion on language: sentences versus words. It asks if meaning is conveyed by language that is transparent or opaque, common or private, and so on. [C] muses that "deeper meaning," comparable to love, is something private but still communicable, cf. my "good wishes."

Of course, discourse coherence in "language poetry" is a liminal case. This form of poetry exploits—sometimes with great mastery, I think, as in these examples—the dynamics of dialogical, intersubjective, face-to-face oriented communication patterns as an ephemeral and precarious coherence-creating force.

The human mind works and thinks in "pulses," in rhythmically delivered *quanta* (portions) of utterance-like units that are approximately sentence-compatible. This means that its flows of thinking and of discourse are flows of such minimal quanta. The advantage of this pulsational mental format is that it opens opportunities for the *other* to kick in and respond or react between any two pulses—as we have seen in the initial, trivial example, again in the simulated prayer, and even in the final, less-than-trivial, poetic example, where the implicit intervention of the reading *other*, the enunciative instance of the *second person*, is the core engine of the text.

Notes

1 The author in fact received this letter; it is reliable data, not another armchair illustration made up for the occasion.
2 The dialogue continues rather explicitly in the P.S.: "Already mailed your payment? Sorry—our letters must have crossed in the mail. Just disregard this notice."
3 Cf. Sorin Stati (1990).
4 In construction grammar (Goldberg 1995), all entities (lexemes, phrases, clauses, sentences, utterances) are seen as form-meaning pairings and are called "constructions." A problem with this model, whether Goldberg's or mine, is that it does not account for the syntactic structure of sentences, unless we explicitly specify that it has to be elaborated at the level Meaning-II. A leveled model allows lexical, syntactic, and discourse meaning to cooperate.
5 Ronald Langacker (2001).

6   The question *Is X the case?* would then mean: *I don't know if you think that X is the case.* So, if that is correct, *if* contains an implicit reference to P2.
7   For the mental space network model, see next chapter and Brandt (2004).
8   There is a limit to how much *snow* is compatible with *journey*. So, the relevance must also comprise a normative evaluation schema, apart from the causal schema itself.
9   Rosmarie Waldrop (1993), *Lawn of Excluded Middle*, Providence: Tender Buttons. Poems reproduced with kind permission of Tender Buttons.

References

Brandt, P. A., 2004. *Spaces, Domains, and Meaning*. Bern: Peter Lang Verlag. European Semiotics No. 4.
Goldberg, A. E., 1995. *Constructions. A Construction Grammar Approach to Argument Structure*. Chicago: University of Chicago Press.
Langacker, R., 2001. "Discourse in Cognitive Grammar." *Cognitive Linguistics*, 12 (2).
Sorin Stati, S., 1990. *Le transphrastique*. Paris: P.U.F., Coll. Linguistique nouvelle.
Waldrop, R., 1993. *Lawn of Excluded Middle*. Providence: Tender Buttons.

6

Mental Spaces and Discourse

The Problem—Short Version

Cognitive semantics is the study of meaning in the embodied human mind. The notion of semantics in this context is functional and representational, in the sense that meaning should be approached as it functions in online processes of thought and communication and therefore in the mental representations that are active in online production of meaning addressing some situation of the cognizer. However, mental space theory (MST)—though claiming to be a branch of cognitive semantics—continues in certain respects to approach meaning as nonrepresentational and as a real-world matter of veri-conditionality, staying in these respects bound to analytic philosophy. Due to this philosophical background view of meaning, which is historically rooted in Spinoza's empiricism and logicism, the analysis in terms of mental spaces fails to grasp the dynamic-schematic properties of meaning production and the semantic implications of mapping and blending. It fails to show how meaning actually *makes sense*. I intend to show how the theory could be changed and further developed in order to avoid this blind alley.

The Ontogenesis of Mental Space Theory

The following is a nonstandard account of the principles and problems of mental space theory.[1] However unusual, the nonstandard criticism I intend to offer might elucidate some peculiarities of its current style of research, that is, of actual analyses using mental spaces and blending. My hope is that this "problematization" will also help the theory to further develop.

The notion of a *mental space* was born some decades ago—curiously enough as a blend of French discourse linguistics and Anglo-Saxon analytic philosophy—namely in Gilles Fauconnier's book in French on the construction of meaning (Fauconnier 1984), where it arose in the context of formal logic, philosophy of language, and early (mentalistic) cognitive approaches to "natural language."[2]

In his book, Fauconnier first introduces logical "connectors" that operate on "mental objects," namely the semantic items appearing in discourse, and then goes

An earlier version of this chapter appeared in *Journal of Pragmatics*, Vol. 37, 2005, pp. 1578–1594.

on to present and develop a model of connective, mental constructions and their corresponding linguistic processes. These constructions integrate objects into larger units of meaning, the description of which involves the enigmatic entities here represented by logical sets[3] and called "mental spaces"—inheriting the adjective "mental" from the objects they are supposed to contain (p. 32, my italics):

> A cette fin nous introduisons la notion d'*espaces mentaux*, distincts des structures linguistiques, mais construits dans chaque *discours* en accord avec les indications fournies par les expressions linguistiques. Dans le modèle, les espaces mentaux seront représentés par des ensembles structurés et modifiables—des *ensembles* [sets] avec des éléments a, b, c, ..., des relations satisfaites par ces éléments (R1ab, R2a, R3cbf,...), et tels qu'on puisse leur ajouter de nouveaux éléments, ou établir de nouvelles relations entre leurs éléments. (Techniquement, un ensemble modifiable est une suite ordonnée d'ensembles ordinaires—il sera commode de parler d'*espace mental construit au fil du discours*, plutôt que de mentionner la suite correspondante d'ensembles.)/Des expressions comme "Ra1a2...an est valide dans l'espace mental M" signifieront que a1, a2, ..., an sont des éléments de M et que (a1, a2, ..., an) satisfait la relation R.

What these "spaces" are supposed to be, apart from being thus represented by a set model, is never made quite clear. They are evidently not simply formed as arbitrary lists of objects. The first examples[4] make the reader intuitively think of imaginary settings,[5] situations, or states of affairs. What are they, and what are they not? The question is not trivial, but curiously enough not directly addressed. After having introduced M, R, and the ax series (cf. above), the text adds a relation of inter-space *inclusion* and the notion of *introductors* (space builders):

> "les expressions qui établissent un nouvel espace ou qui renvoient à un espace déjà introduit dans le discours..."

In this inaugural text, mental spaces are defined not in relation to minds but in relation to discourse, so they could perhaps as well have been called "discursive spaces." In a previous note (Fauconnier 1984, p. 24), we are warned against philosophical "possible world" readings, which would imply ontological stances. Mental spaces are not, strictly speaking, possible worlds, but they may be some sort of "worlds" anyway, depending on the notion of *world* chosen. The issue is left in the note without further comment.

So, what is a mental space? The theory of mental spaces (TMS or MST and in French, TEM) is now known as a prominent trend in cognitive semantics. But still today it does not technically relate neither to existing disciplines of *textual* analysis, for example in literary criticism, literary rhetoric, or poetics, nor to existing disciplines such as pragmatic *discourse* analysis; and its relation to grammar and theoretical linguistics remains almost as rudimentary and "promising" as in its first days. My hypothesis is that the import from analytic philosophy and particularly its inherited "logical cognitivism" have blocked its way to a scientifically sound semantics of language—in the sense of real discourse, real text—and thought, in the sense of real human cognition and communication.

Let me briefly explain my view of the way MST thinks. If we find it meaningful to say things like (Fauconnier, op. cit., p. 25)[6]:

— Lisa, qui est déprimée depuis plusieurs mois, sourit sur la photo —
— Lisa, qui sourit sur la photo, est déprimée depuis plusieurs mois —

then the logical formalization has to make Lisa inhabit two contrasting or contradictory semantic contexts, worlds, or "spaces," one in which she is smiling happily and one in which she is unhappy and depressed (and consequently not smiling happily). The relative construction of the French sentences is explicative (not determinative) and has a concessive meaning (*qui*... here means *despite the fact that she*...), so the same sentence can present two versions of Lisa, or two states of Lisa, or two Lisas right away, depending on how the analysis goes.[7] This is grammatically possible, because the two clauses of the sentence have different temporal and veri-conditional properties. This is of course more of a challenge to the logician than to the grammarian. If the meaning of a sentence (in logic, a "proposition") is—as analytic philosophers are trained to believe—its truth conditions, that is, an account of the state of affairs in the real world that would make the sentence ("proposition") true, then such a bi-propositional sentence, whose two parts are equally meaningful, we suppose, must be semantically anchored in *two worlds*, mutually contradictory but both real. Lisa must really be both happy and unhappy to offer the truth conditions under which the sentence is meaningful. This paradox of course makes the analytic logician feel uncomfortable. So—since grammatical constructions and what they do are irrelevant or unknown to him and totally unrepresented in his model—because he cannot accept a paradoxical veri-conditionality, and so must reject the *realistic* two-worlds solution, he needs to redefine the veri-conditional double-world as a *mental* instance, a "mental world" or, still better, a world of unverifiable "mental spaces." Metaphysics is apparently involved here, right from the start. Meanings are treated either as truths or as mental events. This is just what the ancestor of analytic philosophy Baruch de Spinoza[8] would have done and in corresponding cases in fact did (in his *Ethics* 1677): either an idea is true, and its meaning is in its truth, which is in the real physical world, where its reference is found, and there is no difference between the signified meaning and the referential context (so there is no "mental space"), or else, if the idea is not true, and there is no referent, then it is a meaningless mental affect, an idle imagination, and it is instead true that there is a physical brain-body that has it, as if it were a headache. So, there is still only one real world, and the principle of truth-conditional meaning is saved. But the supposedly "lying" photograph of Lisa is veri-conditionally true about the liar, whoever he is. The Spinozist price paid for the salvation is to accept the physical existence of "imaginations," here: *mental* spaces. The mind (which is, in this conception, the physical brain) can effortlessly hold two non-worlds, or imaginary spaces. But again, how can they both be meaningful? The logician, in casu Fauconnier, who cannot see or care about the grammatical pronoun *qui*, can see the expression *sur la photo* and can see that it builds one of the involved imaginary spaces out of the other: the mental object <photo of Lisa> is present in one space and shows something that happens in the other, while this other space does not contain objects that show what happens in the first space—the photographic connector is thus a one-way sign, it establishes a nonreflexive relation and creates a path from the more (discursively) real to the less (discursively) real of the two non-worlds, or spaces.

This is, I believe, the factual genesis of the notion of mental spaces in the perspective of a history of ideas. The truth-conditional view of semantics was stressed by discursive examples of the bi-propositional and paradoxical type. Instead of being stuck with contradictory truth conditions, rendering technically meaningless what is intuitively meaningful, *the logical semanticist then decided to accept a classical mentalistic solution and thus consider contrasting verbal expressions as meaningful if represented by constructed connections of items in mental non-worlds: in networks of mental spaces.*

Now the crucial problem arises: Is a mental representation of a real situation, that is, of a situation of communication in which mental spaces are set up by "space builders" like *sur la photo*, itself a mental space? Yes or no. The alternatives are the following: Yes, because the communicating persons are having this mental representation, and they distinguish it from the imaginary spaces they are thereby presently involved in setting up; such a mental space is a *Base space*.[9] Or: No, because it is real and therefore not mental; we cannot have true representations of the present and different from the present; their truth conditions would be fulfilled, and they would be *identical* with the present, they would not be "about" the world but would instead "be" the world itself; this last view is, again, directly and clearly Spinozist.

Spinoza's view of meaning, namely that meaning is "reality," in a sense,[10] is also Fauconnier's view,[11] and as far as I can see, the general view in MST. This theory cannot grasp the meaning of, or represent, actual and occurring communication, simply because the reality of communication makes the space model collapse, for Spinozist reasons inherited by the analytic semantic mode of thinking. MST cannot take into consideration and recognize online phenomena in cognition as cognitive processes occurring within or during communication, for example as discourse, dialogue, expressive exchange, because the "spaces" that the involved persons set up in order to understand present events—in medias res—do not count as mental, or imaginary, at all. They are real and thus imply God's infinite universe. So, they are not mental spaces! Again, as Spinoza would say: true ideas about things are not ideas about things but coincide with, are identical with, the things they cognize.[12] The curious result is that MST fails to analyze meaning in actually occurring discourse, text, dialogue, language, and signs in general, in expressions as used in contexts by humans. MST has to *extract* and *isolate* the expressions it wishes to analyze from all real contexts or simply invent these expressions as examples of what the analysis is about but not as data the meaning of which the analysis should try to grasp and explain.

This Base space problem is absolutely crucial to the destiny of MST as either just an entertaining modeling style in analytic philosophy (excluding Base spaces and discourse) or a modeling practice in the cognitive semantics of human semiotics (including Base spaces and discourse).

In Fauconnier and Turner (2002), a section, "Ways of Thinking about Compositionality," indirectly addresses this issue. In logic, it tells us, meaning is based on truth-conditional compositionality, which can be strict (Fregean) or looser. If it is strict, "any syntactic combination of propositions that is itself a proposition encodes a computation of the truth value of the whole form from the truth values of the parts." Compositions have truth tables. Correspondingly, one would expect that "linguistic expressions in isolation have truth conditions that are computable from the truth-conditional properties of their parts." But even if that goes for [something is] *brown*, [something is a] *cow*, and [something is a] *brown cow*, the truth value of many compositions can only be computed if elements from the context are allowed to come into the computation. In difficult cases, like "Athena is the daughter of Zeus" (Fauconnier and Turner 2002), a sufficient specification of the context to include in the computation would have to include information on how Greek mythology lets Zeus be the "mother" of Athene. Still, in such cases, "there is compositionality at the level of the general mapping schemes themselves and at the level of the syntactic forms that prompt for those schemes." What does this mean? That compositionality is no longer truth-conditional, quod erat demonstrandum. Compositions are thus stable mappings that are independent of what they mean. So the compositions "Language is the fossil poetry of the soul" and "Las Vegas is the American Monte Carlo" are both syntactically *NP1 is the NP2 of NP3*. The compositions "Ann is the boss of the daughter of Max" and "Prayer is the echo of the darkness of the soul" (where does this line of dubious poetry come from?) are syntactically identical and have the same mappings. So, from this point of view, "the network model shows a relationship between syntactic composition and composition of mappings that holds independent of reference to domains, situations, and contexts."

They are "of-constructions." Then the authors add, concessively: "Of course, context is all-important—but for the imaginative elaboration of the blends, not for the mapping scheme." What does this mean? That the blends cannot be understood without a huge, perhaps infinite, display of contextual specifications of elements to include in the computation of truth value and thereby meaning. The mappings precede the blend, and the mappings are *asemantic*[13] syntactic combinations! *NPx blabla NPy*, and so on.

I am aware of the fact that the two authors do not understand my criticism on this point, and that they are convinced of having shown, in the section I have been quoting from, that their semantics is not truth-conditional. I can only conclude that plain and simple theoretical debate is not yet on the menu of MST. Such references to Spinoza are met by incomprehension and surprise, given that this philosopher is not (yet) on the reading list of cognitive semantics but only present as the historical instigator behind its unshakeable style of thinking.

The whole issue of involved veri-conditionality is still nonstandard in current metatheoretical debates. So, I assume it still sounds unfamiliar to new-coming scholars. To these readers, a slightly more technical presentation would perhaps be more suitable. Let me rephrase the basic question. Why are certain propositions containing conflicting predications possible, why are they *meaningful* instead of being impossible, why are they not meaningless since they should be self-contradictory, such as all metaphorical propositions stating that in a sense, "something is something else that it is not"...? The MST explanation, still wrought in analytic terms and thought habits of veri-conditionality[14] (semantics is about truth, and to be meaningful is to be true in some world; meaning is thus reference), is the fresh idea that this "not"— in "something is something else that it is *not*"—does not induce self-contradiction but instead indicates a *contrast* between copresent, competing, and structurally[15] cooperating semantic "worlds" (in the plural, like fictive worlds, also called fields, frames, domains) underlying propositional meaning. These brave new worlds were then, in 1984, christened *mental spaces*, as if they were a sort of *places* in 3D space. This new solution to the old problem—of how, for example, the eyes of a girl could have two different and mutually excluding colors in a sentence about a portrait—let the theory discreetly produce a new cognitive ontology according to which there is an abstract, purely mental realm in which several separate and simultaneously active "local-worlds-of-thought" or local semantic wholes (with truth-values) are indeed copresent and actively involved in being parts of a mapping system. There had to be a purely mental region of reality where different representations of things could integrate and form syntactic constructions. There was an urgent need for such an inclusive ideo-sphere, and there was a mentalistic or "cognitivistic" mode of satisfying it. Construction or composition was now seen as referring to an *inner* reality—a hypothetical world of the mind, in fact a Cartesian *res cogitans*, but, against Descartes and following Spinoza, essentially unconnected to any *res extensa*, unless we ask for its meaning. The constructional whole is unconnected to any functional meaning it might have.[16] This is still, apparently, the implicit thinking of MST: it is halfway analytic and halfway structural. The problem it is basically supposed to solve is *not* how the *human mind* really works but instead how an analytic account of paradoxical propositions is still possible and how it is accessible at the price of referring to the human mind, as an isolated (but according to Spinoza: entirely embodied) *res cogitans*. It corresponds to views of human cognition as a system of unconnected, individual, private, inner processes governed by principles, almost *more geometrico*, in the "geometrical" manner where content does not matter to form, not because MST subscribes to such a psychological belief but because its own theorizing is based and relies upon such a way of thinking.

Therefore, MST literature only or mainly offers applications to homemade or decontextualized "examples," rather than to full-scale empirical occurrences, real texts, or situated communications, whether literary or pragmatic. Sense-making in the *semiotic behavior of humans* is not what interests it. Nevertheless, MST seeks ontological support in the actual cognitive sciences (neuroscience, psychology, linguistics, anthropology, etc.) that have a genuine interest in semantics. In this sense, it is indeed "cognitiv-istic." But its inherent analytic way of thinking and understanding semantics is indifferent to and incompatible with an interest in studying how the human mind really works, in so far as the mind and its cognitive semantics are not veri-conditional or based on inner rumination, but instead is grounded in the conceptual and schematic organization occurring in the very interaction, expressive as well as practical, that incessantly connects real and really communicating human minds.

A cognitivistic or mentalistic semantics of this kind is thus not yet a *cognitive* semantics, the latter being committed to a systematic methodology of research, interacting with existing empirical studies of meaning in all accessible fields and subscribing to scientific realism and naturalism. It is instead mainly and primarily concerned with the mere *possibility of constructional and integrative representation*. The way in which humans really *do* represent is then a secondary matter. The main difference between a cognitivistic and a truly cognitive approach is thus that the former only intends to logically *justify* the semantic paradoxes, metaphors, counterfactual conditionals, and so on—by showing that they are still *in principle* possible and virtually meaningful—whereas the latter intends to obtain a full-scale study of their *reality*, including discussions of the structural and functional grounding of cognitive and affective productions in the architecture of the socially and culturally committed human mind and of its pragmatic and semiotic dispositions. Analytic cognitivism—the historical origin of MST—is essentially but a logico-philosophical[17] representationalism. By contrast, cognitive semantics, and especially cognitive semiotics, intends to study how representational meaning can be modeled as dynamically related both to the imaginary and to the experiential world in which meaning is meaningful.

A "mental space" is one thing in the perspective of formal justification and something quite different in that of an exploration of the *process* of dynamic meaning construction. In the former, it is a new tool of representationalism, whereas in the latter, the notion refers to an all-important semantic phenomenon of a hitherto unknown kind, which seems to be responsible both for the deeply entrenched trivialities of human cognition and for a host of strange and enigmatic occurrences, of unstable and creative structural creations that we need to understand in order to make conceptual change and human historicity conceivable. The advantage of MST over cognitive grammar is admittedly its intellectual passion for the bizarre; analyses of semantic monsters are in fact often shortcuts to the understanding of the mysteries hidden in simpler things; this is in fact one of Fauconnier's guidelines. But the analyses must learn more from the material analyzed than demonstrations can learn from their own context-less "examples."

My partial conclusion here is an open question: since, historically, the notion of mental spaces emerged in an analytic context and was developed in a fascinating but profoundly ambiguous logico-cognitivistic style, will MST then now turn into a genuine part of semantic research that can be interpreted as a *cognitive* discipline and recognized as a significant contribution to contemporary research on mind and meaning? In this case, as in the case of speech acts and performativity, analytic philosophy will once more have, if not made then at least inspired, a substantial contribution to a *scientific* project in which it was itself unwilling to participate.

Mental Spaces and Mental Architecture

In the theoretical perspective of a semiotic exploration of cognition and meaning, a mental space is not a genetically modified possible world or a veri-conditional artifact, intended to solve special problems of natural logic (logic in natural language).

Semantics as such is instead understood structurally[18] and so is the notion of mental spaces. Here, the term "mental space" denotes a structural format organizing certain contents that human consciousness naturally responds to and which on a specific level of content organization significantly integrates other contents formatted on lower levels of integration. Conceptual integration, or semiotic integration more generally, appears to be a useful notion, if we want to understand this principle of leveled meaning. Semiotic integration of meaning takes place stepwise, and if the "steps" or levels are canonical, which I will argue is the case, then the canon forms a *stable mental architecture* whose formats the analysis of meaning can refer to. Sensory processing lets us perceive mono-modal *forms*, or qualia, in time and space; and further processing lets us cross-modally identify and categorize *objects* in which such forms are assembled and appear as aspects and properties. Objects are thus integrations of forms. Configurations of objects are further conceptualized in such spatiotemporal connections to the embodied cognizer that they are imagined or experienced as existing in *situations* relevant to this cognizer as a "self." In this sense, situations integrate objects. These situational units further constitute the complex semantic wholes that orient linguistic and gestural syntax (grammar). They are not only "cognizable" but also communicable and, hence, recognizable. It may be their communicability that also makes them accessible to recombination—we can take them apart and combine them in innumerable ways, hence the creativity of semantic construction on their level. They constitute the basic imagery that makes it possible for us to *represent* items of meaning: forms and objects, events and states, acts and attitudes, instead of just experiencing them and "presenting" them to others.[19] They are universally shaped as finite, or local (not infinitely extended), more or less vivid and dynamic[20] wholes, bounded by the span and margins of our attention. As to their spatiotemporal extension, they can usefully be compared to that of dramatic *scenes* performed on the stage of a theater, and we may think of them as episodes in imaginable plays including ourselves or some character we take as our proxy. These "theatrical" wholes are *mental spaces*. By contrast, single objects, or lists or configurations of objects, are not per se mental spaces but can evoke such superordinate organizers. Similarly, and a fortiori, single forms, a color, a sound, a feeling, or the contour of a cup, are not per se mental spaces.[21] They are preparatory, preliminary perceptional integrations. Whereas situational wholes, whether imagined or perceived on-line, are indeed mental spaces in this sense. Our episodic memory is theatrical in the sense that it exclusively or predominantly operates on information from this level of integration—the level of "experience." A cognitive MST will therefore be an important part of a theory of real mental architecture that explores all levels of integration; it will itself explore the ways in which mental spaces further integrate when real higher-order meanings are built, from these situational mental contents, through processes involving what we—following Fauconnier and Turner's structural idea—call conceptual *blending*: reflections, notional meanings, such as those appearing in causal descriptions of events and changes, narrative accounts of intentional doings, normative comparisons and judgments, and so on. So, reflective, abstract thinking integrates mental spaces in larger *networks*, of which, admittedly, we presently only know what we find in the study of discourse, their communicative representation. What we do know is that creative abstract thinking, and therefore conceptual blending, is an important ingredient in emotions and moods: feelings, affective meaning, implied in volition and action planning. *Affects* may constitute an ultimate instance of semantic integration, a top level of mental architecture which also terminally, so to speak, "lands" creative abstraction in the dynamic embodiment of action, close to where it initially took off in the dynamic embodiment of sensory perception.

Mental architecture would seem to be shaped like an afferent-efferent arch: perceived forms → categorized objects → integrated situations (MS) → action-planning reflections → evaluating affects. Before and after this semantic arch, there is situated bodily "behavior," including (afferent) sensation and (efferent) action.

Semantic Domains

Behavior is physical, but it can of course not be reduced to simple physical motion and locomotion. It "takes place" in a physical world that has "pheno-physical" and "pheno-psychological" properties such as the fact that it contains intentional communication. The fact that this intentionally informed world is experienced as preorganized in different "spheres of experience," so to speak, may be a phenomenon emerging in our mental architecture on the level of mental spaces and networks of conceptual integration. Conceptualization of realia is importantly specified by these "spheres": for example, kinship-related concepts (such as Family) belong in a sphere different from that of metrical concepts in physical space and time (such as Distance). In other words, when human beings connect perception and action beyond the semantic arch of "levels" or "steps" in conceptual integration, they do not just move around and sense. They connect perceptive and active behavior in such a way that their action will modify their perception, and their perception will modify their action. This reciprocal modification will convey a certain general *mode* of experiencing, characteristic of the *sort* of reality the individual is currently attending to and intending to interact with. We might say that the individual mind pre-categorizes its cognitive processing altogether by "inscribing" it in a domain of meaning, an experiential *semantic domain*. Such a domain is a phenomenologically significant "region in being," and it is likely that we will have to acknowledge the cognitive existence of a finite, generic, and naturally given set of semantic domains that language, thinking, feeling, and living altogether relate and react to: an articulated phenomenological ontology which is not discourse dependent but that discourse types inversely depend on and are based on.[22]

Semantic domains are involved in the sort of predication we call metaphor. As claimed by standard theory of conceptual metaphor, mapping relations must show a difference in semantic domain grounding of source and target contents, if a given predicative expression is to be understood as metaphorical at all.[23] Otherwise, the semantics of the metaphorical expression is possibly analogical within one domain. This criterion is not just terminological; if an expression is indeed metaphorical, its immediate figurative meaning mediates a dynamic higher-order meaning (a compelling "meaning of meaning," most often reflective, affective, and evaluative) to which the communicative agents will be sensitive. Metaphoricity in meaning is a particular intentional resource, and it can therefore even be used as a valid criterion for semantic domain difference. The constellation of semantic domain differences will then hypothetically (Brandt 2004) yield a picture of a human lifeworld articulated in a finite series or system of naturally occurring and universally shared semantic domains. From these domains, cognition derives its "image schemas" and the vast collection of relational concepts by which things in all domains are construed. *Cross-domain migration of schemas* is probably one of the great mental achievements that human language made possible and common; *language*, in view of its "closed-class" semantics of morphology and syntax, is itself a striking example of schematic migration: same morphemes and same syntax can be used for talking about things in whatever domain!

According to my personal investigations, the basic semantic domains, which we naturally acknowledge and distinguish in gesture and language, include a pheno-physical domain (D1), a domain of social interaction (D2), a mental domain (D3), and a speech-act domain of direct, face-to-face intimacy and interpersonal communication (D4). Higher-order domains appear to be built out of the first four by dual combination, of course excluding the mental domain (e.g., the domestic domain, housing notions of kinship, marriage rules, nursing schemas, etc., is obtained by combining D2 and D4—it has social interaction *and* face-to-face intimacy).

Space Delegation

The hic et nunc of awareness and present thinking is a "self-remembering present," and a *presently represented presence*, that we experience—I suggest—through the mental space format. We also feel that other minds are using the same here-and-now space format while addressing us or attending to our signs. The finite "mental spatiality" of mental spaces, including the Base space of presently represented situational presence, is a natural product of the mind's own design and therefore common to human minds and active in all situations of communication, in which minds can experience reciprocal attention. The mental space format of Presence thus allows the individual to semantically structure interactions not only with the surrounding pheno-physical spatiality but also with *other minds*: other individuals, with collective instances, and even with abstract entities of "higher-order" sociocultural domains.

Other minds have other thoughts; the Presence space or general Base space gives us a format for holding "my thought" and "your thought" at once, simultaneously and in parallel, as it occurs when dialogue, debate, quarrelling, and negotiation in general take place. It allows us correspondingly to hold other mental spaces present in consciousness in addition to the one representing the present, and then to let active arrays of our own or others' out-of-presence mental spaces generate meaning relevant for the present. Blending of "alien" and "own" contents—present or non-present—during dialogical interaction may thus be the original source of complex meaning construction and of linguistic semantics in general. Constructions or compositions that include "your meaning" and "my meaning" and yield impersonal, blended "whoever's meaning," meaning tout court, may thus be the operations by which our minds "blend their way to abstract thinking," to discourse-based or symbol-based reflection.

This view no longer emphasizes the mere plurality of {MS} and their mutual mappings and blendings as such, but rather draws attention to the existence of a structurally stable *semiotic syntax of spaces and space types*—creating networks of MS by "space builders" in Presence or Base space that send or delegate part of our attention, so to speak, and of the attention of our addressee, if there is one, to other regions of reality, to whatever we wish to think of or refer to: a *Reference space* out of presence.[24] These thematic or referential mental sites differ from Base space by being signified from there; the signifying connectors or space builders regularly specify the type of reference intended by this operation of *space delegation*.

Reference is typically distant from the Base in speech-act distance, in *time* (cf. the morphologies of tense) or *place* (cf. the locative adverbials), or both, but can also be neutral to time and place and instead deviate from the Base by deliberately adding extra *modal* features or constraints (as in games, rituals, and conditional thinking), and furthermore it can shelter transmitted, encapsulated, singularized, and *symbolized* representations (reported myths and beliefs, fictions and fantasies, signed by or ascribed to singular intentional entities, i.e., given under the seal of a proper name; cf. the (singular) photo of the fictive Lisa).

Some types of delegation from a Base space to a Reference space:

Epistemic distance	"I claim/think/know ... that X"
Spatiotemporal reference	"Some years ago/In Baghdad, X"
Modal—conditional	"In chess, X"; "If Y, X"; "Maybe X"
Fictional—imaginary	"In Ulysses, X"; "In your dreams, X"

There might be still many other reference types, or these may be ill-named; this fascinating question of space delegation is still in its initial phase. The delegations by epistemic distance, time, space, modality, or fictional-imaginary representation can apparently take place in all semantic domains. In this sense, all semantic domains have unlimited depths of intelligibility.

Space delegation creates reference "sites" in thought and language. I claim that when this happens, and a *Reference space* is thus set up, with material from some domain, then a parallel space will very often accompany it, namely a "site" containing a way to imagine, remember, or otherwise access the reference, a way in which it may be present or presented to the cognizer: a *Presentation space* of contents (from the same or other domains) that our mind tries to map onto the referential content in order to prepare a (blended) *Representation*. The "presentative" content is in a very general sense *predicated* of the referential content. It functions in fact like a *map* to a territory. If a blend of this predicative and this referential content further obtains, then the blend, the Representation, will offer to the cognizing mind an instance of the referent as possessing the properties predicated of it. Fauconnier and Turner predict an "emergent meaning" to sometimes turn up in the blend. It can be shown, I think, that this "emergent" miracle is rather the result of a *schematization* that stabilizes the blend. In fact, when a blend is set up, there is, I further claim, a third input from the Base, a semantic component we have suggested to call a *Relevance schema*, and which contains contextual semantic prerequisites and dynamic schemas projected onto the blend and stabilizing its meaning. There are therefore two states of the blend, the first being *figurative* and uninterpreted, the second *dynamic* and interpreted by the induced schematic structure from the Relevance instance. The two states of the blend are to be distinguished as the pre-schematic and the post-schematic state; the latter is a "Meaning space" and *reenters* the Base space.

These six spaces form an elementary processual network, a sort of MS network molecule, which turns out to constitute a minimal composition or meaning construction.[25] The normal case is a message-formed utterance manifesting a nested structure, using the elementary network recursively.

Two Examples

Let us first consider a simple example, a "material anchor" (Fauconnier and Turner's expression), namely the use of a thermometer. The user in Base space sets up a reference, namely the current *temperature* of his apartment. The user looks upon the graded scale of the artifact, in a Presentation space of the temperature request setting, in order to identify the position of the top of the mercury column. This scale on the "thermic probe," the idea of temperature's quantitative potential in the apartment of Reference space, and the actual numerical result are connected by a mapping and form an imaginary blend in which the temperature "is" the number indicated on the probe. If the thermometer is believed by the user to be a good probe, then the semantic result is a thermal information imported into Base space.

The corresponding network is shown in Figure 6.1.

The *dynamic schema* making the thermometer *relevant* for obtaining information about current temperature is, in casu, that of a *probe*: the subject is barred by an epistemic wall from accessing an object, but the barrier lets the subject penetrate it with an imaginary tube through which specific information can pass between the subject side and the object side of "reality," and thus allows the subject to obtain knowledge of the object despite the barrier (Figure 6.2).

This intuitive, schematic notion of an instrument allowing information to pass through the wall that bars us from immediately sensing what is going on in the "outside" world underlies the use of watches, compasses, alarm controls, and measuring instruments of many sorts.[26]

Networks in meaning construction apparently occur in all forms of communication, not only in language but—according to current research—also in music, gestural semiosis, and pictorial expressions. The connection of these semantic structures to *verbal language* is still to be explored. The basic "syntactic" structure of MS networks, as sketched out here, may be a prefiguration of predicative sentence syntax and a prerequisite of the transformation of non-propositional, direct, experiential, phenomenological, and non-predicative online meaning into propositional offline

Mental Spaces and Discourse 77

Mental-space blending in the experience of use of a thermometer.

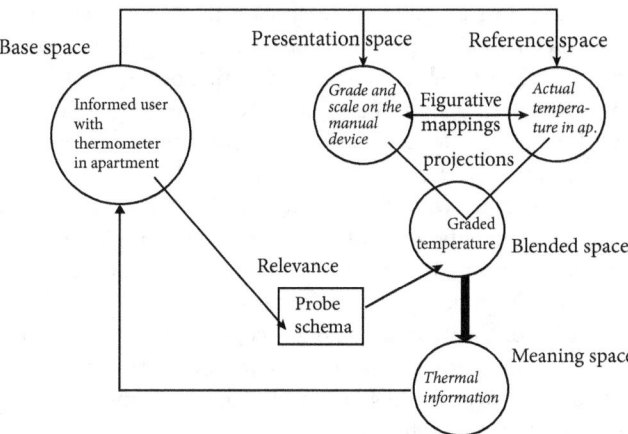

Figure 6.1 Thermometer as a material anchor.

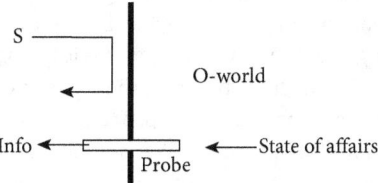

Figure 6.2 Probe barrier schema.

meaning. Language seems to pick up and use meaning structures from all levels of cognition but only to structure *utterances* on the situational MS level of mental architecture. In poetry, the pre-predicative and the post-predicative dimensions of its grammatical potential are drawn into the foreground, so that the extremes, its roots in perception-related form and its ultimate horizon in affect, are, in a sense, exposed.

In painting, an elementary example, our second in this chapter, could be a portrait, say Henri Matisse's *Woman with a Hat* (1905), showing a female face[27] painted in a historically significant fauvist style. The painting is in the MoMA of San Francisco, and if a visitor finds it there and takes a look at it, he will be in a Base space from where he may be prompted to view the picture as a portrait of the painter's wife; this portrayed person will then be positioned (by space delegation) in the visitor's MS network in a biographical Reference space, whereas the canvas in the museum will be contained in a Presentation space whose structures will map onto some details of the face of a person, in Reference space. The scandal provoked by this painting was due to the blend: are you allowed to represent a woman without respecting the real colors of her lovely face? In the picture, her nose is green (cf. above, on Fauconnier's contradictory information about a person depicted). This is because some colors are allowed to stay on the 2D canvas and thus to be pure events of the act of painting and to be expressive gestures independent of the ongoing mimesis. The 3D motif is not the meaning of the painting; this mimetically rendered motif is itself a sign of a higher-order meaning, a (relevantly stabilized) metonymy of a nonfigurative idea, for example Beauty, or the Force of Love, or What Life Is About. So, there is a network embedded in the (Referential) motif. Our aesthetic sensibility will of course notice the vital relation between the style, *l'écriture*, of the representation and the nonfigurative higher-order (metaphysical) meaning of the painting. This relation between two relevance contents, Style and Sense—one at the "signified" level, the other at the "signifying" level—is the axis of aesthetic meaning of a work of art; and it is cognitively interesting to observe in this double network a semantic composition obtaining both a focus on formal beauty and another on abstract meaning, a complex-focus composition that could well be the semiotic origin of symbolization.

Figure 6.3 shows the nested network accounting for space structures like the one the painting offers and probably accounting for pictorial expressions at large, allowing drastic differences in the invested contents of the articulated mental spaces.

The MoMA visitor has to imagine the artist in his atelier (internal Base space, upper network) working up the portrait and vividly experiencing the relation between what he is achieving with his brushes, the stylistic code that supports it, and the existential sense it makes; imagining this process helps the contemporary viewer of the painting "understand" it properly. We notice that a virtual intersubjective relationship is being structured by this double network: one subject is in the internal Base space, the other in the external Base space. This is also, I think, the relationship that is experienced when we read written texts—the (idea of the) sender is in the internal Base space (upper network) of an analogous double network.

MS semantics and its basic networks may be an early paleolithic, proto-symbolic, and proto-linguistic cognitive creation of the human mind, which is still with us; anyway, it certainly remains as active and creative as ever. The particularly rich meaning unfolding that can be found in our technical and artistic practices, in artifacts and works of art, testifies to its transhistorical presence and perhaps also to the importance of tools and art to the development of *the blending brain*.

Conclusion

In this chapter, I wished to stress a major methodological problem in current MST, namely its historically inherited veri-conditional habits and the negative effects they have on the semantic sensibility of the analytic work—especially if they stay undetected and unacknowledged—and the confusion they cause on the level of critical debate in cognitive semantics. I further tried to show some recent developments in MST analysis as practiced and theoretically elaborated at the research group in cognitive semiotics of the University of Aarhus since the 1990s. The critical study of mental spaces has

Mental-space blending diagram of the real act of painting

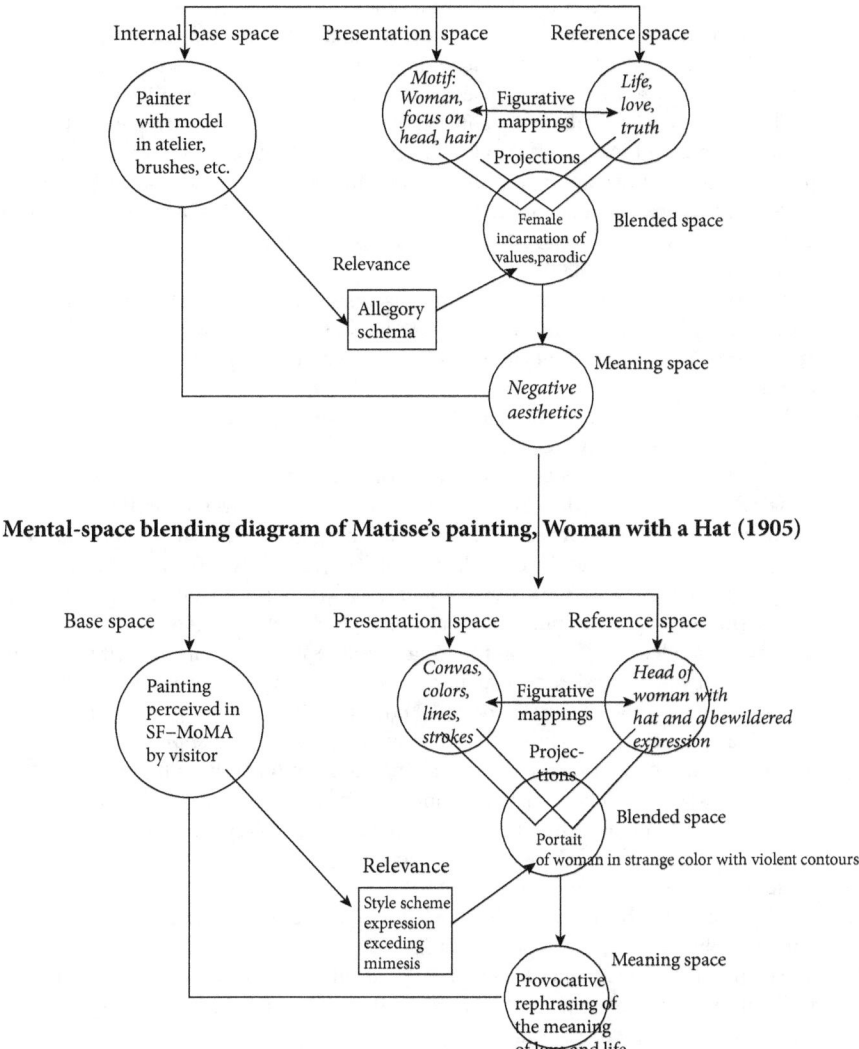

Mental-space blending diagram of Matisse's painting, Woman with a Hat (1905)

Figure 6.3 Double network in painting.

attracted many cognitive researchers, and this discipline may soon be adopted by editors of handbooks in cognitive semantics as a standard field. Its institutionalization will then either add to the stock of confused doctrines or contribute to our knowledge of meaning production in cognition. To some extent, the outcome will depend on the quality of critical debate, including the evaluation of current Spinozist motives, such as the meaning skepticism and its implicit mysticism, in its style of research.

Notes

1. As summarized in Fauconnier and Turner (2002).
2. In the introduction (p. 11), in a note, we learn that "nos préoccupations ne sont pas indépendantes de la philosophie du langage, mais les objectifs sont souvent différents... les problèmes sont posés en termes cognitifs et" mentalistes"; la méthodologie est " linguistique": appel au plus grand nombre d'exemples et de situations, possibilité ou impossibilité de telle ou telle forme, ou interprétation." The project concerns the construction of meaning in discourse in so far as its logical reconstruction can be made in terms of a (specially designed) set-theoretical model.
3. The set representation of mental spaces soon disappeared and is not to be found in Fauconnier and Turner (2002).
4. These examples are not taken from actual discourse but are fabricated by the author for the sake of illustration and sound like the following: "Max croit que, dans le tableau de Luc, les fleurs sont jaunes." Where is then the alleged discourse, one may ask.
5. The French semiotician A.J. Greimas (Greimas 1979) would call these imaginary object contexts (figurative) *isotopies*.
6. "Lisa, who has been depressed for several months, is smiling on the photo" versus "Lisa, who is smiling on the photo, has been depressed for several months."
7. There need not be any contradiction, of course, since one information concerns Lisa's appearance (*paraître*) and the other her being (*être*). Depressed persons can smile.
8. I have the impression that many contemporary semanticists are not aware of the importance that Spinoza's philosophy, especially the chapter on the mind, in *Ethica*, has had on modern Anglo-Saxon thinking—despite Wittgenstein's explicit reference. The modern anti-Cartesian campaign, cf. A. Damasio's books, including his work on the chapter on the affects (Damasio 2003), which has been very salient in the cognitive sciences, is entirely Spinozist. I already discussed this *supra*.
9. This is the notion of Base space later explained in Brandt and Brandt (2005).
10. Though this sense will have to be explained in terms that allow comparison over four centuries of philosophy—those that separate Spinoza's spiritual realism from modern, truth-conditional analytic empiricism.
11. A view stated again in Fauconnier (1997).
12. I am here drawing heavily on K. Hvidtfelt Nielsen's thesis on meaning skepticism in Spinozist philosophy (Hvidtfelt Nielsen 2003).
13. The combinations may well be semantically meaningful but the syntactic structure relevant to the mappings is indifferent to what they mean; so the relevant syntactic structure has *asemantic* relevance.
14. In *Mappings*, Fauconnier (1997) protests energetically (e.g., p. 48) that the new theory is *not* veri-conditional. I am here trying to explain why this protest and the view it opposes are both likely to occur.
15. Here is where veri-conditionality gives way to structural semantics, at least in principle.
16. By functional meaning, I refer to the intentional meaning an utterance has and is understood to have by speaker and addressee. This is the core semantics of communicated meaning, but MST ignores it. So if a joke is analyzed, its mappings and blends can be modeled, but not the reason why it is funny.

17 In the sense of L. Wittgenstein's Spinozist paraphrase of a Tractatus Theologico-politicus, the Tractatus Logico-philosophicus.
18 Truth and meaning no longer coincide; truths are relevant to meanings, if they are structural parts of meanings—as is the case in irony.
19 This stage of cognitive integration is the level of semantics implied in intentional communication in general.
20 A dynamic whole is a scenario dominated by an intelligible force schema—typically rendered in language by deontic, epistemic, or other types of modal expressions.
21 What I am saying is that the integration of *blue* and *cup* in the composition *a blue cup* is not, as Mark Turner has suggested, a mental space that "blends" a *blueness* space and a *cupness* space—a blue cup is not at the right level of integration, in mental architecture, for qualifying as a mental space construction.
22 The system of semantic domains was introduced in Brandt (2004), chapter 3.
23 Characteristically, MST intends to avoid this point and to present metaphor as a subjective matter of imaginative construction of meaning having little to do with mapping and "language forms" (Fauconnier and Turner 2002, p. 152). Imaginative operations of the mind yield different "feelings" but no different objective structures in lifeworld.
24 My colleagues suggest that I call this distinction between in-presence and out-of-presence *on-line* and *off-line*, respectively. The internet is becoming the model of presence.
25 Our minds do not seem to preferably set up, from the Base, just one simple delegation to one Reference space. To "think of something" is often, maybe always, to think of it *in some way* (through some Presentation).
26 The metaphorical notion of material "anchor" has been created and developed by Ed Hutchins (1995). Fauconnier and Turner (2002) comment upon some examples, in chapter 10, but offer no convincing network analysis of the discussed use of a watch, pp. 195–198. Watches are, however, chronometric probes.
27 http://www.abcgallery.com/M/matisse/matisse80.html

References

Brandt, P. A., 2004. *Spaces, Domains, and Meaning. Essays in Cognitive Semiotics*. Series European Semiotics, 4. Bern: Peter Lang.

Brandt, L. and P. A. Brandt, 2005. "Making Sense of a Blend: A Cognitive Semiotic Approach to Metaphor." *Annual Review of Cognitive Linguistics*, 3. John Benjamins.

Damasio, A., 2003. *Looking for Spinoza. Joy, Sorrow, and the Feeling Brain*. New York: Harcourt & Co.

Fauconnier, G., 1984. *Espaces mentaux. Aspects de la construction du sens dans les langues naturelles*. Paris: Ed. de Minuit.

Fauconnier, G., 1997. *Mappings in Thought and Language*. Cambridge, UK: Cambridge University Press.

Fauconnier, G. and M. Turner, 2002. *The Way We Think. Conceptual Blending and the Mind's Hidden Complexities*, New York: Basic Books.

Greimas, A. J., 1979. *Sémiotique. Dictionnaire raisonné de la théorie du langage*. Paris: Hachette Université.

Hutchins, E., 1995. *Cognition in the Wild*. Cambridge, MA: MIT Press.
Hvidtfelt Nielsen, K., 2003. *Interpreting Spinoza's Arguments. Toward a Formal Theory of Consistent Language Scepticism. Imitating Ethica*. New York/Ontario: The Edwin Mellen Press.
de Spinoza, B., 1677. *Ethica. Ordine geometrico demonstrata*, in Spinoza Opera. Vol. 2. Heidelberg: 1925 (72).

7

More on Mental Architecture, Spaces, and Blending

Space Delegation

The notion of *mental space* has interested cognitive researchers and thinkers who have found that alternative notions such as "mental objects" or "mental contents" are too vague and less useful in semantic analysis. A "mental space" is a "portion" (as Umberto Eco would say) of meaning that comes with an internal conceptual structure, a minimum of imagery, and a phenomenological status as a scenario that can be referred to. The present situation of a subject is therefore a mental space, in so far as deixis, a deictic phrase or gesture, can refer to it. Any other scenario or situation is experienced as a mental space when referred to, anaphorically or cataphorically, by some semiotic means, which thereby link a non-present mental space to the present or to an already established, present-linked non-present space. The procedure of referring to non-present spaces is called *space building* in Fauconnier (1985). The basic representation of space building is a diagram with an arrow from one container to another.

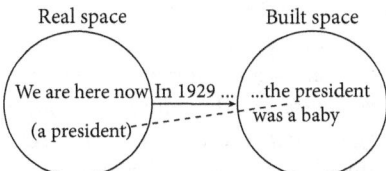

Figure 7.1 Mental space building. "In 1929, the president was a baby."

(It is not the case that the country was ruled by a baby president in 1929; two spaces are required, as everybody understands immediately.)

Spaces contain entities, for example persons and functions, and these can either be specific of a particular space or be shared by different spaces. In Figure 7.1, relative to the mental construction of the sentence "In 1929, the president was a baby," presidency is a function specific of one space, whereas the filler of the function, a person, is represented in two spaces.[1] The adverbial *in 1929* is a "space builder."

This phenomenon of linking an "off-line" space to the "on-line" space is both trivial and fundamental in human thinking and communicating. Still it is nontrivial to analyze it as a matter of mental spaces, rather than just as a matter of tense and similar verbal morphology, and only recently attention has been paid to the richness of the semantic field it opens.[2]

The pragmatic-semantic background of "space building" is, in our view, the intersubjectivity of enunciation: *I say to you that X*. This implicit ditransitive stance allows a *first person* (P1) to stay in the "on-line" space while sending off the avatar of a *second person* (P2) to some other, "off-line" space, X. So P2 is an *enunciational role* that has its base in P1's space and is delegated by P1 to this other space, X, where P1 is currently not present. In this view, space building is *space delegation*.[3] The interesting problem is to further analyze and classify the pathways of space delegation. Simply put: To what sorts of spaces can humans mentally send each other?

First a formal consideration, which will help us model the mechanism of delegation itself. If, for an entity—such as P2—capable of moving between spaces, a mental space is cognitively not only a scenarial container but also a locative attractor, the dynamical topology introduced in semantics by the mathematical philosopher René Thom may offer an adequate model. One of his elementary catastrophes, the *cusp* topology, describes dual attractor conflicts and changes of system states.[4] The convention used in our application lets the attractor minima represent spaces and the system "under the influence" be P2. The path through the control topology represents space delegation (SD); the retroflexed part of the path shows the recursive character of SD. The recursive path shows the event of one attractor space giving rise to another attractor space, which in turn gives rise to a third, and so on, in such a way that the "system" controlled (here P2) is sent from space to space along a sequence of spaces embedded in other spaces (Figure 7.2).

This enunciational operation, by which a change (by b variation while a is negative in the cusp equation) in the relative weights of the conflicting attractors (P1's space and the space X) "sends" P2 from P1's space to X, describes the path of bifurcation from one actant attractor to two, of which one can again allow a bifurcation, and so on, by the recursion called "hysteresis." By contrast, it does not yet describe the *semantic dimension* of the bifurcation, that is, the delegation. The study of a large number of examples shows that at least the following dimensions or delegation types are constantly active in human semiotics and meaning production: delegation by change of *place, time, voice* (evidentiality),[5] *modality* (including epistemic, deontic, root,[6] speech-act), *volition* and *representation* (frozen text worlds, etc.), and finally *activity genres* (games, institutions, discourses, etc.). These types of offline (X) spaces describe the extensions of human imagination, as it were. Conditional, counterfactual, fantastic, magical, grotesque, absurd, and even totally impossible scenarios and beliefs are perfectly commonplace in human semiotic practice, whether they are just happening in single minds or they are shared intersubjectively.[7] Each type of delegation follows a mentally available and potentially shared encyclopedic interpretant, for example a geographical map (of places), a calendar (of times), a sociogram (of voices), a domain map (of modalities), a cultural map (of activity genres). By contrast, on the delegating (P1) side of the process, there is a "degree zero" enunciation space, where speaking, communicating in general, is *internally* unspecified (I am just saying something to someone about things in the world…)— however not externally unspecified, since a semiotic Base space can be specified as determined on many levels.[8] Figure 7.3 summarizes the most salient types of delegation, arranged by increasing complexity of the interpretant.

Mental Architecture, Spaces, and Blending

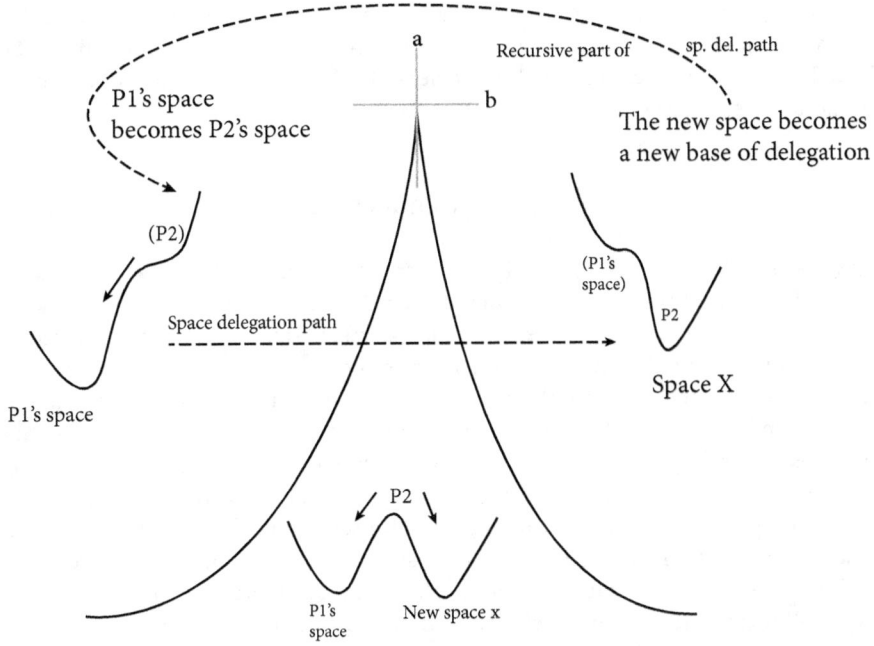

Figure 7.2 The space delegation cusp.

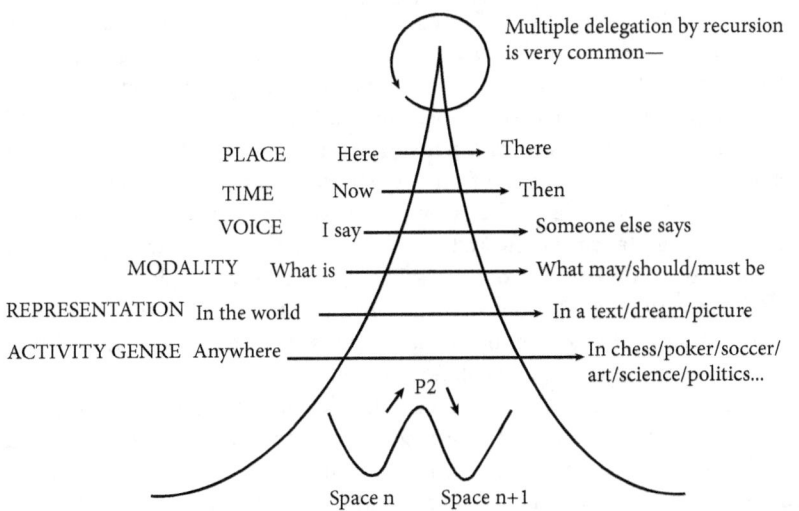

Figure 7.3 Space delegation types.

The six types listed here are by no means meant as an exhaustive typology; the list is probably longer and may be conceived otherwise; however, it does not appear to be reducible to a shorter version. The problem of delegation types is one of the most beautiful ones I know of.

Mental Architecture

The content of a mental space is experienced by P2 (and P1) as a mental-phenomenological whole.[9] Hearing the sentence "In 1929, the president was a baby," the enunciatee (the default addressee) mentally experiences an imaginary scene with a baby starting his political career, maybe by crying in a particularly compelling manner. In fact, when we think of something somewhere, we either ruminate or think *something about it*. We predicate something about our theme, and I think this happens by sending more material along the channel that the delegation opens, so that the X space in question gets gradually "filled" with information of many kinds. We not only set spaces up but also hold them for some time during conversation or just during our solitary states of pensiveness. The enunciational split between P1 and P2 allows us to mentally play both roles and thus attend to online perception and offline reflection simultaneously, and to stay in both and even in several delegated spaces simultaneously for a long time, whether we are daydreaming or concentrating on hard theoretical problems, or both. The advantage of holding many spaces in parallel is that we can then, from memory or external input, recruit and send material from certain spaces to others and revise spaces in the light of such new material.

In particular, our working memory needs to hold recent experiences while feeding prospective and action-oriented spaces from these experiential sources.[10] In an operation of *comparison*, for example, the components of the comparative array are mental spaces held in parallel, while a schematized superposition of these spaces is mentally performed. In a *counterfactual conditional* setup, the factual and the counterfactual components form a network of spaces where a conditional (modal) delegation, the protasis, from the factual space leads to another (modal) delegation, the apodosis.[11] An example will be given below. Among other things, we are going to briefly discuss the standard network for structural metaphors. However, before giving my examples of prominent network types, I have to situate the semantic content of such mental spaces and networks in a realistic context of human mental architecture.[12] In fact, the possible contents of human consciousness are organized in an "architecture" of levels and connections that we will now recapitulate.[13]

Within a scenario perceived or recalled, or even only imagined, we can move our focus of attention around and also change the conceptual distance to its target ("zoom in" and "zoom out"). If we observe this semantic mobility of our attention, we will notice that voluntary modifications of its focus tend to happen in qualitative "leaps" between levels of complexity. Whereas the default setting is situational[14]—oriented toward the present spatiotemporal *situation* of the subject—it is trivially possible to only attend to specific *objects* within this scenario, typically for technical reasons: the need for online causal interpretation of present dynamic object constellations.[15] Along the same line, objects can be perceived by their aspects, such as timbre, color, hue, shadowing, or tactile character—what the tradition calls *qualia*. Qualia are essential in aesthetic perception of things. The experience of an object in space and time is a complex result of a mental integration of qualia; a situation is in turn a complex result of a mental integration of objects. In both cases, there is much more in the result (the object, the situation) than in the ingredients. The organizing process called *Gestaltung* (in classical Gestalt psychology) adds the cognitive design for an "object" and likewise, on the next level, the cognitive format of a "situation." Objectal meaning includes spatiotemporal constancy (which qualia do not have). Situational meaning includes subjectivity and agency (which objects do not have). Those factors pertain to the sort of structure characterizing each level as such. There are levels of integration beyond the three mentioned so far. Situations integrate into what I propose to term *notions*; thus, notions are "exemplified" by situations or by the situational cascades we call narratives, including "tragedies," moral legends, and "fairy tales". A notion, by contrast, contains normative authority; it allows us to compare, evaluate, and regulate doings and states of affairs. Rules and laws are notions in this sense. Language, which is thoroughly notional itself, helps us develop notional systems, accomplish the evaluative tasks of human communities, and adjust existing notions to changing social realities (juridical systems are core examples of this inter-notional regulation). The evolution of a notional level in the human mental architecture is an essential prerequisite for the emergence of ethnic and political cultures, educational routines, and institutions in general. The final stage in semantic integration anchors "notionality" in the core of the individual subjectivity: the system of *affects*.[16] Notions integrate to form the semantic ground of human affectivity. All singular affects—moods, emotions, passions—are rooted in agglomerations of notions; the mood called "happiness," traditionally a basic normative motif in political thinking, presupposes notions such as (presence of sufficient manifestations of) Freedom, Justice, Peace, Respect, and absence of Misery and Impotence. An emotion like "anger" presupposes Offense (lack of Respect), "fear" presupposes Danger and Impotence, and so on. A passion like "love" presupposes Fidelity, Respect, Desire. Human aesthetic activity—visual arts, music, dance, theater, narrative and poetic literature—essentially contributes to the maintenance and updating of relations between notionality and affectivity.

A cascade of integrations and degrees of complexity thus takes our conscious awareness from qualia (I) to objects, from objects (II) to situations, from situations (III) to notions, and from notions (IV) to affects (V). Below the level (I) of qualia, and beyond the level (V) of affect, there is *soma*, *body*, neuronal, hormonal, muscular—so the stratified architecture describes mind in the dual context of its material carrier, situated between *pre-mental* perception and *post-mental* "psycho-somatism."[17] Consciousness is a glade in our opaque bodily being. Figure 7.4 summarizes this analysis.

Mental spaces, as discussed above, basically represent situational meaning (Level III) while allowing background "resonance" from notional and affective meaning to enter the stage, typically as *schemas* regulating the space blends. In this sense,

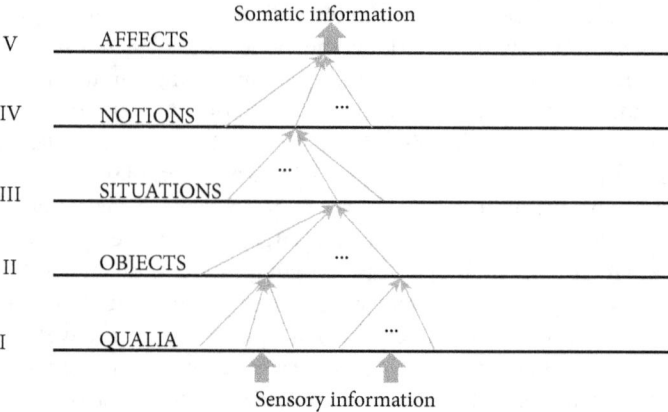

Figure 7.4 The mental architecture of perceptive integrations.

our imaginary is basically figurative; our abstract and symbolic thinking in fact figuratively imagines "situations" of interacting symbolic objects (instead of massive, nonsymbolic objects), each carrying specific notional meaning.

However, symbolic objects do not emerge from nature;[18] they are produced by cognitively active subjects and thus result from symbolic acts. This implies a complementary aspect of mental architecture, namely the existence of cascades of semantic integrations from level to level that *descend* from Level V. The active, *agentive mind* interprets its higher-order contents in terms of lower-order contents, when it translates, or converts, feelings, ideas, and reactions to things "downwards" into motivated action plans, acts, and motoric bodily doings. A symbol is a notion (IV) translated into an expressive object (II) manifested by a graphic movement (I); an icon is an imaginary scene, a scenario (III), translated into an object, a picture (II) manifested by the motion of drawing (I). Subjectivity as *intention* is the descending integration of meanings as a whole; we intend to act while at the same time paying (ascending) *attention* to the world in which we act and to the unfolding traces of the act itself. Attention is afferent, and intention is efferent.

The ascending, afferent, attentional flow and the descending, efferent, intentional flow exploit the same structurally stratified architecture. Ample crossover connections between the flows are equally happening, as we know from the many individual forms of synesthesia and from the collectively stabilized forms of semiosis (indicated by the dotted lines in Figure 7.5; e.g., symbols: IV → II; icons: III → II; deixis: V → I). The flows and processes of meaning construction must of course be much more intertwined, distributed, and quasi-holistic than what we have considered in this brief outline; the huge amount of specific partial processes characterizing the human mental architecture is still to be studied in depth and detail. A minor subset of these processes consists of mental space networks; some illustrative examples are given below.

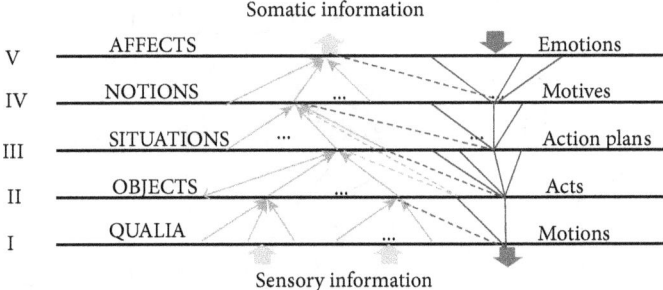

Figure 7.5 The mental architecture of agentive integrations.

Mental Space Networks

When we think or communicate, we often use semantic constructions that are networks of mental spaces and often are combinations of *attentional* and *intentional* meanings. The blending model apparently determining a core part of known conceptual blending processes is a structural network of five preestablished spaces that humans use as a pragmatic-semantic format for fast and seamless comprehension of different but all important elementary mental operations in meaning production—that is, on a certain level of "abstractness" (III). Let us briefly consider and revisit some classical cases.

If I Were You I Would Avoid Me ...

P1 is talking to a friend P2 who is in trouble (X) and gives him the advice to do Y. He uses the counterfactual conditional formula *If I were you...* to perform this communicative act. In P1's address, delegation goes to a Reference space containing P2's problem (X) and to a separate space containing and presenting P1's knowledge (Y); the point is precisely that P2 is in trouble because Y is not in his space (i.e., his situation incl. his knowledge). In order for Y to be in the space of X and not confined to the space of P1's situation and knowledge, P1 would have to merge with P2. This happens in a third space, created (in English) through the relevance-establishing *IF + Subjunctive* morpheme of epistemic modality signaling the value/*impossibility*/.[19] This third space is a counterfactual *blend*, where Y solves the problem X (by a causal schema making the connection Y → X relevant) and generates a non-counterfactual recommendation of Y in a speech-act modal mode, roughly equivalent to the message: "I am hereby giving you the modest advice that you should do Y." In this sense, the *blend space* issues by local delegation a meaning space, whose content is the pragmatically relevant semantics of the utterance *If I were you...* in the context of the Base space (Figure 7.6).

This five-space[20] network, as the example illustrates, constitutes a whole of interdependent parts, which yields a generalizable format for certain processes of meaning construction.

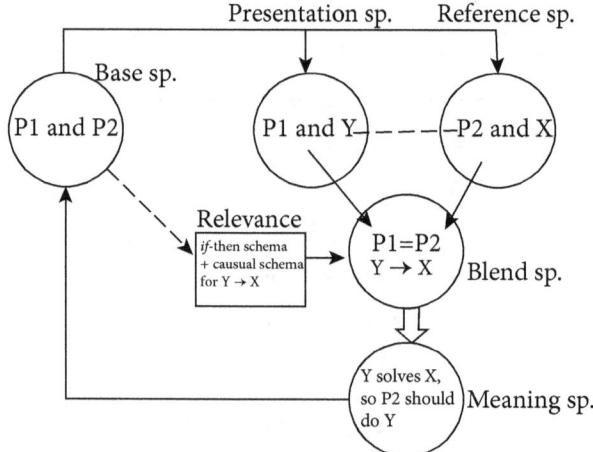

Figure 7.6 *If I were you ...*

X Is the Y of Z. Louis Armstrong Is the King of Jazz.

As illustrated in the previous sections, blends are often predicative: the non-referential input space contains contents that are predicates to core contents in the referential input space. In expressions like "Louis Armstrong is the king of jazz," *the Y of Z* is a predicate to the subject X. However, it is evident that Z and X pertain to the *same semantic domain*, culture: the realm of jazz music, whereas Y refers to a *different semantic domain*, national politics: royal dynasty.[21] This network again emphasizes a certain parallelism and consequent mapping between two input spaces, of which one is referential—*Armstrong, jazz*—while the other—*monarchy*—presents a certain perspective on the content of the former. So, in the blend, Armstrong "rules" in the land of jazz; this figurative superposition and merger of two activities, one cultural (playing), the other political (ruling), attracts a relevance schema of /qualitative superiority/and/uniqueness/. Remarkably, this schema does not stem from any accurate historical knowledge of kings; there have been many unworthy rulers, and the notion of ruler does not essentially contain features such as /qualitative superiority/ and /uniqueness/. The evaluative meaning really "emerges in the blend" (in Turner and Fauconnier's phrasing), in so far as it is rendered stable and operative ("meaningful," relevant) by the specific schema, whose structure, I suggest, consists of a covariation: when quality increases, the number of owners of the quality decreases, until only one is left (shorthand: $Qn = -f(Ql)$).

The schema, binding in our mind to the blend, makes it "ferment" and produces a meaning space of praise, viewing Armstrong as "*the* best" jazz musician ever. This meaning is what is communicated in the example, if our interpretation is correct. The network is shown in Figure 7.7.

The formula *X is the Y of Z* may be considered a rhetorical figure, since it is a figurative form of praise, blame, or at least of emphatic evaluation in some parameter,

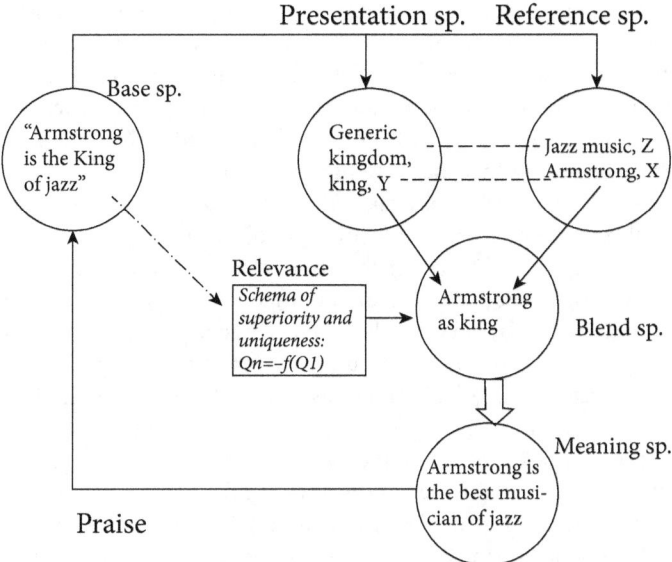

Figure 7.7 XYZ. Louis Armstrong is the king of jazz!

and as such, emotionally efficient, more forceful than a literal statement involving a vocabulary of evaluative comparison would be. The force stems from the domain difference, which calls for a clear and forcefully salient schema!

Metaphor

In metaphor, domain difference between inputs is again decisive; there are two input spaces pertaining to two necessarily different semantic domains.[22] The presentation space has a generic content (cf. the indefinite determiner a *butcher*), while the content of the Reference space is either generic or deictic (cf. the definite demonstrative determiner this *surgeon*... in the much debated metaphor: *This surgeon is a butcher*, Brandt and Brandt 2005).

Animal metaphors are prominent in all human cultures. *Achilles is a lion. Nielsen is a snake.*[23] Different animals are used for different meanings in different cultures; what is transcultural is that these metaphor formulae have morally evaluative meanings for human targets and that these "meaning effects" cannot be induced directly from the animal species as known zoologically by the culture using the metaphor. The metaphorically obtained meanings are due to specific schematizations binding to specific blends.

To say that animal metaphors are instantiations of a conceptual metaphor HUMAN BEINGS ARE ANIMALS[24] would, strictly speaking, be incorrect; this predicate formula is a *theoretical model* describing a type of metaphors (apart from describing a biological truth). This type is not itself a metaphor, or a conceptual metaphor, as cognitive jargon often has it. It is at best a hypothesis for useful classification of certain metaphors. The *A IS B* model is insufficient, because it does not take into account the fact that "inference," or meaning production, is not happening by the predicative relation itself, as a regular transfer from B to A (as from surgeon to Jensen in the non-metaphoric predicative statement: "Jensen is a surgeon.") To believe that meaning production in metaphor is due to ordinary predicative transfer is a serious mistake. The predicative semantics of the domain-different double-space components in metaphor instead brings about a *figurative alienation* of the referential target. It thereby creates a salient figurative instability, hence its potentially idiomatic rhetorical force; this instability is then, as an instantaneous semantic mystery, riddle, or challenge for the addressee, "solved" by the stabilizing relevance schema that culturally binds to the figuratively unstable, "strange," defigurated, referential target absurdly halfways merging, in the blend, with a domain-different "source" predicate from Presentation space.[25] Predicativity in metaphor semantics creates momentary *absurdity*, which triggers a specific schematization that makes the metaphor meaningful.

The snake-in-the-grass examples (see note 23) illustrate the basic principles or properties of metaphor—namely the domain difference, here between natural kinds and interpersonal matters, the schematic import of dynamic-strategic logic, the evaluative meaning effect, and the structural stability of the network itself, which may explain the velocity and smoothness of the processing of these semantic cross-domain predications.[26] The network is shown in Figure 7.8.

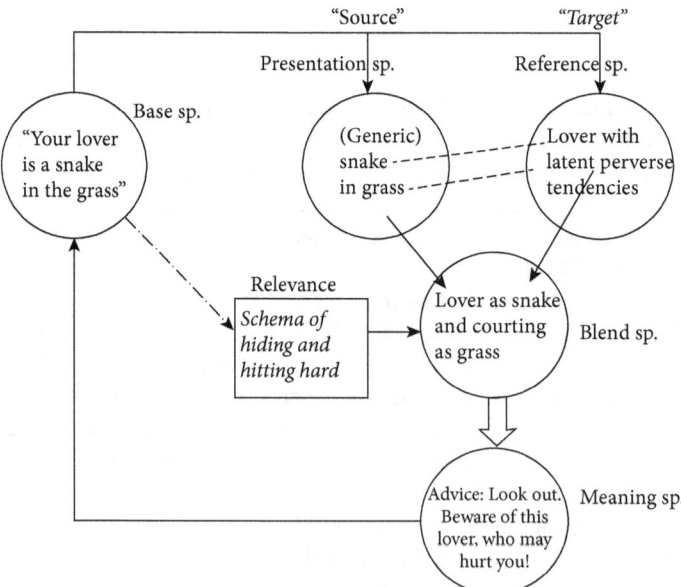

Figure 7.8 Metaphor. *Snake in the grass* blending.

The performative effect seems to be easily and readily obtained through metaphor. The "alienating" mental procedure of blending entities of blatantly different nature may in general enhance the expressivity and the salience of the schematic "logic" in the message.[27]

Adherents of "conceptual metaphor" theory tend to think that the link between source and target binds the conceptualizer to structure inherent in the source. As this example illustrates, this is far from being the case (snakes can do many other things in the grass than biting occasionally passing humans); and same source-target links can express culturally different meanings, because the crucial semantic process only happens when *a schema binds to the blend*,[28] and the cultural choice of schema is variable. It therefore serves no purpose to just list source-target pairs in the "empirical" study of metaphor; what is important is the study of schemas as such—through culturally interpreted metaphors and otherwise.

Metaphor, in the conceptual-cognitive tradition, was further supposed to prove a philosophical point dear to empiricism, namely the physicalist idea of unidirectional mappings from the more physically concrete (sources) toward the more immaterial and abstract (targets), which would explain the origin of abstract meaning: metaphor making the mind abstract. The human mind would primarily perceive physical things and events and then use them as source structure for more abstract targets, and so on. Thereby it would be shown that Locke, Berkeley, and Hume were right: *nihil in intellectu nisi prius in sensu* (in short: perception creates all concepts). However, social experience turns out to be as primordial as physical experience, and even purely mental experience—such as the feeling of the difference between sensing and imagining and thus, for example, between having and wanting—is probably primordial. Speech-act experience ("Don't do this! Don't do that!") is as primordial as macro-physical experience (of bumping into tables and chairs, spilling milk, falling, etc.). The semantic, experiential *domains* involved in the recruiting of space contents for metaphor do *not* follow any such directional ordering[29]; sources can easily be more "abstract" than targets. Abstraction is, as we have mentioned, instead a matter of mental architecture, independent of metaphor. What metaphor *does* or *creates* is not abstraction but schematic foregrounding and most often emphatic messages.

Hypothesis

When we suddenly stop in our tracks surprised by an unexpected view or a state of affairs we had thought would be otherwise, we undergo an experience opposing what we indeed see and what we had reasons to believe would be there to see. We are then *surprised*, because the continuity between the past and the present is broken; we do not immediately understand how a known state could become the perceived new state. What we are presented with contrasts what it refers to, namely the known state. There is a mapping between the two states, by sameness and "unsameness," but also a causal gap that makes us wonder and often express a corresponding interrogative attitude. Returning to a familiar place and finding things changed, as Ulysses returning to Ithaca, would be an illustrious example. The superposition of the contrasting states of affairs in a blend will then trigger a call for "explanation" (making "plain" the bumpy discontinuity). Overly easy suggestions, like ad hoc magic, will be rejected, and the more critical the cognizer, the more specific the type of causation proposed will have to be. Once such a hypothetical explanatory schematization is suggested, and a view of the process of change is obtained, it will in general undergo further examination—if schema X is correct, then (by deduction) other facts should be manifest, and if so, then (by induction) these other facts should point to the same explanation, rather than to a different one.[30]

The standard network here takes on its most trivial but still its most important task in everyday cognition and in our narrative life: the "making-plain" of experience by filling the causal gaps, thus yielding the impression that our lifeworld is somehow, in principle, homogeneous and "rational," causally coherent, despite its contingencies and dark spots.

Once a causal schema is actualized, a new "running" of the network with new inputs may successfully show that the hypothetical explanation is not entirely ad hoc, since the same schema is recognized as being at work in different contexts. The most evident example may be the analysis of a metaphor (with a strange and surprising imagery), eliciting a hypothesis about the schema that would make it signify what it does signify in its (Base space) context. Then that schema in turn calls for examination as to its inner consistency and its possible efficiency in other semantic compositions.[31]

The essential effect of a hypothesis is to offer a construal of a *change* in terms of a causally acceptable *transition*. Still, causal acceptability is insufficient for explanatory acceptability, hence the epistemic process following the hypothetical stage toward establishing a belief. The network of hypothesis suggested is shown in Figure 7.9.

The subjective (emotional) state of cognitive *surprise* contains as such a contrast between two spaces, corresponding to the brute experience of change, as shown in Figure 7.9, and it starts a network, when the problematic superposition of the

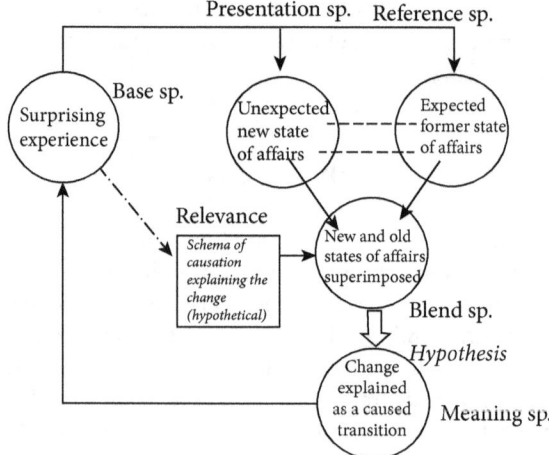

Figure 7.9 Hypothesis. What on earth is going on here? Could it be ... X? Or Y? ... Or ...

two contrasting versions of a state of affairs, one expected and one unexpected but perceived, is bridged by a causal schema. The hypothesis, in the meaning space, is the result of the application of this schema to the unstable blend. Since many different schemas may occur alternatively in the same position of "stabilizer," "explainer," a hypothesis is often surrounded by other hypotheses (stacked in Base space). If no schema emerges, we just have to keep "wondering."

Surprising and intriguing experiences are favorite topics in human communication; the exchange and evaluation of hypotheses are therefore a standard game in dialogue ("Why this?—Why that?"). It is easy to see that the blending network of *hypothesis* is a special case of the network of *comparison*; the latter is already a favorite topic in conversation.[32]

Agency

As discussed, the point of mental representation is to allow us to use the same mental architecture, and thus the same representations, in both directions for semantic interpretation of what we sense and for our planning and monitoring of intentional, voluntary action. The famous *source-path-goal* schema[33] is really a representation of—perceived, planned, or monitored—voluntary action.[34] The semantic setups for voluntary action are *telic*, that is, they are completed when a represented goal state is reached, and they are started when an initial state is represented. They therefore necessarily contain a mental space for the desired terminal (goal) state, established by a *desire* ("dream") delegation, and a mental space for the current, initial state of affairs; the dynamic, causal-intentional[35] schema representing anticipated obstacles and their overcoming is what makes a trajectory from the initial state to the terminal state relevant as a *project* (Figure 7.10).

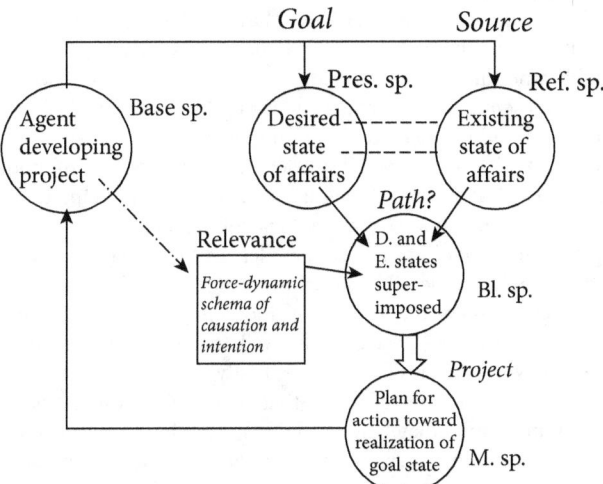

Figure 7.10 Agency as a blending network.

In the "existing state of affairs," there may already be a story of *change*, yielding an embedding of network in network and allowing a transfer of subject from experiencer to potential agent, and even a transfer of schema, if the goal is to revert to an unchanged situation. (The dotted mapping lines indicate the desired contrast, or "unsameness," that animates any project.) The motivation for a project is "to make a difference"—to change the world on some point.

This presentation and discussion of mental spaces, blending, and mental architecture offered a summary of preliminary results of a cognitive-semiotic approach to analysis and theory of (some aspects of) meaning production. We have considered five prominent cases of such production and thereby illustrated a model that allows analysis to be theorized in the framework of a more general, and hopefully more realistic, view of consciousness and meaning.

Notes

1 Why would the here-and-now "real space" be a mental space at all? Because we have to mentally represent this part of the real universe, that is, represent it as a real-situation space, in order to be able to perform the mental operation of transporting entities between distinct "contexts"—and in this example, to enjoy the weird interpretation according to which a baby could be elected as a president.... (Later, this however happened with a certain Trump.)
2 Fauconnier and Sweetser (1996) is a first example of this fruitful new approach.
3 In many languages, the P2 pronoun *you* (or a corresponding morpheme) is used impersonally: "If you ever go to Copenhagen, you should have a beer in Nyhavn..."; *you* is the standard delegate—as is the German *man* and the French *on*—allowing reference to the "off-line" part of experienceable reality that we call the "world."
4 Thom (1972) initiated a new approach to dynamical phenomena both in science and in the world of experienced meaning (which I call *pheno-physics*); Petitot (2011), Wildgen (1985), and Brandt (1992) have explored a range of domains where Thomian "catastrophe theory" applies and opens unexpected horizons; there is now a considerable amount of literature on the subject—an explorable source of reflection for cognitive and semiotic researchers and for philosophers at large.
5 See "Evidentiality and Enunciation," Brandt (2004b).
6 Sweetser's (1990) term "root" modality refers to the expressions of modal dynamics understood as physical force; she writes: "Let us view *can* as being the equivalent of a full gas tank in a car, and *may* as the equivalent of an open garage door" (p. 53). According to Talmy—but not to Sweetser (idem)—the physical meaning of modality would be the "root" of all possible modal meanings, whether social, epistemic, or speech-act. Sweetser keeps the term "root" modality as a tribute to her colleague.
7 How can mental spaces be "shared" at all? Well, this is what this entire project is about. Here are two principles for a starter: firstly, we are set up to organize meaning of a certain complexity in mental spaces that are fit for representation and memory, and we are set up to immediately refer to that format in communication with other minds by language and other semiotic means. Secondly, all semiotic means of communication, including music, contain instructions for filling certain spaces with certain contents.

8   Brandt and Brandt (2005).
9   This statement may need some explanation. A mental space is not a sum of contents but a spatiotemporal format in its own right, a "scenario," which can be held while contents change. As such, a temporal minimum for conceiving of a mental space may correspond to the temporal frame of basic situational consciousness, approx. three seconds, according to neuropsychologist Pöppel (1997). The situational content of course comes with its own temporal horizon, sometimes experienced by projected presence, protention, retention, and other Husserlian properties (Husserl 1980 (1928)). This difference between the involved temporalities makes it possible to voluntarily "hold" a space while filling, emptying, or changing its content: we may control and monitor the format while we let the content of the format flow on its own terms.
10 Alan Baddeley's (2007) models on working memory may be useful for understanding the role of represented content in online phenomenology of perception. The mental space networks may be among the devices connecting the "central executive" to his "slave systems." There is much to discuss here. In general, memory research will hopefully be better connected to phenomenology in the future.
11 See Sweetser, "Mental Spaces and the Grammar of Conditional Constructions," in Fauconnier and Sweetser (1996).
12 Without a discussion of the status of mental spaces in mental architecture, we would miss the opportunity to study their possible "density" and phenomenological consistency. We would run the risk of getting convinced that a *blue cup* is a result of blending a space of "blueness" with a space of "cupness." Such an understanding of mental space semantics would just be guided by lexicon ("blue," "cup") rather than by any consideration of space building or delegation—P2 cannot be sent to "blueness." There is no such type of space delegation. In an early critical note, Line Brandt (2000) writes: "Some theorists sometimes tend to forget that blending is a process that takes place at the conceptual level of consciousness and thus applies to *conceptual* phenomena and not to basic phenomenology of *Gestaltung*. In such moments of overgeneralization, conceptual integration theory is also claimed to explain phenomena such as identity and the capacity to perceive a blue cup (i.e. to perceive a cup as blue), a claim which in my mind has come to be characterized as 'the blue cup fallacy.'" This example refers to Fauconnier and Turner (1999). To my knowledge, this is the first criticism of the arbitrary use of the notion of mental space in Fauconnier and Turner.
13 See Brandt (2006).
14 Chapter 4, above, discusses corresponding levels of selfhood and subjectivity in consciousness; please note that mental architecture (of phenomenal objectivity) and hierarchical subjectivity partly overlap but do not coincide.
15 Classical gestalt phenomenology knows that we perceive object relations. My point is that we do perceive object constellations as dynamically constituted even when we still are not able to specify the dynamics, which appears in an underdetermined way; we will then further question its causal schematization.
16 This idea—that notions finally feed into affects—is of course based on elementary emotions: surprise presupposes expectations, grief presupposes loss, and so on. In these examples, affects are semantically loaded. There are of course simple affects, like fear, that are triggered by reflex reactions to qualia and objects or by nothing at all; and even idiots can be "happy," without having to juggle with a lot of political philosophy. The "higher" levels are cross-connected to "lower" levels in many ways.

Genetically, there may have been just one level, then a bifurcation qualia/affect, then further branchings that nevertheless keep the formerly direct connections alive, as reflexes.

17 Affects in fact *affect*, or impact, our body; *stress* would be a good example. You are persecuted by deadlines, and you end up with fatigue and depression, or worse.

18 An example would be Barry Smith's (1996) analysis of boundaries: *bone fide* boundaries interpret natural differences (rivers can be country frontiers), whereas *fiat* boundaries are projected onto an undifferentiated natural support (frontiers as lines drawn in the sand).

19 The conjunctional morpheme *if* creates a space delegation by epistemic modality, signaling either /possibility/ or /impossibility/. This is the case in both interrogative and conditional grammatical constructions.

20 The component called Relevance is not, strictly speaking, a mental space, since its content does not necessarily appear in the consciousness of the involved subjects, as do the other components of the network (by introspection; still, admittedly, many subjects deny their own introspection). In the example, modal delegation and causal relevance are implicit but indispensable operations in the process. The Relevance is an open collection of schemas imported from the Base space, which is a multilayered source of such schematic contributions (specified in Brandt and Brandt 2005). They can stem from the dialogue itself, from the narrative context of the communication, from the cultural background (as "common ground"), or from the naturally shared cognitive competence of human minds trained by experience in lifeworld. In analysis, we track and infer the implicit schematic stabilizers of a blend "backwards" from the result, that is, using our human capacity to understand the meaning-making intended and often achieved by the utterance.

21 Searching the internet for "the king of" or "the queen of" formulae will give you an impression of the popularity of this evaluative construction. Note that the domain difference is crucial to the evaluative meaning of the construction. *So Peter is the father of Mary* is not to be considered as a blend, and it is certainly not the case that *Peter* and *Mary* are in one space, while *father* is in the other space—such a conception (Turner and Fauconnier 2002) confuses once more the grammatical construction with the semantic operation we are considering, and it entirely ignores the phenomenological semantics of mental spaces, which do not separate "values" and "roles" as a formal analysis of propositional structure may do. By contrast, *father* is in the non-referential presentation space in "George Washington is the father of our country," because the speaker is not believing in G. W.'s literal fatherhood in relation to a country; the blend instead binds to a schematic notion of founding. On the notion of *domain*, see Brandt (2004a). George Lakoff refers to domain difference in his conceptual metaphor theory, where the format A IS B ("LOVE IS A JOURNEY") presupposes that the *domain of target A* (referential, in our terms) and the *domain of source B* (presentational, in our terms) must be different. Lakoff's problem is that he does not explain or even explore the domains of human and lexicographically relevant experience. His theory has essentially just a physical domain, source of all sources (B) and everything else, target (A). This physicalism is contradictory to both empirical metaphor studies and general phenomenology.

22 Since morphemes, that is, closed-class words, are indifferent to domain differences, they cannot work metaphorically. So "Jensen is on drugs" or "Petersen is in love"

do not use *on* end *in* metaphorically, as conceptual metaphor theory claims. These prepositions work in any domain, because they refer to *schematic* structure, not to *categories* in *domains*. Thus, *on* signifies a relatively "flat" situation that you can get *off* under certain circumstances, whereas *in* signifies a relatively "deep" situation, not so easy to get *out of*. Again, here, "flat" and "deep" are not physically spatial but schematic structures that work in imaginary spaces of many kinds, because they relate to mental graphics—the way we think by mental diagrams.

23 The grammatical manifestations of metaphor are variable—*predication*: "That guy's a real snake in the grass, don't waste your time." Or *substitution* of the noun phrase: "How could I ever have trusted that snake in the grass?" Here, *that* ... is deictic, whereas *snake* is generic within the same noun phrase. The generic mode is explicit in the following, contextualized example: "Hear that rattle, fear that hiss/Beware of the Judas kiss/Watch your step, cover your back/Can't trust *a snake* in the grass" [From a Jedd Hughes song about a female seducer].

24 Wei and Wong (2012). Besides, human beings *are* animals. There is no domain difference between A and B.

25 "Source" and "target" are therefore very unsuitable terms for the input components of this process.

26 If the networks were as unstable and irregular as those proposed by Fauconnier and Turner, processing and thus interpretation would be slow and uncertain, and both the meaning effect and the communicational value of such compositions would be null.

27 The principle may be the following: since we cannot express a schema without investing it with categories, which then hide it in their figurativity, a strategy of anti-figurative superposition of figurative categories in turn gives the schema a chance to be foregrounded.

28 All blends have to be stabilized by some schema, otherwise they are almost immediately dissolved (dismissed)—the mind does not "get the point" and decides to forget the nonsense. So, the schema is decisive to the possible meanings of a metaphor, and to misunderstand a metaphor is to apply a culturally "wrong" schema to its perceived blend. Metaphors therefore are good detectors of schemas—and of cultural knowledge.

29 So, biologists will say that the immune system "recognizes" a pathogen, but without having to believe that immune systems have thinking minds capable of recognition. They have to use metaphor—even so often that it becomes unnoticeable to themselves.

30 Niño's important study of C. S. Peirce's notion(s) of abduction through the American philosopher's entire work proposes a basic view of the connection between abductive, deductive, and inductive thinking, in this order, roughly corresponding to the perspective on hypothesis proposed here (Niño 2008, 2012).

31 Causation is cognized by an open family of schemas: "billiard-ball" causation, causation by "spreading," by the dynamics of "making," or that of "letting," and so on. See Brandt (2004a).

32 I am referring to conversations like the following. A: I experienced X and was astonished; B: It reminds me of Y, which was due to Z; A: So maybe X could also be due to Z... The network would take X and Y as inputs and try Z as a schema for the blend.

33 See Tincheva (2012).

34 Mirror neurons in our motor system are known to react to perceived, imagined, and planned acts and agency. See Rizzolatti and Sinigaglia (2008).
35 Intention does not simply "intend" to move along a path, but instead to search for its inherently represented goal state while accepting various paths, depending on the (causal) resistance they offer to the "intent" to move toward the goal state. The "source-path-goal" schema is therefore really a force-dynamic schema, unless that schema describes a ritual process, a ceremonial act (where the path is indeed important, and its completion constitutes a goal in itself).

References

Baddeley, A. D., 2007. *Working Memory, Thought and Action*. Oxford: Oxford University Press.
Brandt, L., 2000. *Explosive Blends—From Cognitive Semantics to Literary Analysis*. Thesis, University of Roskilde.
Brandt, P. A., 1992. *La Charpente modale du sens. Pour une sémiolinguistique morphogénétique et dynamique*. Amsterdam, New York: John Benjamins.
Brandt, P. A., 2004a. *Spaces, Domains, and Meaning. Essays in Cognitive Semiotics*. European Semiotics, Vol. 4. Bern: Peter Lang Verlag.
Brandt, P. A., 2004b. "Evidentiality and Enunciation." In: (Ed.) J. Marín Arrese, *Perspectives on Evidentiality and Modality*. Madrid: Ed. Complutense.
Brandt, P. A., 2006. "Form and Meaning in Art." In: (Ed.) M. Turner, *The Artful Mind. Cognitive Science and the Riddle of Human Creativity*. New York: Oxford University Press.
Brandt, L. and P. A. Brandt, 2005. "Making Sense of a Blend. A Cognitive-Semiotic Approach to Metaphor." In: *Annual Review of Cognitive Linguistics*, Vol. 3, 216–249, John Benjamins.
Fauconnier, G., 1985 reed. 1994. *Mental Spaces: Aspects of Meaning Construction in Natural Languages*. Cambridge: Cambridge University Press.
Fauconnier, G., and M. Turner, 1999. "Analysis versus Global Insight: How and Why Do We Blend Cause and Effect?" Berkeley: University of California.
Fauconnier, G., and M. Turner, 2002. *The Way We Think. Conceptual Blending and the Mind's Hidden Complexities*. New York: Basic Books.
Husserl, E., 1980 (1928). *Vorlesungen zur Phänomenologie des inneren Zeitbewußtseins*. Tübingen: Max Niemeyer Verlag.
Niño, D., 2008. *Abducting abduction. Avatares de la comprensión de la abducción de Charles S. Peirce*. (Doctoral Dissertation). Bogotá: Universidad Nacional de Colombia.
Niño, D., 2012. "Abducción e Inducción en Peirce: evolución y criterios." To appear in: *DeSignis. Revista de la Federación Latinoamericana de Sémiotica*.
Petitot, J., 2011. *Cognitive Morphodynamics. Dynamical Morphological Models of Constituency in Perception and Syntax*. European Semiotics, Vol. 11. Bern: Peter Lang Verlag.
Pöppel, E., 1997. "Consciousness versus States of Being Conscious." *Behavioral and Brain Sciences*, 20 (1).
Rizzolatti, G., and C. Sinigaglia, 2008. *Mirrors in the Brain. How We Share Our Actions and Emotions*. Oxford: Oxford University Press.

Smith, B., 1996. "Mereotopology. A Theory of Parts and Boundaries." *Data and Knowledge Engineering*, 20, 287–303.
Sweetser, E., 1990. *From Etymology to Pragmatics. Metaphorical and Cultural Aspects of Semantic Structure*. Cambridge: Cambridge University Press.
Sweetser, E., 1996. "Mental Spaces and the Grammar of Conditional Constructions." In Fauconnier & Sweetser (above), 318–333.
Tincheva, N., 2012. *The Source-Path-Goal Schema in the Structure of Political Speeches. Political Speeches: A Cognitive Perspective on Text and Structure*. Sofia: Askoni.
Wei, L., and B. E. Wong, 2012. "A Corpus-based Study on Snake Metaphors in Mandarin Chinese and British English." *GEMA Online™ Journal of Language Studies* 311, 12 (1).
Wildgen, W., 1985. *Archetypensemantik. Grundlagen für eine dynamische Semantik auf der Basis der Katastrophentheorie*. Tübingen: Gunter Narr Verl.

8

Blending in the Poetics of Songs: Leonard Cohen's *Hallelujah*

What Is a Song?[1]

Songs are just poems built into music, one might think. However, there are structural differences that have to be accounted for if we want an accurate description of both genres in modern culture.[2] By *enunciation*, we mean the interpersonal act and relation between the *personae* in communication, as represented in language.[3] There is special contract between *enunciator* and *enunciatee* in songs. The enunciation of poetry is characteristically situated close to that which uses the autobiographical voice of the poet, including the use of pronouns referring to existing persons;[4] by contrast, the enunciation in songs, the *melic* enunciation, as opposed to most forms of *poetic* enunciation, includes role-playing strategies that make interpersonal references depend on the narrative situations signified, and situates melic semantics closer to drama and fiction. Songs are often performed collectively, which invites collective identification with roles represented in the "drama" of the texts of songs; it is evidently easier for a collective singing subject to share in "playing" the role of a fictive person than to identify with a biographical one.[5] The literal existence of poetry as text is therefore radically different from that of the textual existence of songs; in poetry, a suite of stanzas cannot be responsibly read while omitting parts or inverting their order, but in songs, the order of verses[6] is often changed, verses are skipped over, and lines are varied in performance. As we shall see, this is also the case in the song we will analyze in this chapter.[7]

Given that the syllabic and the phrase structure can be mapped directly onto notes and musical phrase structure, songs project tonal gestalts onto verbal gestalts,[8] in such a way that the tonal syntax overdetermines the verbal semantics. In particular, the constellation of the same melodic phrase with different verbal content produces semantic similarity effects in the textual meaning. We are going to show how this principle works in the melo-textual meaning production of our song.[9]

Ulf Cronquist, University of Gothenburg, Sweden, coauthored this chapter.

The Text

By text, we mean both the music and the verbal text. For reasons of space, we will presume that the reader knows the melodic form of *Hallelujah*. It consists of a variable series of verses followed by the one-word refrain. The verses, comprising eight bars in a 12/8 meter (tempo 90), correspond to six lines of grosso modo iambic prosody with the following pattern of strong accents (Ø=empty):

// 4 /4 / 4 + 2 + Ø Ø / 4 / 4 / 4 + 2 + Ø 1 //

The refrain has five bars in the same meter, covering four Hallelujahs, of which the fourth partly inhabits two bars.

The chord sequence is the following (in C):

verse: // C Am / C Am / F G / C G / C F G / Am F G / G *E7* / Am //
refrain: // F / Am / F / C G / C (G) //

The chord sequence is interesting, since the first verse in all versions refers to its own chords: "It goes like this: the fourth [F], the fifth [G], the minor fall [Am], the major [C] lift"; and the "secret chord" in the first line could refer to the solitary *E7* in the seventh bar, the chord that hits the important word *broken*.[10]

The precise wording of the song's lyrics is variable, but if we follow the maximal list of verses and their order in Cohen (1993),[11] we get the following seven standard stanzas, which will be our reference corpus:

HALLELUJAH
[1]
[12] I've heard there was a secret chord
that David played to please[13] the Lord,
but you don't really care for music, do you?
It goes like this: the fourth, the fifth
the minor fall, the major lift;
the baffled king composing Hallelujah!
[2]
Your faith was strong but you needed proof.
You saw her bathing on the roof;
her beauty and the moonlight overthrew you.
She tied you to a[14] kitchen chair
she broke your throne, she cut your hair,
and from your[15] lips she drew the Hallelujah!
[3]
You say I took the Name in vain;
I don't even know the name.
But if I did, well, really, what's it to you?
There is a blaze of light in every word;

it doesn't matter which you heard,
the holy, or the broken Hallelujah!
[4]
I did my best;[16] it wasn't much.
I couldn't feel, so I learned[17] to touch.
I've told the truth, I didn't come[18] to fool you.
And even though it all went wrong,
I'll stand before the Lord of Song
with nothing on my lips[19] but Hallelujah!
[5]
Baby[20], I have been here before.
I know[21] this room, I've walked this floor.
I used to live alone before I knew you.
I've seen[22] your flag on the Marble Arch,
but[23] love is not a[24] victory march,
it's a cold and it's a broken Hallelujah!
[6]
There was a time you let me know
what's really going on[25] below
but now you never show it to me, do you?
I remember when I moved in you,
and the holy dove[26] was moving too,
and every breath we drew was Hallelujah!
[7]
Now maybe there's a God above
but all I ever learnt[27] from love
is how to shoot at someone who outdrew you.
And it's no complaint[28] you hear tonight,
[29] and it's not some pilgrim[30] who's seen the light –
it's a cold and it's a broken Hallelujah![31]

A Semio-semantic Model

The scenario of the performance is a source of the meaning production taking place during the singing. The performer always sings *to* the audience as actors on a stage, and his *you* and *I* are roles theatrically played within the dramas of the text, in front of the audience as a resonant chorus. The minimal and normal extension of each such drama is the verse. Enunciation patterns (types of address, prayer, question, statement, etc.) and semantic filling of personal pronouns often change from verse to verse. Musicians and singers on stage or in the studio deliver the *signifiers* *to* the audience, which participates in the imaginary unfolding of the *signified* panorama that the performers then metonymically embody, especially in concert performances.[32] And new signifiers incorporating the returned signifieds follow, so that a circular process of feeding and feedback spirals into a shared experience of semantic saturation, a phenomenology of melo-dramatic communication and, almost, aesthetic communion, which gradually fills and saturates the performance space with structure and emotion.

This anchoring performance scenario is what we call the *semiotic Base space* of meaning production. Semantic content spaces, also called mental spaces, are set up mentally by the participants according to a principle called conceptual integration or blending.[33] The participants share the phenomenology of the scenario they are participants of, and behind this, to a certain extent they share their musical culture, their language, and their lifeworld, from which an undetermined number of semio-cognitive schemas can be mobilized as relevance-makers in the process of meaning production.

We think it is a major discovery that there are two semantic "input" spaces that are created, or "set up," by the communication in Base space, namely a "Presentation space" and a "Reference space," and that these will enter into two sorts of interrelations, first a *mapping* of contents and then a *projection* of contents to and a *merging* of these contents in a new space of virtual meaning, the blending space, where new meaning can be stabilized by *relevant schematization* also drawn from Base space.[34] In metaphor, the Presentation space will contain the imagery, whereas the Reference space will hold the items that the speaker intends (and the hearer would understand in the context) the metaphor to be "about." In non-metaphorical utterances, the Presentation space will still hold the conceptual imagery, in a *metonymical* key, and the Reference space will contain the intended "message." In everyday language, the blends are often not even noticed, but rather experienced as evident, natural, that is, naturalized, meanings of what is uttered.[35] In artful and ritual communication, especially in literature, there is (often) an eventual instance of blending, where the total imagery of the text, in the Presentation space, is mapped onto a "deeper" existential meaning in the Reference space, and the resulting blend can be experienced as the emotional "output" of the work in question, that is, the semiotic effect that returns to Base space as the final meaning, which (literary) interpretation is expected to detect. In this case, the formal patterns of the text deliver the relevance schemas that eventually stabilize the blends as emerging new meanings. Figure 8.1 is a graphic representation of the blending model itself.[36]

The network constitutes a circular flow from the Base space to the elementary input spaces, Presentation space and Reference space, and back to Base space (as experienced meaning) from the schematized space of blending. New schematization of the blend is necessary, because the schemas from imagery and intended content are in general formally incompatible when imported to the blend; the *re-schematization* is the factor explaining the emergence of new meaning through the process. Once the spaces are set up and invested semantically, *their network stays active* and receptive to more inputs from Base space, so that the space of the blends will contain a growing and changing mass of virtual meanings, gradually stabilized in the course of the performance of the text.

Semiotic blending: the processual network of meaning production

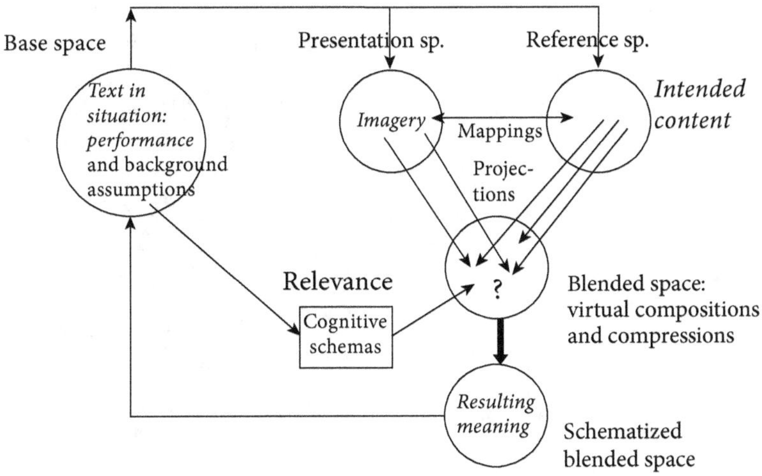

Figure 8.1 The semiotic blending model.

The Blending Process at Work

Let us show right away how the model works by looking at the autoreferential first verse of *Hallelujah*. David, the psalmist king, plays to the Lord and is baffled by a chord that he finds by chance while composing his psalms (the *Tehillim*). That is the reference; the presentation has a first person (*I've heard*) who explains to a second person (*but you don't*) what David did, in terms of fourths and fifths, and so on. In the blend, the first person with his guitar becomes David and the contrast between *you* and the Lord becomes dramatic, unless the Lord in fact cares as little as the present second person about the secret chord and music in general. The music actually played, with the fourth occurring on the word *fourth*, the fifth occurring on the word *fifth*, and so on, emotionally creates and supports the blend of the present and the ancient moment compressed into one and the same magical instant, where the role of *you* is thus *contrasting and merging with* that of the Lord as "pleased" listener to David's psalm. The word "hallelujah"[37] follows immediately the "secret chord" (*E7* in our analysis) on "com-*posing*." When the question sounds: *do you?*, one may already hear: *do yah*—as in *hallelujah*.[38] In the first-person to second-person address, we will by default hear an intimate exchange between persons who know each other (*you don't really care for music...*). So the uncertainty of the second person's response becomes both erotic and religious.

The network will look like Figure 8.2.

This network will run for as many verses as the singer chooses to perform; and the emotional meaning arising will be built on the changing inputs and the (ideally, shared) memory of the semantics already invested in the spaces.

Hallelujah, first verses

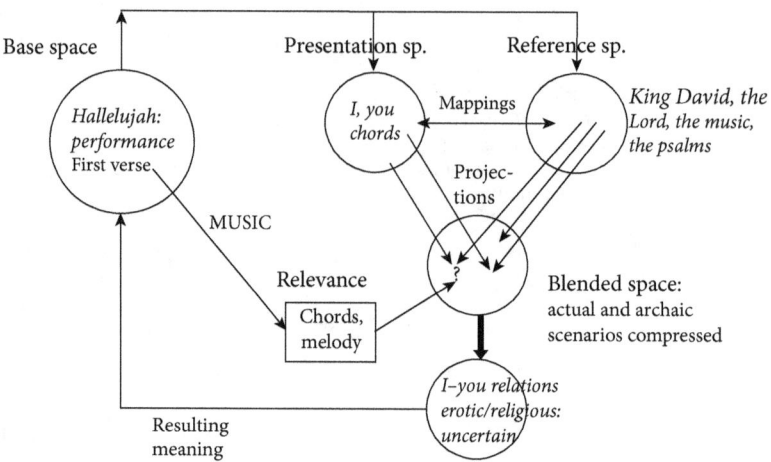

Figure 8.2 The first blend.

In the second verse, the enunciative personal pronouns have a non-embodied first person and a scenario involving second person and third person, supposedly a male and a female character, respectively. The first person could be a (male) narrator addressing himself as *you*, the male. The first line's religious reference ("your faith was strong…") recalls the religious reference in the first verse, but the female "bathing on the roof" must be "proof" of a different relation, an erotic attraction that becomes a power play ("she tied you …," "broke your throne," "cut your hair" as the traitorous Delilah did with the faithful fighter Samson (*Book of Judges*, 16)), ending in submission. From this biblical but actualized erotic show in Presentation space, we therefore get a mapping to a corresponding religious drama in Reference space, and the *Hallelujah*[39] in the same musical position as before again sounds ambiguous, this time forming an explicit erotico-religious blend. The mirror relation between traitorous earthly love and betrayed divine love is established; the love relations in both spaces are "broken," and the tension will yield a *broken* Hallelujah in the third verse.

A new *you* blames a new *I*, in this verse, for taking "the Name in vain" (*Leviticus* 24, a capital sin: you get stoned to death). Maybe the second-person character coincides with the one appearing in the first verse (*do you?*), and we are clearly back in the intimacy of quarrelling.[40] Maybe it is a female reproach addressing the male character who had ironically answered "hallelujah" to something she had said? The ironical version is then the broken one. We swear when we quarrel. We invoke divine entities in the swearing. Hence, in this verse, we may venture that the religious second person activates the sacred (Reference) space, while the ironizing first person activates the profane intimacy (Presentation) space, which he enriches with the claim that in principle, *every word* is enlightening, containing a *blaze of light*. It does not matter if the "hallelujah" is *holy* or *broken*, which might mean that the relation to the Lord is critical, in a state of breaking.

This first person stays stable throughout the remaining verses, 4–7. In the fourth verse, there is in the erotic space a past-oriented statement of break-up (from: *I did my best*, to: *it all went wrong*), and then, in the religious space a "standing before the Lord," presumably in the moment of dying, with nothing but praise—that is, maybe gratitude for life and admission of personal incompetence.[41] This is again an emotional attitude that maps directly from the situation in erotic intimacy to the situation in religious intimacy with a difficult, maybe capricious divinity. So in the blend, and in the perceived flow of words and music by which it reaches us, there is no difference between the two experiences. The love relation is over, or a life is over, the feeling is the same: irreversibility and some sort of embittered happiness.[42]

Whereas verses 3 and 4 are more explicit on the religious than on the erotic side, in verses five and six the erotic space is foregrounded. *I* am alone again, and love was less triumphant (*Marble Arch*) than *you* thought it would be.[43] Loneliness, lack of communication (*now you never show it to me*), and fleshly, carnal knowledge (*... when I moved in you*) gone and now just a memory, albeit a sacred one (*every breath we drew was h.*). Carnal love is of course the topic of the *Song of Songs*, or Song of Salomon, a celebration of desire and sex, and in the Jewish tradition an allegory of the relationship of God (the male) and Israel (the female), as in the Christian tradition it becomes an allegory of the relationship between Christ and his Church. It is the last part of the *Tanakh*, and it is very much appreciated and read; but Jews are not allowed to interpret it as not being allegorically a representation of the divine loving union, that is, a huge metaphor. The network of spaces we have suggested captures directly this macro-metaphor as Cohen's likely underlying structuring principle. Still, this Salomonic love song is, by contrast, *cold and broken*—as modern love songs are and maybe must be.

In the seventh verse, the first rhyme again juxtaposes divinity (*a God above*) and earthly love, from which not much was learnt (how to be jealous?—*shoot at someone who outdrew you*), but then there is a significant return to the autoreferential mode of the first verse: what *you hear tonight*, namely this very song, is neither a complaint nor the expression of an illumination but a certain form of a *Hallelujah*. The reference to the song itself, in the song, is what we will call the *deictic* moment—since it can only happen momentarily.[44] The deictic moment in the first verse (*a secret chord ... it goes like* **this** *...*) and here in the seventh verse (*it's no complaint* **you hear tonight**, namely: now) are verbally explicit, but the musical unfolding of the key word, the reiterated, exclamatory *Hallelujah!*, always coupled, in the verses, to the second person by the rhyme on /uː jaː/, represents an even stronger form of deixis: in the moment of hearing the word and its chords in the refrain following each explanatory verse, the existential, erotico-divine state of mind in question is *called into being* within the musical here-and-now. The deictic function of music is in fact always *calling*—recalling, evoking, making things present in the imaginary of the here-and-now.

The last word of the verses, followed by four repetitions of it in the refrain, yields a total of five hallelujahs, and these are expressed, first through the "falling" Am, then the "rising" F major, then again the "falling" Am, the "rising" F major, and finally the melodically "falling" (e-d-c) but harmonically "raising" cadence: C-G-C, which thus fulfills the merge of deception and praise in one deictic word.

Conclusion

The following general semantic investment of the mental space model of semiotic blending summarizes the meaning production that is happening in the song. From verse to verse, the effect is reinforced by the core deictic exclamatory carried by the music. Verses can be repeated or omitted, as long as the chemical process, so to speak, of the meaning fabrication is stabilized as an intuitive framework shared by performers and audience. After the last verse sung, the refrain is repeated, and it now carries the load of the entire semantic narrative and theological inventory mobilized, in its one and only word. As we just saw, this word *(H.)* becomes, in the blending space, itself an instantaneous blender of *deception* (D.) and *praise* (P.), those apparently contradictory concepts that now merge—D. + P. := H.—into a feeling that is no longer a concept, but rather an unnamed emotional state, embodied by the musically connected persons in Base space. In Figure 8.3, we tentatively call this "meaning effect" a (erotico-religious) *reconciliation*. In this effect, a love story *is* a life story, and what we experience in relation to others in intimacy *is* what the relationship or exchange with the divinity is and means.

Through this analysis, we hope to show the principal process of the ongoing meaning production but of course not all its details. As the song—this song as any other that lives on beyond the first instances of performance—may still be subject to variations on the musical or the verbal side, an exhaustive account of its details is not our main interest. We hope to have exemplified an approach to the study of songs that is prepared for integrating the musical and the verbal developments and discover the forces of their interaction.

The semantic (content) and semiotic (signifying) structure of a song can be much more complex than it is in this beautiful case, networks can be embedded in other networks, and the music can affect the verbal meaning in many other specific ways.

Hallelujah, through the verses

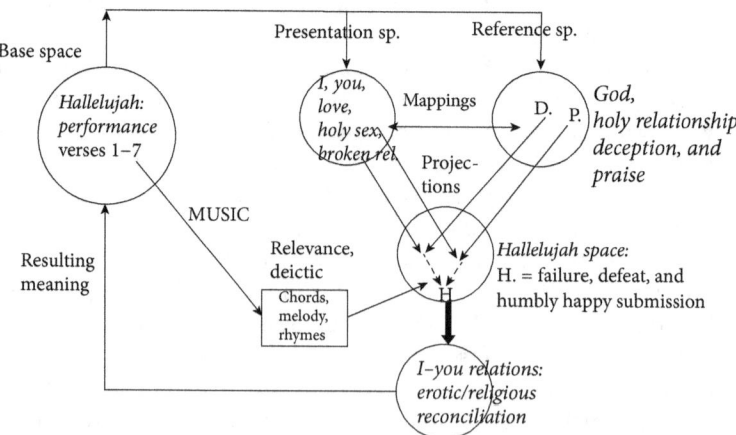

Figure 8.3 The resulting blend.

Our interest is to develop a cognitively and semiotically informed poetics that can finally do justice to the most important and probably the oldest of all human cultural manifestations, the use of the voice—and of language and music—we call *singing*.

Notes

1. See Brandt (2017).
2. The split between song and poem happened in Western culture in the Renaissance when the printing technique (Gutenberg) produced a separation of written and oral poetry: recital versus concert, so to speak. In the ancient cultures, texts were not read silently, and people would gather to listen to the poet's lyre. Cf. the important work of Ong (1982).
3. The term renders the French *énonciation*, used by the linguist Émile Benveniste in his groundbreaking chapter, "L'homme dans la langue," in Benveniste (1966).
4. In poetry, personal references are generally gendered, so female poets will refer to themselves using the feminine gender in languages that have such distinctions (constructions like the French "Je suis fatiguée …," feminine predicate) and male poets using the masculine gender. Germanic languages do not mark the distinction, but romance languages indeed do.
5. So in Hallelujah, when you sing "I heard there was a secret chord," *you* personally are not supposed to have heard this piece of information, but only to perform and enact the first person's utterance as a line of a theatrical role. In poetry, apart from theater, the situation is different; poetry (lyrical) is not fiction and role-playing. Here, the first person refers to the biographical author. Poets know this better than modern academic critics who have learned to always separate the text from everything else.
6. In songs, the terminology distinguishes "verse" and "refrain," where poetry has "stanzas."
7. Leonard Cohen (1934–2016) first published as a poet, *Let Us Compare Mythologies* (1956), *The Spice-Box of Earth* (1961), and continued to publish two novels, *The Favourite Game* (1963), *Beautiful Losers* (1966), before going to Nashville to record his first album *Songs of Leonard Cohen* (1967). He continued his life both as a publishing poet and as a singer-musician, saying au revoir just prior to his passing with the album *You Want It Darker*. Cohen's melo-poetic œuvre of course may blur the distinction between song and poem.
8. A "gestalt" is a perceived whole of parts. For example, the ticks of the metronome can be heard as following a 4/4 or a 3/4 meter; such a "grouping" is a gestalt.
9. Leonard Cohen's song Hallelujah lived a quiet life for many years before becoming one the most well-known and loved songs in contemporary popular culture, now recorded in more than 300 cover versions and featured in a number of films, TV series, and talent shows. The song was first released in 1984 in Canada (in Europe 1985), in the album *Various Positions*. Columbia Records refused to release the LP in the United States, considering it not commercially viable.
In 1991 John Cale released the first cover of the song on the tribute album to Leonard Cohen, *I'm Your Fan*. Cale also provided a live version on his 1992 record *Fragments of a Rainy Season*. This version of the song was also used in the film *Shrek* (2001), while a version by Rufus Wainwright is used on the audio release of the soundtrack.

John Cale's recording of the song includes verses that are not in Cohen's original song lyrics but nevertheless written by him. Cohen has said that he worked with the song for more than five years and wrote about eighty-eight verses. His original recording from 1984 consists of four verses. In 1988 John Cale asked Cohen to see the lyrics and received fifteen pages in his fax machine. Out of these he selected three previously unrecorded verses that are now officially included in the song's canon (see the following note). There is no official record of the other seventy-plus verses. These are in the Leonard Cohen Archive at the University of Toronto, Canada, yet to be made available.

10 This is the only seventh chord in the song, and as such it stands out. A variant, Em, is found on the internet in a score signed "Ludy."

11 The lyrics is found on pp. 347–348. Cohen was actively engaged in editing the book. The careful punctuation is noticeable. Referring to our numbering of the stanzas 1–7, only 1–4 appeared on the original recording from 1984. Then, as mentioned, John Cale got a hold of more stanzas, faxed by Cohen. Of these he chose to use number 5–7 but left out 3–4. His version—the first cover—thus consists of 1–2 and 5–7, and this became canonical for another 300 covers! Jeff Buckley follows Cale in his equally powerful version.

12 Jeff Buckley (1994) begins lines 1 and 4 with the word "well." Other singers, including Cohen, also put in words (in different spaces) like well, but, and, um that do not change the semantics.

13 John Cale (1992) changed "to please" into "and it pleased." It has become the standard.

14 Buckley (1994) sings "her" instead of "a."

15 k. d. lang (2010) sings "her" instead of "your." So who is crying victory or submission (hallelujah) here? Is the answer to be found in verse 5?

16 k. d. lang (2010) adds "I know" between phrases.

17 Wainwright's variant: "tried."

18 Cohen, beginning in 1988, adds "all this way" after "come."

19 Cohen changes "lips" to "tongue" already in 1985—the only difference by then to the original recording.

20 Wainwright (2001) sings "Maybe."

21 Buckley and lang change "I know" to "I've seen."

22 lang changes "I've seen" to "Then I saw."

23 lang changes "but" to "our."

24 Cohen (1988) changes "a" to "some kind of."

25 Wainwright: "what's real and going on below." It may change the meaning of "below." From "in your sexual life" to "behind the surface" in your thinking, in general.

26 Wainwright changes "dove" to "dark"; Allison Crowe (2004) instead sings "ghost." Cohen (1988) adds "she" after "dove."

27 Cohen (1988) sings "seem to learn" instead of "learnt."

28 Cohen (1988) changes "no complaint" to "not a cry." Cale sings "not a cry." lang sings "not a crime that."

29 Cohen (1988, San Sebastian) changes the verse into: "not the abandoned laughter of someone who claims to have seen the light." Cohen (1988, Reykjavik): "not some laughter from some newborn mystic who's seen the light."

30 Cale changes "pilgrim" to "somebody."

31 In a live recording from Warsaw 1985, Cohen sings verses 1–4, as on the record: https://www.youtube.com/watch?v=qF8MrGyeeqg (Accessed February 10, 2020).

A version from Montreux 1985 also has verses 1–4:
https://www.youtube.com/watch?v=S6KLK_8Tg6Y (Accessed February 10, 2020).
1988 Live San Sebastien, verses sung 5-6-7-5 (slight change of lyrics in 7)
https://www.youtube.com/watch?v=Ke77LhLGQ6o (Accessed February 10, 2020).
1988 Live Reykjavik, verses sung, 5-6-7-5/6 (the last verse sung begins with first three lines of 5 and ends with last three lines of 6).
1988 Live St Austin, verses sung, 5-6-7-4.
1993 Live Barcelona, 5-6-7-4.
https://www.youtube.com/watch?v=FC1dqx0urmE (Accessed February 10, 2020).
2008 Live Montreal, 1-2-7-5-6-4.
2009 Live London, 1-2-7-5-6-4.
2013 Live Oakland, 1-2-4-3-6-4.
https://www.youtube.com/watch?v=oFqOAJkIUIo (Accessed February 10, 2020).

32 *Signifiers* and *signifieds*: expressions and their contents.
33 A first-generation blending model is presented in Turner and Fauconnier (2002). The second-generation model we will use in the present analysis is explained in Brandt (2004) and in depth in L. Brandt (2013). The main difference between the two models is that the former has no Base space and does not stabilize its blends by relevance schemas; this is due to its lack of phenomenological grounding and semiotic perspective. As Schorlemmer et al. (2014) note, the first-generation blending theory is "silent on issues that are relevant if conceptual blending is to be used as a mechanism for designing creative systems … [It] does not specify how novel blends are constructed" (2014, p. 2).The idea of centering the semantic analysis on *mental spaces* instead of itemized contents is the merit of this pioneer model. The second-generation model allows us to understand the process of meaning production in greater detail and within the framework of a shared canonical semiotic space structure that precedes its filled "slots." The canonical part is the default setting of input spaces to the blend.
34 We apologize for the compact explanation here. The described mental space structure is shown in detail for metaphorical meaning in Brandt and Brandt (2005) and in L. Brandt (2013).
35 The contents of mental spaces correspond to what the Paris school of A.-J. Greimas called *isotopies*, that is, coherent semantic wholes or scenarios from some semantic domain. See Greimas and Courtés (1979).
36 In the diagrams, mental spaces are indicated by circles and all other relations or processes by arrows. Diagrams like this one may illustrate the general disposition of the elementary blending network and its instances. They also serve as heuristic tools helping the researcher focus on specific parts of the analyzed processes.
37 From Late Latin hallelujah, alleluia, from Greek allelouia, from Hebrew hallalu-yah "praise ye Jehovah," from hallalu, plural imperative of hallel "to praise," also "song of praise," from hillel "he praised," of imitative origin, with primary sense being "to trill." Second element is yah, shortened form of Yahweh, YHWH, the tetragrammaton, the Lord's name. G.F. Haendel's great oratorio *Messiah* (1741) has made this word and the chords that carry it in the final hymn unforgettable.
38 All verses, 1–7, have this /u: ja/ending in third line: *overthrew you/to you/fool you/knew you/do you/outdrew you*. This makes it possible to note the rhyme structure of the verses: a a b c c b.
39 The exclamation can be attributed to the male or to the female character, depending on the chosen possessive pronoun (see note 14, 15, 26). The general framework

except in the second verse supports the male *hallelujah* and the female *you*, pronounced *yah* in the rhyme of the third lines. So the second person "rhymes" on the divinity.

40   "In the late eighties, Bob Dylan performed Hallelujah on the road as a roughshod blues with a sly, ascending chorus. His version sounds less like the prettified Jeff Buckley version than like a work by John Lee Hooker. 'That song Hallelujah has resonance for me,'" Dylan said. "There again, it's a beautifully constructed melody that steps up, evolves, and slips back, all in quick time. But this song has a connective chorus, which when it comes in has a power all of its own. The 'secret chord' and *the point-blank I-know-you-better-than-you-know-yourself aspect of the song* has plenty of resonance for me" (Dylan on Cohen, *The New Yorker*, October 2016; italics added).

41   The Lord of Song—how do we understand this expression? Is it, as in the Greek polytheism, the god of music, poetry, and truth (verse 4, *I've told the truth…*), namely Apollo? Greek and Jewish theology, locally blended.

42   Compared to the Greek tragedy's *anagnorisis*, there is no purification and no illumination here. No *epiphany* or sudden insight.

43   Cohen bought a house in 1960 on the Greek island of Hydra, where he worked on his art especially in the 1960s and 1970s. Every year there is a *victory march* over the Turks, *Miaoulis Day*: Captain Miaoulis was a hero in the war of independence. The local *flag* is then on display; its heroic inscription goes back to the ancient Spartans. It says: "With it or on it." It means, referring to the shield of the warrior, "Come back bringing it back, or come back on it [dead]."

The Roman Arch of Constantine spans the *Via triumphalis*, the way taken by the emperors when they entered the city in triumph. The Marble Arch in London was displaced, set aside, so to speak, being too narrow for the royal carriage to pass.

Cohen was a great admirer of Federico Garcia Lorca. In concert he used to introduce his homage "Take this Waltz" with a quote from his hero: "I want to pass through the arches of Elvira, to see your thighs and begin weeping" (from the poem "Gacela del Mercado Matutino"). The Elvira Arch in question is situated in Granada, Spain, Lorca's city of birth. Cohen also significantly named his daughter Lorca. For a fine book on Cohen and Lorca, see Manzano (2012). Beyond our scope here, we hope to return with more research on this subject.

44   Deixis is the "pointing" effect of certain linguistic entities like "this," "that," "now," or "here" or of nonlinguistic signs that are sometimes called indexical, like an actual pointing finger.

References

Benveniste, É., 1966. *Problèmes de linguistique générale*. Paris: Gallimard.

Brandt, L., 2013. *The Communicative Mind. A Linguistic Exploration of Conceptual Integration and Meaning Construction*. Newcastle upon Tyne: Cambridge Scholars Publishing.

Brandt, P. A., 2004. *Spaces, Domains, and Meaning. Essays in Cognitive Semiotics*, European Semiotics, No. 4. Bern: Peter Lang.

Brandt, P. A., 2017. "De l'énonciation poétique." In: (Ed.) A. Biglari, and N. Watteyne, *Scènes d'énonciation de la poésie lyrique moderne. Approches, critiques, repères historiques, perspectives culturelles*, 27–39, Paris: Classiques Garnier.

Brandt, L., and P. A. Brandt. 2005. "Making Sense of a Blend: A Cognitive Semiotic Approach to Metaphor." *Annual Review of Cognitive Linguistics*, 3.
Cohen, L., 1993. *Stranger Music. Selected Poems and Songs*. New York: McClelland & Stewart.
Greimas, A. J., and J. Courtés, 1979. "Isotopie" (entry), *Sémiotique. Dictionnaire raisonné de la théorie du langage*. Paris: Hachette Université.
Light, A., 2012. *The Holy or the Broken. Leonard Cohen, Jeff Buckley & the Unlikely Ascent of 'Hallelujah'*. New York, Toronto: Atria Books
Manzano, A., 2012. *Leonard Cohen: Lorca, el flamenco y el judío errante*. Barcelona: Ediciones Alfabia.
Ong, W. T., 1982. *Orality and Literacy: The Technologizing of the Word*. London and New York: Routledge.
Schorlemmer et al., 2014. "COINVENT: Towards a Computational Concept Invention Theory." In *5th International Conference on Computational Creativity* (ICCC).
Turner, M., and G. Fauconnier, 2002. *The Way We Think. Conceptual Blending and the Mind's Hidden Complexities*. New York: Basic Books.

9

Forces and Spaces—Maupassant, Borges, Hemingway

The aim of a semio-cognitive narratology,[1] as I see it, is to develop the literary and generally semiotic study of narratives through cognitive modeling and to develop cognitive studies of mind and meaning by integrating insights from literary scholarship. In this chapter, I first examine the concept of narrative discourse (versus descriptive and argumentative discourse). Second, I discuss the principles for distinguishing narrative subgenres (realistic, fantastic, marvelous, grotesque, absurd stories); and third, I propose a model of the constitutive architecture of narrative meaning as manifested by "good stories," stories that make sense by conveying a view of the human condition.

In order to develop and test the model, I analyze a selection of acknowledged literary masterpieces: three short stories by Guy de Maupassant ("Deux amis," "La Ficelle," "La Parure"), two by Jorge Luis Borges ("Emma Zunz," "La otra muerte"), one by Ernest Hemingway ("A Very Short Story"). Through these analyses, including succinct literary interpretations of the texts, a new view of narrative dynamics is outlined. Agents operate in spaces that have specific dynamic properties, in that they display characteristic forces determining acts and events. There is, I postulate, a canonical set of narrative and situational spaces, each encompassing and contributing a significant part of the meaning of a story. The model distinguishes four such spaces, which are typically also staged as distinct locations: an initial *conditioning* space, a *catastrophic* space, a *consequence* space, and a *conclusion* space.

Forces are described as causal or intentional. The causal forces are either trivial (habitual, regular, default, whether physical or social) or "fatal" (sudden, special, contingent, singular). The intentional forces are agentive (volitional and located in agents) or magical (supernatural and non-agentive but still volitional).

The scenario-framing and dynamically invested spaces are linked in a default diegetic order allowing forces to fire forwards and backwards in time, which explains how stories progress and end, and in particular, eventually, how they can mean what we report them to mean. Interpretation and interpretability depend on the dynamic "logic" of this spatial diegesis, rather than on reader identifications in a story or on ideologies ascribed to the narrator.

Narrative Discourse

If by "discourse" we mean the whole of semantic properties that sentences must share in order to make sense as parts of the flow of communication by language, we can distinguish types or genres of such flows of discourse with distinct semantic properties.

It is thus possible to distinguish *narrative, descriptive, and argumentative discourse*,[2] on the grounds that these genres differ in terms of their basic semantics. *Narrative* discourse contents unfold a spatial and temporal continuity, and at least a certain continuity or constancy as to states, events, objects, and characters, whereas *descriptive* discourse contents display inventories of synchronically viewed entities that share a specific space;[3] and *argumentative* discourse contents essentially consist in deriving representations from other representations, whether narrative or descriptive, by combining their conceptual properties. Furthermore, it is evident that narratives can contain descriptions and argumentation; that you can argue about narratives and descriptions (this is what historical scholarship does); and that everything can be described (still, to describe a story is not to tell it and to describe an argument is not to argue).

I would like to mention an additional structural feature characterizing narrative discourse: it is the only discourse type that comes with a constitutive semantic duality in space representations, namely a split and a mapping between a *perceptual* and a *conceptual* representation of the same event space—in other words, between an experiencer's *proximal* and "concrete," phenomenological space-time and a narrator's *distal* and "abstract," knowledge-based (or, in some cases, ignorance-based) version of the same space-time. By contrast, pure argumentative discourse is in principle only conceptual and distal (abstract), whereas pure descriptive discourse is in principle only perceptual and proximal (concrete). This *double representation* of the narrative space-time is operative in pragmatic narrative genres such as accounts of navigation (typically, travel reports) and of warfare (incl. strategic plans), where *maps* are central means of reference: to be "on" a map is to integrate *and blend* a perceptual deixis and a conceptual geography.[4] Double representation is particularly prominent in literary narrative, and constitutive of fiction in general, since fictive perception must take place in a context created by overt and playful conceptual manipulation of common knowledge.[5]

All manifestations of narrative discourse, the semiotic entities we call stories,[6] whether fictive or "factive" (e.g., documentary), present a core set of "persons" or "characters": subjective instances, including a primary series of (protagonist or observer) *experiencers*; a supplementary series of (agonistic and antagonistic) *agents*; and the voice of a (conceptual) *narrator*, transcending in principle the chain of events of the story but often embodied in a (primary or supplementary) subjective instance, thus giving rise to a specific "vantage point."[7] These instances, including the grounding narrative voice itself, only unfold in so far as they participate in or attend to one and the same chain of events, namely *the story as such*. There has to be a story *an sich*, so to speak.[8] This principle of a distinction between *narration* (voice-based) and *story* (event-based) is, I think, a cognitive presupposition of all narrative discourse, a condition of its making sense, of its cognitive and semiotic possibility, and therefore the natural starting point of a semio-cognitive narratology.[9]

Events are linked into a chain of events that constitutes a story to the extent that they take place in a temporal continuum forming a trajectory in a spatial continuum and that some of these events are critical. A critical event is a "significant" *change of state* occurring somewhere in this spatiotemporal continuum.[10] I will argue and show that it results from the work of forces creating states in spaces. A critical change results from a variation of the relative magnitude of locally conflicting and concurring state-maintaining forces, which induces other local variations of forces. The interesting consequence of this dynamic view is that represented spaces, as limited operative fields of forces that uphold and change states, must be "local" and articulated, each "locality" containing a setting that frames a characteristic unfolding of forces.[11]

It would therefore seem phenomenologically relevant to study and elaborate a representative typology of forces[12] occurring in reported experiences had by human beings in what phenomenological philosophers after Husserl call our lifeworld, *Lebenswelt*. These forces would form the natural cognitive inventory of forces likely to occur in narrative spaces, whether literary, religious, or otherwise cultural (e.g., mythological). Here we will venture a short list of immediately perceptible types supposedly active in the dynamics of everyday life.[13] There are the potentially conscious *intentional* forces that—by "mental causation"—motivate the doings of embodied subjects, who, so to speak, "contain" them as *agentive*, unless the subjects encounter them or manipulate them as *magical* forces of nature; both the agentive and the magical forces are intentional, in the sense that volition is involved, so magic is easily re-embodied in fairies, trolls, phantoms, spooky places, and divinities of all kinds (but it does not have to be thus embodied). There further are the "blind" *causal* forces that these subjects count on or encounter in the physical and the social domains, some of which are *trivial*, that is, culturally habitual, to be expected, experienced as inherent in things and states of affairs, and quasi-necessary, unavoidable in a given circumstantial space, while others by contrast are not to be expected: contingent, possible but rare, sudden, punctual, singular, and locally *fatal*, that is, in spite of their singularity and punctuality, decisive to the narrative course of events: significant, critical.[14]

I intend to show that it is possible to meaningfully understand the *event logic* of stories in terms solely or mainly of such interacting forces and thereby to circumscribe the core structures of basic narrative sense-making that all narrating presupposes, whether artistic or not. The artistic, literary form often proceeds from everyday episodic narrative structure by supplying additional descriptive and argumentative accounts of the implied subjective experiences or by describing or arguing about its own narrating; in general, the event logic remains the same (Figure 9.1).

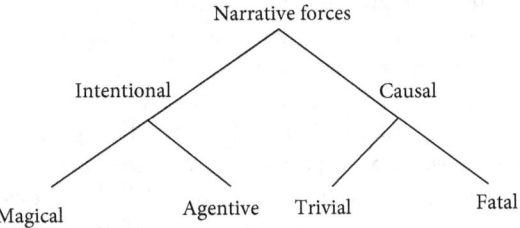

Figure 9.1 Narrative forces.

Narrative Genres

In order to understand and evaluate a story, we often implicitly decide which "genre" it represents. In the semiotics of stories, genres are the analogues of species in biology—we apply them for fast and useful categorization. However, here we are dealing with the human imaginary, and its semantic representations will follow the cognitive-semiotic format of things imagined, however "naturalistic" or "creative" they may be. Narrative genres are spontaneously distinguished with respect to their dynamic properties; so, a "good" hagiographic legend and a "good" testimonial account given by a witness in court, both following a perfectly narrative format, are seldom "good" or well formed by the same criteria; the former often displays significantly more fatal and magical forces than the latter.[15] If we perceive different narrative genres, such as fantastic versus socio-realistic stories, grotesque or absurd stories versus fairytales, as being distinct by their dynamic styles, their allowance or non-allowance of specific (force-driven) event types, we may further develop this view by conceiving a total narrative sequence of temporally linked and dynamically connected spaces as a *story world* configuration or the manifestation of a dynamically specific narrative *world type*. In some narrative worlds, in this sense, intentional forces dominate, and magic is welcome, while the rest is trivial causality; in other narrative worlds, nontrivial, historiographical, fatal causation dominates. And so on. The dynamic properties of distinct narrative genres apparently differ by the nature of the conceptual worlds to which their dynamic spaces pertain. The tone and temperature of the voice of the "Olympian," unembodied narrator may then be perceived as the mode of expression of a given narrative-conceptual world.

The following is an elementary sketch of such a "world"-oriented account of narrative genres.

We can stipulate a neutral, naturalistic anchoring base, a plainly *realistic* world R, corresponding to the realm of ordinary human, macro-physical, mental, social, and pragmatic everyday life and cognition. This basic, realistic world can be *narratively deformed* in two directions, by addition (R^+) or by subtraction of forces (R^-).[16] We add narrative forces if we allow magic acts to co-occur with realistic causes in a given world; this increases its dynamic density, so to speak, and the result is either the *fantastic* genre (where magic is local) or the enchanted, *marvelous* genre (where magic is global).[17] By contrast, if we instead subtract forces, we allow events and acts to occur that have no trivial causal or intentional reason to occur or to be executed; this decreases the story's dynamic density, so we get a "crazier" world; this operation yields either the *grotesque* or the *absurd* genre. Here, the trivial and the fatal forces are increasingly left alone on stage, while typically the intentional forces decrease: a conjuncture that often gives rise to humor or to impressions of "madness" or incomprehensible occurrences and behaviors. Narrative realism can thus be deformed in two opposite directions, either (R^+) toward the fantastic and the marvelous (increased dynamic density) or (R^-) toward the grotesque and the absurd (decreased dynamic density). Magic is intuitively a *marked* form of intentional force (while agentive intentionality is unmarked, "default"); and correspondingly, fatal causal force is *marked* (whereas trivial causality is of course unmarked). Realism is therefore the most unmarked genre; the *marvelous* and the *absurd* are the most marked (in Roman Jakobson's sense of markedness).[18]

The question of the status of genres in literature is of course much more comprehensive than the one we are discussing here; narrative genres are only subgenres of *the* narrative genre and could be mistaken for arbitrary subdivisions of the former. But there are reasons to believe that the dynamic specifications are really operative in human cognitive organization of meaning in such a way that they "generate" meaning differently: they are, so to speak, organically distinct. For instance, psychological specification of characters is decreasingly possible as magic increases, or as absurd fatality increases. The very length of stories also tends to decrease by the same parameters: fairy tales and absurd stories are typically short. Only cognitive references can explain such correlations, I think. Magical awe and absurd humor are short-time processes in the human mind.

Figure 9.2 is a tentative, slightly simplified graphic summary of this view of narrative genres (worlds are circles).

In this view, a narrative scenario, an episode, a sequence of events and acts, any diegetic unit, is a part of a "world" characterized by a specific "mix" of dynamic properties, realistic or deformed in either direction. Some stories can even change "world" in the course of lengthy developments comprising important amounts of scenarial spaces, such as García Márquez's *Cien años de solidad* or Lewis Carroll's *Alice's Adventures in Wonderland* and *Through the Looking-Glass*, which oscillate radically on the "world" axis from the marvelous to the absurd.[19] Authors have "world" preferences by which we often know them (Kafka: grotesque; Kharms, Ionesco: absurd; Cortázar, Borges, Poe: fantastic; Breton, Aymé: marvelous). This is probably a matter of writers' general cognitive profiles, but evidently, the same author is not bound to only one genre.

Narrative subgenres are important to the interpretation of stories, because they determine the way in which narratives make sense (or beautiful nonsense) to us: a grotesque or fantastic story does not make us believe that life is grotesque or fantastic; it may make us laugh or shiver, while we extract life-relevant meaning from its world, which we distinguish from our own world. Our cognitive minds essentially

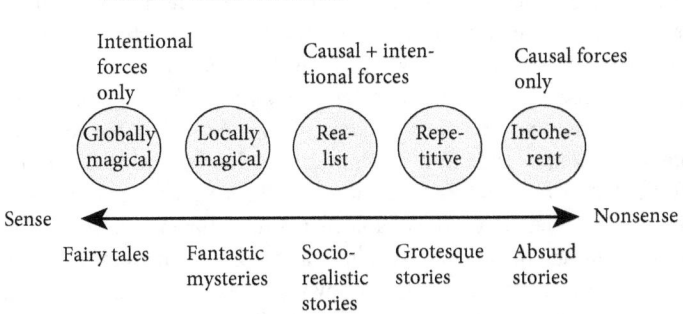

Figure 9.2 Narrative world variations.

enjoy visiting nonrealistic, marked worlds. Paradoxically, such worlds are felt as more meaningful than the plain, unmarked lifeworld; evidently, our emotional minds prefer them to lifeworlds.

This was the first main point of this chapter. The second main point is the following hypothesis: In each story, a narrative world is instantiated in terms of a sequence of *event spaces*, that is, more or less clearly defined *places* set up by locative indications or descriptions, where characters are actively or passively connected to the play of conflicting forces of different types and affected by these forces through narrated sequential time. The *interconnection of spaces and forces*, allowing us to detect a canonical diegetic series of dynamic spatiotemporal stances through which a story makes sense, is the central idea of this hypothesis. Please note that event spaces are not "mental spaces"; a mental space is a part of a network anchored in actual *semiosis* (cf. Brandt 2004a), whereas an event space is a spatial frame of a narrative content situated in the *diegetic process* of a story. A semiosis can contain a diegesis, namely as a narration contains a narrative. Maybe it will take a new initiative, the building of a consistent semiotic and cognitive text theory, to further determine this relation and articulation. Discourse semantics as in so-called *Text World Theory* (Gavins 2007) might offer a significant contribution to such a project but still does not feed into the interest in the immanent dynamic structures of narrative causation that is the main concern of the present chapter. Is it possible to identify a canonical set of narrative event spaces? The following section attempts to answer this question through analysis.

I will illustrate this approach by presenting a brief sequence of space-and-force models intended to extract the basic narrative meaning of a sample of short stories by Guy de Maupassant ("The Diamond Necklace," "Two Friends," "A Piece of String"), Jorge Luis Borges ("Emma Zunz," "The Other Death"), and Ernest Hemingway ("A Very Short Story"). Let me note that in an analytic and schematizing enterprise such as the present, mistakes are likely to occur; the advantage of using explicit schemas and models, however, is to make them easier to detect and discuss.

The Specific Force Dynamics of Narrative Structure

Guy de Maupassant's "The Diamond Necklace" ("La Parure")[20] is a sad story about humiliation, the cruelty of destiny, and social ambitions letting a misunderstanding and a dream destroy a life. Mathilde, of a modest family, but who dreams of luxury, is married to a poor ministerial clerk. When her husband gets an invitation to a ball at the Ministry, she manages to get him to pay her a new gown; she finds that she also needs jewels and somewhat reluctantly goes to her wealthy friend, Madame Forestier, a former schoolmate, and asks her to lend her something. Adorned with a diamond necklace, she goes to the ball with her clerk husband and enjoys a great personal success on the dance floor. At a very late hour, the couple leaves the ballroom, hastily so as not to be remarked for their lack of elegant coats, and arriving at their modest home discovers that the necklace has disappeared. The following week they panic; at last they find a similar necklace that they cannot afford, but use a heritage, borrow a fortune, and buy the adornment, then return it to Madame Forestier. The couple spends the next ten years living miserably and working several jobs, day and night; Mathilde's youth and beauty wither away. Then suddenly she meets her former friend, who is walking with a child, still looking beautiful, on the Champs-Elysées. Mathilde tells her story, in order to explain why she has changed so much that she was not even recognized. She then learns from her friend that the necklace was just an imitation, paste, worth very little.

The story sets up an *initial space*, A, presenting the protagonists at home and summarizing the initial conditions of the events to happen: the modest situation of the couple, the ambitions of the young woman, then the opportunity, and the preparations for the ball.[21] The *second space*, B, the scenario of the ministerial ballroom, contains the metamorphosis materializing the desire of the female protagonist and the fatal catastrophe that ends it. The *third space*, C, is a time-space of ten years, unfolding the consequences of the preceding states, events, and acts. Finally, the *fourth space*, D, the elegant main street of Paris, contains the fortuitous meeting and the revelation concerning the value of the object whose loss so massively influenced and deteriorated the life of the protagonists.

Four spaces or stances are articulated.[22] Let us take a look on their dynamic inventories and connections.

A: The modest middle-class life space-time.
A1. The *agentive intentional force* of Mathilde, her desire of luxury and glamour.
A2. The *trivial causal force* of the social condition she comes from and has again married into.
A3. The *fatal causal force* of the invitation to the glamorous ball.
A4. The *agentive intentional force* of the ball preparations, including the borrowing of the necklace of Mme Forestier. A2 → (A3 → A4).

B: The ministerial ballroom.
B1. The *trivial causal force* of the actual joy and glamour of the ball, matching A1.
B2. The *fatal causal force* of the loss of the necklace, supplemented by the permanence of A2.

C: The social space-time of many years of economic hardship.
C1. The *trivial causal* consequence of B2, the incurring of important debts.
C2. The *trivial causal* consequence of C1, ten irreversible years of hard work and misery.

D. The space of the encounter, Les Champs-Elysées.
D1. The *trivial causal* consequence of C2, the attrition of Mathilde.
D2. The *fatal causal* encounter of Mathilde and the lender (A4).
D3. The *trivial causal* consequence of D1 that Mathilde is not recognized and has to tell her story to Madame Forestier.
D4. The *fatal causal force* of the discovery by Mathilde that B2 → C1 was based on a misunderstanding, which persisted because of A2 + A1 (Mathilde was ashamed of her condition and did not want to see Madame Forestier). The content of D4, the misunderstanding, invalidates B2 → C1 but unfortunately after C1 → C2. A classic case of tragic, Aristotelian, anagnorisis.[23]

We will call A a *Condition Space*, B a *Catastrophe Space*, C a *Consequence Space*, and D a *Conclusion Space*. These narrative spaces are displayed as distinct experiential locations, here clearly so in B and D, whereas A and C are more vaguely described but still clearly distinct from their neighboring spaces. The entire spatio-causal network can be summarized and visualized in Figure 9.3.[24]

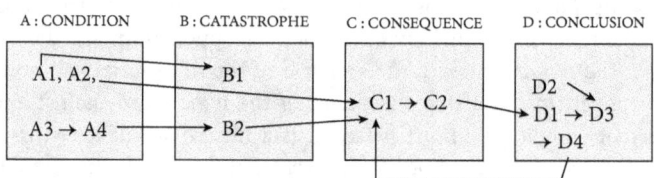

Figure 9.3 Diegesis of "The Diamond Necklace."

The anaphoric arrow from D4 to the linking arrows between B and C would seem to counterfactually cancel the content of C altogether. A3, B2, and D2 are fatal events. Only the Consequence Space, typically, has none. The feedback from D4 leads our attention back to A2 and from there to the sad fragility of the moment of dream realization (A1/B1), triggering the ensuing social humiliation (A2 and C, D).

In "Two Friends" ("Deux amis"),[25] we learn about the fate of two Parisian citizens, Mr. Morisot and Mr. Sauvage, a watchmaker and a draper, who used to go fishing and enjoy nature and each other's company on idle days at the river Seine, but who under the siege of the city, caused by the French-Prussian War (1871–1872), are now blocked from going to their place at the river. On a winter morning, they happen to meet in the street, and after a couple of absinthes had in cafés, they decide to brave the military lines and take up fishing. They get leave to pass and readily walk, bend, creep through the occupied terrain down to the Seine with their angling equipment. Soon they enjoy catching abundant glittering fish and "indulging in a pastime of which they had long been deprived." But they are soon discovered by a group of Prussian soldiers and brought to a small island in the river, l'Ile Marante, now a military camp. An officer explains to them that they are French spies and will be executed. He asks them for their password, promising them to let them go if he gets it. They do not answer. The officer ceremoniously asks them one by one and gets the same answer, silence. The two friends say goodbye to each other, are shot and thrown into the river. The officer finally orders the fish they had caught fried for him.

The story offers an initial space, Paris under the siege (A). Then a second space, the riverbank, where the protagonists enjoy the realization of their dream (B). The third space (C) is the island, where they have to assume the consequences of their act, namely to be formally identified as spies, even if the identification is only formal—the officer does not have to believe in the inherent truth of this attribution, he just states their identity according to their location and their provenience, since the qualification as spies is the result of a simple strategic calculus.[26] So, they have to die, whether they deliver a password or not; it does not even appear that they have one that they could have decided not to reveal.[27] The fourth space (D) is or includes the river, flecked by their blood.

Let us try to achieve a dynamic overview.

A: Paris besieged.
A1. The *agentive intentional force* of the two anglers' desire to go fishing.
A2. The *trivial causal force* of the wartime condition: urban famine, deprivation.
A3. The *fatal causal force* of the fortuitous encounter of the two friends.
A4. The *agentive intentional force* of their contacting the French officer and obtaining the leave to pass.[28] And A3 → A4.

B: Fishing by the river.
B1. The *trivial causal force* of their happiness of fishing again, matching A1.
B2. The *fatal causal force* of their being discovered by the Prussian soldiers.

C: The Isle Marante.
C1. The *trivial causal force* of their being declared spies by the officer.
C2. The *trivial causal force* of their verdict: execution; the rules of war followed. C1 → C2.[29]

D. The river shore of the island, place of the death scene.
D1. The *agentive intentional force* of the two friends' dignified reaction to C2.
D2. The *agentive intentional force* of the officer's ritual interrogation of his "spies."
D3. The *agentive intentional force* of the two friends' mutual goodbye gesture.
D1 → D3.
D4. The *trivial causal force* of the execution itself, whose figurative aspects refer back to the A2–B2 complex that led to C1: the wartime rules; the annulation of interhuman rules of respect and solidarity (soldiers are not allowed to act according to ordinary ethics).

The dynamic network of "Two Friends" is formally[30] quasi-identical to that of "The Diamond Necklace," in the sense that the forces are linked in exactly the same way, except for the link A4 → B2 in the "Necklace" but not in the "Friends." The forces are not of the same kind, but they drive the same feedback result D4-to-C1, which in both cases directly generate the uncanny meaning of the story[31]: humanity rendered precarious by social class separation or by war. Maupassant's prose offers a rich display of details supporting this reading.

In "A Piece of String" ("La Ficelle"),[32] we are in Normandy, and the peasants, rich or poor, are going to the marketplace in a small town.[33] Our protagonist, Maître Hauchecorne, arriving in town, picks up a little piece of string from the ground—a habit of his, expressing of course his peasant attitude to the economics of life. Then he discovers that he is being observed by a person he is on bad terms with, Maître Malandain, who stares at him from his doorstep. Overcome by shame at being seen picking up an item almost without value, he pretends to look for something else without finding it, and finally walks off, embarrassed. In front of the inn, at noon, suddenly the drum sounds, and the public crier announces the loss of a pocketbook containing 500 francs and business papers. A little later, the police corporal appears and asks for Maître Hauchecorne! He is there, answers, and follows the corporal to the mayor's office. The mayor declares that he was seen picking up the pocketbook in question. Malandain has reported on him. Hauchecorne shows the string he has picked up and swears on God and his soul's salvation, but the mayor just adds that he was even seen to look for more money from the pocketbook. Malandain and Hauchecorne are confronted; nothing can be concluded. But the story spreads. Hauchecorne tells his version, which is not believed, and he is laughed at. He angrily keeps telling his story, and he repeats it in his village. Nobody believes him. Next day, the pocketbook is reported found on the road and returned; the illiterate finder had carried it home and given it to his master, who finally delivered it to the owner. Hauchecorne triumphs and retells his story; he insists, on the roads, at the cabaret, in front of the church, to strangers. People listen jokingly, not convinced. In the town, he is even attacked physically and called a "great rogue." At last, during a nasty conversation in the tavern, he understands that he is accused of stealing, lying, and then having had the pocketbook brought back by an accomplice. He goes home and now has a confusing feeling of perhaps being capable of having done what he is accused of, including the boasting storytelling. The story grows longer and longer, and it exhausts him and weakens his mind and body. A winter day he takes to his bed and in the ravings of his death agony recounts the story; he revives the scene where he explained to the mayor that it was only a little bit of string: "See, here it is…"

The sequence of spaces is rather clearly articulated—though geographically (A) includes (B) and (D) includes (A) and (C). The story starts on the road to the marketplace: this is the conditioning cultural space, amply unfolded (A). Then, the catastrophic place of the string and the fatal simulation (B). The mayor's office allows Hauchecorne to reveal the truth and be rejected (C). The rest of the narrative uses the entire landscape to develop the consequences of his counterproductive story (D). In his final agony, he goes mentally back to C.

- A: The road to the Norman market.
- A1. The *agentive intentional force* of the protagonist's desire to profit from even extremely small advantages and findings.
- A2. The *trivial causal force* of the local, mean-spirited peasant culture.
- A3. The *trivial causal* circumstance of the market day: oral broadcasting.

- B: The string scene on the road.
- B1. The *fatal causal force* of finding and picking up the piece of string. A1 → B1.
- B2. The *fatal causal force* of being seen by a malevolent person, Malandain, and of Hauchecorne's subsequent simulating.

- C: The mayor's office.
- C1. The *fatal causal force* of the broadcast loss of the pocketbook.
- C2. The *trivial causal force* of the report by Malandain to the mayor. B2 → C2.
- C3. The *trivial causal force* of the accusation of Hauchecorne by the mayor. C2 → C3

- D: The entire rural community space.
- D1. The *agentive intentional force* of Hauchecorne's narrative response. C3 → D1.
- D2. The *trivial causal force* of the community's reaction to this defense. A2 → D2.

D3. The *fatal causal force* of Hauchecorne's (counterfactual) feeling of guilt, which supposedly contributes to causing his narrative overdoing, causes him to relive the fiasco of his defense in front of the mayor and finally kills him.

Again, we see a semiotic return from the Conclusion Space to the core content of the Consequence Space. This time it happens to the protagonist, at least in some confused mode, whereas it easily occurs to the reader that overdoing a defense is counterproductive; in a sense, the subject is again guilty of being *where* he is (in a place where any exposure or blunder can kill), not *what* he is (innocent). The tragedy is, as I understand it, based on the contrast between what the honest sharing of narrative experience should achieve among humans and what instead happens when the hyperbolic *enunciation* of this narrative is read as evidence to its falsehood. This is again an opposition of the global and the local, of global peaceful humanity and local hostility and cruelty.

This analysis translates into a dynamic network as in Figure 9.4, slightly different from the former.

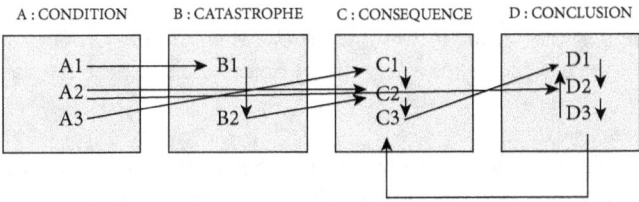

Figure 9.4 Diegesis of "A Piece of String."

This network is, as we see, extremely dense, which may be why we feel the intensity of its depressive meaning, experienced by the reader through the feedback (D3 → C3) and the subsequent C-D loop that leads to the death of the protagonist.

Let us change century and take a look at another masterful story, Jorge Luis Borges' "Emma Zunz."[34] Emma is a 19-year-old worker at the textile factory run by Aarón Loewenthal, in Buenos Aires. One winter day, she receives a letter from Brazil stating that her father has committed suicide. He had worked for the factory as cashier but had been dismissed, accused of fraud six years earlier; before going into exile, he had confidentially told his daughter that the real culprit was in fact Loewenthal himself, at that time a manager, who later became the co-owner of the company. Emma, in shock, decides overnight to take her just revenge on this fraudulent author of her father's death. She waits until Saturday afternoon after work, goes to the harbor and finds a sailor of a boat about to leave, offers herself to him as if she were a prostitute, whereas the story stresses her abyssal horror of sexuality. She accomplishes this feat, but tears into pieces the money left besides the bed by her "customer" (as she had torn to pieces the letter); instinctively, she regrets this impious act.[35] As there is a strike looming at the factory, she calls Loewenthal on the phone and asks to see him personally, pretending she wants to inform against her colleagues. Having repeated to herself the words of accusation she was going to deliver, she enters his office, starts talking to him, hesitantly, about her coworkers, then asks him to get her a glass of water, and while she is alone, takes the revolver known to be in the drawer of his desk; but instead of first telling him about God's Justice and her knowledge of his crime, disturbed by the urge to punish him for the outrage she has been through before coming, more than driven by the wish to avenge her father, she shoots him right away, twice. In his agony, he swears furiously, the guard dog starts barking, and finally Emma starts her discourse: "I have avenged my father, and no one can punish me ...," but the victim is already dead, probably without understanding. Then she disarranges the sofa, the clothes of the corpse, removes his blood-stained pince-nez, and calls the police to give her story of what happened: a false call by Loewenthal about the strike, then the rape, and her legitimate defense. Her story is believed, because as the narrator comments, it is essentially true and told with conviction, as to the tone, the shame, the hatred, the outrage; false are only the circumstances, the times, and a couple of proper names, as Borges comments.

Emma receives the triggering letter at home, where she also remembers her father's secret, and conceives her plan: a first, *conditioning* space (A). Then she is in the harbor tavern and the adjacent room upstairs, the space of her *catastrophic* experience (B). The *consequence*, thus prepared, is the visit to Loewenthal's office (and home, since he lives on an upper floor of the factory), the site of the murder (C). The last space (D) includes all of the judiciary sites where she will successfully repeat her plausible story.

A: Emma's apartment.
A1. The *agentive intentional force* of the remembered fraudulent act of Loewenthal.
A2. The *fatal causal force* of (the news of) the paternal suicide. A1 → A2.
A3. The *agentive intentional force* of Emma's revenge plan. A2 → A3.

B: The harbor.
B1. The *agentive intentional force* of the sexual sacrifice made by Emma.
B2. The *fatal causal force* of the ritual mistreatment of the money. B1 → B2.

C: Loewenthal's office.
C1. The *agentive intentional force* of Emma's killing Loewenthal. A3 → C1.
C2. The *fatal causal force* of her omission of the speech to give before killing, as the revenge act requires if the target needs information in order to decode its symbolic meaning.[36]

D: Implied places: police office, courtroom, factory. The community.
D1. The *trivial causal force* of Emma's coherent and successful explanation.
D2. The *trivial causal force* of her lasting frustration at the symbolically unsuccessful act, paid by her humiliation.

The dynamic network of this narrative is given in Figure 9.5.

The plan is blessed with success, physically, but still cursed with bad luck mentally. Emma's emotional frustration (D2) is due to the horror of B1, even worse for her than the grief at A2; and it is further fueled by the incomplete symbolic act truncated by C2. One of the most "meaningful" narrative themes in literature and life, *revenge*, the search for an-eye-for-an-eye justice, ends in an utterly meaningless and painful state of affairs covered by triviality and frustration.

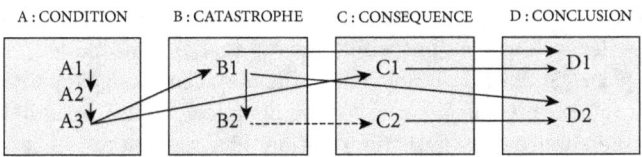

Figure 9.5 Diegesis of "Emma Zunz."

The second story by Borges, "The Other Death" ("La otra muerte"),[37] is overtly fantastic.[38] The first-person narrator receives a letter from his friend Gannon, telling him that he is about to send his Spanish translation of the poem "The Past," by R.W. Emerson, and adding that a person they both know has died of a lung inflammation: the peasant Pedro Damián, of Gualeguay, who had fought in the decisive battle at Masoller four decades ago, in 1904, with the Uruguayan rebel Aparicio Saravia (who was defeated in that battle and died of his wounds); in his fever-ridden agony, Damián had relived the bloodshed of Masoller. He had returned to his province after the battle and stayed in his lonely farm all this time. The narrator had met him and talked to him in 1942, but he was very taciturn. Gannon had sent him a photo of Damián, but now he has lost it (and would be afraid of finding it; we don't know why he says that). Then in Montevideo, some months later, the narrator goes to see the colonel Tabares, who had fought in the same battle, a circumstance that interests the narrator for a fantastic story he is preparing. Tabares tells him about the horrors of the battles of this civil war and with many details. He turns out to remember Damián, an Indian type who first makes him laugh and then stop; poor Damián had been boasting in the bars but turned out to behave embarrassingly cowardly in the fights themselves. The narrator had seen a possible hero in Pedro, but now he understands his solitude, silence, and reservation. He was Argentinean and should be a brave gaucho, fighting with the Uruguayans; Tabares despised his lack of courage and attributed it to the Argentineans. For the same reasons, still researching for the story resisting him, the narrator meets Tabares again some months later, in the company of another elderly gentleman, doctor Amaro, who also had been fighting in Saravia's revolution, and the two are precisely talking about Masoller. After some anecdotes, Amaro mentions this young sheepshearer, Damián, who had been in the valiant vanguard of the troops and died heroically from a bullet in his chest while leading an attack from his horseback, shouting "¡Viva Urquiza!"[39] Amazingly brave for someone not even twenty years old. Now the colonel gets confused; he is sure he has never heard about any Damián at all. Later, the narrator encounters in a bookstore his friend Gannon, who now denies ever having written about translating Emerson and certainly not knowing anything about any Damián either. Then the colonel writes to him, no longer confused, and now clearly remembers the young hero Damián from Masoller. In the summer, the narrator happens to be in Gualeguay and wishes to interview the man who saw him die; he has died already in the fall. Damián's farm has disappeared. The narrator tries to find the photo of Damián he has; it turns out to be of someone else, a famous opera singer. He finally tries to find an explanation of these strange facts. There could have been two Damiáns; or the narrator could have dreamt the first one; a friend suggests that Damián could indeed have died at Masoller, but while praying that God would let him return to his beloved place; God, who cannot change the past, can change the future, and has let his ghost return to Gualeguaychú, where his image finally faded like a shadow. Along this line, the narrator finds the solution after reading the treatise *De divina omnipotentia* by Pier Damiani (!), about God's power, discussed in Dante's *Paradiso*.[40] Damiani argued, against most others, that God can indeed change the past. So, the solution the narrator presents is that Damián indeed turned out to be a coward at Masoller, survived, and dedicated the rest of his life to correcting this shame, back in his province, by his hard work. For forty years, he hopes and prays to get another chance to prove his courage, and he finally gets it in the hallucinations of his agony, in 1946. God at last hears him. He relives the battle and now is very brave; he dies in the attack, hit by a bullet in his chest, in the early days of 1904. In a sense, first he dies in 1946, then a second time, in 1904. God therefore has to correct the past. For example, he has to change the memories of all who remember him; and he has to kill the man who saw him die in 1946. Since the narrator has also met him, he too seems to be in danger! But he will, he hopes, save his life by soon, around 1951, being convinced that the entire story was just an invention created by Emerson's poem, by the analogy of the names and by Damiani's arguments, in the process of writing a fantastic story. Now poor Damián has achieved what his heart desired, albeit a little late, but maybe there is no greater happiness, the narrator concludes. And of course, we must agree, he has indeed written a fantastic story.

This narrative seems to insist on the epistemic research problems of an embodied narrator who is a writer.[41] Nevertheless, it is easy to see that the reconstructed story itself yields the same cognitive characteristics as the former in our series. Pedro is a young Argentinean peasant living in Entreríos (Condition Space, A). He joins the Uruguayan rebels and fights at Masoller (Catastrophe Space, B). He then returns to his province and for the rest of his life ruminates on the outcome of the battle in terms of his lousy moral performance (Consequence Space, C). But in his agony his desire is heard by God who allows him (in the Conclusion Space, D) to return to Masoller and to replay the decisive scene and this second time have the glorious death he so intensely desires.

A: Gualeguay (1904).
A1. The *agentive intentional force* of the young and bragging Damián's wish to prove his courage.
A2. The *trivial causal force* of Damián's enrollment in Saravia's revolutionary army.[42]

B: Masoller (1904).
B1. The *trivial causal force* of the violent battle. A2 → B1.
B2. The *fatal causal force* of his psychological weakness in the moment of truth. Damián's first non-death, then of his second death.

C: Gualeguay (1904–1946).
C1. The *trivial causal force* of the shame now filling Damián's entire life.

C2. The *agentive intentional force* of his dream-filled agony in which he relives the battle and fights.
C3. The *magical intentional force* of the omnipotent divine decision to let him have the death he has prepared for during these years and intensely desires.
D: Masoller (1904 revisited).
D1. The *agentive intentional force* of Damián's remade, now brave fighting and heroic death during the fierce battle.
D2. The *trivial causal force* of the ontological consequences of God's changing the past: erasure of traces and even human lives and memories, including the first-person narrator's life.

Again, we summarize this dynamic network in a spatiotemporal unfolding (Figure 9.6).

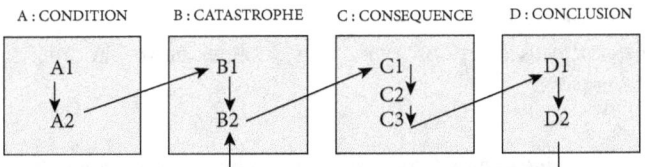

Figure 9.6 Diegesis of "La otra muerte."

Magic is of course not always working backwards in time as here, where the past causal traces have to be removed; we know however that the desire to change the past can be very strong even in contemporary minds, and it is, I think, such an intentional disposition that the—very scholarly developed—theme of this story exploits. As formerly mentioned, human cognition is dynamically generous: it allows a wide range of narrative deviations from the trivially real world, as philosophers and storytellers know or find out. Borges found his inspiration for this imaginary experiment in medieval theology.

Ernest Hemingway's "A Very Short Story"[43] takes place during the First World War. A wounded American soldier in a hospital in Padua is taken care of by an Italian girl, Luz, and the two engage in an apparently serious love story. He is operated and tries to live up to his beloved.[44] Before he—no name—returns to the front, the two enter the cathedral of Padua, Il Duomo, and pray. They would have liked to get married, but there is no time left, and they have no birth certificates; so, the ceremony does not happen. A period of separation is bridged by Luz's fervent love letters, which he opens after the armistice. Then he has to go home to the states. She refuses to follow him and asks him several things: to get a good job, to see no friends (!), and to not drink; these are her conditions for following him later, if he can pick her up in New York. They quarrel sadly about this on the train from Padua to Milan, where they part, and he leaves, via Genoa. Luz returns to the North-East to work at a hospital in Pordonone and is lonely. But in the same sentence, she meets the major of a battalion of the *Arditi*—"the daring" and glorious storm troops—who makes love to her. She is very impressed by this Italian relationship, so she writes to the states, Chicago, and tells our man it's over, theirs was only a childish affair, and she is going to be married shortly.[45] The major however turns out not to marry Luz. She gets no answer from Chicago; and the only "contract" our young American gets, on the other side, is by contracting gonorrhea from a girl while riding in a taxicab. And that is all.

In this sad two-pages long story, the Condition Space is the hospital in Padua (A); then I propose that we have a Catastrophe Space (B), the Duomo, where the lovers emphatically do *not* get formally married. Here is where the decisive symbolization does not happen.[46] Third, there is an unfolding of the Consequence, the crisis in the train to Milan (C). Finally, they stop communicating, each in a separate country (D), both ending up absorbed in their respective misery, succinctly stated by the narrator. In terms of space-time logic, we thus have the following instances:

A: Padua. The hospital.
A1. The *fatal causal force* of love.
A2. The *trivial causal force* of trying to be a better person in order to protect a growing love.

B: Il Duomo.
B1. The *agentive intentional force* of seeking symbolic confirmation.
B2. The *fatal causal force* of the circumstances preventing marriage.

C: The train from Padua to Milan.
C1. The *agentive intentional force* of Luz's categorical reservations.
C2. The *fatal causal force* of their unfinished quarrel: the train stops in Milan but the content of the quarrel is not settled.
C3. The *trivial causal force* of their separation.

D: Chicago and Pordonone.
D1. The *fatal causal force* of Luz's infidelity.
D2. The *trivial causal force* of the ex-soldier's careless sex.

In this reading (incl. B2 → C1), which I do not pretend to defend as the only possible, the dynamic network would be as in Figure 9.7.

The feedback from D2 to A2 is a cruel retrospective way in which D2 resonates after A2 and thus lets us reread the story emotionally; cognitively, this theme of trying-to-be-a-better-person ("shaping up") or letting-go ("shaping down") is, I suggest, a universal of moral behavior as linked to love.

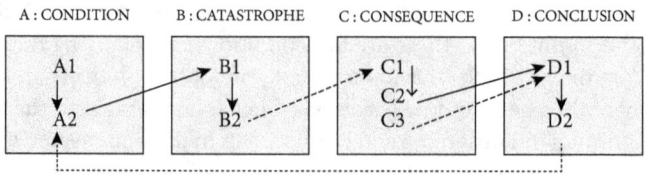

Figure 9.7 Diegesis of "A Very Short Story."

An Overarching Schema of Narrative Dynamics

If we compare the event structures reported above, we can additionally grasp a cross-spatial dynamic pattern. There is a subject desiring something, then accessing and achieving it, but then having to pay a sad price for the access or achievement. The path to glamour ("The Necklace"), to hours of shared happiness ("Two Friends"), to lucky findings ("A Piece of String"), to vengeance ("Emma Zunz"), to honor ("The Other Death"), or simply to love ("A Very Short Story") goes through misery, humiliation, lifelong suffering, death right away, or other sacrifices; subjects in a sense get what they want but have to pay a *price* for it that might have modified, maybe cancelled, their initial desire, had they known it before experiencing it.

In terms of linguistic semantics, a special version of force dynamics, the force-barrier schema, which is primarily used for analyses of causation, modality, and similar semio-syntactic phenomena in grammar (cf. note 11, above), may serve as a diagrammatic representation of this view (Figure 9.8).

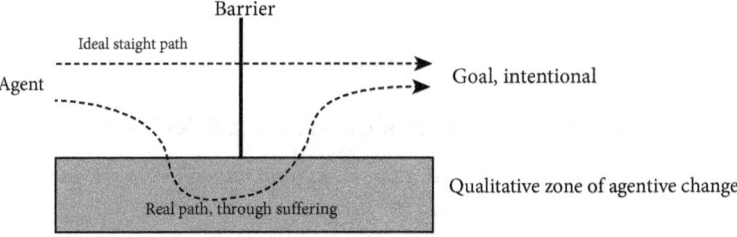

Figure 9.8 The force-barrier schema.

Per aspera ad astra—The subject has to circumvent the existential barrier that makes the ideal path of desire impossible and so has to cross a qualitative boundary beyond which life takes its toll. So, in retrospect, the subject agent will ironically have reached its destination, object, goal, in a "winged" state, marked by the heavy price paid in terms of life span, dignity, and so on.[47]

There may be many different meta-stories underlying the diegetic spatio-dynamic products of human imagination, but this overarching sacrificial format is at least a prominent one of them.

Conclusion

The reader will have worked through the preceding dynamic networks and will have had a chance to evaluate the particular relations established and postulated. These relational networks are at the core of the meaningfulness—the production of meaning, if you will—of these stories, in so far as they imprint themselves on the reading minds and challenge them in respect to their experiences of what can follow from what and what feeling you can have of what happens and will happen.

In short stories like these, we may grasp an elementary narrative unfolding, a sort of narrative molecule, whose atoms are the dynamic spaces involved; the forces are then the particles of these atoms, to spin this metaphor. In larger narrative creations, we would expect to see overarching networks of such elementary networks, in parallel or in serial articulations and combinations. This generalization evidently calls for empirical examination.

However, the basic dynamic analysis is possible to the extent that active narrative forces[48] can be identified and localized spatiotemporally in a format allowing description and comparison. If the dynamic logic of narrative meaning we have sketched out is stable under generalization and empirical cultural variation, it may make it possible to eventually reach a level of analysis contributing both to a narrative phenomenology of natural *human imagination*—not only of perception (although perception is narratively impregnated[49])—and to an understanding of human cultures as more or less elegant, intricate, dramatical, spiritual, or humoristic ways of phrasing the intricate web of things we do and things that simply seem to happen to us, to our gods, saints, martyrs, heroes, fairies, colleagues, friends, and significant others—people we care about.

Appendix

Letting, Making, and the Dynamics of Causation. A Brief Note

Force-dynamic modeling has been developed for grammatical expressions of causation (Talmy 2000) and modality (Sweetser 1990, Brandt 2004a) in various versions, either as wheels-and-brakes or as paths-and-barriers. The present discussion examines a format of representation allowing the modeling both of the basic *letting* concepts and of the basic *making* concepts. The result is a dynamic schema model that offers possibilities of further elaboration as a model of narrative event sequences and eventually as a format for interactive and context-anchored cognitive robotics.

The forces-and-barriers model[50] offers a simple means of representing the relationship holding between a process or a project that we refer to and a circumstance that its realization depends on. In the case of a project, a "path to realization"[51] leads through a stance of conditions to be fulfilled and circumstances to take into account. The condition or circumstance is cognized (conceptualized schematically) as a barrier that either does or does not *let* the process or project follow its course toward fulfillment. *Letting* something happen means not stopping it; it means lowering the barrier or opening a gate in it; *letting* and *not letting* determine an axis of corresponding modal meaning values: the reference entity therefore *can/cannot* pass. This modal result (involving the modal verb *may*) also includes the deontic set *permission/prohibition* (of some act) and the epistemic set *possibility/impossibility* (of some event). This axis is one of the semiotic dimensions of the dynamic square for causation presented below.

Letting is passive, whereas *not letting* is active. By contrast, *making* is active, whereas *not making* is passive. This striking phenomenon of inverse correlation of negative and positive values is due to the semiotic correlation between *letting* and *making*, a disposition that current literature on the subject has not considered. In fact, *making* (making something happen) is an active, often even agentive concept, though its dynamic representation is far from being clear. By contrast, *not making* (not making something happen) is passive and equivalent to *letting* (something stay in its present state). The modal meaning values (involving the modal verb *must*) corresponding to the positive form of *making* include the deontic modal set *obligation/facultativity* and the epistemic modal set *necessity/contingency*.

Let us summarize, first using the verb *be* to refer to the states involved:

Making corresponds to not letting be; active (= changing), whereas:
Not making corresponds to letting be; passive (= leaving unchanged).

There are two more meanings to attend to in the basic group of *letting* effects. They appear if we instead apply the infinitive *do* and allow a paraphrase using the verb *stop* (in the sense of *prevent from*):

Letting do corresponds to *not stopping*; passive (=non-intervention).
Not letting do corresponds to *stopping*; active (=negative intervention).

So, we have four meaning values: *(not) letting be*; *(not) letting do*. Two active, two passive. Only the *letting do* forms have been taken into account in standard force-dynamic modeling. Adding the *letting be* forms solves the problem of modeling active *making* through force dynamics.

My aim here is just to show that these meanings can be represented within the framework of one and the same dynamic schema, accounting directly for their cognitive kinship, apparent in the fact that they share verbs of the *letting* type (Fr. *laisser*, G. *lassen*, da. *lade*, Sp. *dejar*, Port. *deixar*,[52] etc.) characterized by their transitive constructions with verb-phrasal objects by examples (1)–(4):

(1) The open cage door let the birds escape.
(2) Paul never let anybody criticize him.
(3) Mary let her boyfriend down. She made him unhappy.
(4) Please let me stay with you. Let things be as they are.

Figure 9.9 shows the semiotic square[53] corresponding to these main forms.

This Greimas-like presentation of two intersecting "contradictory" values (2) – (1=non2) and (3) – (4=non3), forms an axis of "contraries" (3) – (2) that opposes the strong, efficient, positive, active values, *making versus stopping*, whereas the axis of "subcontraries" only distinguishes two weak, concessive, negative, passive values (1) – (4). This semantic square summarizes the schematic structure of the involved dynamic concepts.

The corresponding, unified schematic representation—a force-barrier diagram—is based on four elements: (a) **P**, a process or a project, or simply an intentional agent driven by a goal and trying to "reach" it; (b) a flexible *path* in space (or time) from an initial position of **P** and oriented toward the fulfillment, completion, or goal to be

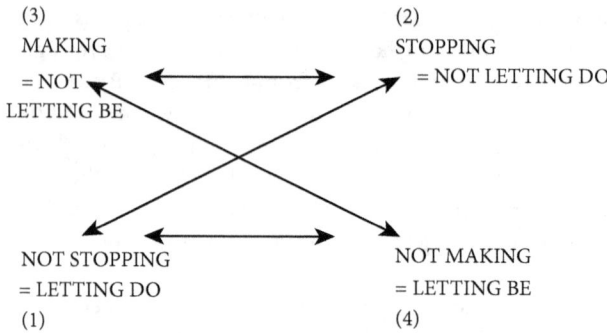

Figure 9.9 Semiotic square of *making* and *letting*.

reached, namely the continuation of a process or state or the realization of a project; (c) a *barrier* **B**[54] showing the particular circumstances affecting the path of **P**; and finally (d) a division of the dynamic space in two qualitative strata with a *critical line* separating the two parts, one in which movements, acts, or events do not change the state of the agent: thus a stratum of *Same state*, and one representing a *Different state*.

In ordinary "letting" causation, like (1) and (2), the barrier coincides with the critical line, and the passage through (across, around) this critical barrier leads from Same to Different state. The barrier **B** lets or does not let the process or project **P** happen or lets the Agent reach his goal (Figure 9.10).

If by contrast the critical qualitative line crosses the barrier instead of running parallel to it, we are able to represent a transition from **P** to **P′** within one and the same state, when an open barrier **lets P** stay the same; a closed barrier can force **P** to go into a qualitative different state, so the actively impeding circumstance will be precisely the one changing or **making P** into a **P***, as in Figure 9.11.

The "harassment" of **P** by the barrier **B** corresponds to an active intervention that **makes P** go into a state determined by this dynamic circumstance. **B** changes **P**.

It had formerly been suggested (Brandt 2004a) that a *making* schema includes a transforming instance, a multiple input into this instance, and a critical boundary that the process crosses before unfolding a result scenario that shows the change that the input undergoes. This result scenario—a morphological change such as dividing, crushing, splitting, growing, shrinking, or the set of mereological changes such as filling, emptying, ordering, disordering—would characterize **P*** as a figurative revision.

It is plausible that the *letting* and the *making* forms of causation are basic in human cognition. They should therefore be studied and modeled with particular care and accuracy. The present account only contributes to the elucidation of two important aspects of their behavior that have intrigued semantic research: how come they can use the same *verb* and in very similar constructions? And how can a *barrier* possibly *make* anything at all?[55] The verb *let* unfolds, with and without *negation*, the verbal categories *be* and *do* as a variable dynamic scenario, yielding a diagrammatic representation which may be part of an elementary set of thinking tools of the human (and animal) mind. *Making is what we do when we do not let things be what they already are.*[56]

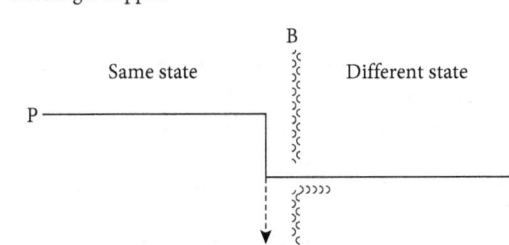

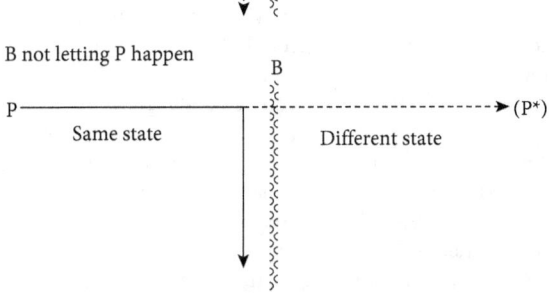

Figure 9.10 Force-barrier schema of *letting* and *not letting*.

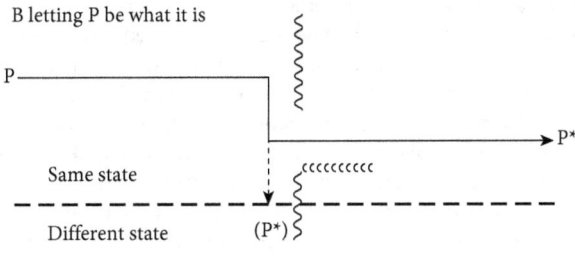

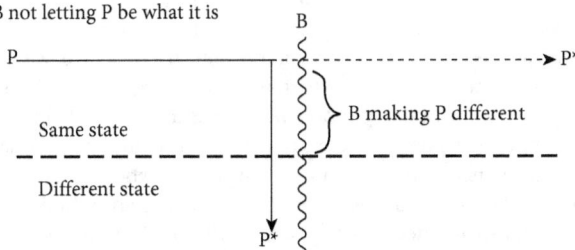

Figure 9.11 *Letting* versus *making*.

In narrative unfoldings, **P*** can further achieve overcomings and reach goals that **P** could not do; one dynamic scenario can *make* the subject competent for overcoming a barrier in another scenario. The subject can thus be doing one thing in order to do another sort of thing, not because the goals are linked but because the first experience prepares the subject for the second task.

Notes

1. The term "narratology" is due to Todorov (1969: 10). The expression "cognitive narratology" is very recent and was first used, I believe, in the sense adopted in this chapter by David Herman (2000). The term "semio-cognitive" refers to a recently developed line of research drawing particularly on semiotics (structural and philosophical) and cognitive semantics; see the journal *Cognitive Semiotics* (2007–) and Brandt (2004b).
2. In the sense of: discourses of telling, showing, and proving, respectively. Benveniste (1966) studied the structural differences of *récit* (story) and *discours*, essentially distinguishing the narrative mode and everything else.
3. The referential space of a description can be purely conceptual, notional, and in that case, the display of the notional distribution can of course be temporal. Examples include cooking recipes; such texts are not narrative just because the prescribed actions are not to be performed simultaneously. Recipes are still descriptions—like walking through a museum following the numbered sections.
4. On blending, see Chapter 7.
5. The *fictivity* of fiction is not our concern in the analysis of narrative event logic; this feature of well-wrought stories probably has to do with their closed structure—the impression of completion they convey. They make us think: *se non è vero, è ben trovato!* However, fictivity is a semiotically and cognitively challenging phenomenon, difficult to explain. Personally, I think Roman Jakobson (1960) was on the right path when he proposed his concept of a poetic function based on self-reference of the "message": if a story offers a structure so salient and compelling that it no longer matters if it is true, then it will be artfully told out of the context of true things and typically transmitted in verse or writing to be enjoyed by audiences with no knowledge of its referential circumstances. Its "artfulness" makes it into a "meme," you might say. A compelling alternative but compatible view is that fictivity results from the insertion, in discourse, of an artificial, "fictive" narrator—an enunciative, theatrical role, which then determines everything under its scope as unreal, as unreal as itself. The *narrator role* would define fiction, whatever be the story told.
6. Turner (1996) uses "story" in a broader sense of any state, event, or act involving a subject; his view eliminates the dramatic meaning of the term.
7. When the narrator is embodied in a primary subjective instance, we often feel that the "Olympian" narrator of the *third-person narration* (as an unembodied, external voice) disappears; we get a *first-person narration*. But it is equally justifiable to hear the latter as a discreetly polyphonic narrative: "It was a fine summer day in Cleveland. I was sitting on a bench in the park and having a beer, when suddenly ... "—the first sentence still being "Olympian," whereas the second has an embodied narrator. The embodied voice does not necessarily erase *the unembodied voice*, hence the eventuality of a duo, or in general a plurality, of voices, one of which stays unembodied.
8. This idea is by no means trivial or evident. Greimas (1966) proposed to situate his actantial narrative dynamics at a level between the deep level semiotics of pure oppositional semantic "logic" and the surface level of enunciational and rhetorically invested discourse, in a "generative" semantic theory of meaning. Colm Hogan (2003) starts a chapter by stating: "A central distinction in narratology is that between story and discourse, what happens and the presentation of what happens." What happens is what I call the story *an sich*.

9   I do not of course claim that narratology should be exclusively the study of story structure, only that the difference between the two main aspects of narratives must be acknowledged. While the study of narra*tion*, narrator styles, viewpoints, strategies of telling, and so on, that is, the rhetoric of narratives, has been a central part of literary scholarship for a century, the "story" part has been neglected to such an extent that it is now common to believe that there *is* no story structure to be found in narrative texts, just a narrating process and a corresponding process of ongoing reception—a view that suits the empiricist thinking style of certain philosophically biased scholars (the great David Bordwell (2008) would be a recent example). So, a primary goal of this chapter is to show *that there is indeed a story structure*, which is independent of narrator styles, just as in linguistics it is indeed possible to distinguish an *énoncé* from its *énonciation* (Benveniste 1966, Cervoni 1987). To be clear: that "there is a story" does not mean that it exists on a screen, a sheet of paper, in the materiality of the medium, just like the semantics of a sentence does not live in the materiality of the speech sounds. So where *does* it live? In the cognitive content of minds that semiotically share meaning in communication.—Can minds share meaning? Yes.—How? By following the semiotic mental instructions given by the signs of the medium. What is a sign? That is a long story... What if a story is passed on from a realistic narrator to a fantastic narrator, I am being asked. A story can of course undergo transformations such that it becomes fantastic, for example, if it has been realistic (or the inverse), but that is not a matter of changing narrator, though it is often a matter of changing author! Please distinguish author and narrator. Realistic biography can thus become hagiography (fantastic).

10 When is a change "critical"? Criticality in this context may be determined as the property of having effects that include contributing to the occurrence of other events, not necessarily immediate but happening in the spatiotemporal continuum of the story in question. A dynamic change is "critical" if *somewhere* it induces another dynamic change. Some basic analytic ideas on criticality and the roles of causation in narration in terms of mental space blending were presented in Brandt (2004a), chapter 4.

11 We know force-dynamic schemas from cognitive grammar (Brandt 1990, Geeraerts and Cuyckens 2007, Sweetser 1990, Talmy 2000), but the force-dynamic semantics of causation and modality, which is now known to be lexically and syntactically expressed in sentences, has not yet been systematically studied in the framework of entire narratives. However, force dynamics is evidently a default part of all source-path-goal schemas and all mediated subject-object relations. The role of *forms and forces* in human perception accounts for the cooperation of spatial and temporal cognition in immediate experience. Narrative cognition builds on this cooperation in perception and reactivates it in human imagination, especially in anticipation and preparation of acts and reactions. All experiences of time are dynamic. See Evans (2006). I have added a research note, "Letting, Making, and the Dynamics of Causation," as an appendix to this chapter, just to offer a view of the way some cognitive or semiotic linguists are handling the dynamic semantics of causal language and thought.

12 What I mean is simply the following. When something happens to us, we think: this was mainly because of X... That is, X represents some sort of force causing the thing that happened.

13 Our episodic memory (Tulving 1983) is made of experiences of this kind. This does not mean that human beings experience their lives as a *sustained* narrative (Stafford (2007) protests against such existential pan-narrativism), but it does

mean that narrative event logic is directly related to the episodic structuring processes of human memory and thus that it is a phenomenon that belongs in our neuropsychological reality. Zacks and Magliano (2009) very usefully summarize a wide range of studies of narrative cognition in film and offer an updated neuroscientific perspective.

14   These *fatal* forces—cf. Baudrillard (1983), one of the most inspiring and challenging essays on human acts and motivation I have read—are experienced as "more contingent than the contingent," so uncaused that they seem to express an underlying or overarching determination, destination, or destiny. Example: the critically ill person's address to Destiny, Fatum: "Why me?" The fatal becomes an attraction in ludomania. Should we discard such things in narratology? They are irrational, in so far as human cognition is (partly) irrational, but they are still semiotically rational, that is, components in sense-making.

15   As mentioned above, our tentative classification of forces contains so far only the following: *intentional* {*agentive* versus *magical*} versus *causal* {*trivial* versus *fatal*}. This may of course turn out to be too simple. But the set of force categories does certainly not contain fewer elements than these. See the analyses below for an exemplification.

16   The idea of a variable dynamic density by "addition" or "subtraction" of forces is due to L. Brandt (2013). The idea of a default realistic starting point for variations and derivations goes directly counter to Roland Barthes' suggestion in a famous article, "L'effet de reel" (Barthes 1968), namely to conceive the realistic genre as built on a special descriptive "effect," obtained by adding arbitrary details, thus seeing realism as a particularly artificial construction.

17   The French term: *le merveilleux* refers to fairy-tale worlds. Cf. Todorov (1970).

18   See Jakobson (1972).

19   Cf. "Curioser and curioser." In Brandt (1994, 1995).

20   Maupassant (1974: 1198). *Le Gaulois,* 1884.

21   The structure is so far analogous to that of the fairy tale of Cinderella (Aarne-Thompson, type 510A).

22   By spaces I mean either concrete geographical places or less concrete socio-géographical habitats and situations. The terms for their designation proposed below are generic; the term *catastrophe* refers to René Thom's so-called catastrophe theory (Thom 1980, Brandt 1992): a catastrophe is a dynamically induced, significant change in a reference situation.

23   D4 is *mentally fatal* to the protagonist, since it tells her that all her sufferings were meaningless. What you don't know and what you then get to know by chance or accident, instead of not knowing it and be happier in the middle of misery, is fatal but does not change anything in the event logic, only in the conclusive reflection of the protagonist and the empathic reader. So, it leads to an epistemic event: the understanding that much of your life is spent on severe consequences of tiny misunderstandings, that is, expensive and destructive nonsense.

24   The suite of spaces—instantiated directly as places of variable spatiotemporal extension—is canonical, I claim, and it can thus be compared to the classical rhetorical models (exposition, complication, climax, resolution …, cf. Gustav Freytag's 1863 analysis of Greek dramas; and in modern poetics, Sternberg 1993) but this suite is independent of rhetoric. It is inherently event-dynamic. It does not

(like "climax") refer to the appropriate feelings of the hearer-reader, but rather to the unfolding in space and time of the event logic involved in a story.

25 Maupassant (1974: 732). *Gil Blas*, 1883.

26 If the two friends were allowed to return to Paris, they would be able to tell the French army where their enemy was hiding; they would potentially, retrospectively, be scouts, hence spies. Anglers or spies—this depends on the viewpoint: to themselves, historically, they are anglers, as we know; to the player in the war game they entered, they now play a different role, as truthfully as they embodied the former.

27 Greimas (1976), in his book (summarized in Brandt 1983, chapter 6, where "Deux amis" and "La Ficelle" are reanalyzed) also entirely dedicated to the analysis of this short story, assumes that they had a real password (not only an oral or written license to pass) and that they were therefore, while staying silent under the interrogation, performing a heroic deed by opposing the "Stalinist" Prussian officer instead of saving their life, which would have been possible and likely to happen if they had disclosed that password. J.-Cl. Coquet (1997: 25–26) found this not to be a correct analysis of the situation, and I share his conclusion: They could not have saved their lives; they do not even have a password, and even if they had had one, it would evidently not have helped them, because the officer cannot let them go; they are not heroic combatants of resistance but simple human beings caught in the logic of place and power, finding themselves in a location where they should not be. It's war: they are (now, potential) spies, given *where* they are.

28 "Ils se remirent en marche, munis d'un laissez-passer." That is, undoubtedly, a piece of paper with their names on it, not a memorized password.

29 Again, the Consequence Space is plainly, trivially R and without any marked fatality. Hence the stone-face cruelty of the story.

30 Well, in this story, the "upper-cut event" D4 is trivial, whereas it was fatal in the former story. The execution is trivial in the basic sense that it follows from the rules of the play—and this is precisely what feeds the tragical meaning: if you find yourself in the wrong place, no intentional auto-interpretation can save you from being allo-interpreted in accordance with that place.

31 Since the force/space model turns out to yield a quasi-identical structural network in these two stories, our *figure 9.3* will cover both of them.

32 Maupassant (1974: 1080). *Le Gaulois*, 1883. The editor comments (p. 1605): "Un des plus célèbres contes de Maupassant n'évoque pas seulement la terre normande, avec ses coutumes et ses hommes, il montre aussi comment un homme devient prisonnier de sa propre mésaventure. Il y a là quelque chose de kafkaïen et de labyrinthique, au point que le conte ne peut se refermer que sur lui-même pour recommencer à nouveau: "Les plaisants maintenant lui faisaient conter 'la ficelle'." Le conte ramené à son statut de pur objet fonctionne comme un piège de la conscience."

33 "It all smelled of the stable, of milk, of hay and of perspiration, giving off that half-human, half-animal odor which is peculiar to country folks." Naturalism summarized in one sentence; humans are still animals.

34 *El aleph* (1949). An editor and critic of Borges, Marcos Ricardo Barnatán (1981: 149) writes that this text, one of very few in Borges containing a sexual reference, is in fact a double story, of a revenge and of a repetition of the suffering of the avenged beloved being.

35 The text says: "Romper dinero es una impiedad, como tirar el pan; Emma se arrepintió, apenas lo hizo. Un acto de soberbia y en aquel día...." My reading has to

36 accept the narrator's comment on the tearing up of the money: it is a symbolic act and could have consequences, especially on such a day. Only if it does have magical consequences is the story fantastic; else it stays in psychological realism.

36 The magical intentional feeling remains, that B2 can have caused C2, namely, if so, by *magic*. In that case (see note 22), one fatality causes another, since the first is additionally to be seen as negatively *magically intentional*—it offends a taboo, a (supernatural) intentional instance protecting symbolic items (money, bread...) from destruction. By B2 → C2, this story would qualify as fantastic.

37 *El aleph*, 1949.

38 It is also very complicated; so, discussing it in this context is a challenge. Its argumentative aspect is overwhelming, compared to the reference narrative; it is a story about a story—the latter is the one we are focusing on.

39 Anachronically so: Urquiza was a caudillo general who led the army that deposited the dictator Rosas in the battle of Caseros, 1852.

40 Pier or Pietro Damiani, 1007–1072, theologian and saint, appears in the seventh heaven of Dante's *Paradise, XXI*, 112–126.

41 The effect on the reader of the epistemic mysteries of the narration is admittedly essential to the aesthetic force of this text. Reading is a process, and in the emotional display invited by this process lies much of the artfulness of a narrative of this kind, and in general, of fantastic stories (investing as they do in ambiguity). Nevertheless, the story *must* deliver a network of intelligible dynamic causal relations to reconstruct during the process in order to make sense, even as a (initial) mystery (and a terminal paradox). Without asking what "really happened" the reader will not be sensible to the mystery.

42 The text stresses sufficiently that the motive for his participation in the uprising is not political (Urquiza!).

43 *In Our Time*, 1925, 1930.

44 "He went under the anaesthetic holding tight on to himself, so he would not blab about anything during the silly, talky time." The reader wonders what to think here.

45 "She loved him as always, but she realized now it was only a boy and girl love. She hoped he would have a great career and believed in him absolutely. She knew it was for the best." The narrator's mordant irony cannot be missed in sentences like these.

46 "They felt as though they were married, but they wanted everyone to know about it, and to make it so they could not lose it." The feeling as such is not sufficient, the symbolic ritual has to take place, and it doesn't.

47 The change occurring when the real path traverses a qualitative boundary affects the subject's circumstances in many respects and often determines other narratives involving the subject, as we clearly see in "The Necklace." The Faustian motive—selling one's soul to the devil—is another forceful example. The dynamic narrative links as those we have studied will then often correspond to whole arrays of interconnected force-dynamic scenarios. How come that we so easily and intuitively grasp these complex connections in the course of a story we read? I think the answer is the same as to the problem of our fast and automatic understanding of the grammar and meaning of sentences: we use default cognitive formats and schemas. We do not need to know them in order to do that.

48 Again: by *forces* we mean all sorts of causal and intentional instances that narratives can refer to or imply—eventually, we may therefore be able to find a rich set of force types in literature and then, for the sake of cognitive psychology, include these in

the inventory of forces that the human mind can use in its explanatory thinking. It is already evident that this set is not reduced to trivial physical causation but includes at least three other types from the start, that is, without any metaphoric transfer. The mind is not physicalistic; it would be more accurate to see it as naturally "surrealistic" in a broad sense. Hence a "naturalization" of narratives (Fludernik 2005: 313), constructing "narrativity on the basis of real-world cognitive parameters (handled in a flexible manner)," will have to be flexible enough to understand that genuine, human, embodied experience is inherently full of magical wonders and absurd humor or sadness. However, I doubt that "naturalization" will stay a suitable term for such a theoretical endeavor.

49   Animal consciousness is dramatically narrative in the sense of offering an apparently constant, present, dramatically catastrophic space to the subject (see Chapter 4, above).

50   The standard force-barrier model works as follows. A mobile entity follows a path toward a goal but encounters a barrier in the middle; the resistance of the barrier to the movement of the entity determines what further happens. The barrier can be "overcome," or it can "stop" the moving entity, unless it instead follows a path around it. An opening in the barrier can *let* the entity pass. *Making* is not represented by this standard model. Sweetser (1990), Talmy (2000). Geeraerts and Cuyckens (2007) have a useful chapter on force dynamics.

51   Source-path-goal schemas are inherent in all concepts of intention, volition, planning, projects, and conscious acts in general. This is why "LOVE IS A JOURNEY" in Lakoff's (1987) list of "conceptual metaphors." "Love," here, is a project and is conceptualized by a force-barrier schema; in the metaphor, the source is another project, the "journey."

52   Silva (1999 et passim) is no doubt the scholar most consequently immersed in the study of dynamic semantic aspects of grammar of contemporary literature.

53   A semiotic square—*un carré sémiotique*—is a diagram proposed by A.J. Greimas (Greimas and Courtés 1979).

54   The barrier can be interpreted as a physical obstacle (a mountain, a wall), as a social artifact (traffic lights and lines, locked doors), or as a person, interacting with P in communicational ways.

55   If the Agent is intentional, that is, is internally driven by a tendency to move toward a goal, then a barrier forcing the Agent to take a detour, if this detour leads through a field of imprinting experiences, will affect and change the Agent; this change is *made* by the (closed) barrier causing the detour. *Making* in this analysis is thus a concept presupposing an entity undergoing the change which is intentional; even inanimate things "want to" stay as they are and oppose our efforts to change them. This non-physicalistic, intentionalistic view is intuitively easy to understand but has not been admitted in cognitive semantics—probably for philosophical reasons.

56   Curiously, Sigmund Freud had the idea that negation cannot be imagined (so people would be forced to imagine positively what was conceptualized negatively). Of course, an isolated operator called "not" does not prompt us to imagine anything. But formal logic is not the format of elementary thinking; in life, it is easier to imagine negation as a door (or a factory) that closes—that's negation in the human scale, the form that cognitively grounds abstract thinking. Admittedly, a static image does not open or close anything; modeling has to be kinetic and dynamic in order to account for our mental doings.

References

Barnatán, M. R., 1981. *Jorge Luis Borges, Narraciones*. Madrid: Cátedra.
Barthes, R., 1968. "L'effet de reel," *Communications* (11), Paris: EHESS.
Baudrillard, J., 1983. *Les stratégies fatales*. Paris: Edition Bernard Grasset, série Figures.
Benveniste, E., 1966. *L'homme dans la langue*, chapter in *Problèmes de linguistique generale*. Paris: Gallimard.
Bordwell, D., 2008. *Poetics of Cinema*. New York: Routledge.
Brandt, P. A., 2004a. *Spaces, Domains, and Meaning. Essays in Cognitive Semiotics*, European Semiotics Series, Vol. 4. Berne: Peter Lang.
Brandt, P. A., 2004b. "Toward a Cognitive Semiotics." In: (Ed.) P. Fastrez, *Recherches en Communication*, Vol. 19. Dossier Cognitive Semiotics. Leuven: Université catholique de Louvain.
Brandt, P. A., 1995. *Morphologies of Meaning*. Aarhus: Aarhus University Press.
Brandt, P. A., 1994. "Curiouser and Curiouser—A Brief Analysis of Alice in Wonderland." In: (Ed.) C. Marello, *Semiotics and Linguistics in Alice's Worlds*, Berlin, New York Ed. Walter de Gruyter, Series Research in Text Theory/Untersuchungen zur Texttheorie.
Brandt, P. A., 1992. *La charpente modale du sens. Pour une sémio-linguistique morphogénétique et dynamique*. Aarhus, Amsterdam: Aarhus University Press & John Benjamins.
Brandt, P. A., 1990. "The Dynamics of Modality: A Catastrophe Analysis," RSSI (*Recherches Sémiotique/Semiotic Inquiry*), 9, 1-2-3, Université du Québec à Montréal.
Brandt, P. A., 1983. *Sandheden, sætningen og døden. Semiotiske aspekter af kulturanalysen*. [Truth, Sentence, Death. Semiotic Aspects of Cultural Analysis]. Copenhagen: Basilisk.
Cervoni, J., 1987. *L'énonciation*. Paris: Presses Universitaires de France, série Linguistique nouvelle.
Colm Hogan, P., 2003. *Cognitive Science, Literature, and the Arts*. New York, London: Routledge.
Coquet, J. C., 1997. *La quête du sens. Le langage en question*. Paris: PUF.
Evans, V., 2006. *The Structure of Time: Language, Meaning, and Temporal Cognition*. Amsterdam, Philadelphia: John Benjamins, series Human Cognitive Processing
Fludernik, M., 2005 (1996). *Towards a "Natural" Narratology*. London, New York: Taylor & Francis.
Gavins, J., 2007. *Text World Theory. An Introduction*. Edinburgh: Edinburgh University Press.
Geeraerts, D., and H. Cuyckens, 2007. *The Oxford Handbook of Cognitive Linguistics*. Oxford: Oxford University Press.
Greimas, A. J., 1976. *Maupassant. La sémiotique du texte. Exercices pratiques*. Paris: Editions du Seuil.
Greimas, A. J., 1966. *Sémantique structurale. Recherche de méthode*. Paris: Larousse.
Greimas A. J., and J. Courtés, 1979. *Sémiotique. Dictionnaire raisonné de la théorie du langage*. Paris: Hachette Université.
Herman, D., 2000. "Narratology as a Cognitive Science." *Image & Narrative*, 1, Cognitive Narratology, www.imageandnarrative.be
Jakobson, R., 1972. "Verbal Communication." *Scientific American*, 227, 72-80.
Jakobson, R., 1960. "Closing Statements: Linguistics and Poetics." In: (Ed.) T. Sebeok, *Style in Language*. Cambridge, MA: MIT Press.

de Maupassant, G., 1974. *Contes et nouvelles*, Vol. I, ed. Louis Forestier. Paris: Gallimard, Bibliothèque de la Pléiade.
da Silva, A. S., 1999. *A Semántica de Deixar. Uma Contribuição para a Abordagem Cognitiva em Semântica Lexical.* Lisbon: Gulbenkian.
Stafford, B. M., 2007. *Echo Objects: The Cognitive Work of Images*. Chicago: University of Chicago Press.
Sternberg, M., 1993. *Expositional Modes and Temporal Ordering in Fiction*. Bloomington: Indiana University Press.
Sweetser, E., 1990. *From Etymology to Pragmatics*. Cambridge: Cambridge University Press.
Talmy, L., 2000. *Toward a Cognitive Semantics*, I–II. Cambridge, MA: MIT Press.
Todorov, T., 1969. *Grammaire du Décaméron*. The Hague, Paris: Mouton.
Todorov, T., 1970. *Introduction à la littérature fantastique*. Paris: Le Seuil.
Thom, R., 1980. *Modèles mathématiques de la morphogenèse*. Paris: Christian Bourgois Ed.
Tulving, E., 1983. *Elements of Episodic Memory*. Oxford: Clarendon Press.
Turner, M., 1996. *The Literary Mind. The Origins of Thought and Language*. New York: Oxford University Press.
Zacks, J. M., and Joseph P. Magliano, 2009. "Film, Narrative, and Cognitive Neuroscience." In: (Eds.) D. P. Melcher and F. Bacci, *Art and the Senses*. New York: Oxford University Press.
www.classicreader.com/book/ Guy de Maupassant, "A Piece of String"
www.classicreader.com/book/933/1/ "Two Friends"
www.classicreader.com/book/463/1/ "The Diamond Necklace"
www.classicreader.com/book/518/1/; http://records.viu.ca/~lanes/english/hemngway/vershort.htm (Accessed February 10, 2020).

10

The Meaning of Translation

In its cognitive function, language is minimally dependent on the grammatical pattern because the definition of our experience stands in complementary relation to metalinguistic operations—the cognitive level of language not only admits but directly requires recoding interpretation, i.e., translation. Any assumption of ineffable or untranslatable cognitive data would be a contradiction in terms. But in jest, in dreams, in magic, briefly, in what one would call everyday verbal mythology and in poetry above all, the grammatical categories carry a high semantic import. In these conditions, the question of translation becomes much more entangled and controversial.

Roman Jakobson, see note 1, below.

On the Possibility of Translation

If signifiers and signifieds are strictly interdependent, as many modern semioticians and linguists—including Louis Hjelmslev and maybe Ferdinand de Saussure—would think, then translation should be impossible, since a shift in signifier would entail a shift in signified. But translation is supposed to *trans–late* (transfer) a signified meaning from one regime of signifiers to another.[1] The simplest formula for the idea of possible translation may in fact be the following (Figure 10.1).

$$\frac{\text{Signifier1} \rightarrow \text{Signifier2}}{\text{Signified}}$$

Figure 10.1 The semiotic formula of translation.

According to this formula, a signified (meaning) stays stable under a change of its signifier when translation happens. Can signifieds, that is, meanings, do that? It is quite common to answer negatively. Of course, the imputed generic impossibility of translation disappears if the interdependence of signifiers and signifieds is no longer considered as an absolute, but rather as a special condition.[2] In that case we would have to admit that meanings sometimes can indeed stay stable and be invariable under variation of the signifiers that express them. Meanings can always be signified by signifiers and thus become *the* signifieds *of* certain signifiers, but meanings are not created by their signifiers or entirely constituted by social acts of signification.

Instead, they are mental creations issued by human cognition, including perception and conceptualization on many levels of mental complexity.[3] This view is supported by huge evidence, that is, by the results of extensive and intensive research during a century[4] but is still not accepted by all modern philosophies. So, certain meaning skeptics claim that in principle, meanings cannot be accessed or understood, because their signifiers change incessantly and thereby constantly erase what they signify.[5] Nevertheless, what we call thinking—whether narrative, theoretical, moral, poetical, musical, or other—is indeed constantly being translated, not only interlingually, from language to language, but also inside a single language (as in paraphrasis) and between language and other semiotic media. This happens every time an idea is rephrased, expanded or compressed, reformulated, diagrammed, critically reexamined, discussed, and compared to similar or contrasting ideas (as we just did with the idea of the possibility of translation). Thinking is essentially rephrasing; an idea takes on its contours when it is represented in more than one way. This is why dialogue is such an efficient means of contouring and developing ideas. Roman Jakobson's distinction between *intralingual* and *interlingual* translation, and between *intrasemiotic* (such as interlingual) and *intersemiotic* translation, which just served us above, generalizes usefully the scope of the notion of translation: synonymy, paraphrasis, summarizing, expanding, interpreting in real time, translating to other languages within genres or between genres, narrative transposing from novel to cartoon or opera—all are instances of meanings being "transferred," "carried on" from one manifestation to another, or rather of meanings re-manifested and identified, acknowledged, as being (more or less, but sufficiently) the "same" meanings. In this sense, translation is rather—in all of its forms—an art of variation. We "understand" through variation. Meanings circulate, migrate, without really moving in the physical sense.[6] Only their signifiers present a physical aspect giving rise to Reddy's famous "conduit metaphor" of communication,[7] which naturally extends to translation as soon as the "reception" of a message is testified by a new rendering of the "received." But the signifiers involved are not necessarily moving from place to place either; they are just "taking over" from each other. This observation stresses the semio-cognitive reality behind the "conduit," namely that minds that "connect" are essentially only exchanging *signifying forms*, and that these forms are mental instructions that trigger receptive processes of conceptual reconstruction of meanings counting intuitively as "same" as the meanings expressed. After some dialogical checking, we then experience a "sharing"[8] of ideas, affects, intentions, and so on. Meaningful content is to be phrased in multiple ways, *pollakôs legomenon*, as Aristotle said about being. It is shared. That is what makes translation possible.

However, some meanings are definitely untranslatable. If an expression in a special context means what it means by being that particular expression, then the text passage, or sentence, where this happens is by definition untranslatable. The effect is laughter.[9] So this is the case of puns. Consider the following examples:

(1) I'm reading a book about antigravity. It's impossible to put down.
(2) Did you hear about the guy whose whole left side was cut off? He's all right now.

(3) It's not that the man did not know how to juggle, he just didn't have the balls to do it.
(4) I couldn't quite remember how to throw a boomerang, but eventually it came back to me.

In (1), the expression *put down* creates in the thematic context of antigravity the absurd scenario of a reader trying to hold on to a book that escapes him by flying upwards while he reads. This semantic scenario is generated by the particular English expression, and its absurdity is ascribed to the particular ambiguity created by expression and context. It is the foregrounding of the expression that triggers the comical effect. Likewise, in (2), *being all right* is forced to take on an absurd literal and *lateral* meaning. In (3), the colloquial sexist metaphor *have the balls to...* is de-metaphorized and re-literalized by the context of juggling; in a blended scenario,[10] the hearer may even imagine an artist juggling with testicles. In (4), the idiomatic metaphor *coming back* in the sense of remembering is de-metaphorized by the boomerang in the context, but in a blended scenario, the hearer may imagine the mental return of the remembered skill as hitting the person physically. Idiomatic expressions normally do not draw our attention to their figurativity; so when a prominent element in the close context invites both a figurative and a nonfigurative reading, and the result is absurd, we get a *pun*. According to this analysis, puns can at least often be described as caused by the semantic absurdity resulting from a contextual de-figurativization of a figurative expression and calling the hearer's *attention to the signifier* responsible for it. We are apparently laughing at the signifier! This looks like an anthropological fact. The de-figurative context causes the content to lose its figurativity. The formula of the untranslatable would be the following (Figure 10.2).

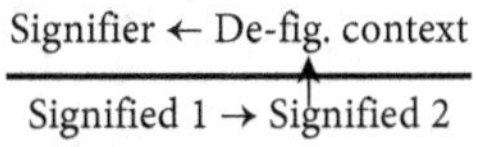

$$\frac{\text{Signifier} \leftarrow \text{De-fig. context}}{\text{Signified 1} \rightarrow \text{Signified 2}}$$

Figure 10.2 Formula of the untranslatable expression and its semiotic loop.

By contrast, jokes are often translatable, namely when the foregrounded language is not idiomatic but still gives rise to alternative semantic scenarios, which are not necessarily absurd but always implicitly traumatic in some way:

(5) COMEDIAN: Every night I get women banging on my door backstage. Sometimes I let them out.
(6) Two hunters are out in the woods, one faints, eyes glazed, and seems to have stopped breathing. The other hunter pulls out his cellphone and calls 911. He gasps to the operator "My friend is dead! What can I do?"
The operator in a calm voice says "Take it easy. I'll help you. First, let's make sure he's dead." There's silence, and then a shot is heard. Back on the phone he says, "OK, now what?"

In (5), we expect the scenario of *letting in*, but are instead offered the scenario of *letting out* these women, who must have been caged in a perverse comedian's room. *Banging on a door* is done either from the outside or from the inside. In (6), *making sure X* is alternatively interpreted as *causing X*, because the agent is a hunter, and X is *death*.

We might conclude on this point that it is the strongly autoreferential character of the pun text that makes it difficult or impossible to translate. *Autoreferentiality* also happens in poetry and in rhetorical prose, namely when an expression is demonstratively chosen not only for its meaning but for its sound or its expressive relations to other expressions. The content then seems to justify itself by reference to its own expression. In such cases, the poetic text appears to be untranslatable. Or rather, more optimistically put, it obliges the interlingual translator to "negotiate" or "navigate" between solutions that follow the meaning and solutions that follow the expression while trying to keep the syntax in close contact with the original.

Interlingual Translation, Language, and Text

A text written "in" a language has properties due to the grammar of the language in question but also possesses certain other properties that stem from the "strategy" used by the writer in order to approach his subject or in order to signal a textual or pragmatic genre. A *text* is thus made of the language it manifests, but it also manifests a formal structure that transcends this language while characterizing a certain genre, a poetic mold, a compositional principle, a personal idiomatism—we will call this aspect the writing (*l'écriture*) of the text.

The *semiotic structure of a text, as a manifestation of a language and a writing*, in the large sense of grammar, enunciation, and pragmatics, can be summarized in terms of Expression/Content functions on two main levels. A basic linguistic or "immanent" level comprises the grammatical relation between the classical "plane of expression" and the classical "plane of content" in Hjelmslev's model (following Saussure), but the expressive "plane" must again be analyzed as a relation between its own expressive graphics and gesture, which we subsume as *writing*, and the signified *phonetics*. Likewise, the content "plane" comprises a meaningful *syntactic* form and a signified *semantic* whole equivalent to a cognitive act.

The superordinate or "transcendent" textual level inscribes this basic structure into a content of *enunciation*, the instance that shapes the intentional profile of an enunciator approaching a specific subject, and into an expression of a referential *pragmatic* content that projects the conceptual content into the world of reception. All of this is of course important to translation theory and practice, because the understanding of both immanent and transcendent functions of *language and text* affects the translator's attention to the input and the output of his work. The distinction made between conceptual meaning and referential meaning corresponds roughly to the classical distinction between *denotative* meaning and *connotative* meaning of texts; the former is "immanent" and structural, the latter "transcendent," context-dependent, and dependent on pragmatic codes. All texts operate in cultures of reception whose coding has decisive impact on the process of *phrasing*, for the writer, and on the process of *rephrasing*, for the translator. So, writers and translators

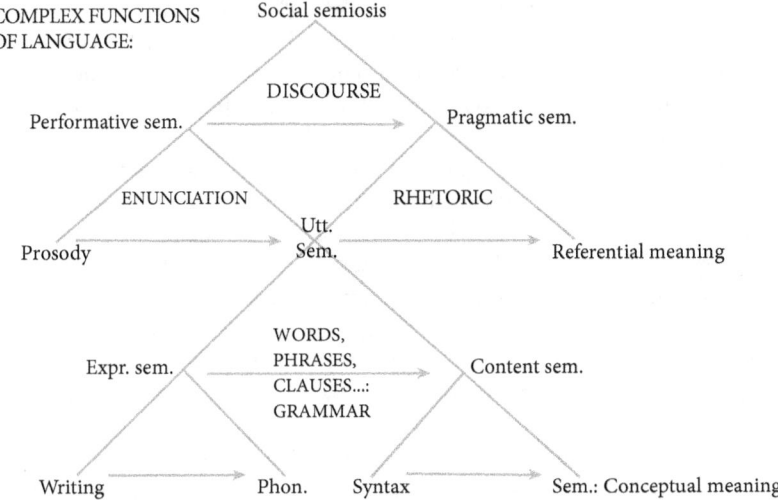

Figure 10.3 Six semiotic instances and their interaction.

share an intuitive attention to the structural properties of language as it appears in its actual phrasal functions affecting subjects that shape texts. Figure 10.3 summarizes the complex (immanent and transcendent) *semiosis*, or semiotic functions, of language and text, as it can be modeled on the basis of a recursive sign model.[11] This is what language and text look like in a general semiotic configuration, if each semiotic function is represented by a triangle of signifier (expression), signified (content), and sign function, semiosis.

The *utterance* ("Utt. Sem.," utterance semiosis, in the model) is the highest immanent sign function, whereas *discourse*, or social semiosis, is the highest transcendent function. *Enunciation* is the expressive function under *discourse* that lets the utterance be signified by an utterer, an enunciator. *Rhetoric* is the content function under *discourse* that lets the utterance signify a meaning in the pragmatic field of its use (e.g., in a social ritual).

The two extreme expressive instances, *prosody* and *writing*, must be coordinated by the speaking/writing subject; this correlation corresponds to what we perceive as the *tone* or *temperature* of the resulting text.

When the translator is working within a specific discourse, or textual genre, the functions on all levels of this complex architecture are affected by that condition. In particular, this is important to the main "ethics" of translation that varies significantly from the *literary* pole to the *commercial* pole. Translation within the literary "discourse" stays as close as possible to the graphics, the sounding, the phrases, the figurative language, the enunciative/writing tone of the source text, and it is sensitive to the degree of idiomaticity of the source text as a text in the source language—some texts being more or less "strange" or alien in their language. The translation should neither eliminate nor exaggerate the relative idiomaticity of the source text, which is in principle an important part of its particular "music." One might say that literary translation gives privilege to the "rendering" of the immanent lower level of linguistic structure (and to conceptual meaning) and accepts to run the risk of hurting or shocking the sensitivity of the receiving end, of ignoring the default settings of pragmatic meaning at the reception, to offend (or contribute to reshaping) the cultural norms of the target culture and its readers.

By contrast, *commercial* translation directly targets the pragmatic meaning and aims at assuring an optimal immediate reception of the intended "message," which is often or always tied to a commercial (performative) act of some sort. The conceptual meanings, their figurativity, and especially their metaphors do not count if following the source text closely would be pragmatically counterproductive. So, one might say that commercial translation opposes literary translation by giving privilege to the transcendent upper level of linguistic structure. This genre accepts substantial changes in the "inner" structure of the text, in order to obtain maximal efficiency of its "outer" structure.

If the genres of literary and commercial translation are determined by a clear opposition of literary and commercial *discourse*, in this respect, it seems useful to add a third genre, which offers similarity with both opposed genres, in so far as it both depends on particular stylistic features, including neologisms and idiomatic expressions that can make it sound rather poetic, and depends on being understood straightforwardly, without undergoing textual analyses and hermeneutic interpretation as practiced in literary criticism. This genre is the *philosophical* translation, an important aspect of philosophical discourse.[12] It allows close rendering of the source idiomaticities, but also the introduction of strategically placed interpreting terms around new expressions, *explicative* circumlocutions, in short, the sort of rephrasing found in commercial translation. Philosophical translation may be called a hybrid genre in this sense. It navigates between the literary and the commercial norms.

Finally, we have to mention *literal* translation, which only appears in the context of comparative linguistic analysis; the linear order of lexemes and morphemes in the source text, normally just a sentence, is replicated by a string of signs, natural or theoretical, produced by the linguist in the act of primary decoding, an act that may eventually give rise to a translation in ordinary prose. I suspect that language learners spontaneously use the same format when decoding unknown texts syllable by syllable.

The four main genres of interlingual translation mentioned can be projected onto a Greimasian[13] semiotic square of oppositions separating the major "contrary" relations and the subordinate "contradictory" relations obtained by negation of the contrary terms (Figure 10.4).

The deontic requirements of these genres vary significantly. Nevertheless, there are certain basic deontic principles underlying these variations. An ethics of translation contains the elementary requirement that the source text, even if it is commercial, should not be substantially "improved" by the translator; the latter is not the editor of the text. This is worth mentioning because the temptation to correct is almost irresistible when the source text is experienced as being suboptimal, weak, broken, and in need of repair at certain points. The translator then can hardly avoid a crisis of *solidarity*: he would like to defend the supposedly important essence of the text against the weaknesses of its author by altering and "improving" the text he translates—by

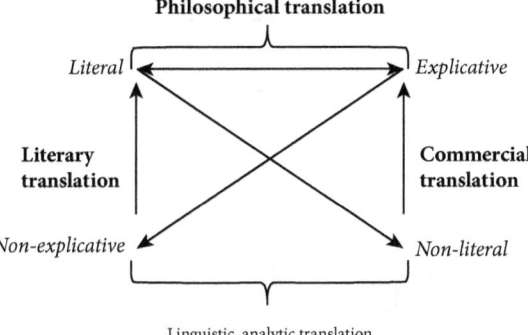

Figure 10.4 Genres of translation.

deviating from the details of its crafting. But the result is necessarily a weakness of the translation *as such*. The ethical solution to the problem (which is not often mentioned in such subjective terms in the literature on translation) is for the translator to avoid having to translate texts, especially literary texts, if she is not entirely comfortable with them or if she finds them problematic. Psychoanalysts would perhaps say that there needs to exist an identification-based transference from the translator to the implied author of the text.[14] The subjectivity of the literary or philosophical translator[15] is invested in the work on a deep level; writers who translate will experience a long-term effect of being bodily and mentally, and especially linguistically—in their own writing—influenced, involuntarily (unconsciously) changed, by the source texts and the auctorial *subjectivity* they carry with them. This phenomenon can be compared to the way a friendship influences and changes a person. A text is virtually a person. It has a voice.

The Dynamics of Writing. Translation as Transfer

The structural semantics of A.J. Greimas[16] proposed a curious model of general narrative semantics, the *actantial model*. This model combined three axes: an axis of *transfer* (of an entity from a source or origin to a destination), an axis of *project* (a subject's desire to accomplish the transfer), and an axis of *conflict* (opposing an adjuvant and an opponent to the subject's project). Figure 10.5 is a representation of the relations between the six involved actants.[17]

In Figure 10.5, an Object of value is moved by a Subject from an Origin (French: *Destinateur*) to a Destination (French: *Destinataire*), if the conflict and balance of powers of Adjuvants and Opponents make it possible. In a folktale, the model must be used twice and in a circular sequencing, namely for the Object to be abduced by a Villain (Subject 1) and for the Hero (Subject 2) to rescue the Object and bring it back to the Origin. In political ideology, Subject 1 nurtures the project of transforming the society in one direction, with the help of the people but against the will of

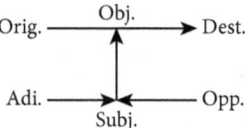

Figure 10.5 Greimas' model of actant structure.

reactionary antagonists; while Subject 2 inversely desires to bring the society back to its former situation, again with the help of the people and despite the resistance of some bad guys. If two actantial models are used for circular transports of this kind, their combination will correspond to their inscription in a semiotic square with a circulating Object in the middle. However, the number of actants would then ideally be reduced to four. The actantial model and its dynamics could eventually schematize any intentional project on an elementary semantic level.

A single investment of the actantial model may illustrate the narrative project of writing a piece of literature of some kind and especially the rather demanding task of writing a book of poetry, a novel, or a drama. In this version, the subjectivity of the writer corresponds to the Subject actant whose transfer project is to extract some meaning (Object) from an aspect of the world (Origin) and to deposit it in a text (Destination). The writer's available language of course resists the task, which otherwise would be easy and without merit. Language, the ordinary language of speech, which is an Adjuvant in communication, is thus experienced as an obstacle, an *Opponent*, when the project is to discover new perspectives or properties of the world, including the mental world, the affective world, and to create knowledge thereof. The *Adjuvant* in these cases is the *writing*, that is, the battery of special methods, models, forms, rhythms, mathematics, and other nonlinguistic means of symbolization at the disposal of the researcher and the writer. In literature, this battery may be called *Form* (in poetry: metrics and expressive designs, in narrative prose: formats, narrator profiles, rhetorical figures, styles of enunciation and evidentiality, etc.). Every writer has his own arsenal of special formal devices that assists her in the fight for meaning, the *mining of meaning*, so to speak. The *dynamics of writing* is this conflict between Opponent and Adjuvant in the use of language and form. The following actantial representation corresponds to such an analysis of the dynamics of writing (Figure 10.6).

If this representation is correct or plausible, it is of interest to translators, since it presents the text as a dramatic result of a dynamic process. Language may tend to oppose or block the formal work, while the formal devices mobilized by the writer to help her grasp and represent a meaningful content may tend to make the verbal rendering of this content even more difficult. To translate a text is to inherit the resulting text and thereby also to inherit its agonistic *actantial presuppositions*, the story of its "birth." Understanding the source text includes obtaining knowledge about the conditions of its production. Translation is in fact a similar dynamic process. Inversely, for the translator, however, language is of course an Adjuvant, not an Opponent, whereas the Forms mobilized by the writer have to be matched by new

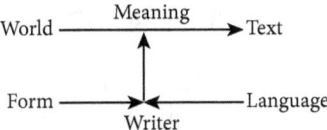

Figure 10.6 The actant dynamics of writing.

Formal properties, which are obstacles to the fabrication of the new text, in so far as they often cannot simply be copied from the source but still have to be represented somehow. For example, the rhymes and the metrics of a classical poem translated to a modern language and culture may be matched by new rhymes and new metrics similar to those of the source text, but rhyming in the new text costs considerable rewording and consequent loss and deformation of content; and metrics may have to be altered from the source verse or left aside, whereby the nerve of line and line break is damaged. Form cannot be neglected in the translation, but neither can it be copied directly from the source; it has to be invented anew by the translator. Form is now an obstacle. So, in summary, the dynamics of Opponent and Adjuvant is inversed, when we sequentially represent the actantial scenarios of the two processes involved, the writing of the source and the writing of the translation. We will eventually have to produce an actantial diagram as in Figure 10.7.

In this perspective, what we call a translation, in the sense of the *translatum*, is the format in which the meaning and the form of the translated text are given back to the world, namely to a culture of readers different from the culture of readers in which it originated. The possible contrast between the involved two cultures may affect the transfer, but in particular, it contributes to the exchange of ideas, norms, concepts, and formal aesthetic sensitivities in a multicultural world. The perceived cultural "strangeness" of a literary "translatum" is in itself a value, in the sense that it widens the horizon of the receiving culture. A pragmatic normalization of the alterity of the translatum would be a culturally protective gesture keeping the reception limited to intra-cultural translata and thus limiting the effect of the exchange.

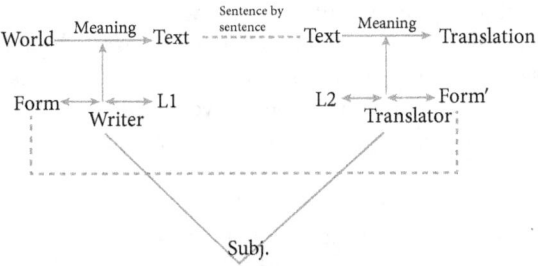

The subject as writer and as translator

Figure 10.7 The actant dynamics of translating.

A Poetic Translation

To illustrate the inter-actantial dynamics of form and language in the two actantial settings, here is a recent translation of a Swedish poem by a modern classic, the great Swedish-speaking Finnish poet Edith Södergran (1892–1923) into the English of a young American poet, Brooklyn Copeland (b. 1984):

Edith Södergran	Brooklyn Copeland
Animalisk hymn[18]	*Animalistic Hymn*

Den röda solen går upp	The red sun rises
Utan tankar	without intent
Och är lika mot alla.	And shines the same on all of us.
Vi fröjda os åt solen såsom barn.	We play like children under the sun.
Det kommer en dag då vort stoft skall sönderfalla,	One day, our ashes will scatter –
Det är detsamma när det sker.	It doesn't matter when.
Nu lyser solen in i våra hjartans innersta vrå	Now the sun finds our innermost hearts,
Fyllande allt med tanklöshet	fills us with oblivion
Stark som skogen, vintern och havet.	Intense as the forest, winter and sea.

This translation of a poem almost a century older by a young contemporary poet is rather characteristic of the work we currently find in international journals dedicated to poetry. It respects elementary formal requirements such as a number of lines equal to that of the original; its punctuation and syntax stay in contact with that of the source text,[19] albeit with some variation, and thereby obtains a tone of voice close to the source.

Variations from Södergran (ES) to Copeland (BC) include the following:

1. Line 2: ES: *tankar*, thoughts, plural, becomes BC: *intent*; the sun has no special intentions. In the original, the sun does not have *thoughts* at all, which is a bit more radical. It does not *think* that some people deserve special treatment.
2. Line 3: ES: The sun treats everybody the same way. BC: it *shines* the same way on all. In ES, the sun is thus an intentional person who is an egalitarian and acknowledges others without discrimination; in BC, it just shines equally on the shinees, like any meteorological state or event would do. The original is again more radical; the sun is actively egalitarian, not just a neutral mechanical luminary.
3. Line 4: ES: we *rejoice* (fröjdas) at the sun like children; BC: we *play* under the sun. Lexical error. Children are likely to play, but that is not what the ES text has, and ES is both more hymnic and more emotional than the behavioral BC, who plays but does not rejoice.
4. Lines 5–7: ES the fatal future, *shall*, BC: *will*... not so fatal, rather probabilistic. ES has a longer line (5) to fatalize the point, but ll. 5–7 still generally work out

well. In l. 7, when ES has *lyser* (shines), this time BC has *finds*, personalizing the sun. I suspect that the *shining* here means blessing, reflecting the Bible's Psalm 66 (Hebrew 67), the morning prayer. The poem's first line describes a sunrise. Intertextuality should oblige the translator to let such a reference be heard. The title of the poem would support it.

5. Line 8: ES: filling everything with *thoughtlessness* (*tanklöshet*); BC ... *oblivion*, negation of remembering, which in a sense comes close but does not take up the clear and evident correlation between ll. 2 and 8: the absence of *thoughts*, the animalistic blessing.
6. Line 9, the cadence: ES: *strong* (stark), BC: *intense*—does this predicate qualify the sun or the thoughtlessness? The syntactic parallelism *fyllande* (filling)/*stark* would seem to indicate that the subject is the sun; the absence of parallelism in BC gives privilege to the alternative, thoughtlessness, which may explain the lexical choice of a mental concept (*oblivion*). ES's filling *all things* becomes filling *us* in the translation! (translators, beware of the quantifiers, they scaffold the text). But again, if we follow ES's syntax, the strength of the sun is compared to that of the *forest*, the *winter*, and the *sea* (why does BC drop the articles on the latter two nouns but not on the first? ES keeps all three articles, monumentally). So, the strong sun, connoting a summer scenario, is aligned with winter and strong cold; life and joy are aligned with death, ashes and dust (*stoft*). The forest and the sea can freeze, as they can flow or grow—strength in life and strength in the approach to death would characterize the optimistic Nietzschean enunciation of the existential attitude of the human animal. The entities mentioned, forest, winter, and sea, are not (BC) *intense*, as the *experience* of Californian subjects in the sun at the beach may be—but *intensity* here would lead to a different philosophy, a modern carpe diem figure, or a doctrine of desire, more likely to be present in BC's own writing.[20]

We see how sensitive an interpretation is to the apparently simple lexical choices of the translator in poetry.

A Last Consideration

Translation is essential to the existence of *meaning* as such, since mental contents have to be signified, and *variably signified*, by the mind, and to itself, in order to be consciously intended to potentially be shared by other minds. Mental contents become impersonal *thoughts* of some kind, when this happens. Animal minds do not seem to variably signify their immediate concepts, so in that sense, animals do not "think," as Descartes mused; phenomenologists may call their mental activity *prereflective*.[21] But humans, as other animals, do practice prereflective experiencing, of course, and this is what Södergran refers to. She writes masterfully around it—writing around things is what poetry basically does—and treats it as a source of strength, as we have seen. It is a prereflective and pre-semiotic source of meaning, without *yet* being meaningful—not yet being a "thought." It can be described, as can everything

else, but it cannot, in itself, be translated. Here is the radically untranslatable. Only strong empathy can approach it: Love. Therefore, literary translators must love the text they translate, and therefore, Love, Meaning, and Translation are inseparable.
Quod erat demonstrandum.

Notes

1. Roman Jakobson, in his totally wonderful little essay "On Linguistic Aspects of Translation" (Brower 1966, an important anthology of specialists' reflections on translation), elegantly distinguishes *intralingual* translation, that is, rewording within the same language; *interlingual* translation (proper), transfer of textual meaning from one language to another; and *intersemiotic* translation, transfer from text to signs of nonverbal sign systems. The quotation is from Brower, p. 236.
2. The effect of the belief that translation is impossible by definition is to consider (good) translations as *miracles* and never to criticize translations, since you are not supposed to criticize miracles. This is damaging to the ethics of translation.
3. The individual mind communicates to itself and to other minds, present or absent, incessantly, by the fact of having and representing thoughts; and in order to be able to have thoughts at all, the mind must possess an *eidetic format* allowing it to build, hold, vary, copy, negate, change single ideas within each thought; a huge cognitive set of capacities is involved.
4. The view itself has been defended since the logical rationalism of the seventeenth and eighteenth centuries and further developed in the nineteenth century by the new science called psychology, before cognitive psychology and *Gestalt*-based phenomenology in the twentieth century took it over and made it relevant to linguistics and semiotics.
5. My favorite example is Danish philosopher K. Hvidtfelt Nielsen (2003), *Interpreting Spinoza's Arguments*. The first three sentences of his volume read: "In this book, I shall argue that verbal meanings are unique events happening in two equally problematic elements, or regions: mind and time, the mental and the temporal. Strictly unrepeatable and transient by nature, verbal meanings defy direct accessing by any kind of cognitively motivated understanding. / Further, I shall argue that verbal meanings happen in ways, or under circumstances, to make us systematically suppress or overlook their incompatibility with understanding." Martin Heidegger, Ludwig Wittgenstein, and Jacques Derrida are often associated with this anti-semantic and sometimes "deconstructive" stance.
6. See Brandt (2015).
7. Example: "She gave me a good idea." A conceptual metaphor: COMMUNICATION IS EXCHANGING OBJECTS, according to Reddy (1979).
8. The expression *sharing ideas* would of course manifest another metaphor: IDEAS ARE CAKES ..., if we use the A-is-B conceptual metaphor formula; however, this A-is-B model is not the only one in the field. Blending can explain the sense-making of metaphor. See Brandt and Brandt (2005) and L. Brandt (2013).
9. Apparently, human beings are laughing at language itself or at the absurd semantic scenarios that language generates in these cases.
10. Semiotic blending theory would in fact be an efficient analytic tool here. Cf. note 8, above.

11 Semiotic recursion simply means that both the instance of Expression (E) and the instance of Content (C) in a semiotic function (f) can be unfolded as other semiotic functions: E f C → (E f C) f (E f C), and so on.
12 Philosophers mainly write for philosophers, and they need to both singularize their work and make it known and influential. They also constantly have to translate each other's thinking into their own singular idiolect, including interlingually, which gives rise to quite a lot of despair and confusion and to a rich field of intertextual exchanges.
13 The semiotic square is a simple representation of semantic oppositions distinguishing contraries and contradictions, inspired by the Danish linguist V. Brøndal. See Greimas and Courtés (1979).
14 Umberto Eco's famous *lector in fabula* (1979) should be supplemented with an *author in fabula*, which would be the entity concerned by this transference.
15 This effect is less important in commercial translation; here, the intersubjective "binding" that exists in literary and philosophical translation is less strong, and the emphasis is instead on the pragmatic "message" of the translated text, not on the full range of expressive properties of the source text, including the singular *enunciative personhood* that "binds" the noncommercial translator.
16 See Greimas (1966).
17 Greimas imported the notion of *actant* from Lucien Tesnière's stemmatic syntax, where the notion corresponds to that of nominal complement.
18 From: *Framtidens skugga* ([The shadow of the future] 1920). Translated by Brooklyn Copeland IN: *POETRY*, June 2011, "The Translation Issue," p. 235.
19 This is by no means a trivial requirement, since it is not respected in commercial translation. In philosophy and poetry, by contrast, it is essential, because every sentence comes with its own specific enunciative quality and intentional (performative) value, so sentence embeddings and sentence cuts will change the discursive sound of the result. In poetry, metrical and free verse lines must be respected, as they are essential to the rhythmic textual flow; line breaks are musical events, since they can happen in counterpoint to grammatical structure and instead be motivated by principles of prosody/writing.
20 Brooklyn Copeland, who lives in Indiana, is the editor of a journal of poetry, music, and translation, *TAIGA* (Russian word meaning boreal forest, snowforest).
21 In the sense of Merleau-Ponty (1945).

References

Brandt, L., 2013. *The Communicative Mind*. Cambridge: Cambridge Scholars.
Brandt, P. A., 2015. "Culture, Creativity, and Conceptual Dynamics. A Structural Hypothesis." In: (Ed.) P. Hanenberg, *A New Visibility: On Culture, Translation and Cognition*. Lisbon: Universidade Catolica Editora.
Brandt, L., and P. A. Brandt, 2005. "Making Sense of a Blend. A Cognitive-semiotic Approach to Metaphor." In: (Ed.) F. Ruiz Mendoza, *Annual Review of Cognitive Linguistics 3*, 216–249 Amsterdam: John Benjamins.
Brower, R. A. (Ed.), 1966. *On Translation*. Ney York: Oxford University Press.
Greimas, A. J., 1966. *Sémantique structurale. Recherche de méthode*. Paris: Larousse.
Greimas, A. J., and Joseph Courtés, 1979. *Sémiotique. Dictionnaire raisonné de la théorie du langage*. Paris: Hachette Université.

Hvidtfelt Nielsen, K., 2003. *Interpreting Spinoza's Arguments—Toward a Formal Theory of Consistent Language Scepticism. Imitating Ethica.* New York: Edwin Mellen Press.
Merleau-Ponty, M., 1945. *Phénoménologie de la perception.* Paris: Gallimard.
Reddy, M. J., 1979. "The Conduit Metaphor: A Case of Frame Conflict in Our Language about Language." In: (Ed.) A. Ortony, *Metaphor and Thought.* Cambridge: Cambridge University Press.

11

Elements in Poetic Imagination

Hans-Erik Larsen in memoriam

Introduction

The purpose[1] of this chapter is to demonstrate how cognitive and traditional poetic interpretations can be complementary, using as examples two familiar nature poems. William Wordsworth is one of the first romantics, and the modern poet William Butler Yeats called himself one of the last. "I Wandered Lonely as a Cloud" (1802) and "The Wild Swans at Coole" (1917) were written about a century apart, the first in the Lake Country of Britain and the second in the west country of Ireland.[2] Both poems depict the poets as solitary individuals on walks who come upon extraordinary natural sights—a vast field of daffodils and a large flock of swans, respectively. They even give their experiences similar poetic forms: six-line stanzas, each with alternating rhymes and a closing couplet. Upon later reflection these events come to have very different yet equally profound personal meanings for the two poets.

The meanings of experiences like these are not inherent in the immediate perception of ongoing events in the present but are developed in the imaginary of the experiencer. The human imaginary has a structure of its own, which determines basic features of what makes experiences meaningful. The experienced space, including the interplay and contrasts of the natural elements, has emotional meaning for the subject; proximal and distal phenomena recalled have or take on distinct thymic values, euphoric or dysphoric. The hypothesis of the cognitive existence of not only one but three distinct imaginaries—a bio-imaginary, a socio-imaginary, and a phantasmatic imaginary—makes it possible to decode and more distinctly interpret spatial descriptions present in these texts, and thus to elucidate the functioning of events and spatial unfoldings in the meaning production of poetic texts.

A Cognitive System of the Elements

Humans, and probably higher animals as well, experience the outer world in terms of foregrounded *objects* and backgrounded *elements*. We perceive the difference between *solid* soil, rock, and *liquid* streams, ponds, lakes, oceans; our bodily and technical behavior while traveling along paths—which is what we mainly do—depends on the substances we have to interact with. The *air*, the wind, the sky itself with its clouds, changing weather, and heavenly bodies are all instances of another element that competes with the solid and the liquid in authority. Human cultures have imagined divinities defined by these elements, and pictorial art has celebrated the beauty of their appearances. Even musical imagination is predominantly element-driven; we easily associate "landscapes" and "sound-scapes."[3] The elements are frequently active in metaphorical imagery describing our moods, emotions, and passions. If it is true that we most often "think" in terms of objects, we typically "feel" in terms of elements.[4]

The elements are of course almost omnipresent in our sensory perception;[5] while they are all given to us in more than one sense modality, there is, however, an experiential difference with regard to their physicality: an element is *proximal* as opposed to *distal* if it is associated with tactile, olfactory, or gustative sensing, and it is distal if it is mostly only seen or heard. So /water/ is proximal, and /air/ is distal, while /earth/ is in between, so to speak. Our body relates to them by observing and emulating swimming, walking, and flying beings. The elements form a simple binary paradigm with a neutral middle value. Our hypothesis, following Larsen (1996),[6] is that this paradigm, and its phenomenological variations, forms a significant and strongly structuring scaffolding of the human spatial imaginary as manifested by aesthetic expressions and by affective representations in general.

Space with its foregrounds (objects) and backgrounds (elements) is a "grounding" property of the imagination. However, it comes in significantly distinct versions in the human imaginary.[7] In one version we cognize and recognize ourselves as having sensitive bodies that breathe, sleep, and wake, have a beating heart, and give us both pain and pleasure. The presence and the absence of other persons in this space of intimacy, the first space we experience when newborn, are felt as proximal and distal states of these others. A "bath" in the "waves" of caresses (cf. the liquid element, by analogy) will contrast the dry and windy emptiness and loneliness (cf. air, by analogy) felt when the (significant) other is away. By default, presence and proximity are evaluated as *euphoric*, whereas absence and distance are evaluated as *dysphoric*. The paradigm now carries a system of "phoric" or *thymic*[8] values. In this version or register, which is called the *bio-imaginary* (Larsen), the proximity of the other is euphoric, while distality is dysphoric. Objects and Others will circulate between these opposite zones in the bio-imaginary.

A dynamic model of the bio-imaginary can be obtained by using a cusp topology (Thom 1972, Brandt 1995, Larsen 1996), as in Figure 11.1.

This is a thymic paradigm that is extremely frequently found in existential descriptions: loneliness, solitude versus togetherness, company. In Greimas' formal terminology this is the "junctive" logic, disjunction versus conjunction, of Subject and Object (Greimas and Courtés 1979).

There is a second version or register of the imaginary, this time corresponding to the social domain in general cognition and correspondingly named the *socio-imaginary*. It offers an *inverse thymic investment*: the distal is now "perspective," "vision," and "mission," and so on, euphoric valorization of political idealism as opposed to proximal promiscuity, "amiguismo," "mafia," too close connexions, conspiracy,

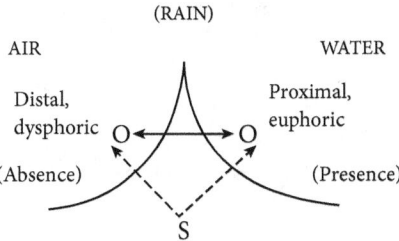

Figure 11.1 The strata of the bio-imaginary space.

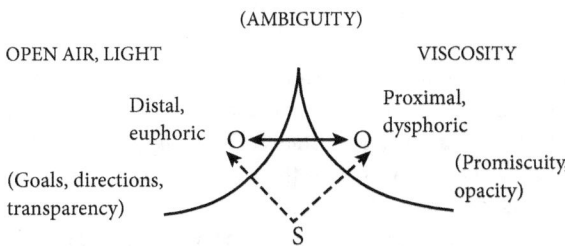

Figure 11.2 The strata of the socio-imaginary space.

corruption, and so forth. Furthermore, the dysphoric masses (massively proximal) contrast the distal, euphoric hero who stands forth, stands alone, and indicate the direction of "progress," and so on. Far from being a modern phenomenon, the social cult of the "outstanding" individual or performance is manifest in historiography worldwide.

A dynamic model of the socio-imaginary therefore looks like Figure 11.2.

Social space, the socio-imaginary, is as important to humans as the intimate bodily (bio-)space; however, its thymic orientation contradicts that of the bio-imaginary, because the Subject experiences it as "emancipation" from intimacy. There may be an ontogenetic dimension in this phenomenon—the passage to adulthood seen as entering a new space of possible identities, built either on "sticky" alliances or on bright general ideas, exemplary deeds for others to follow (or on both). This paradigm is of course independent of particular ideologies; these are, in turn, emotionally dependent on the socio-imaginary, and much discursive *pathos* is built on imagery copied directly from its dynamic morphology. On the other hand, neurotic agoraphobia may be a suffering grounded in a Subject's socio-imaginary dysphoria.[9]

Thirdly, there is a "post-social" space, a wider, more abstract, often more "mental" and fantastic, dream-like, *phantasmatic imaginary* (Larsen). Here, the context of the Subject is nature, *physis*, the universe, cosmos, and identifies as a (spiritual) Self enjoying, as in the first paradigm, the presence of others—animals, other spirits, for example in a religious community—while fearing the infinite, silent, inscrutable world. Individual solitude is as existential as in the bio-imaginary, but now it is cosmic, metaphysical.

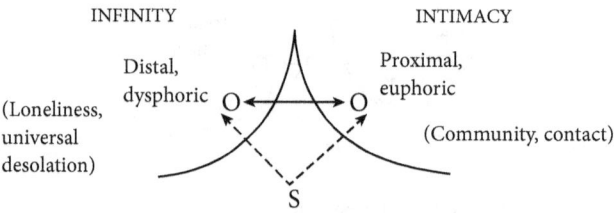

Figure 11.3 The strata of the phantasmatic imaginary.

There is often, as in the former versions, a complex zone in which the opposed elements merge, so that the distal and the proximal coincide ecstatically: a sacred fusion of the infinite and the communitary. In states of love, mystical elevation, or psychosis, the Subject will experience contact with the divine, an oxymoronic closeness of the infinitely distant, the intimacy of the universe.

A dynamic model of the phantasmatic imaginary then looks like Figure 11.3.

This paradigm is oriented thymically the same way as the bio-imaginary, and it can appear superimposed on it, which often happens in dreams and hallucinations.

The human imaginary, analyzed in a series of thymic element spaces (where each element can carry opposite values, depending on which imaginary space it is an element of), constitutes a series of representational settings and of avatars for the Subject. It experiences the "I" as a body, a social identity, and a self—facing corresponding avatars of the "you" or the "other."

In art, and thus in poetry, we find expressions of processes that can be read as itineraries through each of the imaginary topologies and as changes, transitions from one to another topology. In some poetic texts we even find processes leading us through all of the three registers, the bio-imaginary, the socio-imaginary, and the phantasmatic imaginary. This is what we intend to show in the following section. We are not aware of other cognitive inquiries into such thymic unfoldings of the experienced space and its figurative relation to the natural elements.[10]

Readings of the Poems. The Bio-imaginary

Wordsworth's poem (Wordsworth 1932) foregrounds the Subject from the first word on.[11] Yet with the surprising cloud simile (mirrored on the page by the poem's floating title), he also distances himself by an analogy narrowly based on parallel motions of walking and floating rather than on its shared shape or consciousness:

I Wandered Lonely As a Cloud
I wandered lonely as a cloud
That floats on high o'er vales and hills

When all at once I saw a crowd,
A host, of golden daffodils;
Beside the lake, beneath the trees,
Fluttering and dancing in the breeze.

His feeling isolated and cut off from the nature around him is expressed by euphoric water particles that are dissipated in the dysphoric element of air. We know from his sister Dorothy's *Journal* (Wordsworth 1941) that she accompanied him on this walk in April 1802, so his loneliness is Wordsworth's poetic strategy to exclude human society. In fact, her own more literal account offers some instructive contrasts to his poem. She reports that along the way they happened to see an empty boat "floating in the middle of the bay" (131), a likely source for the cloud simile once Wordsworth had naturalized and displaced the boat from the euphoric water. Psychologically, he is in two places at once—walking along the ground and looking down from the sky on the lakeshore where he would appear as just a speck. His surprise at coming upon the daffodils in the otherwise unremarkable rural landscape brings him back down to earth, like water, euphoric in the bio-imaginary.

In his own opening stanza (Yeats 1933) Yeats takes a more gradual approach, delaying the Subject's actual appearance on the scene by using the autumnal setting to reflect the minor compensations of his own dry autumnal stage of life. As Hazard Adams writes, "The swans float among the stones at Coole in a real and allegorical autumn" (109, Adams 1990). The collective objects—trees, paths, stones, swans—have as their background the singular and unifying water:

The Wild Swans at Coole
The trees are in their autumn beauty,
The woodland paths are dry,
Under the October twilight the water
Mirrors a still sky;
Upon the brimming water among the stones
Are nine-and-fifty swans.

He has apparently walked to the lake, but the only visible activity is in nature where the "brimming" water "Mirrors a still sky," bringing its vast distance close. The poem's manuscripts show that Yeats originally wrote "the water is low" (Bradford 49), a common condition in the autumn, but he makes it share the contagious energy of the swans, whose presence is delayed dramatically until the stanza's last word. The swans themselves are close to shore "among the stones" and stationary enough to be readily counted. Fifty-nine is an unusually large number of swans, and Yeats, unlike Wordsworth, emphasizes the exactitude of his census. In the manuscript he had first tried both 45 and 47, numbers also approximating his own age of 51, and he makes them all odd to match his own unpaired condition (Bradford 59). Overall this first stanza reflects the proximal elements of earth and water; in contrast to Wordsworth's alienated self-image as a cloud, Yeats' sky is grounded visually in the lake water.[12]

The Socio-imaginary

The lonely Wordsworth suddenly "saw a crowd, / A host, of golden daffodils." Before he identifies them as flowers he uses collective human terms. Positioned like Yeats' swans, they are "beside the lake, beneath the trees." He next activates the static crowd so that they are "fluttering and dancing in the breeze." Their "fluttering" suggests a frustrated flight propelled by the wind, and the dancing metaphor implies an ongoing pattern of movement that is naturally limited to a unified bending in the breeze. If the distant cloud conveyed his melancholy, his visual distance from the flowers releases positive feelings, as the socio-imaginary valorizes the air and space necessary for observation. It is essential to both poetic experiences that the daffodils and the swans are large collectives and also wild. Their power to surprise would be neutralized if found in the more common setting of a city park, for example.

Wordsworth's second remarkable simile extends far beyond his earlier self-image as a cloud to the cosmic space of the Milky Way, a striking visual parallel to the yellow flowers, although what he stresses is their continuity:

> Continuous as the stars that shine
> And twinkle on the milky way,
> They stretch in never-ending line
> Along the margin of a bay:
> Ten thousand saw I at a glance,
> Tossing their heads in sprightly dance.

The reader's imagined background shifts abruptly from a sunny day to a clear night sky of infinite space, and the fiery twinkling gives the stars an illusory motion. His sister Dorothy had faithfully noted that the few daffodils scattered before and after the full field do not "disturb the simplicity, unity and life of that one busy highway" (132), a conventional metaphor with the same point. Wordsworth confirms the Milky Way metaphor with "stretched in never-ending line / along the margin of a bay." Continuity in space is matched by unity in time: he sees them "all at once" and "at a glance." Instead of Yeats' precise fifty-nine, Wordsworth numbers them emotively as "ten thousand," as innumerable as the stars themselves and contrasting implicitly with the singular observer.

Returning to the dance metaphor, he next adds to their personification "Tossing their heads in sprightly dance." Although dancers normally make more use of their arms and legs, the flowers are, of course, rooted in the earth. Dorothy noticed that some flowers even "rested their heads upon these stones" (131) as if on pillows, but any hint of their fatigue is banished from her brother's vision. Unlike Yeats' paired swans, the daffodils confront Wordsworth with a huge unpaired and asexual collective. Water is still present in this socio-imaginary phase, but it is also subject to the wind and subordinated to the breeze-blown flowers that "outdid the sparkling waves in glee."

While Wordsworth's enthusiasm is implied in his lively description of the flowers, when he comes to express it directly it sounds more like his professional duty than a spontaneous impulse: "A poet could not but be gay / In such a jocund company," where "company" reduces the earlier "crowd" and "host" to a more manageable domestic gathering. Instead of himself swaying with the flowers in the wind, for example, he keeps his visual distance: "I gazed—and gazed—but little thought / What wealth the show to me had brought." His fascination excluded all thoughts of the future, but in retrospect he unifies and reduces the flowers to an artificial "show" that provided unexpected "wealth" with its buried metaphor of golden flowers.

Like Wordsworth, Yeats presents himself as a solitary person confronting an uncontrolled and active natural collective. Unlike Wordsworth he delays his Subject until the scene has been well established, and even then he identifies himself not by his passing mood but as the regular census-taker of Coole's swans over nineteen years:

> The nineteenth autumn has come upon me
> Since I first made my count;
> I saw, before I had well finished,
> All suddenly mount
> And scattered wheeling in great broken rings
> Upon their clamorous wings.

His own contact is not a once-in-a-lifetime surprise, but his regular end-of-summer ritual. His Subject that enters the poem with a historical precision like that of the fifty-nine swans has remained constant, whereas their number and identities are bound to vary from year to year, an obvious fact he omits. The first time he counted the wild swans they almost eluded his enumeration, an event he recalls so vividly that his memory becomes a present experience for the reader. Like Wordsworth's sudden seeing the field of dancing daffodils, Yeats had seen the swans "suddenly mount..." In the manuscript he admits that his intrusion had frightened them into flight (Bradford 1965, 50), but here he gives them their own agency. To emphasize their effortless "conquest" of the air, he also omits the ornithological detail that swans are so heavy that they must first gain momentum by "running" on the water, a fact his friend George Moore had noted at this very location (191). Yeats also has them "climb the air" like humans scaling a ladder.

While Wordsworth's daffodils move as an undifferentiated unit, Yeats' swans are less organized in their flight, although terms "scatter" and "broken" are shaped by "wheeling" and "rings." The flowers sway silently to the wind's uneven rhythm, whereas Yeats emphasizes the swans' noise both in the present and nineteen years earlier when the ordered, harmonious "bell-beat of their wings" prompted his own sympathetic response and as he "trod with a lighter tread," as if sharing their levitation in the euphoric element of air:

> I have looked upon those brilliant creatures,
> And now my heart is sore.
> All's changed since I, hearing at twilight,
> The first time on this shore,

The bell-beat of their wings above my head,
Trod with a lighter tread.

A vivid memory recurs for Yeats as it does for Wordsworth, but its psychological impact is quite different. Both poets have kinesthetic responses to the collectives in nature; for Yeats this is physical and set in the past, whereas for Wordsworth it is metaphorical and set in the future. Yeats' swan memory only reminds him of the losses of aging, the difference he feels in himself between then and now. As Hazard Adams writes of the swans, "Time is their milieu even as they seem to be beyond time as the poet understands it" (109). Wordsworth can dance in his imagination as he could not in person, while Yeats can no longer fly with the swans in his imagination. His memory also requires annual renewal, although his diminished response is sudden rather than gradual. Yeats' heart is "sore" with loss, whereas Wordsworth's heart "with pleasure fills."

Recalling his youthful response leads Yeats to describe the "unwearied" swans in terms that contrast implicitly with his own situation:

Unwearied still, lover by lover,
They paddle in the cold
Companionable streams or climb the air,
Their hearts have not grown old;
Passion or conquest, wander where they will,
Attend upon them still.

They are "lover by lover" while he remains painfully solitary.[13] In the swans' own bio-imaginary realm the cold streams are "companionable," because they are insulated as humans are not, making water dysphoric for Yeats. "The streams, like Keats's 'cold pastoral urn,' have an oxymoronic quality..." (Adams 110). Yeats assumes that "Their hearts have not grown old," implying that his has, and the swans are still driven by the energy for sexual "passion or conquest" that he lacks. Even worse than his aging is the fact that time also reduces the "desire from which he derives his power to transfigure the world" (Bell 2006, 38) through his art. Of course, the daffodils' fleeting mood of gaiety is much easier to share than the swans' continuous and active passion. Like Wordsworth on his walk, the swans "wander where they will," while Yeats seems tied down by fatigue and duties. He feels that he should be able to match their vitality; however, unlike Wordsworth Yeats doesn't make explicit his special public role as a poet, which would be already well known to his readers.

For both solitary poets these nonhuman collectives are appealing as natural communities, but as uncontrollable masses they also threaten their independence as heroes of the human imagination, so they appreciate them but they keep a safe distance. As Michel Serres (Serres 1995) points out, "the aggregate as such is not a well-formed object; it seems irrational to us" compared to either a unity or to distinct individuals (2 or 3). To the poets these appearances of irrationality in nature are both memorably attractive and unsettling.

The Phantasmatic Imaginary

That the swans are wild and, therefore, always free to wander elsewhere leads Yeats to imagine their disappearance from Coole Lake and from his own life. The poem originally ended with the previous stanza, a more despairing conclusion. In adding the final consolation, he first reconfirms their stable positions as in the first stanza. At this point Yeats can risk conventional adjectives because the swans' sustained power and passion have been firmly established:

> But now they drift on the still water,
> Mysterious, beautiful;
> Among what rushes will they build,
> By what lake's edge or pool
> Delight men's eyes when I awake some day
> To find they have flown away?

In this phantasmic phase water regains its euphoric value, and it is "still" rather than "brimming," while the sky becomes the dysphoric means of their imagined disappearance. This "now," the second one after "now my heart is sore," turns impersonal. In this wide-angle pictorial view, they "drift" rather than actively "paddle," and he feels no further need to humanize them.

Like Wordsworth's poem, this one ends with Yeats' move from outdoor nature to indoor reflections perhaps in his bed at Coole Park where he spent many summers from 1897 on. For the last stanza he omits the walk to the Lake along those "woodland paths," imagining a future when he "awake[s] some day / To find they have flown away," having left permanently during the night rather than just circling before relanding on Coole Lake.[14] The future location of their new home is the poem's final and unanswerable question: Where will they build nests and raise the next generation? If it happened at Coole, this would be a good omen as Yeats suggested to Lady Gregory (Jeffares 1968, 156). That they will "delight men's eyes" elsewhere is his generous projection into future time and space, even though the pleasure he imagines for them sounds conventional enough—they won't appreciate them as intensely as he has. In practical terms the swans' departure would spare him the contrast bound to become more painful as he ages, yet it would also end his reassuring census ritual. In theory he could treasure his many swan memories to excite his own "inward eye," but unlike Wordsworth Yeats needs repeated contact to feed his imagination, so the final feeling in his poem is one of an anticipated future loss that is philosophically accepted rather than a heightened feeling of imaginative recovery and renewal.

In keeping with Wordsworth's well-known theory of poetry-writing as motivated by "emotion recollected in tranquillity" rather than immediate experiences (Bate 1991, 344), he describes how visual memories of the daffodils repeatedly "flash upon that inward eye," apparently prompting him to write the poem some two years later:

> For oft, when on my couch I lie
> In vacant or in pensive mood,

They flash upon that inward eye
Which is the bliss of solitude;
And then my heart with pleasure fills,
And dances with the daffodils.

Corresponding to the phantasmic phase he has moved indoors where he is alone and lying on his couch—the opposite of dancing by the lake. His spatial experience of the daffodil-filled shore that he extended metaphorically to the vast Milky Way has contracted to within four walls. However, his initial mood is similar: he may not feel cloud-lonely, but he is "vacant" or "pensive"—empty or almost melancholy. The sudden memory of the daffodils demonstrates the "bliss of solitude" that he believes in. Instead of a one-time sight, this memory of the daffodils recurs spontaneously in his "inward eye" without him feeling alienated from the earth and the collective of flowers. When this visual memory happens to recur, its effect on Wordsworth is both physical and emotional: "And then my heart with pleasure fills / And dances with the daffodils." The euphorically fluid emotion generated by this vivid scene energizes his heart to dance with the flowers, whereas in their actual presence he merely felt "gay." If he had chosen to do so, Wordsworth could have returned every spring to view these vivid perennials; in Yeatsian fashion he could even have measured the expansion of their bed as they self-propagated along the lakeshore. But his fantasies of the daffodils provide a more intense satisfaction to him than did the experience itself.

Conclusions

In terms of the cognitive theory of the elements in artworks, it is revealing that in these poems both poets progress from outdoor encounters with unexpected and thought-provoking objects to indoor feelings and reflections, as different as they are for Wordsworth and Yeats. Having observed these large collectives from a distance, both poets withdraw to a "post-social" mental space of solitude in keeping with the phantasmatic imaginary. That they find there "a sacred fusion of the infinite and the community" is less apparent for Yeats than for Wordsworth. If for the latter nature is almost divine, the images that flash on his "inward eye" bringing the distant daffodils up close create the sacred "bliss of solitude" in which he can also join them in their communal dance, momentarily fusing the individual and the collective.

As a romantic/modernist writing a century later, Yeats' progression through the three imaginaries is inevitably somewhat different from Wordsworth's. Yeats' experience of nature is primarily one of loss. From the beginning of the poem the Subject is subordinated, first to a description of the landscape and later to the swans for whom he has been the dutiful census-taker over nineteen years, and he is now the elderly man envying the sexual energy of their pairings. Nevertheless, Yeats feels that the swans retain the life force that he is losing with age, so when he reluctantly imagines their disappearance from Coole Lake, he is also contemplating his own disappearance in death. His phantasmatic "fusion of the infinite and community" is one of imagining his immortal soul being still in contact with the eternal swans and their anonymous appreciators. Just as Wordsworth ends by reflecting on the source of his poetic creativity—the images that "flash upon that inward eye"—so Yeats' swans suggest an analogy to his poems that he hopes will "delight men's eyes" after his death. As Jahan Ramazani (Ramazani 1990) notes, "Overcoming the sad thought of loss, Yeats celebrates indirectly his aesthetic gain" (145).

If the cognitive poetics of the elements does bring a new perspective to more traditional readings of these two well-known poems, revealing patterns that might otherwise be overlooked, we cannot claim for our approach any universal relevance, even to the other nineteenth and twentieth-century nature poems in the long romantic tradition. However, it is instructive to find a similar sequence of imaginaries in "Watching Fireflies" by the eighth-century Chinese poet Tu Fu:

Fireflies from the Enchanted Mountains
come through the screen this autumn night
and settle on my shirt

my lute and my books grow cold

outside, above the eaves
they are hard to tell from the stars

they sail over the well
each reflecting a mate

in the garden they pass chrysanthemums
flares of color against the dark

white-haired and sad
I try to read their code
wanting a prediction:
will I be here next year
to watch them.[15]

Notes

1 This chapter is coauthored by Professor John Hobbs of Oberlin College, Ohio. It was published in *Cognitive Semiotics*, 2, 2008.
2 Wordsworth first published the poem in 1807. He later added the second stanza, the version we will discuss here. As Yeats' most recent biographer R.F. Foster (2003) points out, Yeats had been studying Wordsworth's poetry around the time that he wrote "The Wild Swans at Coole" (82).
3 For descriptions of musical imagination, see Brandt (2013).
4 Elements are unbounded objects. The Aristotelian metaphysical distinction between homeomeres, unbounded masses, and anhomeomeres, bounded things, corresponds to the distinction in René Thom's semio-physics, between continuous and discontinuous being. See Wildgen (2004).

5   Outdoors perception is element-dominated, whereas indoors perception is object-dominated. This phenomenological difference is crucial to the representation of space in poetry. Lautréamont's celebrated simile *"beau comme la rencontre fortuite sur une table de dissection d'une machine à coudre et d'un parapluie"*—"as beautiful as the chance meeting on a dissecting-table of a sewing-machine and an umbrella" is clearly an indoors construction and perhaps also a signal of a change in space apperception in certain forms of modern poetry.
6   In this pioneering book, Hans-Erik Larsen applies an elaborate element morphology to readings of poetry by Kierkegaard, Bjørnvig, Johnsson, Grotrian and to interpretations of paintings by Turner and Hopper.
7   The three space forms we are going to consider—the bio-imaginary, the socio-imaginary, and the phantasmatic imaginary—correspond closely to the experiential-semantic domains D5-7, that is, *oikos, polis, hieron*, as presented in Brandt (2004: 55).
8   "Thymic" means bodily valued (euphoric means bodily attractive, dysphoric means bodily repellent). The term is used as in Greimas and Courtes (1979).
9   Political metaphors of navigation (Mao the Helmsman), of kinship (Garcia Marquez' La Mama Grande), and so on, can be understood in this spatial context.
10 A comparison with earlier element readings of this type would be Gaston Bachelard's (1964) work, inspired by phenomenological philosophy, psychoanalysis, and structural literary criticism.
11 While some interpreters might distinguish between the poets and the speakers of these two poems, there are such obvious biographical aspects to each that the effort seems unnecessary. And since poems are not fictions, they do not depend on a fictive narrator—but instead on a certain identity of tone. The first person in poetry is in general much closer to the author's first-personhood.
12 Yeats had his own occult theories of the elements. While staying at Coole Park, he told his friend George Moore (Moore 1985) one morning that he "felt a great deal of aridness in [his] nature, and need of moisture, and was making the most tremendous invocations with water" (Moore 189).
13 As he told an American professor, the poem was written in a mood of intense depression, having again failed to persuade his lifelong love Maud Gonne to marry him and having no other prospects (Jeffares 154–155).
14 As Yeats informed Moore, these swans visited lakes all over Galway and Mayo, but they always had returned to Coole in the autumn (Moore 191).
15 From Young (1990: 110). Reproduced with kind permission of the translator and publisher.

References

Adams, H., 1990. *The Book of Yeats's Poems*. Tallahassee: Florida State University Press.
Bachelard, G., 1964. *The Poetics of Space*. Trans. Maria Jolas. New York: Orion Press.
Bate, J., 1991. *Romantic Ecology: Wordsworth and the Environmental Tradition*. London: Routledge.
Bell, V., 2006. *Yeats and the Logic of Formalism*. Columbia, MS: University of Missouri Press.

Brandt, P. A., 1995. "The Onto-morphology of Meaning. Elements of a Structural Analysis of the Imaginary. *Morphologies of Meaning*. Aarhus: Aarhus University Press.

Brandt, P. A., 2004. "The Architecture of Semantic Domains." In: *Spaces, Domains, and Meaning. Essays in Cognitive Semiotics*, 33–67, Bern: European Semiotics, 4, Peter Lang Verlag.

Brandt, P. A., 2013. "Weather Reports: Discourse and Musical Cognition." In: (Eds.) A. H. Clark and K. Chapin. *Speaking of Music. Addressing the Sonorous*. New York: Fordham University Press.

Bradford, C. B., 1965. *Yeats at Work*. Carbondale: Southern Illinois University Press.

Foster, R. F., 2003. *W. B. Yeats: A Life, Vol. II: The Arch-Poet 1915–1939*. New York: Oxford University Press.

Greimas, A. J., and J. Courtés, 1979. *Sémiotique. Dictionnaire raisonné de la théorie du langage*. Paris: Hachette Université.

Jeffares, A. N., 1968. *A Commentary on the Collected Poems of W. B. Yeats*. Stanford: Stanford University Press.

Larsen, H. E., 1996. *The Aesthetics of the Elements: Imaginary Morphologies in Texts and Paintings*. Aarhus: Aarhus University Press.

Moore, G., 1985. *Hail and Farewell: Ave, Salve, Vale*. Ed. Richard Allen Cave. Washington: Catholic University Press.

Ramazani, J., 1990. *Yeats and the Poetry of Death: Elegy, Self-Elegy, and the Sublime*. New Haven: Yale University Press.

Serres, M., 1995. *Genesis*. Trans. Genevieve James and James Nelson. Ann Arbor: University of Michigan Press.

Thom, R., 1972. *Stabilité structurelle et morphogenèse. Essai d'une théorie générale des modèles*. Reading, MA: W. A. Benjamin, Inc.

Wildgen, W., 2004. "Le problème du continu/discontinu dans la sémiophysique de René Thom et l'origine du langage." *Cahiers de Praxématique*, 42, 121–143.

Wordsworth, D., 1941. *Journals*. Ed. E. De Selincourt, Vol. I. New York: Macmillan.

Wordsworth, W., 1932. *The Complete Poetical Works of Wordsworth*. Boston: Houghton Mifflin.

Yeats, W. B., 1933. *Collected Poems of W. B. Yeats*. New York: Macmillan.

Young, D. P., 1990. *Five T'ang Poets*. Field Translation Series 15. Oberlin, OH: Oberlin College Press.

12

Words in Language and Thought

The Structures of Language

The problem I will address in this chapter is the following: in languages, we find several components that fiercely resist reduction to a simpler representation as parts of one holistic, coherent Structure that could define language and *a* language (in Saussure's sense, *une langue*). We find a *phonetic* component, including phonology and prosody, which can of course never be identified with syntax, despite the importance of certain phonotactic regularities; *syntactic* structures create forms such as transitive, double-transitive, passive, impersonal, or reflexive constructions and introduce dependency networks that do inform sentence prosody but differ categorically from phonemic and syllabic networks. *Semantic* structures in their turn certainly inform syntactic constructions, but again cannot be merged with these; for example, metaphorical, metonymical, and other semantic forms use the same syntactic formulae as literal semantic forms, and the cognitive schemas that are active in the semantics of sentences are generally not directly represented in syntax at all. Beyond sentence semantics, there is a *discourse-semantic* component responsible for narrative, argumentative, descriptive, and performative functions that are necessary in the textual organization of language and in dialogue; it contains encyclopedic meaning relations (terminologies of "knowledge," including affective beliefs) and cognitive frame networks ("thinking") without which coherent speech and writing would not be possible. And finally, there is a region of language that organizes the deictic, intersubjective, emotional, and referential relations in what has come to be called *enunciative* structures. From enunciation to pronunciation, there is evidently a gap or a "jump," but also a close relationship, so these five instances— *phonetics, syntax, sentence semantics, discourse semantics,* and *enunciation*—may be modeled as forming a non-closed ring, a spiral,[1] around the most important and prominent entity in language: the *word* itself and its lexical morphology. Words indeed have *phonetic* properties, *syntactic* properties (functions), *semantic* (word class) properties, *discursive* properties, and *enunciative* properties,[2] but they still resist reduction to any of these structural domains in language.[3] Instead of representing language, and *a* language, as one holistic and quasi-logical Structure, we could therefore propose an architecture as follows (Figure 12.1).

Any *word*, or lexeme, whether of a closed class or of an open class,[4] has a phonetic and a semantic "filling," as Ferdinand de Saussure said: a constitutive biplanary format, *signifier* over *signified*. Or as Louis Hjelmslev rephrased it: form of *expression* over form of *content*. This rather obvious biplanarity corresponds to the vertical axis in the

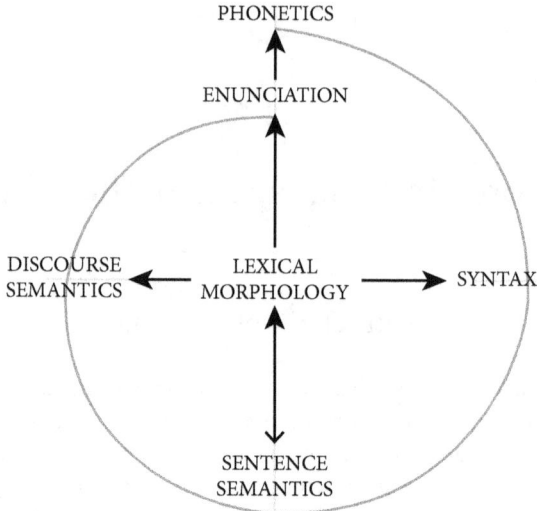

Figure 12.1 Language, seen from the *word*.

model (Figure 12.1). But words also fill syntactic functions in phrase structure, since there would be neither phrases nor sentences without words as their parts. And the final meaning of a word in an utterance is a much more complex discourse-dependent effect, furthermore dependent on the personalized use of it in the emotionally based performative and rhetorical addressing of a hearer or a reader through the deictic enunciative instance. Thus, the word can safely be considered as a central instance in the architecture of language. *Lexical morphology*—the unfolding of roots and flexives taking on syntactic, sentence-semantic, or discourse-semantic meanings—is the very center of this complex of instances and is in itself distinct from all of them.[5]

The spiral organization, that is, the neuro-cognitive networks hypothetically corresponding to it in brain and mind, may have evolved from primitive (*I–you–this*-structure, personal, deictic) enunciation, which originally may have carried musical[6] or gestural expressions (dance) and ritual contents and which probably first sedimented proper names, mainly used for calling on or announcing persons. Names in this hypothesis would become nouns or shape nominal phonetics, and inspire the articulation of word classes, giving rise to class-combining phrases and then to sentences with propositional, predicative semantics.

The Saussurean distinction between language *use* and (a) language as (a) *system*, *parole* versus *langue*, will have to be strongly modified in this new perspective. Since there is really no such unified *langue*, we will have to understand how speech and writing affect each of the autonomously structured instances of this spiral architecture in every moment of "use." The spiral itself is a representation of the way the actual processes feed into each other in *parole*, that is, in production and reception of language. The "unification" of structures happens in the *use* of language, rather than in a systematic *langue*.

Both production and reception of language originate in speakers' and hearers' attention to the *word*. We pick up each other's words and then try to unfold "their" structures of meaning in a context; we do not consciously think of syntax when we speak but we do consciously attend to words (namely those to use or to avoid using in dialogue with specific others), while the structures automatically grow around them.

If we consider syntax as an autonomous instance underlying phonetics, and again propositional semantics as an autonomous cognitive instance underlying syntax, then discourse semantics must again "underlie" sentence semantics, and finally, enunciation must "underlie" encyclopedic, discursive semantics, because the domains and frames selected and activated from our personal "encyclopedia" depend on the present enunciational situation. But structured enunciation is equally directly presupposed by *pronunciation* or, more generally, by the materialization of signifiers uttered and recognized as such. The result is a ring-shaped model where structures are neither "deep" nor pertaining to a "surface," since the maximal "depth" is to be found where the "surface" would be—that is, in the architecture of the spiral model, where the open gap between enunciation and phonetics is located.[7] The processing of language, in production and reception (often simultaneously, as in dialogue), must immediately activate all involved, yet autonomous, instances at once. Otherwise we would not experience such a wonderfully instantaneous coherence between sound, grammar, meaning, thought, feeling, and personal voice, for example when reading good literature. This experience can even leave us momentarily speechless—because we do no longer attend to any specific word within the coherent whole, or on the contrary, because one word suddenly seems to concentrate in or around itself an entire universe of meaning, created in a text. We will study the word's connections to the autonomous structures of language in the following sections.

Enunciation, Personhood

As mentioned, a word can be considered a biplanary entity (two planes: expression over content) that is likely to become hard-wired in the mind and the memory of a person speaking the language *of* the word in question. When a word of an open class[8] (nouns, verbs, adjectives, and their derivations) is memorized, it often carries with it, in the mind of the subject, the memory of what its particular content, reference, and meaning is or was to some person and of what its expression sounded like in the mouth, pen, or hand of some person, not necessarily the same. In this way, the word links us to other persons and to the domains of experience we share. The difficulty of learning words in foreign languages is that without such links to specific others, words are not readily memorized. The reason for this is that words are then frozen as abstract phono-semantic units, whereas they have to become, be and stay connected to enunciation, which is a semiotic structure involving persons in communicative contact (though their frozen format may help the mind use words for neutral, impersonal thinking).

Enunciation is a structure that allows us to be signified as speakers (in the first person, P1), as hearers (in the second person, P2), and as communicating beings prepared to

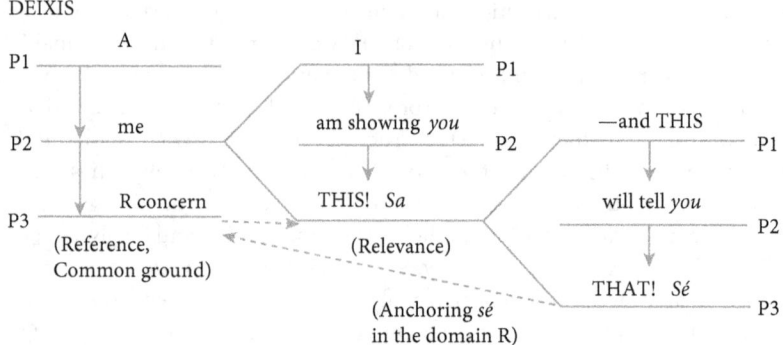

Figure 12.2 Enunciation as a deictic structure.

"do things with words."[9] The core form is the deictic *giving* stance: *I* or *we* (P1) give *you* (P2) *this* signifier (O=P3), which (P3 → P1) further will give *you* (P2) a content (O'=P3) to interpret. The interpretation importantly depends on a pre-understanding of the entity that informed P1 in the first place, as an epistemic and evidential source and authority (A) in some field (R) relevant to the ongoing communication. The word is firstly represented by its phonetic signifier (*Sa*) and then, when the signifier is acknowledged as such, in a specific language, and as part of a relevant common ground and concern, R, given to the speaker by what he feels is a shared culture or immaterial reality, as communicating a signified content (*Sé*) (Figure 12.2).

The model says: I, endowed by the instance A with the concern R, am showing you THIS (signifier), in order for THIS (signifier) to tell you THAT (signified).

The semantic domain of R, under the authority of some A, makes sense of the word content *Sé*.[10] The deictic enunciational structure shows the speaker, *I*, in two roles, first as P2 and then as P1; and the hearer, *you*, as P2 in two instances.[11]

A word of open classes (approx.: noun, verb, adjective) refers to categories, that is, to things, states, or events, in the semantic domains that our minds know of.[12] When a word is used while referring to a semantic domain (in R) of which the referent of the word is known as a part (culturally), it is used "literally." Otherwise, it is used figuratively, in particular "metaphorically." Words of closed classes, by contrast, such as prepositions, determiners, core or satellite adverbs (*in, out, up, down, etc.*), are used in all semantic domains without difference in meaning, since their meaning is *schematic*, reflecting only the relational *conceptual schemas* by which the mind organizes its experiences and thoughts.

Things, states, events, and acts, that is, the main open-class *categories* of a domain, can be modified in many directions, as to number, gender, status, time, aspectual style of occurrence, epistemic value, and so forth, and such variations are often expressed by the *flexives* of the (extremely variable) lexical morphology of the language in question. Words are universally identified by their "roots," which are basic concepts signified by certain phonetic invariants, from a couple of consonants to a series of syllables, surrounded or filled by variants, obtained by flexives, expressing syntactic or semantic modifications. In principle, flexives have *schematic* (relational) meanings, whereas lexical roots have *categorial* (classificatory) meaning. The flexo-lexical result is thus a word with both categorial and schematic meaning.[13] In grammatical phrases, the linear order of flexive words is more rigid than the syntactic word order, probably because it belongs to the lexical instance and is really a matter of the inner phono-articulation of the word, characteristic of the language in question.

Trees of Syntax

Words feed into phrases and sentences: syntax. Lexical morphology readily indicates the syntactic functions of words. The syntactic organization of words, when we speak, takes place within a time span of very few seconds, and the resulting constellation of phrases and clauses, sealed by a phonetic or graphical pause that makes the syntactic whole into a sentence (whether finished or not), works as an intuitively *structured mental space*, rather than as a memorized linear and additive sequence of accumulating elements of possible grammatical meaning. Meaning notably occurs at once, when this syntactic space is thus marked as saturated and closed (again: whether finished or not). Word "order" is primarily a matter of relative distance between connected words, not a matter of direct linear contact: spatial closeness expresses structural connection but only relatively. Connections are established by something quite different from word-to-word contact. They obtain between words and groups of already connected words through the operations of a canonical mechanism that activates a series of proto-semantic *nodes*, whereby words are combined and their meanings integrated to build elementary scenarios corresponding to various syntactic constructions. In the view of this theory, the connecting mechanism itself, and the series of nodes that can be activated, remains the same for different constructions; it consists of a maximal set of possible phrase and sentence complement types, or proto-semantically informed cases, a subset of which is used for each construction.[14]

Apart from displaying a certain construction, a sentence is facultatively specified by epistemic or modal adverbials, spatiotemporal complements, and other specifiers—indicating causality, finality, instrumentality, and so on.[15] Since the point here is not to argue thoroughly in favor of a particular syntactic model, but rather to present a global view of the spiral architecture of language, I shall only venture a short demonstration of the sort of sentence analysis that would suit this view.

Here is a random sentence from Fénéon's *Novels in Three Lines*[16]:

(1) In a café on Rue Fontaine, Vautour, Lenoir, and Atanis exchanged a few bullets regarding their wives, who were not present.

The stemmatic node structure[17] integrates substructures with verbal and nominal heads (Figure 12.3).

The linearized version (1) of the syntactic tree, or *stemma*, of the sentence is obtained by a series of projections from the (everywhere binary) phrase nodes to the phonetic string, where prosody is added accordingly. Several different linear manifestations of

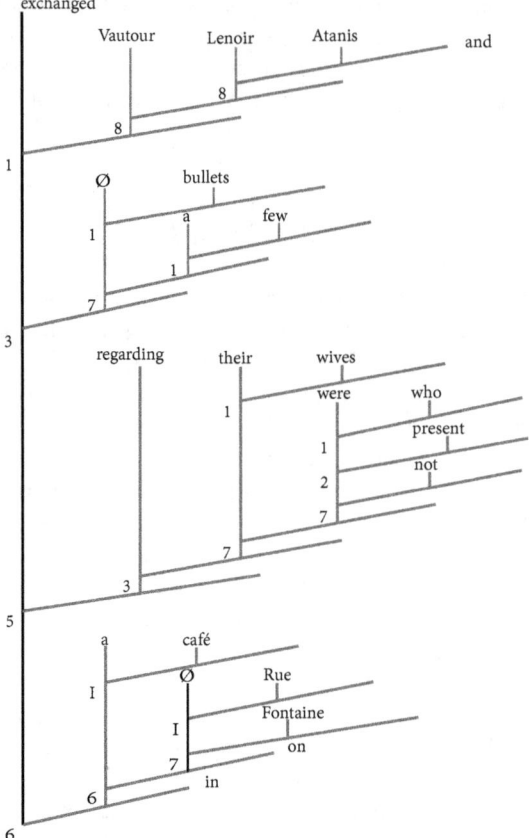

Figure 12.3 Stemmatic representation of (1).

the same stemma are often possible, but prosody must signal the meaningful phrasal parts of the sentence. To read a sentence, or to grasp its meaning from heard speech, is to immediately set up the *global sentence scenario*, here a scenario containing three male characters in a café who shoot at each other after discussing their respective wives.

Exchange Semantics

The proper names, we have to imagine, refer to male customers seated at a table in the café and having a conversation concerning their respective wives. We must further imagine that the conversation becomes a rather vehement debate involving offensive comments on the virtues of the ladies. The verbal *exchange* then becomes violent, and since the three gentlemen are armed and maybe intoxicated, it goes from niceties to less polite verbal provocations and then to gunfight. The semantics of the concept of exchange displays its full range from positive to negative. In conversations, we mainly offer friendly comments on the world, each other and ourselves, but teasing

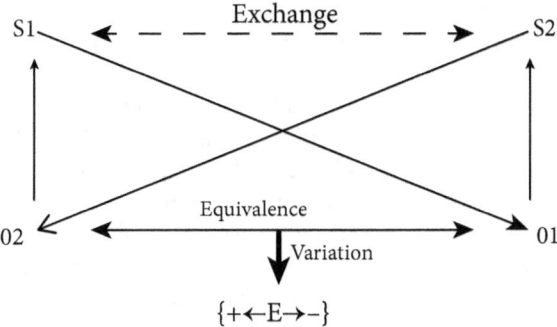

Figure 12.4 Unstable exchange.

can be *offensive*, trigger *anger*, and escalate into *violence*. We do not know what these gentlemen were drinking, but the degenerative course of events may invite suggestions.

The semantic schematizer of the situation is thus that of exchange, in the positive sense of reciprocation and of its negative, retaliation. Speaking and shooting illustrate the extremes. Between the extremes, exchange implies the idea of *equivalence* of the entities that circulate among the agents, but also the idea of instability and possible imbalance characterizing the playful aspect of many informal exchanges, where responses therefore easily escalate. Male comments on women would be a privileged category of occasions for such developments from respect to disrespect and thus from equilibrium to extremism.[18] In an exchange relation between S1 and S2, where the response to O1 from S1 is O2 from S2, the unstable equivalence E can radically change the value of the Os on a scale from good to evil. Figure 12.4 shows a Greimasian semiotic square in a kinetic version, where Objects thus move between Subjects.

Fénéon's *very* short "story" (French: *fait divers*) consisting of only one sentence activates a semantic awareness of this aspect of our intersubjective condition, which can readily be recognized in many contexts and at different historical scales. It is also involved in the functioning of money in exchanges; monetarized exchanges intend to limit the instability of the equivalence of "values" by explicit quantification.

Discourse Semantics

Nouvelles en trois lignes (News in three lines) was really the name of a column that appeared in newspapers at the beginning of the twentieth century, such as *Le Matin*, where the author, the writer, critic, and editor Félix Fénéon worked for some months in 1906 and wrote 1220 of those before finding another job. As the English translator Luc Sante reminds us in his preface to his translation of the book (2007), newspapers were the immensely important new media at that time and marked both literature and modern art profoundly, as their appearance in cubist paintings illustrate. The format of the *fait divers*, the laconic anecdote, reduces the citizen to a ridiculous or tragic miniature figure, mainly bound for statistics. Fénéon was an art critic and a literary editor who had worked for Thadée Nathanson's famous *Revue blanche* for eight years and who had edited Rimbaud's *Illuminations* as well as Lautréamont's *Chants de Maldoror*. His personal publishing house later published the first French translation of James Joyce, *Dédale* (1924). A disciple of Mallarmé, Fénéon was famously exercising "his considérable talents for compression, distillation, and skeletal evocation, making the items something like haikai. He managed to engineer the most minimal, Swiss-watch examples of suspense (making them a special challenge for the translator, since word order is often crucial)" (Sante p. xxiv in Fénéon 2007). Here are three examples of his *nouvelles*:

(2) Responding to a call at night, M. Sirvent, café owner of Caissargues, Gard, opened his window; a rifle shot destroyed his face.
(3) Mme Fournier, M. Vouin, M. Septeuil, of Sucy, Tripleval, Septeuil, hanged themselves; neurasthenia, cancer, unemployment.
(4) On the bowling lawn a stroke leveled M. André, 75, of Levallois. While his ball was still rolling he was no more.

This is the sort of almost silent prose that forms the context of our syntactic example (1). Remember that 1905 had been a turbulent year in France and elsewhere; separation of Church and State; failed Russian revolution; roaring declamations and hyperbolic discourse filled the public spaces as well as the newspapers (while the radio and the cinema were not yet socially present and operative).

As the examples show, the semantic core of the "stories" is often the theme of death. The lethal events are framed by very salient schematisms, such as the inverse transitivities: passively looking *out*, actively shooting *in* (2); suicidal despair (3) caused by mind, body, and society, as if these three instances were of the same kind, all just being fatal circumstances: neurasthenia = cancer = unemployment. Capitalist economy, lethal illness, or madness: intransitivity (it just happens) =/≠ transitivity (the world just does this to you), causality "is" chance.[19] M. André, in (4), throws his ball and dies; the ball runs for some time, and he dies *within* that time span, not knowing where the ball goes: durative (rolling) and aoristic (dying) aspects are superimposed; what you do has life-indifferent temporal consequences and effects, erratic or goal-directed, that you will never know.

The minimalist writing of Fénéon foregrounds schemas like these and point to an overarching aesthetic sensitivity that lets silence vibrate metaphysically, so to speak. The absence of a reassuring narrator's voice becomes a question addressing the world as experienced from within—namely within the three news-column lines of each anecdote. The universe is as silent as the narrator. As Marquis de Sade had stated a century earlier, horrible crimes and sad stories abound, as well as good deeds, and the sky stays blue, empty, indifferent.

As the examples show, discourse semantics can add a wider semantic resonance to what is literally present in a sentence: words that build scenarios also build different kinds of significant silence around themselves, reflecting the *discursive resonance* they create in the universe of history, politics, aesthetics, metaphysics, ideology, and general attitudes of the informed mind to the experiential and cultural world. This is due to the specific structure of discourse semantics: the micro-narrative texts of our examples are not integrated into a macro-*narrative* form, a real "story," but are instead thrown into a *descriptive* format that conveys to each micro-text the status of a verse in a long poetic list, the book.[20] This long "poem" is in turn interpretable as an *argumentative* whole, in which the episodic elements are premises and a certain human condition is the implicit conclusion. Semiotically speaking, discourse is in fact organized by either *narrative, descriptive*, or *argumentative* networks of sentence-semantic elements. *Narratives* are temporally and agentively linked aggregations of situational spaces under a narrator's voice. *Descriptions* are spatiotemporally linked aggregations of observations, "data," under an observer's gaze. *Argumentations* are finally collections of arguments (whether narrative or descriptive) serving as orienting vectors in a space of interrogation. The three discursive principles, and the three overarching subject roles, the narrator, the observer, and the interrogative thinker, are cognitive operators guiding the mind toward certain eventual forms of meaning. Knowledge is thus constituted by more complex uses of these principles: *historical* knowledge is mainly narrative and descriptive; *science* in general is mainly descriptive and argumentative; and *philosophy* is narrative and argumentative. Religious and ideological discourse seem to be narrative and anti-argumentative, using sets of arguments as disorienting vectors in interrogative space; the result is their focus on the subjective attitude, rather than on an intended reality; the emotional subject becomes its own disoriented reality. However, in all cases, the discursive subject will potentially be a subject of enunciation (a first person, P1).

Conclusion Returning to Enunciation

Reading a text or listening to someone's speech implies activating a feeling of "where it comes from," an attempt to find the common ground and the sort of authority (i.e., genre of truth) that is active behind the voice, imagined or perceived, of the enunciator. The deepest level of discursive-semantic resonance of the literal meaning apperceived will invest this basic and grounding instance of enunciation and orient the receptive attention, as well as it will determine the subsequent *response* of hearer or reader. In a sense, starting to write or to speak is always responding to some portion of language, recent or remote, perceived or remembered with a sufficient degree of saliency to trigger word-based cognitive activity. The spiral model (see Figure 12.1) situates the moment of speech initiation in the hiatus spanning from pre-speech enunciation to actual phonation or digital expression. In that moment, a second or third person becomes a first person, and an intention to continue or discontinue the thought of another person, or several, naturally becomes an urge to participate in the common project of "saying what (we think) *there is*"—the basic project that follows from sharing words, that is, from being part of a linguistic community: *Say what has to be said!* This is what words are for, what they call for; their meaning lets us and urges us to *speak up*—we can therefore even sometimes suffer a sort of speech compulsion and experience the difficulty of "holding our tongue." By contrast, as we have seen, there also exists an emotional need *not* to speak but instead to mentally inspect the words that present themselves to us as candidates for triggering an outburst of language: a critique of available language that can lead to irony, poetry, or a preference for silence, as our author, Fénéon, has shown. Fénéon said: *J'aspire au silence* (I aspire to silence). This "anti-prose" attitude is apparently, maybe universally, obtained through an intense attention paid to words themselves. They make us speak, when the mind lets them be transparent,[21] as windows toward the world, and they can silence us, when we turn our attention to their own strange and linguistico-textual existence.

Notes

1. The idea of describing the architecture of language in this way, as a spiral, comes from my inspiring colleague Lene Fogsgaard (2000), who in turn refers to Culioli (1968). Culioli calls this spiral model, in French, *la came*.
2. *Enunciation*, in French *l'énonciation*, is Émile Benveniste's (1966) term for the grammatical presence, in language, of markers of speaker and hearer roles and properties, including personhood, status, deixis, referential indicators. See Brandt (2016a). The concept of enunciation and its communicative importance in cognitive linguistics are discussed in L. Brandt (2013).
3. This point is where current linguistic theories may deserve fierce criticism, especially the so-called "construction grammars." But we will not be fierce.
4. On *closed-class semantics* and the general importance of the distinction between open and closed word classes, see Talmy (2000), chapter 1, "The Relation of Grammar to Cognition."
5. See, on this point, the account of multifunctional morphology in Brandt (2016b).
6. See Merker (2015).
7. There is of course a gap between *enunciation*, the semantics of personhood (who is addressing who in what way and with what authority, etc.) and *pronunciation*, the act of actually pronouncing and producing syllables, words, sentences: speaking, gesturing, writing.
8. *Open* word classes take in or adapt new words for new concepts by more or less adjusting their phonetic and written shape, if their origin is another language, and otherwise just following the phonetic and morphological regularities of the receiving language. Closed word classes do not admit new items, unless the entire morphological inventory changes, as from Latin to the Romance languages. Semantically, open word classes express *categories*, whereas closed word classes express *schematic* meaning relations. So in a sense, the closed classes could be said to define *a* language.
9. Austin's (1975) formula refers to the specific phenomenon of speech acts, but the very fact of addressing the other in speech or writing is already to be conceived as an act: a presupposed act of *giving* one's voice and words to the other and thereby promising the other something hopefully both true and helpful, whether an information, an instruction, or just an idea.
10. A speaker communicates what he, according to himself, is "authorized" to share. As a specialist in some field, for example, he is "informed" by the authority, the

"spirit," the methodology, or the rationality, of that field. The French philosopher Michel Foucault used to ask, "Where are you speaking *from*?" The subject of enunciation (P1) is always speaking "from" somewhere, A. The ultimate version of A is quite simply the truth, of interest to Humanity—or the respect for truth we call Reason.

11 The pronoun *we* can be analyzed as P1 + A, where A is either inclusive or exclusive of P2.
12 On semantic domains, see Brandt (2004).
13 So in the word "submission," the meaning of "sub-" is schematic, whereas the meaning of "-mission" is categorial.
14 By proto-semantic nodes, I mean nodes that connect meaningfully but vaguely. The verbal node for *transitivity*, for example (notated C3 below), carries the vague schematic meaning of /change/, whereby the agentive form of transitivity confers change to the object, and apperceptive transitivity confers change to the subject: *Peter helps Mary*, versus *Peter sees Mary*.
15 I gave a first account of this particular view and model of syntax in Brandt (1973), then in Brandt (2004) and passim. This "stemmatic" model is a sort of case grammar in Fillmore's sense, but instead of an infinity of frames and cases it uses a canonical set of case nodes with "vague," proto-semantic contents. See also Brandt (2010).
16 The quoted sentence constitutes the entire story! (Fénéon 2007).
17 *Stemmatic* structures are recursive cascades of schematizing nodes running from 1 to 8. Grosso modo: Head: verb or determiner. Complement 1: subject. C2: predicate. C3: object. C4: directive (indirect object). C5: projective (ground or cause). C6: locative. C7: enunciative: modal adverbial, quantifier, or name. C8: conjunction. The complement nodes Cx each contribute a schematic aspect of the meaning scenario of the integrated constructions; not all have to be filled, but their stemmatic order of integrations stays identical.
18 Especially so since *three* agents are involved. The exchange is asymmetrical. But here we will just consider the minimal dual version S1 ↔ S2. There are three of these involved in the given situation S1–S2–S3.
19 Fénéon was also an active political anarchist and very critical against the cynical bourgeois society he felt he had served as a ministerial clerk in his early days.
20 Published posthumously by Jean Paulhan, in 1948. The author died in 1944.
21 Louis Hjelmslev interestingly observed that "language does not want to be seen" (Omkring sprogteoriens grundlæggelse, *Prolegomena*, §1).

References

Austin, J. L., 1975. *How to Do Things with Words* (Eds.) James O. Urmson and Marina Sbisà. Boston: The Harvard University Press (originally 1962).
Benveniste, É., 1966. *Problèmes de linguistique générale*. Paris: Gallimard.
Brandt, L., 2013. *The Communicative Mind. A Linguistic Exploration of Conceptual Integration and Meaning Construction*. Newcastle: Cambridge Scholars Press.
Brandt, P. A., 1973. *L'analyse phrastique. Introduction à la grammatique*. Bruxelles: AIMAV.
Brandt, P. A., 2004. *Spaces, Domains, and Meaning. Essays in Cognitive Semiotics*. Berne: Peter Lang (European Semiotics, 4).

Brandt, P. A., 2010. "Thinking and Language: A View from Cognitive Semio-Linguistics." In: (Eds.) B. Glatzeder, V. Goel, and A. von Müller, *Towards a Theory of Thinking. Building Blocks for a Conceptual Framework*, 251–259, Berlin: Springer Verlag, Series: On Thinking.

Brandt, P. A., 2016a. "Deixis—a Semiotic Mystery: Enunciation and Reference." *Cognitive Semiotics*, 9 (1), 1–10.

Brandt, P. A., 2016b. "Linguistic Theory in the Framework of a Cognitive Semiotics: The Role of Semio-Syntax." In: (Eds.) J. Zlatev, G. Sonesson, and P. Konderak. *Meaning, Mind and Communication. Explorations in Cognitive Semiotics*, 391–408, Bern: Peter Lang.

Culioli, A., 1968. "La formalisation en linguistique." *Cahiers pour l'analyse*, 9.

Fénéon, F., 2007. *Novels in Three Lines* (Ed. and trans.) L. Sante. New York: New York Review of Books (French original 1906, as a book, *Nouvelles en trois lignes*, 1948.)

Fogsgaard, L., 2000. *Esquemas copulativos de SER y ESTAR. Ensayo de semiolingüística*. Berne: Peter Lang (European Semiotics, 2).

Merker, B., 2015. "Seven Theses on the Biology of Music and Language." In: (Eds.) P. A. Brandt, and J. R. Do Carmo Jr. *Sémiotique de la musique/Music and Meaning*. Liège: Presses Universitaires de Liège (Signata, 6).

Talmy, L., 2000. *Toward a Cognitive Semantics, Vol. I, Concept Structuring Systems*. Cambridge, MA: MIT Press.

13

Numbers Are Things in Time

The Cognitive Origin of Numbers[1]

In a recent volume on the origin of mathematics in human cognition, we find the striking statement that for the embodied human mind, "numbers are things in the world."[2] Humans perceive things in the spatial world of their bodily existence, so they conceive of abstract numbers in terms of concrete perceived things, using a grounding arithmetic *metaphor*. This is the basic idea of Lakoff and Núñez, and it is less than convincing, since it remains speculative and unsupported by evolutionary evidence; in cognitive science, however, to my knowledge, no alternative has been considered.

The metaphorico-conceptual grounding is logically aporetic, since the *source* (things) and the *target* (numbers) of the conceptual metaphor both would have to preexist in order for the projection from source to target to happen. Metaphor can change a target, but it cannot create it. Therefore, numbers cannot have been created by a numbers-are-things metaphor. The same aporia persists if you try to transpose the idea in terms of conceptual integration theory[3]: the input mental spaces must precede the blend that they give rise to. The blend can, and most often do, give rise to changes in the input contents, but it cannot create them ex nihilo.

So: *how does a number of things become a number in itself, seen as a "thing"?* In all its simplicity, this is the unsolved question for cognitive science and semiotics.

Numbers in Language[4]

If the conceptual metaphor were operative, it would be reflected in language. Numbers would be represented as things are, by *nouns*. Nouns are the open-class terms by which humans refer to things: objects, masses, notions. But no; numerals are not nouns. So the determiners (the/a/Ø) do not work with number words:

(1) *There goes *a* two [a couple].
(2) **The* two is on the table [the scissors].
(3) *I do not like ambiguity and two [duplicity].

Numeral words are not adjectives either:

(4) *James felt terribly minus seventeen that day.
(5) *The cats were old and two.

Numerals are instead *quantifiers*. They therefore work well with "logical" quantifiers:

(6) *All* ((of) the) *nine* cats were black.
(7) *Some* of the *nine* cats were black.
(8) *None* of the *nine* cats were black

In (6), there were k (:= nine) of them, and each of these were black; *all k* means k minus zero—thus, without exception. In (7), *some k* means k minus x, thus with exceptions. In (8), *none* means k minus k. In the linguistic representation, *logical* quantifiers refer to *numerical* quantifiers, which in turn refer to nominal contents.

Numerical quantifiers (one, two, three ...) are as rigid as proper names. They are often indeclinable as to case, gender, plexity.[5] A plausible cause may be that these words in fact *are* a sort of proper names, namely of the singularities that human beings experience and share with extreme and dramatic intensity, despite their invisibility: numbers, moments in time.

The Symbolization of Time

Cognitive semantics registers many ways of referring to time. However, the contrast between the following three modes (a, b, c) is particularly important.

(a) *Deictic time*. Time as an embodied *first-person* dimension, represented by adverbial "shifters": *now, tomorrow, yesterday, next week, last year*. The deictic time schema has a path and a present hic et nunc station in the middle, with future positions on one side and past positions on the other side, with possible delegations: there is a past of past, a future of future, a past of future, a future of past, and so on, as interrelated positions on the path. Note that a metrics of minutes, hours, days, weeks, or years is strongly compatible with deixis.

(b) *Epistemic time*. Time as stage of something's manifestation, represented by *third-person* temporal adverbials: *never, always, sometimes, seldom, often*—a series that conveys epistemic statements of probability for everyone and which thus refers to time as *time-of-truth*.[6] This mode does not have intrinsic metrics and thus is similar to logical quantifiers. The schema has a plastic event line (E) running close to a straight reality line (R), and when E crosses or coincides with R, the event in question happens and is true. Otherwise, E is virtual.

(c) *Aspectual time*. Event realization depends on a different event or state. This mode therefore uses mental space delegation of a *second person* to some contextual circumstance and then situates the realization of the event in question within that delegated space-time; there is generally an aspectual relation as between a background *durative* and a foregrounded *punctual* realization or an anchoring sequential relation between the two events: *two days later, after midnight, the following year, ten minutes before, when the moon is full, on Saturday nights*. Those are relative indications, again based on a metric of some kind, that is, grounded in a map of possible time slots according to a paradigm, however vague or precise. This mode directly invites metrics, as a measure of the implied in-between, and thus of numbers, ordinal and cardinal.

Temporal units of the (a) and (c) type rely on named time slots, that is, on serial locative symbolization. Days in weeks have names, months and years equally; in many cultures, even hours are named and numbered. Numbers are possible names for such units, besides names of divinities and of ritual celebrations. These forms of serial symbolization are possible, when each series is finite and used cyclically, articulated on other cyclic series (as foreground on background). Calendar systems function like numerical systems; calendars are even most likely the origin of numerical systems, which were used for counting days, years, and so on and projecting social events onto these units distributively.

Figure 13.1 The Aztec calendar. A (originally colored) rendition of the Sun Stone, or the Stone of Axayacatl. Museo de Antropología, México DF.

This calendar contains a profane system, *Xiuhpohualli*, and a sacred system, *Tonalpohualli*. The first of these is agricultural and its year has 360 days plus five *nemontemi*, useless days, where nothing good could be done. Its year has eighteen months, each with a *name*, and each with twenty *numbered* days. The sacred calendar system comprises years of 260 days, and its twenty months carrying *names* of divinities have thirteen *numbered* days. The two calendars end on the same day every fifty-two years. Years are counted by cycles of four *names* repeated thirteen *numbered* times; so, this "complete" year of fifty-two Xiuhpohualli years contains seventy-three Tonalpohualli years and in three subsystems combines names and numbers.

The only human forms of bodily behavior that offer this multicyclical temporal structure are music and dance. See Brandt (2019), the first three chapters. These forms of symbolic practice are frequently linked to calendar time: night music, morning music, dances and themes for special days, weeks, months, calendar-driven symbolic transitions (the New Year!), and for existential calendars: funerals, baptisms, weddings, and status transitions of all kinds.

It is therefore a highly plausible evolutionary hypothesis that the structure of strongly symbolized, calendaric social time is rooted in the symbolic structure of corresponding music. In musical structure, rhythm is based on meter, which is only possible if beats can be counted cyclically and multicyclically. This is the case when musical beats are grouped, as gestalts, and integrated into regular measures, and the measures into choruses, so that dancers can plan their coordinated moves sharing the beats with (their) musicians.

The counting of beats is necessary for intersubjective musicking. The beat battery and the series of intra-octaval tones linked to specific beats constitute the minimal set of information needed for playing. Dancers will often dispose of specific series of moves, steps, and gestures linked to specific tonal modes, phrases, and rhythms, in parallel with what makes it possible to play together—and thus, to dance collectively and thereby to express specified time and temporal meanings together: to be "contemporary" and experience shared meanings.

A *beat* is of course invisible. It is very often also inaudible. Nevertheless, it exists, it is there, the musician or the dancer will feel and mark it by a secret proprioceptive muscular move; and it can be counted aloud using its name, as often occurs when a piece begins, and the participants seek to be "on the same beat." Cardinal *numerals*— one, two ...—are such *names of beats*. Other cultures, such as the Aztecs, have other, mostly more complicated names for beats, but all are learned as finite series, following a decimal, vigesimal, duodecimal, trigesimal, or otherwise simple and short cycle embedded in other cycles. The basic cycles have to be not just finite but short, in order to generate paradigms of numeral names for its beats and in order to be perceived as grouped gestalts.

The current cognitive dogma that space determines all domains of meaning is not helpful here. Temporal symbolization is not tridimensional, but possibly multidimensional, and its mental visibility is sui generis: a measure (an ordered and iterated series of beats, like 4/4) or a sequence of measures can form a tonal time-space in the sense of an imaginary place, where a tonal phrase can unfold and even allow verbal events to "take place." However, the imaginary place where this happens has no gravitation, the body of the subject is not represented, it has no colors (except for synesthetes, as we will see below), and even no stable scale of objects. But it still has numerical identity! It is entirely immaterial, in this sense, and it is experienced by humans as being shared. This temporal phenomenon of experienced *sharedness* is an elementary and basic form of communication, an emotional continuity between subjects: a primordial form of intersubjectivity as participative temporal togetherness and as expressed by the socially constitutive first-person pronoun *we*.[7]

It is easy to see how this temporal numericity can be transposed into spatial experiences of number, namely by the *rhythmic* gesture of deictic counting-by-pointing. The temporality of the digital deictic *counting* preserves the original abstract (immaterial) version while projecting it onto unmoving or unordered concrete things in space. These things will just have to be perceived as *groupable*, typically by sharing a category determination (e.g., counting sheep, not including cattle). Phenomenologically, projecting beat names—numbers—onto stationary objects corresponds to attaching a label to a physical object; we can, and remarkably often do, attach mental labels to events, persons, and things, even to lacking things (absent objects that we are looking for), in the very act of "paying attention" to them. Seeing something "as" something is applying a categorial label in the act of perceiving; when we count serial things around us, for example bricks in a wall, columns around a Greek temple, windows in a façade, we are using this mental routine of projecting named beats onto visible entities that are perceived under a categorial label.[8] We will then talk about their architectural "rhythm."

Symbols of Time Units

There would of course be no weekdays without the names of the days and the numerical status of the week in the calendar. In this semiotic area of temporal cognition, *we cannot separate the name from the thing!* It would make no sense to say that *four* exists cognitively before emerging as something corresponding to the beat that follows three previous (named) beats in a bar. No four without one-two-three. In spatial cognition, by contrast, nothing is easier than separating name and thing, since the singularity of each thing resists generic categorization. Only hardnosed nominalists reject this evidence.

The reality of temporal units, like Wednesdays, is inseparable from having such a denomination. The days of Wodanaz, Wotan, or Odin are theo-socially dedicated to this god, who is as invisible as time itself. Divinities are typically associated with time units; their service is then inscribed in this slot of the calendar. Gods and numbers are here doing the same symbolic work.[9] One conclusion would be that divinities and numbers are in fact symbolically identical: the one-and-only god is the number: one (1), and the number "one" is that god; however, he cannot functionally "own" all days, so Christians give him the first one of the week: *dies domenica, domingo, dimanche*, day of the Lord.

Maybe the most solid generalization would be to state that humans signify invisible beings that carry strong emotional meanings by *proper names*. In a sense, even *persons* are invisible, since they too differ from their bodies, in sociocultural cognition. Persons (like the divinities) are in their achievements, their deeds, their masterpieces, the great creations they have signed; their names and signatures survive them. Ethnic entities and nations are per se invisible, and their names are existential to the feeling of identity of individuals, often dramatically so. Otherwise, nationalism would not be possible. Remarkably, musical support is essential for ethnicity, nationality, personhood—and love in general. We must sing and play to honor these *identitary* references. Music is therefore closely related to proper names; song texts are often centered on a name call, and of course, national or ethnic hymns are calls to the "spirit" associated with the name of the collective being.[10] If we go down to the detail, the name itself is a melodious suite of syllables, supported by the *tonal accent*— the core link between music and language: poetry. The beat, again, is the referential link between the name and the being that is called upon. Therefore, it is likely that *tonal* entities will be named based on calling, such as *ut–re–mi–fa-sol-la-[si]* from a call on St. John:

Ut queant laxis **re**sonāre fibris (**Ut** was later changed to the open syllable **Do**[**mine**])
Mira gestorum **fa**muli tuorum,
Solve polluti **la**bii reatum,
Sancte Iohannes. [S. I. = **si**]
= ut re mi fa sol la si do.

(So that these your servants can, with all their voice, sing your wonderful feats, clean the blemish of our spotted lips, O Saint John!)

Rhythmic entities are equally embodied in singing; our infants learn numbers and multiplication tables by singing number songs and chanting the tables; coordination of sports competitors starts by countdowns; think of the use of numbers in bodily coordination: coordination of rowers and marching soldiers, and so on. Interbody coordination in *work, worship, and love*, the three universal and elementary categories of social activity, is universally based on counting, singing, and dancing.

Numbers are basic in bodily social life. Furthermore, the development of techniques of *writing*, allowing written numbers to be aligned and manipulated in two dimensions, changes this primordial *temporal* numeracy into the *spatial* symbolic arts of bookkeeping, accounting, economics, mathematics, geometry, and computation in general. *Techné* in general is numeracy. The spatiality of written numeracy is still mental, however, rather than copied off of the space of things in our surrounding lifeworld. Likewise, written tonal and rhythmic music is spatial in two-dimensional scores, prolonging our diagrammatic inner vision rather than the optical dimensions of the visual outer world. Written numeracy emerges in early societies' sacred calendars and myth-based calculations, as in the Aztec and Mayan cultures; it enters philosophy through the Greek school of Pythagoras of Samos, who was also a musician and who taught that the proportions in the planetary system were organized like the intervals between harmonic tones in a scale (intra-octave). Of course, planets are moving, "dancing," according to those proportions, in his Music of the Spheres.

The Rhythmic Body

Humans can control their breathing consciously, so that we can use our vocal chords expressively, talk, eat, and breathe without suffocating. For the same reason, we can dive, merge into water, hold our breath, and then set up a regular drive between arms and legs to achieve the polyrhythmic feat we call *swimming*. At a time when our species was living along coastlines and partly feeding on seafood, this capacity may have been a great evolutionary advantage.[11] Moving our feet in a multiple of the rhythm of our arms and our breathing and keeping a steady "gait" made it possible for us to not only find food but also dance—using the same division and "phrasing" relation between the upper and the lower part of our body while moving as when swimming. Hand movements of many dance traditions still suggest a watery element and makes the air feel "liquid" (such as with Balinese and flamenco dancers). This effect may be important to the human imaginary.[12]

The *voluntary control* of these bodily movements, which can be trained and culturally shaped, gives rise to entire normative disciplines of "correct" moving, walking, marching, and dancing for specific purposes. Human bodies are kinetically rhythmic as well as most animal (esp. mammal, primate) bodies are, but the direct link to *conciousness* and *volition* makes a huge difference. It means that the time scales of conscious monitoring movements and expressions directly and immediately affect our kinetic behavior. This is undeniably the root of intentional action; we can stop it, we can "mean" it and go on; we can repeat it; we can "show" it for others to repeat; and

Figure 13.2 Cave painting: Kondusi stick dance. The painting may date 25,000 years BP. This reproduction is in the Nairobi National Museum.

we can correct it on the fly. We thereby *signify* to each other that our movements are indeed "intended," "meant," so that we can be "responsible" for them and so that they can carry special symbolic, signified messages, connotations.

The most important aspect of this simple fact is that *acts have beginnings and endings*. They are discrete. They are not just arbitrary fragments of an unbroken flow. Acts are *telic* and have aspectual articulation. *One* act can be repeated and simulated mimetically. The multiple of our repetitions then becomes significant ("How many times do I have to say this?!"). The discrete articulations of our acts correspond to the discrete articulations of our voice, when it passes from *one* tone to another. This is crucial. The close and discretely articulated *interaction between consciousness and bodily performance* gives rise to intentional causation, to mimesis, to teaching and learning, to formal cooperation of all kinds (again: in work, worship, and love). No mimesis without discreteness.[13]

We can control each other's acts and gestures as we control our own; *attuning* to what others are doing is absolutely decisive for cultural life to happen; attuning others to our own doing is a natural counterpart. *Knowing* that you are doing what others *know* that they are doing while you and they are doing it is really doing something "together"—which can thus have a shared meaning. Mimesis as a culturally decisive phenomenon depends on this human faculty.[14]

There is an underlying process here that M. Donald and the German neuropsychologist Ernst Pöppel direct our attention to, namely the fact that the brain generates consciousness *in time*. Pöppel's minimal three second window of basic awareness[15] is an example. We speak and think in sentences that have beginnings and endings and a standard duration compatible with their finite grammar. We gesture the same articulate way. We phrase musically and choreographically in a comparably "articulate" way. Thinking pulsates. So, it makes sense to say: "I have an idea, maybe just *one*, but it is worth considering..."—and it makes sense to make one's "point" (even maybe just one). Consciousness *counts* and *pulsates*, therefore there are sentences, propositions, ideas, points to make. To stay focused, to concentrate, to attend to something, is to connect the moments in the pulse, instead of getting off track between two pulses. It is easy to hear this in music, in oral discourse and conversation, in social debate, written simulations of thinking like "essays," and of course, if we pay attention, in our own inner line of simply being conscious. The pulsation of consciousness is of course behind the morphology of aspects in language: morphemes for beginnings, endings, continuations, iterations, diminuations, increasings, and punctuality.

Working memory categorizes while perceiving, which takes time and works rhythmically; Donald (2007) now proposes a "slow process" going on in the background of direct perceiving that makes narrative sense of what we experience, and this sense-making or narrative hook-up again takes time, in terms of seconds and minutes. Things are interpreted in terms of their indirect significations, thus becoming signs—but slowly. It takes time for the "penny to drop." I would like to go further: *The discreteness of being conscious is the origin of the discreteness of signs*. We signify, after having *started* to signify, and then we *stop* signifying. We step on to the stage of signifying, and then step off, down. The addressee understands this as an evident *telic* condition of signification and human contact in general. Nobody can listen forever or speak forever or indefinitely; the turn-taking routines of conversation are rooted in this rhythmic neural reality of the consciousness-making brains. Dialogue is rhythmic; arhythmia in dialogue is, as psychiatrists will know, indicative of a socially impairing pathology.

The Cognitive Construction of Value

The—socially decisive—notion of numerical value is evidently based on the possibility of equating a (counted) *number of things* and a *quantity of a mass*. You will remember K. Marx's simplest "value equation" in the first chapter of *Das Kapital*:[16]

1 coat = 10 yards of linen

Exchanging quantities of different *substances* creates the *form* of value, Marx explains.[17] This happens even in a direct act of bartering. Now here is the first detail he does not attend to: a number (*multiplex*) of discrete objects (coats) is virtually exchanged for a numbered *measure* of a non-discrete mass (linen).[18] However, multiplex and measure are not identical concepts; masses by definition cannot be counted, only measured—by a repeated application of a measuring "stick" of some kind. And here is the second detail Marx forgets to mention: exchanges are acts involving minimally two human beings, "subjects," who accept to *give* in order to receive what they *want* to have. Giving and wanting-to-have are basic socio-cognitive phenomena; the two subjects involved in an act of direct exchange are both subjects of giving, wanting, and receiving. Only if the strength of the wanting is matched by the giving—or the strength of the giving by the wanting—on both sides do we get a Marxian equation; the "equivalence" is not a mysterious or magical hocus-pocus force, as his literary phrasing often invites to suggest, but instead a real, modal relevance-maker that has to be present in the consciousness of the (actively or passively) involved subjects.

The model used below reflects the semiotic modification of the abovementioned Fauconnier-Turner model of elementary blending of mental spaces. Mental spaces are signified from a Base space of communication and exchange between subjects; these "spaces" are minimal situational ideas, and their contents can blend into a new space whose meaning depends on input from a relevance-making schema (or several) which will let it shape a conceptual nontrivial output, imported back to Base space. The blend itself is a *mental topology*, or *mental diagram*, that reorganizes contents from both input spaces.

The appropriate model for cognitive analysis of this process of value-creation through inter-numerical exchange may be this *semiotic blending network* (Figure 13.3). The simple situation of exchange involving two subjects, say, *you* and *me*, gives rise to two distinct *mental spaces* shared reciprocally (interchanging first- and second-person pronouns) by the subjects: in one, *I give you N coats*, and in the other, *you give me M of linen*. The mappings of *I to you, you to me, N to M, coats to linen*, and of course *give to give*, and *take to take* allow the subjects to share a blended space where the corresponding entities merge, so that objects and masses *fuse* and become a third entity, an abstract quantity of "stuff." That "stuff" is, in the imaginary semantic process of cognition, precisely what the subjects *want and get*! The wanting-and-getting[19] of

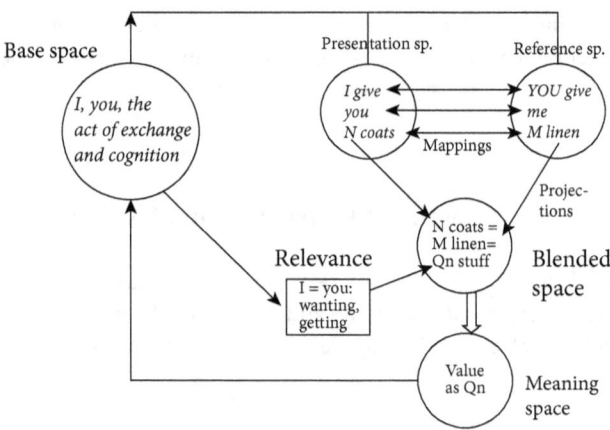

Figure 13.3 A blending network of exchange and value.

a merged subject (since the *we* in question ideally gets both what it wants and what it wants to give) now translates into the phenomenon of *value*, which we experience when we exchange and which is typically expressed by a handshake or an equivalent gesture of mutual satisfaction and politeness, when the "deal is done." "Deals" are finite and framed telic acts, aspectualized into inchoative, continuative, and terminative aspectual phases, and imply such reciprocal processual networks.

In blending networks of this type, quantity finally becomes a real abstraction: *value*. Since the difference between bounded objects and unbounded masses has been eliminated in the blend, the semantic content of quantity can now, if needed, be expressed in a third substance, a "currency," that is, a number of arbitrarily shaped bounded objects cut out of a uniform mass of an available, already valued substance: *money*.[20]

Once number was conceptualized in terms of abstract quantity, which probably happened in many places and cultures in early historical time, it was straightforward to apply this invisible value-"jelly," as Marx said, to physical entities, forms of energy, weights of masses, forces, velocities, and so forth. Mathematics had what was required for its generality. It has stayed particularly close to physics, the physics of bounded objects, bodies, and unbounded elements, hence to engineering, medicine, and so on, due to this inherent affinity of the X-jelly and the abstract dynamic entities, "forces," of the world.

The radical modern finding that math is *about* mathematical reality as such, per se, and that it is therefore indeed a *science*, whose problems and findings are "empirical" in a pure mathematical world or space, is deep and forceful; it leads to the idealistic idea and rational claim that *reality* is more comprehensive than the physical universe and still is a world or space of spaces: *mathematical reality*. If I am right, human numeracy grew out of early evolutionary concerns for temporal control and interaction, in the pheno-physical world of our bodily social life, but it led to explorations and discoveries of a world of forms and inter-quantitative laws potentially applying across our entire universe and referring to an even more comprehensive reality (Cf. note 2).

Figure 13.4 Borneo, Gua Tewet, The tree of life. From Luc-Henri Fage, *Borneo, Memory of the Caves*, Kalimanthrope, 2010.

Back to the Body. The Argument of Synesthesia

Many people "see" numbers draped in colors, when they think of numerical signs or even when they visually attend to numerical graphics. We call this phenomenon synesthesia. Colors seem to particularly often project to numbers, letters, and musical tones. Concepts of time—names of calendaric units, such as weekdays or chronological numbers—are also frequently "seen" in colors or in graphic shapes; some synesthetes even describe numbers as personalities; others see and remember the names of persons in distinct colors. There is still no solid overall theory of this complex family of phenomena.[21] However, I find it striking, on the one hand, that *colors* are qualia that since early cultures have been reproduced artificially and regularly used as identitary signals;[22] and on the other hand, that colors project to the three major forms of digital writing and reading: numerical, literal, and musical. *Numbers, letters,* and *tones* all have phonetic names and they all, in synesthetic minds, attract colors. These graphical signifiers of phonetic names are all essential to intentional *digital* doings (counting, writing, playing) that rhythmically connect our tactile fingertips to our auditive and visual systems while we *communicate* with others. In articulate communication, whether written or not, of course the digital and the corporeal articulations have to integrate (as in counting and dancing, or reading and chanting, or playing an instrument). Digitally expressive fingers and whole, colorful, embodied persons have to move and "swim" together, in a sort of *double articulation*, as the one that André Martinet ascribed to language,[23] and to intentionally coordinate in order for communication to happen and be felicitous—in language and music, as well as in commercial or any other symbolic interaction. Synesthesia may thus be a deeply semiotic phenomenon caused by our communicative nature: *digital units refer to whole-body units that are conceptualized with a color.* This would explain the main directionality from number etc. to color, rather than the inverse; Hubbard and Ramachandran did not notice this.

The emotional impact of intersubjective communication may in fact be the binding factor that confers spatial color or shape to these humanly signifying sounds—beats, syllables, tones—that have configured and still are shaping our thinking, because they are themselves signified by our digital symbolization (writing), while our colored bodies dance to their meaning.

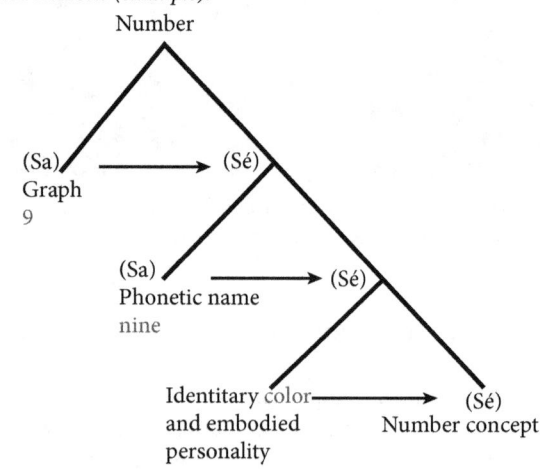

Figure 13.5 The synesthetic cascade.

If this is correct, we have (see Figure 13.5) a structurally stable semiotic cascade of signs,[24] signs-in-signs, one that may describe ordinary Saussurean signs as well, if we accept to include both their "script" and their "emotional color," which any writer or musician would do without much hesitation.

The human voice bridges the distance between digital and corporeal motricity, since it is sensitive to both; we *sing* digitally, note by note, while phrasing corporeally, melodic line after melodic line, and we likewise articulate distinctly while modulating prosodically when *speaking*. We are thus "analytic" (digital) while simultaneously being "synthetic" (corporeal). This double articulation *in time* may be another aspect of basic numerical cognition. First, as plexity, *number* must blend with mass *quantity*, so that a discrete number may paradoxically be cognized as quantity of a continuity; second, numbers, as digital units, must be integrated into multicycle multiples as in calendars and decimal or analogous systems, still connected to bodily movement and thereby creating the real intelligibility of numerical operations.[25]

Notes

1. A part of a former version of this text was published in Bockarova, Danesi and Nuñez (2012).
2. Lakoff and Nuñez (2000: 97). An anonymous, critical Wikipedia article on the book comments: "The idea of Lakoff and Núñez that mathematical objects exist only as *particular instances* of concepts/metaphors in our embodied brains, is an inadequate philosophical basis to account for the experience and de facto research methods of working mathematicians. Perhaps this is a reason why these ideas have been met with comparatively little interest by the mathematical community." It is true that the philosophical strangeness of this book makes it difficult to believe that the authors still refer to mathematics as a *science* in its own right and not as a whim of human psychology.
3. Fauconnier and Turner (2002).
4. See also Fontanille (ed.) (1992).
5. Proper names behave strangely in language; the reason for this may be that they are alien to default predicative syntax, being rooted in an archaic semiotics of *calling* on persons, animals, and spirits and of *naming* territories and people.
6. Answering the question: When is X true? Time-as-truth is a vital epistemic category in grammar. Example: "Do you love me?"—"Forever!" (meaning "yes" plus a certain extension). Not: "*2020."
7. The personal pronoun *we* has an inclusive and an exclusive meaning: I + you (inclusive) versus I + they (exclusive of you). The exclusive meaning may be a distal derivate of the inclusive version, considered as primary. Cf. k minus x, above. "All minus you." Correspondingly, *you* is often either a second-person singular or a plural *you* + *they*. "All minus me." In some languages, *you* is also an inclusive anybody, *you/me/they*. "When *you* hear this rhythm, *you* will want to dance."
8. Being a "number one," "number two," and so on, as in sports games is being categorially labeled, as in institutional ratings of all kinds.
9. When our ancestors discovered that numbers have infinitely many important and nontrivial properties, it may have been straightforward to attribute these mathematical properties to the divinities implied in their symbolization.

10 Calling (for) persons is presuming their absence and desiring and inviting their presence. Tonal (song-borne) calls reach farther targets than spoken calls.
11 I am referring to the still controversial but not negligible "aquatic ape hypothesis," see Morgan (1989).
12 See above, about the dancing daffodils in Wordsworth's poem.
13 On mimesis in this sense, see Donald (the following note). Discreteness, telicity, and volitive control are essential to acts and agentive mimesis; this point deserves all the attention it gets in Donald, and more.
14 The Canadian philosopher and cognitive psychologist Merlin Donald (1991, 2001) has unfolded his monumental vision of human cultural evolution based on *mimesis* as a primordial element.
15 The German neuropsychologist Ernst Pöppel (1997) wrote a short but entirely revolutionary note on this temporal aspect of a "flow" that does not just flow indefinitely but rather unfold a rhythmic rhetoric from extended moment to extended moment and does so for deep neurophysiological reasons.
16 *Capital*, Vol. I, Part I, "Commodities and Money," Chapter One: Commodities, Section 2, "The Twofold Character of the Labor Embodied in Commodities."
17 Marx: "Here two different kinds of commodities (in our example the linen and the coat), evidently play two different parts. The linen expresses its value in the coat; the coat serves as the material in which that value is expressed. The former plays an active, the latter a passive, part. The value of the linen is represented as relative value, or appears in relative form. The coat officiates as equivalent, or appears in equivalent form."
18 Bounded objects (b.o.) and unbounded masses (u.m.) behave differently in noun phrases, especially regarding the compatible determiners. Example: "Do you have a horse?" (b.o.) versus "Do you like horse?" (u.m., that is, horse meat).
19 We could call this modal entity "desire-of-X," a sort of *must-have*, even if such an abstraction does not seem to advance us very much.
20 History shows that *gold* and other precious metals and substances were already "precious" as material for proper, shiny adornment of religious icons (statues, images), qualifying these substances for becoming monetary expressions—on a territory sharing notions of sacredness and corresponding beauty. The origin of what we call "economy" is thus to be found in religion and sacred aesthetics.
21 See E. Hubbard and V. Ramachandran (2005) for a good state-of-the-art account of cognitive research on synesthesia.
22 In ancient cultures, including the Mesoamerican societies, divinities are often associated with specific colors, which are seen as their visual signatures. In modern societies, colors are political and national markers. "Pure colors" are only to be found in modern art and fashion; I suspect that our (somewhat archaic) minds still spontaneously perceive colors as markers of subjectivity, gender, age, personality traits, intentional style: identity.
23 Martinet (1960). Words signify and so do sentences. These two levels of signification constitute a striking "double articulation" of language, according to this linguist. Chess is his example of a "simple articulation" game. I would add: correspondingly, words are typically hand-size and sentences body-size in co-speech gesture.
24 A semiotic cascade is a sign whose planes are again signs, and so on: recursion in the signifier or in the signified.
25 In France, I have personally met a cognitive scientist who was also a dancer and who claimed to be able to dance the arithmetic operations. I believe him, to the extent

that the thinking-for-dancing is a sort of plastic mental topology of grouped steps; dancing-for-thinking would be next step.

References

Bockarova, M., D., Marcel, and Nuñez (Eds.), 2012. *Semiotic and Cognitive Science Essays on the Nature of Mathematics*. Fields Cognitive Science Network, Munich: Lincom Europa.

Brandt, P. A., 2019. *The Music of Meaning. Essays in Cognitive Semiotics*. Newcastle upon Tyne: Cambridge Scholars.

Donald, M., 1991. *Origins of the Modern Mind: Three Stages in the Evolution of Culture and Cognition*. Cambridge, MA: Harvard University Press.

Donald, M., 2001. *A Mind So Rare: The Evolution of Human Consciousness*. New York: Norton.

Donald, M., 2007. "The Slow Process: A Hypothetical Cognitive Adaptation for Distributed Cognitive Networks." *Journal of Physiology–Paris*, 101, 4–6.

Fauconnier, G., and M. Turner, 2002. *The Way We Think: Conceptual Blending and the Mind's Hidden Complexities*. New York: Basic Books.

Fontanille, J. (Ed.), 1992. *La quantité et ses modulations qualitatives*. Collection Nouveaux Actes Sémiotiques. Limoges, Amsterdam: Presses Universitaires de Limoges & J. Benjamins.

Hubbard, E. M., and V. S. Ramachandran, 2005. "Neurocognitive Mechanisms of Synesthesia." *Neuron*, 48, 509–520.

Lakoff, G., and R. Núñez, 2000. *Where Mathematics Comes From. How the Embodied Mind Brings Mathematics into Being*. New York: Basic Books.

Martinet, A., 1960. *Éléments de linguistique générale*. Paris: Armand Colin.

Morgan, E., 1989. *The Aquatic Ape Hypothesis. A Theory of Human Evolution*. London: Souvenir Press.

Pöppel, E., 1997. "Consciousness versus States of Being Conscious." *Behavioral and Brain Sciences*, 20.

14

The Meaning and Madness of Money

Ecological Prerequisites of the Monetary Sign

Monetary signs not only "signify" abstract value but also carry a performative force rooted in their substantiation, that is, rooted in the fact that their *substance of expression*, to use the linguist Louis Hjelmslev's term, is, at least in their basic manifestation as coins, but even still in their indirect manifestations, singularized as material objects.[1] Their "form of expression" cannot be separated from their "substance of expression." The act of "giving signs" is normally *participative* (the giver does not "lose" what he gives, he just shares it), whereas giving money, therefore, is *object* giving and therefore *separative* (moving singular material objects, substantial forces, or privileges from one proprietor to another). This unique condition of monetary signs—money and its generalization: capital—is therefore still a serious challenge to semiotic theory. The understanding of performative force in speech acts offers a similar difficulty, due to the ritual abolition of the distinction between sign and thing in illocutionary uses of language.[2] Economics, the mathematics of monetary practices, is of little help in treating this challenge, in so far as it builds on the assumption that this mysterious ontological[3] condition of the existence of money signs simply holds by definition; in economics, as in philosophy, it is taken as an axiom or an evidence, which should not be explained but just taken for granted and then analyzed in its current contexts.[4]

In this chapter, I will present an alternative, namely a semiotic and ecological, hence semio-ecological, view of the problem of understanding money. I will ignore the axiom that the existence of money should just be taken for granted and instead start from basic ecological considerations, supplemented by a semiotic approach to the issue.[5]

As the French philosopher Georges Bataille pointed out in a metaphysical moment, the living nature and the existence of human civilizations are results of the practically infinite, generous, unrequited, entropic "giving" of the sun, which on our planet causes

---

An earlier version of this chapter appeared in the journal *Language and Semiotic Studies*, Vol. 3, 3, 2017. This journal is published by Soochow University and is freely accessible on the internet. It was equally published in the journal *Cognitive Semiotics*, 2017, Vol. 10, 2, with a critique by Todd Oakley and my reply to the critique. A follow-up to this chapter, "What Is a Global Citizen?," is published in (Ed.) Ellis, Maureen, 2020, *Critical Global Semiotics. Understanding Sustainable Transformational Citizenship*. London: Routledge.

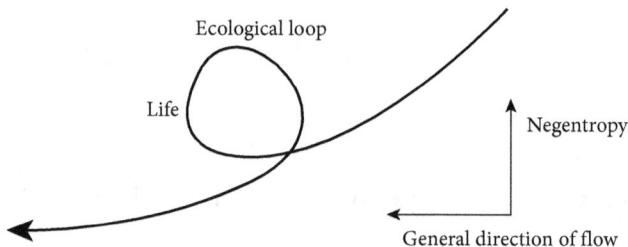

Figure 14.1 A negentropic loop.

a *negentropic* process called *life*.[6] If we follow Bataille on this point and think of the *entropic* temporal flow of matter and energy as one immense stream, we may imagine the negentropic movement that humans and all other living beings are involved in as a local reverse stream, or rather a number of local reverse negentropic streams, branching off from the main entropic flow. These negentropic streams finally *return* to the main, entropic flow and thus form an *ecological loop*. The return happens because death, decay, and waste make these negentropic movements spatially and temporally finite; new negentropic processes have to start from the local death, decay, and waste of the former processes. This ecological loop is therefore never a trivial given; life is fragile and abruptly ends as soon as it cannot feed on a nature that includes life's own litter. See Monsaingeon (2017).

Entropy universally increases but locally decreases where living matter emerges. Life thus consists in a loop by which the universal run toward chaos is momentarily halted and patterns of organization grow, until death and decay resume the universal tendency. This is the elementary general framework I suggest as a general prerequisite of the development of a semio-ecological analysis. When life emerges, it lays the ground for organic species, and again for human life, which feeds on life in general and on life's decay and litter. In the case of humans, however, from the moment civilizations emerge, an empirical observation easily distinguishes three major (sub-negentropic) off-branchings and sub-loops, corresponding to three standard levels of social organization. We can in fact superimpose three negentropic sub-loops in the case of human civilizations.

A first ecological sub-loop is initiated by our direct extraction and consumption of organic matter and water: vegetables, fruits, crops, animals—elements whose preparation mainly presupposes access to soil, water, wind, and fire, and a certain technique—hunting, fishing, gathering, sheltering, and then agriculture. This basic *organic loop* has its own ecology, of course; crops must be kept growing on viable qualities of soil, and so on. Water, soft or salt, must be kept clean enough to remain a fishing environment or a source of watering and drinking. Firewood must be renewable. Deterioration and devastation are always threatening possibilities. Civilizations are ecologically vulnerable, as ethnology shows.[7] Basic ecological consciousness, as found in tribal societies, grows on this essential *organic* loop and may extend to the following two loops. And basic ecological consciousness is ontological, in the sense that it grounds our fundamental existential realism, our constant awareness of the bodily drama of life and death and of personal and shared fragility.

A second loop extracts energy and raw materials allowing further elaboration of provisions, securing life conditions, and creating tools and means to satisfy expanding functional needs of collective life: we may call it the *technical loop*. Systematic production and distribution of artifacts (tools, machines, ships, weaponry) and other complex goods thus require extended *extraction* of energy, stone, metal, wood, building materials, raw materials for all kinds of production and construction: production facilities, infrastructure (roads, bridges, means of transportation and communication), social institutions, marketplaces, shops and workshops, homes and urban settings. Technical production, maintenance, repair, renewal, and development of the entire space of work, transportation, and exchange increase the consumption of energy and of many sorts of nonedible material. Strategies for the disposal and treatment of waste and refuse are again never trivial in view of maintaining a local habitat and a local population's health and growth. The technical loop differs from the organic loop by its most prominent effect, *urbanization*, with its dumping sites and cemeteries. This level of collective life develops shared imaginary conceptions, no longer of the drama of life and death but of forms of life, ways of living, thinking and feeling, institutions for different kinds of care, knowledge, and collective memory, communication, administration, and education. It also notably develops technology, production, and transportation of functional goods of all kinds.

Finally, a third, *symbolic loop* always extracts exquisite elements from nature for transcendent "spiritual" reasons: precious and rare metals and minerals, gold, silver, copper, marble, jade, gemstones, which are extracted for nonfunctional, decorative, and symbolic uses related to the erection of palaces and temples, with their adornments, imagery, and statues, monuments, that is, for ceremonial purposes of many kinds, sacred or profane. In all larger historical societies, religious or profane displays of social power constitute an overall category of *symbolic* construction and activity that shape social life by providing overarching authority, sacred mythology, emotional coherence, bringing both mystery and principles of transcendent "value" and forms of legitimacy—forms of "beauty," "truth," "justice," and "morality"—to the entire complex of practices implied by collective life.[8] Taking care of the need for collective identity is an essential symbolic task of the nominal ruler, the sovereign. Taking care of deaths, births, and individual or collective alliances is an essential symbolic task of the religious category. So, we may call this particular stream the *symbolic loop*. Symbolicity culturally seals the social formation as a whole. The negative output, or product, of the symbolic loop includes aggressive ideology and its consequence, warfare and destruction. In the contemporary worldwide civilization, the symbolic loops still as in all previous civilizations involve imagery and behaviors expressing the typical "spiritual" and violent endeavors embodied in sovereignty and religion. This level develops the very strange human form of behavior we call *rituals*: displays of acts and movements addressing instances above the range of human beings and supposed to dispose of our deepest feelings, our happiness, our right to exist—or in short, our sociopsychological health and sanity. The symbolicity of sovereign rituals on this level overrules all other (institutional) uses of symbols in social life.

These three negentropic, looping streams, all branching off from the main entropic flow and returning to it, can be represented as superimposed levels of *substantial and formal social life*. The substantial differences from level to level will correspond to formal differences in the regulations and concepts appearing at the three levels. I hypothesize that the stratified flow model thus obtained is, so far, generally valid for human social formations throughout our prehistorical and historical civilizations, whether hunter-gatherer-tribal, agricultural-feudal, agri-theocratic, capitalo-industrial, or otherwise formalized.

The three extraction-based loops will further correspond to three levels of vital social activity and life-forms: in a very elementary social formation, that of *organic producers*—agents in agriculture, fishing, hunting, gathering, and so on; that of *technical producers*—craftsmen, workers, engineers, administrators, traders, social and commercial agents; and that of *symbolic producers*—chiefs, rulers, politicians, intellectuals, artists, priests, and bankers. All producers are of course also resource consumers.

Between the three loops, there will always be many sorts of exchange, especially of products from one level serving on another level, both upwards and downwards. It is further necessary to consider the institutions that the constant activities on each level and between them create, as if by sedimentation, and which slowly but surely emerge by the nature of things, namely the needs that the activities themselves generate: needs for norms and maintenance of means, both moral and technical. We can consider them as the modes of *stasis* along or within the flows, and it is possible to postulate a finite set of such major categories of *stasis*, or "establishments"—which may differ in many ways and in their relative importance, depending on the specific structures developed in specific cultures and forms of social production. Here follows my suggested list of default instances of this kind: six elementary categories of stasis.

(1) Firstly, endeavors like assuring the access to water, shelter, protection, construction wood and firewood, a territory of operation, require concrete collaborative measures, certain elementary *communitary systems* for sharing necessary burdens and possible outcomes. This is the rudiment that may evolve into the network of institutions we now call the modern nation-state. The elementary communitary instance primarily connects and interacts with the organic and the technical flows.

(2) Secondly, organic products are immediately distributed and exchanged within a population according to some principles allowing the sharing of food, services, and

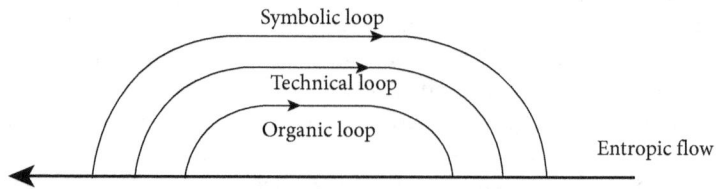

Figure 14.2 The organic, the technical, and the symbolic loops on the entropic flow.

basic goods. A community must therefore create and maintain pathways and places, where transportation, presentation, and exchange of such entities can happen. We may call such accessible places, in a very elementary sense, food *markets*.

(3) Thirdly, as mentioned, we may acknowledge the stasis of urbanization, the creation of cumulative habitats where systematic technical production and products (artifacts) can be sheltered and connected (workshops, factories, storages), and where larger-scale social and cultural communication can happen. This "public" sphere of urbanized activity includes the social accumulation of material goods and corresponding "wealth," and the display thereof. Material wealth in turn leads to the development of abstract juridical concepts of property: principles of ownership, "private" or "public," passed down through generations and expressed by real estate, and legal charters that allow private interests to emerge within the public domain.[9]

(4) Exchanges on the level of "property" lead to higher orders of distribution and market formation. On this level, real estate, land, and human beings (workers, women, slaves) are among the *goods* exchanged. The modern labor market is one of the aspects of this instance of the market, but much else is of course bound to happen before we get that far. This level is where production becomes industrial and capitalistic in the basic sense and where the Marxian theory of Capital, surplus value, profit, and subsequent class struggle then relevantly applies. Here is where societies acquire their so-called political economies (to be distinguished from their "general economies" in Bataille's sense, which include all three levels).

(5 and 6) On the third stream, the symbolic flow, there are two universally unfolding forms of stasis. One is what we call the instance of *sovereignty*, the place and institution of the ruler, the incarnation of the privilege and physical power to make binding decisions for entire populations on a territory and to declare wars: to define a "country," and later, a "nation" or even an "empire." Physically, this stasis is expressed by lavish buildings, displays of provocative architecture with monumental dimensions and emphatic use of extracted and preferably rare and costly materials. The other form is the materialization of *religion*, the equally provocative and awe-inducing temple, which in modern societies, especially after the introduction and generalization of the use of money, is doubled by a parallel variant, the *bank*.[10] The alliance of sovereignty and religion makes possible the creation of locally organized military forces to protect the population and aggress other populations.

Figure 14.3 summarizes this simplified analysis of stases in the formation of a shared human reality. There is of course much more interaction between these instances than shown by the arrows in the graph. The idea is that an elementary deep-structure like the one I propose here must underlie the specification of distinct social formations, modes of production, and politico-economic structures and conjunctures, making them comparable. The contrasts between an isolated tribal society and a modern industrial society are evidently huge, but my claim is that we need a materialistic, "pre-structured" common ecological basis like the one sketched out in this model to even clearly perceive the contrasts and to be able to structurally and more precisely specify and understand the different *historical* formations. History would thus be the temporal and differential unfolding of a largely predetermined structure.

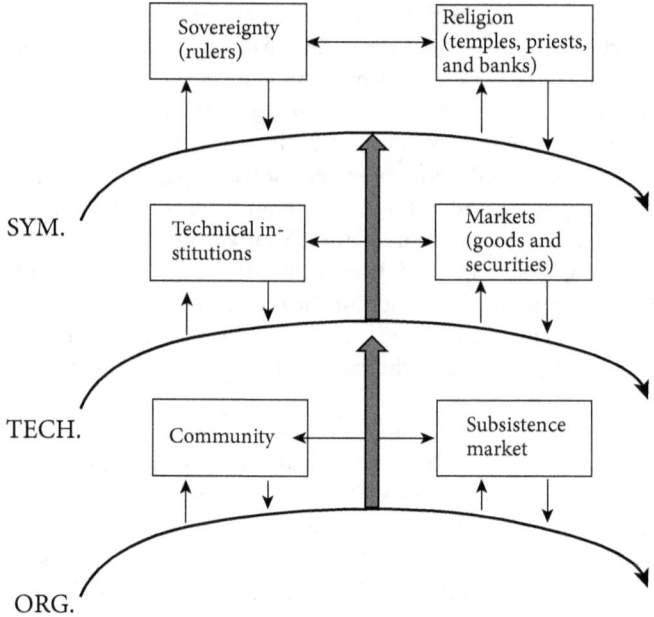

Figure 14.3 Three strata and six stasis categories in the formation of social reality.

The three basic streams articulate the presupposed human population, a part of which is mainly active on the organic level, whereas other parts are active on the technical level of production; a relatively smaller part is active on the symbolic level, where power and sacredness are "fabricated." Hence the common intuitive model of a society as a pyramid. A population[11] will become a class or caste society if the level of activity, in terms of strata, of one generation is transferred to and thus inherited by subsequent generations. The access or nonaccess to property and sovereignty is then of course particularly important to the social status of a population segment. And as Marx and Engels stated, the *extension of private ownership* of collectively produced goods and means of production is one of the preconditions of the formations we call capitalistic. However, a prerequisite of the same magnitude is the existence and functionality of the symbolic entity called *money*.

Money and the Strata of Societies

There are reasons to believe that the phenomenon and the extended use of money, in the form of coins, emerged during the so-called Axial Age[12] and that the religious instance (6, above) is directly involved.[13] Precious materials and, in particular, *metals* are first used for the adornment of iconic representations of rulers and divinities (statues, paintings, drapery, theatrical imagery of all kinds). These metals, gold, silver, electrum, bronze, and so on, are thereby—namely through the magical contact with the artistically represented, embodied sacred entity and divinity—rendered even more precious and are then, we suggest, interpreted as inheriting and containing the power of the divinities they adorn and magically touch. (Magic is thus a cognitive prerequisite for the semiotics of money to develop.) The priests discover that they can have people work for them by "paying" them with these metallic items infused with divine power. Then the priests can "lend" people certain quantities of them for similar purposes but against mortgage. The items acquire an inherent *protective value*[14] that makes them desirable in social life, in the shape of artistic adornments and then in the shape of small *coins* carrying the signs of a ruler and a priest who may in principle be seen as guaranteeing their metallic authenticity and volume, and the intensity of their inherent protective force. The ascribed inherent "value" of pieces of such metal of equal weight and authenticity is then relatively equal and stable. The temple is originally the place where such money is coined and issued, and where larger quantities or amounts of "monetary" value is kept, hence the historical link between (ancient) temples and (modern) banks. But of course, the efficiency of these shining items is abundantly proven outside the temples and especially in marketplaces on lower social levels. The use of uniform metallic units containing the abstract, imaginary property of *protecting* its owner is reinforced by the practical demonstration: in fact, the more you acquire of these entities, the better you are off.[15] You can exchange them for goods, services, including services of material protection. The semantics of money is in fact self-reinforcing.[16] However, let us not forget that trade, distribution, and accounting may well be much older than money. The first manifestations of what would become writing, from the eighth millennium BC, namely the token systems found by Schmandt-Besserat,[17] are dedicated to counting kept animals and therefore probably to the "accounting" of such animals, owned or owed. We know that cattle can be used as trading equivalents, or "capital,"[18] as seen from the Roman distinction *pecunia* versus *familia*, "small cattle" versus "big cattle," the latter not used for ordinary trade but for more radical investments. When money filters into the practices of exchange, maybe five millennia into the agricultural societies emerging after the end of the last glaciation, something radically new happens to social life and cultural activity: a huge growth of societies under unifying rulers and the beginning of monotheism (such as early Zoroastrianism).[19] Both may be causally related to the way social formations are slowly and gradually permeated on all levels by the same massively and intensely repeated symbolic references. The next version of the stratification graph shows the principle (Figure 14.4). We may therefore distinguish three forms of monetary capital: (1) the concrete exchange-based, organic, and reproductive capital, (2) the technical, investment-based productive capital, and (3) the speculation-based financial, or symbolic, capital.[20]

In a sense, the third, symbolic level of monetary practice is primordial, since money originates there, if I am right; so, in the same sense, financial capital *is* a primordial form of money.[21] But as early religious and law texts illustrate, it is immediately used for buying workforce, services, goods, and of course food. On the organic level, it constitutes the *reproductive capital* that circulates between food markets and income from paid work or sold products; small communitary capital formations—created by the invention of *taxes*—cover the necessary infrastructure, education initiatives

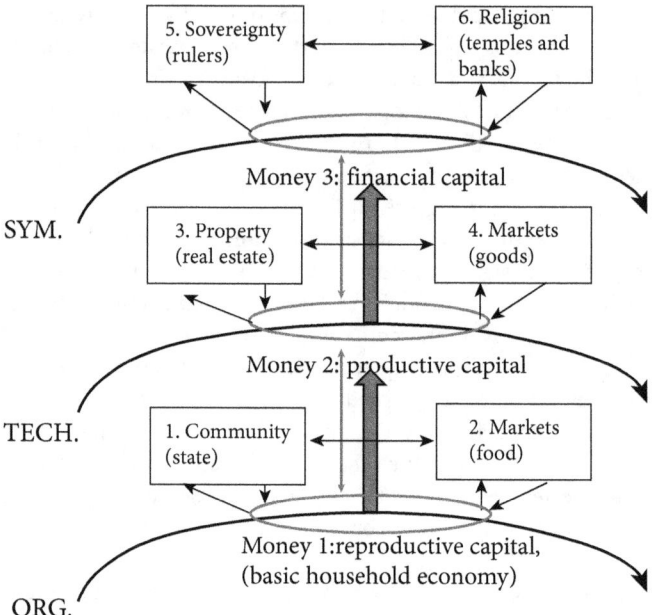

Figure 14.4 The three forms of monetary capital (in grey on the graph): reproductive, productive, and financial.

(schools), health-improving initiatives, and so on. The finality of this basic circulation of money is evidently the *reproduction of human life* in the framework of various sorts of households: the simple meaning of the term *oiko-nomy*,[22] which is further used as a (problematically inaccurate and misleading, hence ideological) metaphor for the political "economy" of entire societies. Societies are not "houses," and societies are in particular the ecological conditions for households.

On the technical level, the *productive capital* offers a different form of monetary circulation and a different set of semantic concepts. Here, money can be stocked in "property" and can be "invested" in industrious or industrial processes of paid work whose products are sold on the market of goods, so that the circular effect of "making money" by organizing production and distribution based on proletarian[23] workers paid by the money just "made," that is, the surplus value ingeniously described by Karl Marx, can create *profit* to reinvest, to stock in property, or to place in "speculative" enterprises on the superimposed symbolic level. If a section of the population cannot access the technical level *as proprietors*, it becomes in fact a "proletariat," and the part accessing and controlling the productive capital becomes historically the "bourgeoisie," the class of classical capitalists—those who *cannot borrow* versus those *who can*.

The *speculative capital*, on the symbolic level, allows a nonworking proprietor elite of a population to "invest" in entire productive enterprises and in other investments in them, and to treat these as abstract "goods" whose profits—typically becoming interests—are objects of conjecture and "speculation," that is, moving capital in and out of entire production zones and countries. Speculative profits are obtained by *investments in investments* and are used in many ethically more or less problematic ways, essentially for political manipulation, lobbying, buying the loyalty of rulers or the language of propagandists, and feeding secret agencies and mafias; for imperial, expansionist, colonial, energy-related or religious warfare; and for controlling illegal and secretive mega-markets exchanging third level reference values such as uranium, gold, drugs, artworks, or jewelry. It is worthy of notice that the activities happening on the symbolic level of capital and power are considered as situated "above" ordinary legality; sovereignty is allied with sacredness and is therefore essentially untouchable and not accessible to formal lawmaking and jurisdiction.[24] Laws mainly exist as immanent regulators of productive and reproductive life, on the second and the first levels of social structure. They presuppose a public sphere of discourse, whereas the symbolic transactions transgress this sphere of discourse; they are only displayed if the "show" serves the imaginary construction of beliefs and support (the social dream factory, so to speak). Money buys lives and deaths, and modern "lobbying" is a good model of the alliance of secrecy and display that dominates on this level. It is, in this sense, constitutively transgressive, which is no doubt the most important obstacle to all political or judicial attempts to limit its dangerous effects on societies and the planet, but it is no doubt also the most forceful motive for individual and pathological aspirations to power—meaning "total," totalitarian, unbridled social power beyond moral restrictions. Power in this sense is psychologically sexy to the point of inducing psychopathy and psychosis: deep and dangerous madness.[25] It can be strongly seductive if supported by submissive social communication, and it has demonstrated its appeal to "the People" throughout the various, more or less irrational, totalitarian populisms, or despotic populocracies, of world history.[26]

The most important effect of the introduction of the systems of capital in a social formation is, however, the modern vertical integration of the instances (1), (3), and (5), community, property, and sovereignty, which finally become levels of institutional, hierarchical Nation-States.[27] *The state* was basically and primordially just the reproductive community, but it is now also materialized in property as real estate, the "property of the people," "res publica," an independent, overarching social Subject that can own and manage productive capital. The holder of sovereignty becomes a ruler of this vertical (three-level) state apparatus, paid by generalized taxation and supported by both a currency-controlling "national bank" and, often, a religious establishment.

The modern phenomenon of an integrative and "national" state is inseparable from the pervasive monetarization of the social formation. The smooth trans-capitalistic (three-level) circulation of monetary values and the subsequent material exchanges are what gives rise to the protective (monetary, currency-based) feeling of social *oneness* we find in nationalisms, paradoxically running in parallel to the still more exacerbated contrasts between the forms of capital—the speculative, the productive, and the organic-reproductive—and the population's class gaps and inequality following from these contrasts. Money, state, and "People" are contrasting but interdependent concepts. But markets currently integrate internationally, and financial operations do that particularly fast, aided by numerical technology; markets and speculative movements expand the domination of money so intensely that it tends to dissolve the national, that is, state-based, legal boundaries in favor of unstable networks of capital streams, a process now referred to by the term *globalization* (French: *mondialisation*). The globalization of money means that nation-states can all be indebted to non national, globally active banking systems connecting the speculative capitals and sovereignties of the world. In this process, money *seems to* lose all reference to currencies and metals and to become a purely *fiat* entity that can be created ex nihilo by issuing debts, as Graeber suggests. Money seems to become radically infinite, since nothing limits its continuous creation and the subsequent creation of indebted instances. This historically important process is now reaching the limits of possible substantial growth of production, and its destructive effects on the planetary society, the entire *sociosphere*, makes it clear that a numerically infinite economy cannot harmonically coexist with a qualitatively finite and fragile planetary ecology.

The political consequences of this dilemma are not yet known, but international confusion is increasingly felt, and the human costs of the political unrest caused by the current frenetic behavior of capitalism are already becoming unbearable. At the same time, the changes in the planetary climate are becoming dramatic, and more populations than ever are becoming aware of the ecological effects of the madness of money.

What we call representative democracy is clearly an effect of the integrated state, where the hierarchical ordering of the levels of stasis can be expressed in terms of formal *representation* of individuals and groups by other individuals and groups.[28] Since the entire system is constitutively permeated by money, and representative status can be handled as a sort of commodity, the representative principle is, however, essentially unstable. Its monetary origin and ground remain manifest in its instability: mafias, lobbies, totalitarian excesses are never far away from the pockets of democratic "representatives." In this framework, social life will thus contain a political life, which mainly regulates the relative strength of the state institutions on all levels and the market interests on all levels, as these functions affect reproduction, production, and sovereignty.

Since political life unfolds in the substance of discourse, the state side opposes the commercial side as a "left wing" opposes a "right wing" in the lateralized space of public discourse or as a "progressive" versus a "reactionary" attitude in that discursive space. We might call this standard variation the *horizontal dynamics* of political discourse, simply put: state supporters versus market supporters. There is, however, a different determination of discursive style to consider, namely the vertical dynamics stemming from the superimposed capital forms. The third, symbolic stream generates a "wild," transgressive motive that conceptualizes social power in terms of charisma-based *despotism*, whether autocratic or theocratic, or both. This style contrasts with the conceptualization of social voices emanating from the productive capital and its institutions in particular, which is and must be *legalistic*. Legislation, based on institutional administration, is central in political life on the level of the productive capital.[29] Despotism and legalism form an essential vertical opposition, or variation in style, crossing the horizontal left–right opposition. So just as we find two forms of "left-wing" discourse, one revolutionary ("hardcore" and more or less despotic) and the other reformist ("soft" and legalistic), we find in "right-wing" discourse a split between "hardcore," despotic reactionaries (populist, fascist) and "soft" legalistic conservatives. However, on the basic first level of reproductive capital, discourse is rather of a third type, namely *pragmatic*. In the perspective of this discourse, on the one hand, even bad solutions are better than bad problems, so in some cases "hardcore," terroristic anarchism, in other cases "softer" and more democratic anarchism will be preferred, depending on the immediate effect of the remedy.[30] On the other hand, short-term pragmatism, opportunism, can contrast long-term pragmatism, grassroot ecology, seriously; short-term solutions to the problem of "getting rid of" waste by dumping it in the oceans, for example, create long-term problems by eliminating aquatic animal life, an important source of human food. Ecology in the sense of this chapter is in fact a form of long-term pragmatism, namely a concern for what economists call "negative externalities"—the fundamental problem being how to maintain the planet as a human habitat. Capitals, that is, the agents of capitals on all levels, are not inherently organic and not naturally interested in questions of preserving the life of humans in general; money itself is not organic, it is allowed to do what it "wants," that is, what its growth in the symbolic level requires.

The Ecological Problem

In the integrated and globalizing capitalistic perspective, coherence can only exist in terms of monetary coherence, which means that the semantics of money must prevail. The *meaning of money* is to circulate—protectively[31]—and in order to do so, since circulation however smooth is costly and implies loss, to increase, instead of decrease, *growth* must happen. So, an ideology of necessary growth is likely to develop. But for material growth to happen, the negentropic-entropic loops exploiting natural resources on all levels (organic, technical, symbolic; affecting soils, oceans, atmosphere, etc.) must be exploited infinitely, that is, must be handled according to the formal infinity of capitals; this has led to such destruction, pollution, and exhaustion of habitats and resources that human and animal life on the planet is now becoming seriously threatened. The metaphorical use of the organic term *growth* for the inanimate, purely symbolic finality of numerical capitals is tragically ironic. Money, or value, is not a living organism that can "grow," as this metaphor has it. The problem is whether it will manage to fully exhaust and destroy its own necessary material foundation, the natural loops that carry it, before it is itself "outgrown" by a healthier principle of human organization, a sustainable form of reproduction, production, and symbolization—in whatever scale of realization. We may have to discuss the possibility of "sustainable symbolization" and thus, of the sustainability of money as such. What is bound to happen globally is a dramatic matter of time, as ecology always is and locally has been. Can money be separated from capitalism and be cured from its apparently inherent madness? Can some human *ethics* finally make money rational and ecologically viable? Or could human civilization, as we know it, exist without the *symbolic* medium we call money? The latter question evidently presupposes an understanding of what money *is*, which is the ontological question that motivates this *semiotic and cognitive* inquiry.

The Political Problem

If the "growth" of the generalized and globalized capital is slowed down by the ecological difficulties it has created for local societies, and in particular by the impossibility of obtaining the quantities of energy needed for increasing material production, then an increasing part of the total capital will move "upwards" toward the pure symbolic and speculative level.[32] This is happening now and may account for the current "growth" of diffuse and irrational outbursts of sovereign insanity, including neocolonial warfare, religious militancy, and, no doubt, a very dangerous general turn to religious *and* neocolonial belligerence, in many parts of the planet— again, capitals must stay active, circulate, flow, move, and be used in order to exist. They exist "growingly," and *symbolic hyperactivity* of this kind can probably only be stopped or slowed down by resolute human acts: political intervention. But such intervention would mainly or only spring from the basic, existential, pragmatic level, where populations are hit by corresponding misery; and here, the weakened monetary flow ironically compels them to just call again for ... protection, that is, more monetary insanity. Intellectual political resistance is additionally inhibited by the lack of conceptual distinctions between capital forms, and the predominant vision of *the* Capital, *das Kapital*, as one tremendous, homogeneous, indivisible, maybe invincible block, not a stratified system whose single strata might be made relatively independent and amenable to regulation. The semio-ecological view may therefore become useful.[33]

The Problem of Knowledge

Institutions for the development and the transmission of knowledge are collective Subjects or Persons that are in the hands of either the state or the market and most often in both sorts of hands. These share the fate of the "public sphere" of information, debate, critical discourse, entertainment, advertisement, and propaganda—namely, to be playthings between states and an integrated, overarching market. Human minds naturally strive for insight and useful, accurate knowledge of the world, and at least what we call *science, history,* and *philosophy*, three main branches of real, relatively and potentially systematic and critical search for knowledge, are essentially the developed collaborative versions of this natural human drive. However, knowledge and its "truths"—however approximate—can be disturbing, and morally challenged persons can be persuaded monetarily to hide, deny, and distort such disturbance. As relevant organic, technical, and symbolic knowledge is becoming increasingly important to the survival of human beings in the current dangerous physical and organic state of the planet, these counter-epistemic, inhibiting factors are becoming particularly problematic. The *technologies of epistemic and counter-epistemic agency*, the industries of information and delusion, including the media of the "public sphere" and of the new "semi-private sphere" of more intimate personal digital media, make the task of politically building on real knowledge, rather than on interested misinformation, extremely difficult. As

Plato already observed, truth should not be a commodity that you can buy (as you could buy and take a course in rhetoric with Gorgias). Neither truths nor money are ordinary commodities; they are "sovereign" symbolic entities.[34] But money can therefore oppose truth, and knowledge is often "taken hostage," "bought": privatized, patented as property, made inaccessible and useless. However, truths are the necessary weapons of an ethical regulation of money-based power, because *truth is a supreme form of authority* that social power in general *must* itself appear to possess. Why else would it bother to lie? The voices of power have to sound as voices of truth, not just as voices of command.

The Problem of Culture

The frequently occurring direct fusion of sovereignty (5) and religion (6) in a conjuncture of inflated financial-speculative capitalism creates a particularly dangerous and explosive situation within a technically fragilized world-system of societies.[35] Religions merging with sovereignty potentially create a dangerous caste of priest-warrior-bankers-rulers on top of weakened political states. In such conjunctures, ethnic passions will replace rationality and inhibit, censure, or exclude deliberative discourse, and the local and global results are utterly destructive. By contrast, when ethno-cultural particularities are maintained and only transmitted on the basic organic level of households, their pretentions are limited, and they mainly assure elementary reproductive functions in family lives: ritualized burials, marriages, baptisms, celebration of events in the mythical calendar. However, these cultural functions of *cult* (in the instances (1) and (2) of Figure 14.4) are easily subsumed by the religious-financial elites (6), who can then mobilize the organic masses, already distressed and disoriented by the destructive effects of speculative capitals, and manipulate them to follow irrational orders and interests of inflated magicians or religious rulers (5–6). This is a formula of atemporal fascism; the first and the third levels suddenly merge into a sort of "sacred mob" to bully the second-level institutions, left and right, cultural and commercial. Only the cultural horizon of warfare subsists, and brutalism becomes a default behavioral style.

(Im)possible Alternatives

Contemporary philosophers frequently argue against the current structural reign of money, which now causes these spectacular disasters, but most often they argue without indicating realistic means of changing the situation. Certain forms of hope are indeed expressed. So, on the one hand, economists hope that more and new, hitherto unseen forms of "growth" will eventually ease the situation and repair the social damage caused by capital-driven violence and destruction. Such expectations generally do not include the devastation of nature, for economy is still not ecology. On the other hand, revolutionary mysticisms thrive among mundane philosophers and intellectuals hoping that the global proletariat will somehow again erect and climb the mythical barricades; and yet the elementary question remains: What to do about the monetary or otherwise symbolic condition, even after a new political revolution, global or local? The question concerns all inhabitable areas of the planet—will mankind be able to reorganize and develop a high-technological global social formation without its "wild" speculative money? Or would societies have to scale down to tribal formats and try to make that work locally? Or again: can money stay with us as a regulator but without capitalism? This sounds like a rhetorical question. But it may become a realistic one and even an urgent problem to solve.

Certain anti-capitalistic views would see the solution in a new strengthening of the state, making it possible to fight the strong integration and hegemony of the markets. But as we are seeing already in some of the largest societies of the planet, states and markets can be strengthened at the same time; we could reanimate or generalize one or two of modern history's particularly unfortunate anti-capitalistic models, but global ecology is not likely to be served.

Neoliberal thinkers are convinced that new technologies of some kind will overcome the hurdles of growth; they hope that increases of energy consumption will therefore not be necessary or that new sources of energy will be found. Production is supposed to grow, while the energy flow will proportionally shrink or stay on current levels or miraculously increase at no ecological cost. The new technology will maybe not need increased extraction, just immaterial smartness. But smartness alone is not relevant in any sense before it produces *more* than is presently the case, which again requires increased extraction, energy, and material consumption, and if growth is just stagnation with lowered costs due to smart robots, the production and maintenance of these new machines will again require increased extraction, consumption, expulsion. A growth with zero-increase in energy consumption and waste is simply impossible. Believing otherwise amounts to relying on miracles. Growth of production is growth of extraction and waste. Less life, more garbage.

Money has created the great human historical world as we know it. And money is now destroying it. Still nothing is in view that could replace it without itself being money (e.g., bitcoin[36]). The remaining question is therefore the deepest and simplest: Can money be changed into something less pervasive and destructive?[37] Or is there another semiotic way to organize an intelligent post-capitalistic society and its symbolic level?

The answer may depend on the interpretation of the underlying flows and the social stasis that these flows must create for human populations to live. Maybe new attention should be paid to the sacred origin of money[38] as an atavistic means of contact with the divine. It should be clear that reducing the capitalistic size and importance of this instance ((6) in the model) and its alliances with political rulers ((5) in the model) *could* reduce the toxic effects, initiatives, and attitudes that flow from this sphere and inhibit human political thinking, creating intolerance, arrogance, fanaticism—irrationalisms of all kinds. No viable solution can be worked out under the dominance of violence, corruption, and financially militarized religion. If the symbolic flow of financio-religio-despotico-speculative capital can be reduced and weakened, *state rulers may gain rationality*, which is a prerequisite for gaining control of the lawless forces at work on this third level and downward. The goal would be a significant reduction of the role of "wild money" in the global circulation, that is, a certain "de-capitalization" of the third level and a corresponding "re-rationalization" of governance.

Instead of yielding to despair faced with the global capitalization of money, it may be possible to dwell on its substantial layering, which subsists despite all types of state and market integration, combination, and conflict. It may be important to remember that the role of money is still *different* from one ecological level to another, and that the danger to mankind of activities being determined mainly by monetary flows increases drastically from level to level upwards, while it decreases in the opposite direction. Money therefore needs to be taken "down" from speculative dominance. The fatal lack of rationality occurs mainly at the highest level; therefore, initiatives to limit the severe ecological and human damages caused by the functions of capital in our contemporary societies should primarily target the symbolic top of the monetary flows and their influential bodies of power, the ties between speculative wealth, politico-economic ruling power, and religious mind control. The theme of growth may be crucial here: it needs to be deeply problematized.

Since the Axial Age, through Antiquity, the feudal Middle Ages, the commercial Renaissance, the agonistic Baroque, Industrial Romanticism, and technological Modernism, money has given rise to many great and impressive technical, social, and cultural developments and achievements worldwide, however often obtained to a saddening price paid by nature and life. Currently, the planetary situation calls for a profound rational reconsideration of the monetary world order, and we must find ways to empower forms of political rationality capable of changing the perspective, and in particular, to reduce the irrational agency caused by the monetary world order *as it is*.

The Symbolic Condition. A Critique of Sovereignty

If I am right, the symbolic flow, which is the main historical cause of the disaster, has an interesting weak spot, namely that it is and remains—*symbolic*. It is semiotically symbolic and refers to itself; symbols grow out of symbols, as Peirce mentioned (*omne symbolum de symbolo*).[39] This is probably the root of all irrationalisms: recursive "meta-language," infinite self-reference. Symbolicity is mainly driven by *language*, which is always self-referential to a certain point. Money has indeed often been compared to language.[40] It is strikingly true that language, in the shape of *discourse*— in fact a rich display of different *discourses*, political, religious, ideological, and so on, each with its own aesthetical norms of well-formedness and rhetorical forms, which constitute the delight of semiotic analysis[41]—pervades social and cultural formations as much as and even more than money. Money itself would not exist without language to negotiate, define, and compare the properties of pieces or quantities of monetary value and to determine their performative force. But furthermore, religious practices as well as political acts are entirely shaped by language—their operations and terms depend on the *intelligibility* and the *credibility* of political and religious discourse and of their combinations. That is why social rulers and religious authorities must spectacularly *display* their agency in constant massive and, of course, ostentatiously costly, lavish, and wasteful theatrical setups. If an equally massive or socially audible rational critique of these displays, and their inherently vacuous futility and essentially stultifying simulacra, could obtain sufficient social and material support to become a real challenge, despite all technical attempts to silence it, then the *roles* of money may in fact be changed, and the fate of mankind be made to look less somber.

An explicit critique of transgressive sovereignty—what sort of discourse could materialize its task? *Where* would it speak from, as Michel Foucault (1971) would ask. While symbolic capital and activities in general are inherently aggressive and transgressive, the authority of the law is inoperative on this transcendent level, and often technically powerless, as demonstrated every day in contemporary social and political life. Still, language has an advantage and even sacred versions of sovereignty have a weak spot where this advantage is located: language and only language can make it exist socially, and language comes with an inherent, built-in *ethics of enunciation*: to speak is to give and to care for the other and for others in the world, to give voice to an elementary ethical claim of respect for life and therefore for truth. Evil is inherently silent or self-contradictory.[42] An *ethical critique of sovereignty*, formulated in the prosaic or poetical language of organic human experience and subsequently in the discourse of a philosophy of responsibility, may be a means to obtain such a change of mind. All humans capable of following a story and grasping its narrative logic in principle do understand the distinction between serving life and serving death, between helping and harming, and between responsible reason and irresponsible madness. The semantics of a fundamentally ethical critique in fact should have a chance to at least transcend ethnic passions and powerful pathological behaviors. Lawyers of the current academic sort will probably reject it, but beyond the unavoidable formalisms of laws, there is an *ethical condition* for human life to make sense, namely the call to *protect the other*, not as money was supposed to do according to its semantic "value," which meant just *protect yourself, as possessor*. This grounding ethical call to protect others around you (the individual you), including those of the still more precarious future, is a strong call, deeply rooted in human nature, and it is, I think, strong enough to fight and defeat the speculative madness of money, when the ecological catastrophes accumulate.[43] As idle capitals accumulate, so do these catastrophes, by direct proportionality—and there will be a tipping point where the discourse of ethical ecology may become the only voice capable of countering radical defeatism. It would however be cynical to passively await such a moment.

The monetary sign is performative, that is, it embodies the same performative force as the utterance of a declaration, a promise, a threat. It is a materialized, declared promise. Either the money is given by A to B or not; either the promise by A addressing B is made or not. If given, made, a situation has changed. But money can only be given and received within a *frame* of specified exchange that must be understood or defined by language. This exchange may be an act of "buying," of "lending," of "donating," or of course of "bribing," and so on. Language is therefore conceptually superimposed on money. This is interesting, because in the last instance, and especially when used for illicit, transgressive purposes, as shown in crime fiction and the corresponding reality, language must follow an inherent principle of *discursive ethics* that forces the user to *do as promised* (*in casu*, even keep a secret, tell the same lie as someone else, etc.), that is, to be linguistically reliable. If this principle is not respected, the subject is excluded even from a criminal community. Only psychosis or brain damage can make the speaker deviate from this fundamental principle of ethics of language use. Ethics in this sense is stronger than morality and law, and therefore it can be *where to speak from* in a future critique of destructive capitals. *Ethics speaks from language itself.* Laws can be bent, ignored, interpreted in many fanciful ways, but the ethics of language use, which is, I claim, the very grounding ethics of the human being as such, cannot. This source, the grounding human ethics of meaning and truth, is from where art, literature, music come, and from where responsible scholars, scientists, and philosophers speak and write, if they have the personal capacity and integrity to assume their task, which admittedly is far from always the case. In particular, one may quite often suspect academic economists to neglect to display such conceptual and ethical integrity.

Money may be pervasive, but in the last instance, it is ruled by language, by enunciation. It may therefore be politically and structurally changeable by language, art, music, emotional expressions of commitments to life, in the name of the very ethics that makes us human. We may have to find our way *into* this critical core of our communicative being if we want to find our way *out* of the current maze of despotic or erratic capitalism, mental confusion, and ecological disaster.

The Realms of Meaning

In Georges Bataille's so-called heterology, which describes experiences and observations of behaviors corresponding to what is happening on the symbolic level in my analysis of eco-social structure, power and madness are linked to excess, transgression of rationality and of norms, behaviors of "sovereignty" both in the collective and in the individual scale. His social phenomenology is indifferent to such scale shifts between the macro-social and the micro-social or even intimate realms. It strikes me that this conceptual plasticity of scale called for justification and that we might now have an explanatory argument at hand.

The three levels of societal organization, including their interactions and interdependent processes, with or without the intervention of money, are matched by three levels of semantic organization that we find in *all human semiotic phenomena of meaning-making*: in language, art, music, affectivity, normativity. We will briefly consider this subjective perspective and its consequences.

There are three main levels of meaning in sociocultural life, as we have seen.

The terminology proposed by the French structural psychoanalyst Jacques Lacan[44] to characterize the core instances active in the human mind, or subjectivity, *the Symbolic, the Imaginary, the Real*, can in fact and meaningfully be transposed to describe these levels of meaning in sociocultural life:

> III. The *Symbolic* level of meaning: authority and ritual force; "identity" and violence; POWER.

II. The *Imaginary* level of meaning: social representations and projects of all kinds; THOUGHT.
I. The *Real* level of meaning: family, friendship, love, births, deaths. Existential aspects; LIFE.

Note that language has a corresponding set of meaning types (SY/IM/RE):

III. *Performative* force; speech-act meaning: promises, orders, declarations. SY.
II. *Informative* force; denotative meaning: statements, dialogical functions. IM.
I. *Formative* force; connotative, affective and evaluative meaning: poetic functions. RE.[45]

We experience social life first by growing up in a collective setting, by being there and taking part in its daily endeavors. Our existential *reality* consists of passionate bindings to others and learning to follow their rules and norms, their "moral" principles. But we soon learn that there are larger social horizons regulated by laws issued by institutions and addressing us as citizens, as principles of "legality" to follow (or fight). We encounter this sort of meaning as an encyclopedic mass of (traditionally: maternal) *Imaginary* entities: projects, political "dreams" and ideologies, references to knowledge, myths, songs, stories, information, propaganda, and so on. At the same time, we discover that there are "higher" orders of decision making, transcendent principles of authority, sacredness, spirituality, and (traditionally: paternal) *Symbolic* acts without rational explanations, which seem to venerate some sort of shared Destiny calling upon our participation. The latter "order" is no longer regulated by the civil and ordinary *law*, nor by the *moral* norms of the basic, *Real* level, but either by the sovereign madness of sacralized rulers or else by some superordinate principles of universal *ethics*—such as what we call the Human Rights and an ethics of care for life and nature: ecology. The existentially grounded personal ethics by which we traditionally oppose, as young adults, the paternal order is a result of our slow and gradual discovery of our own affective life and the existence of conscience in consciousness.

A corresponding division in the registers of meaning characteristic of language is thus straightforward and appears natural. In the register of speech acts, the presupposed authority of the speaker and the relevance of the hearer make it possible to create new interpersonal and social situations by performing declarations, promises, imperatives, curses, conjurations, oaths, and other speech-active utterances in the present tense. This is the "symbolic semantics" of language. But in the framework of the non-performative functions of language, communication simultaneously builds universes of *imaginary* political, educational, aesthetic, narrative meaning allowing human societies to operate as huge networks of connected and collaborative (incl. polemically responsive) minds, open toward the shared past and a shared future. The open-class words that constantly change their meaning and possible reference, migrate between languages, and follow the historical and technical developments of cultures and countries form the necessary grounds of all social life. This is the "imaginary semantics" of language, still to use Lacan's terms. Finally, the phenomenological, *real* register in language is dominated by proper names, place names, pet names, nicknames, markers of singular (numerical) identities that are essential in our affective and intimate life; idiomatic expressions, dialects, sociolects, sexolects may therefore pertain to the same register. This is then the "real semantics" of language. The *vocative* case in certain languages, used for calling and invocations, may be emblematic of this register.

In the enunciational morphology of the personal pronouns, *you (singular) and I* are anchored in the basic, real, phenomenological register, whereas *we and you (plural)* mark the collective imaginary, and the *we (singular)*, as in "we, the king," refers to the symbolic instance.[46]

In these respects, language is, I suggest, shaped by a deep ecological structural folding of human sociality. It can be argued that *signs* in general, not only linguistic signs but visual, auditive, gestural, or otherwise humanly configured expressions, including artistic expression, which are often complex integrations of expressions of various modalities, manifest a similarly differentiated semantic folding and unfolding. One part of a sign always potentially signifies an instruction: the *symbolic* aspect; another part always to some extent indicates what something referred to is or does or means: the *imaginary* aspect; and one part of the sign connotes its context or origin and value to the speaker, the *real* aspect, in Lacan's sense, here adopted. Submission, conceptualization, and affection.

One of the most important categories of subjectivity is of course affect. Human affectivity divides into several independent but interrelated systems, including regulators of our mental and bodily state in different time scales. The "fastest" affects are the shifting *emotions* by which we experience our constantly changing social situations: joy, surprise, anger, fear, sadness, concern, sorrow, shame, pride, contempt, disgust. The time scale refers to minutes of expression and feeling. This category corresponds directly to our insertion in the rapidly changing social *imaginary*.

The category of what we call *moods* cover the somewhat "slower" affective states of excitement, elation, ecstasy, and their opposites: depression, dejection, melancholy. Between these polar extremes, there is a neutral state; the time scale for being in the non-neutral states of mood is the day, since they are regulated by our circadian rhythms and because the *symbolic calendar* and our ritual behavioral routines let our binding to the symbolic instances determine the choice of state, at least to a certain extent. Religion is therefore a regulator of mood and one that easily binds our subjectivity to sacredness and authority.

Finally, the sort of affect we call *passions* relates to our existential feelings: being-in-love, love (itself), grief, affection, bitterness, resentment, hatred. Those states of mind and body are "long-term" affects. Their scale runs from the year to a lifetime; they regulate and often dramatize our real existential life.[47]

Conclusion

In these respects, the architecture of the human mind is literally *identical* to that of society. It is thus a reasonable assumption that the three levels of social flow are imprinted in human minds and bodies, that is, that they have been shaping our subjectivity during the last—at least ten—millennia in which we have been living in stable or unstable social formations articulated in this way. This would explain why social events immediately affect us so deeply and directly, individually; from gossip to news programs and media messages, and to poetry, what "happens around us" directly determine our personal thoughts and feelings to a striking degree: the individual mind experiences society as a part of its bodily self. So social "crises" often become individual crises as well. And madness in one sense becomes madness in another sense: social rulers experience their body as a country; psychotic conditions can induce similar feelings, for example the feeling of being a ruler because the body has become a country, as we see in some forms of schizophrenic psychosis. Psychology and sociology coincide as to their orders, levels, and semiotic processes—the human mind is a radically social machine, one may say.

The ecological order of a society is replicated in institutions and groups of any size, down to the family, so that the resulting structure is fractal, so to speak: the triads SY/IM/RE reappear at any level of experience, which explains that language easily travels from the bottom to the top of social systems, using the same words and categories, the same syntax and the same rhetoric, the same tropes and figures, only with slight variations in preferences, to mark distinction or affect.

If this is correct, at least as a first approximation, we may begin to understand how money can enter the human mind with such a tremendous imperative force, as the semiotic entity that the individual feels it must relate to. Money can enter the mind exactly as language does and by following the very example of language (given that language preceded it in the human symbolic evolution, phylogenesis, as it does in individual development, ontogenesis). Money becomes an irresistible *master sign* in the flows of our affectivity and quasi-automatically regulates our reasoning, giving rise to the so-called *economical rationality* that critical theories have problematized. However, we do not need a theory of authoritarian personalities in order to grasp the endemic logic of monetary submission in modern human psychology.[48] We do not even need theories of "reflection" like Lenin's by which the mind mirrors social processes; our minds *are* directly involved in these processes. What we instead do need in order to fight and limit the madness of money in our personal, political, and variably empowered lives is an understanding of the genealogy and general semiotic economy of money and its underlying general ecology. In the finiteness of our ecology is the remedy for the delirious infinity of our economical imagination.

Notes

1 Walt Disney's, that is, Carl Barks', philosophical and pedagogical masterpiece, the cartoon Donald Duck has a Dickens-inspired character, Scrooge McDuck, who owns a money tank filled with gold coins; it serves as his swimming pool and allows him to physically enjoy his immense wealth by bodily contact with the liquid of his "money."
2 To "give someone your word," in the sense of making a promise, has the same effect of irreversibly depositing an entity of value. You "pawn" your language and must "pay" (fulfill the promise) to get it back ("You have my word!"). Otherwise you lose your illocutive force.

3   On the ontology of money, Antonelli (2018) presents an interesting "deconstructive" analysis.
4   Critical semiotic approaches have been taken by social philosophers such as Jean Baudrillard (1972) or Ferruccio Rossi-Landi (1975). The assumption of these attempts is that linguistic and monetary signs essentially work the same way. Words are the money of our bodies. Both are conventional, and both have performative force. We will return to this analogistic view, which calls for serious modification, a modification that can profit from a closer study of monetary functions.
    I should specify that I am talking about standard neoclassical economics. I admit that several heterodox economists, and the school called Modern Money Theory (MMT), or Chartalism, do place monetary institutions at the center of macroeconomics. They further make a main distinction between metal money and paper money, the latter seen as being created by states through declarative acts (therefore nicely called: *fiat* money; metal money would then be *bona fide* money). The first modern theorist of money, Ferdinando Galliani, whose *Della moneta*, inspired by Hume, appeared in 1751, was a "state metallist": he suggested that metal money emerged spontaneously out of states' need for a manageable tax-paying reference.
5   However, the works of three important modern economists, Karl Polanyi, E.F. Schumacher, and Nicolai Georgescu-Roegen, should not be forgotten; they stressed that economy must be socially embedded, the latter even saw the ecologic perspectives.
6   Georges Bataille (1944). The negentropic loop referred to here also underlies Bataille's (1949) concept and project of a "general economy," which opposes the restricted economy of production, profit, and reinvestment, by also including the instances of systematic destruction of uninvested wealth, as in wars or costly displays, typically related to the symbolization of sovereignty.
7   Cf. the decline of Classic Lowland Maya civilization, The Easter Island civilization, and Angkor Wat. See Diamond (1994).
8   I will argue that money arises from symbolic activity in this sense. The contemporary "Modern Money Theory" economist L. Randall Wray, a student of the fiat-money pioneer Hyman Minsky, supports the view that all these psychological and symbolic aspects of collective life are involved in capital formation (Wray 1990). He rejects the standard and Marxian view that money emerges from exchange of goods. Whereas the exchange-based view imagines that money as such develops bottom-up, so to speak, that is, from barter, he reaches a conclusion similar to that of the present author, namely that it originates in a top-down process, *from the symbolic level*. It then serves exchanges on all levels by expressing "value."
9   This statement sounds like an ideological standard phrase. But understanding the origin of "private" (person-assigned) property is not a problem solved by Morgan, Marx, Engels, or any other modern social scientist. Here, we will bluntly assume that the concept of real estate and property evolves out of ownership applied to objects and entities on the level of the technical flow. How "private" it eventually becomes, or again ceases to be, is a historical question. Friedrich Engels' (1884–1892) work on the subject, *The Origin of the Family, Private Property, and the State*, remains a major contribution to the discussion. Property is one of the schematic meanings expressed by linguistic morphologies of *genitive* relations.
10 In ancient cultures, temples often also served as banks. The biblical Jesus caused scandal by expelling the bankers from the temple of Jerusalem, thus marking the modern distinction—which remains relative. The original unity is recalled by

institutions like the most Catholic *Banco del Santo Spirito*. Apollo's temple in Delphi was an important monetary depository.

11   For there to be a population, there has to be a territory inhabited by people sharing language, moral and technical habits, history, and interpreting that territory in terms of its life-forms.

12   Graeber (2011). The original German term is *Achsenzeit*, the period from about eighth to third century BC, suggested by the philosopher Karl Jaspers (1949) to be a decisive founding phase of the great civilizations that would follow in many areas of the planet simultaneously. In Mesopotamia, gold ornaments first appeared in the fifth millennium BC. Gold played a prominent part in funeral gifts and ceremonial objects. Cult statues were often covered with gold foil. In the mid-second millennium, gold from Egypt was imported from the Pharaoh by the Babylonian kings in exchange for richly worked textiles or war chariots.

13   Brandt (2015a), (2015b).

14   Remember that the etymologically important Juno *Moneta* was a powerful protective Roman goddess, who warned the Romans of an earthquake. The imputed inherent *protective* force of money consequently grounds its semantics of abstract "value." Protection is what value means, historically.

15   Money thus also exists as a store of value. In contrast to *Say's law*, as J.M. Keynes (1919) critically named this well-known belief that money is just a momentary link between two acts of buying, and that the market is thus self-regulating, we in fact hoard money as a bulwark against uncertainty. Jean-Baptiste Say formulated the principle in his *Traité d'Economie politique*, 1803. "Money performs but a momentary function in this double exchange; and when the transaction is finally closed, it will always be found, that one kind of commodity has been exchanged for another."

16   Of course, the affective background of the semantics of money, on this account, is the omni-presence of the universal basic emotion *fear*. Money is experienced as a remedy against this very real feeling. Through the three millennia of the history of organized money, this circumstance has stayed stable. Money is still experienced as protective. This is true even when it is used as female adornment, for example. (Cf. the monetary story in Maupassant's "The Necklace," above). Or when used in wedding rings, protecting the contract. And it is characteristic of sacred imagery to still use precious metal adornment lavishly, as if to constantly remind us of its origin.

17   Schmandt-Besserat (1996).

18   The word *capital* is derived from the same Latin root as cattle: *caput*, "head" (of cattle).

19   Religion and sovereign money seem to cooperate across cultures and through history. On the website *New Economic Perspectives*, L. Randall Wray critically quotes Nobel Prize winner Paul Samuelson's remark that "[…] one of the functions of old fashioned *religion* was to scare people by sometimes what might be regarded as myths into behaving in a way that the long-run *civilized life* requires. We have taken away a belief in the intrinsic necessity of balancing the budget if not in every year, [then] in every short period of time. […]" Wray does not believe in the religion of balancing state budgets for the mythical reason that "one must always pay what one owes." He writes: "We don't need myths. We need more democracy, more understanding, and more transparency. We do need to constrain our leaders—but not through dysfunctional superstitions."

20   Hyman Minsky, one of the founders of MMT, distinguished three forms: commercial, welfare state, and money manager capitalism, fairly comparable to our three strata of capital *in general*. Minsky (1986) noticed that a surplus of productive capital *immediately* spills over into speculative capital, which destabilizes the "system." That is what Bataille already saw.

21   Commodity money (coins) was first replaced by representative money (paper) in China, according to Marco Polo, and became then "represented" by bank notes in the seventeenth century in Europe. Paper money remains anchored in references to gold or silver until the second part of the twentieth century, when the references seem to become autonomous: the pieces of paper finally inherit the protective magic of the metals, if properly authenticated. Paper money consists in documents stating debts to the person owning the documents. The debt statement is a double performative act, a *declaration of a promise*, signed by the issuer of the unique and singular piece of paper to whoever will own it.

   Commodity money represents value as a link between nominal units of currency and quantity of coined metal. A very interesting debate involving the philosopher John Locke took place in the last decade of the English eighteenth century, around the Great Recoinage 1696–1700; guided by the philosopher, the run-down shilling was recoined with as much silver as there had been a century before, and it was decided to keep the rate fixed. Why keep the rate fixed? Because the value *still is* in the metal. The issue was treated as a deep philosophical problem. Soon, the pound was bound to fixed amounts of gold in the same way, by the Bank of England. See John Locke, "Further Considerations Concerning Raising the Value of Money," in Kelly (1991).

22   The *oikos* is of course a house, a home, but it does not yet really count as a value, contrarily to what is the case on the technical level, where it becomes a priced Property. Mostly, either the dwelling is built by the owner or it is rented. On the other hand, the term *ecology*—introduced by the German biologist and philosopher Ernst Haeckel in 1866—refers to the same *oikos*, now in the sense of "niche," and to *logos* in the sense of study: the biological or social study of the interactions between organisms and their environments, or niches.

23   Banks define the difference between capitalists and proletarians directly: the former can borrow money, because they can offer mortgage, the latter cannot, since their "property" is considered null.

24   That sovereign governments apparently can create money "out of thin air" still scares modern citizens.

25   Sergio Tonkonoff (2012) offers a fine and finely written account of Bataille's view of human transgression. Sovereignty in this dramatic sense can be seen as a paradoxically permanent "state of emergency," as in the Italian philosopher Giorgio Agamben's thinking, inspired by Carl Schmitt. See Agamben (1995). Agamben understandably wishes to get rid of it altogether; I doubt the possibility of building a society without a symbolic level. But since the *law* that regulates the conflicts on the second level does not have much effect on the third level, we might instead look at transcendent principles such as the Human Rights to find the ethical principles that can limit the irrationality of this third, dangerously destructive level of sociality.

26   Populocracy is the direct opposite of democracy, although *populus* in Latin translates demos in *Greek*. Populism strives to increase the unbridled powers of sovereignty, whereas democracy tries to decrease these powers.

27   This conception is not far from the Chartalist view of the multiple functions of money (see note 4).

28 The standard semiotic (Peircean) principle of signs and representation as occurring when *aliquid stat pro aliquo* is structurally based on political representation. Communication in a certain level "represents" communications going on in a different level. Enunciation is transitive, in the sense that speaking is *authorized* on a previous level. Political representation is thus representative both of voices on the underlying level, the "people," and of voices from the overarching level of sovereignty—this ambiguity is felt in the duplicity of demagogy and corruption or the muddy waters between populism and democracy.

29 We rediscover in this context Karl Jaspers' friend Max Weber's (1905, 2016) famous opposition of traditional, *charismatic*, and *bureaucratic* power, the latter two superseding the power of *traditions* and conventions, which are of course rooted in the necessities of reproductive life. In my view, Weber's categories are essentially superimposed on each other, like our three levels, and correspond to these, rather than only being historically sequenced.

30 We could call this style of management a *cowboy logic*. The hero of such conflicts and stories is typically a pragmatician, which can be felt as a relief from the stressing higher-order conflict between the four predominant styles described here.

31 The meaning of money is to yield *protection*, if my analysis is correct. The fundamental concept of "value" in economics is based on this semantic effect. Some heterodox economists, from Keynes and Minsky to Wray, may incidentally agree, whereas neoclassical mainstream economists just consider money as a neutral, *insignificant* element of macroeconomics, not in need of any ontological analysis.

32 The Minsky principle: when capitals cannot be immediately invested in production, for whatever reasons, it moves upwards and becomes speculative.

33 There is certainly a dynamic agonist–antagonist relation between productive and speculative instances, and wild speculation stemming from stases 3 and 4 profits can be ruled in and stabilized by stasis 5. There is a feedback loop from stasis 5 to stasis 1: "financial reason," in a sense.

34 Truths are sovereign symbolic representations that "protect" us even better than divinities and money against the dangers of our lifeworld and especially against our own spontaneous behaviors.

35 I insist that there is nothing new in the alliance between sovereignty and religion. Its basic expression is the very existence of money, created at least 3000 years ago. Religion created the "quality" of money, while sovereignty took care of its controlled quantity. Still, stasis 5 and 6 can be kept distinct, as in the world's admittedly few secular regimes. Ethno-religious passions frequently disturb this distinctive condition.

36 My cognitive science colleague Todd Oakley comments that bitcoin is not money, unless you can pay taxes with it. An open theoretical question; I think he may be right, in the sense that to be money is to be able to connect the levels of capital in integrated flows.

37 An anonymous reader of this essay, who evidently is a heterodox economist, comments interestingly on the question: "It depends on the institutions around it. The power of sovereign currency systems to fulfill a public purpose that stabilizes societies is indeed possible, at least for a time, but pathological fears of insolvency (not possible for sovereign currencies) and inflation (not on the horizon) is a great hurdle to overcome. It also means embracing the transgressive prerogatives of the state (which can be used to fulfill the public purpose just as much as to aggrandize the sovereign)." Print more money.

38 Max Weber already pointed out the close connection between economy and religion, but in a different key, namely, as a relation between moral standards of Protestantism, especially Calvinism, and the norms of industrial capitalism. My more general view is that economy is religious in its very origin and core.

39 "What is a sign?" (1894), §8: "Symbols grow. They come into being by development out of other signs, particularly from likenesses or from mixed signs partaking of the nature of likenesses and symbols. We think only in signs. These mental signs are of mixed nature; the symbol-parts of them are called concepts. If a man makes a new symbol, it is by thoughts involving concepts. So it is only out of symbols that a new symbol can grow. *Omne symbolum de symbolo.* A symbol, once in being, spreads among the peoples. In use and in experience, its meaning grows. Such words as *force, law, wealth, marriage,* bear for us very different meanings from those they bore to our barbarous ancestors. The symbol may, with Emerson's sphynx, say to man, Of thine eye I am eyebeam."

40 See Rossi-Landi (1975), Baudrillard (1972), and Bataille (1949). The Swiss linguist Ferdinand de Saussure ((1915) 1962) famously says, in Chapter IV of his *Cours de linguistique générale,* where he discusses what he calls *value* as opposed to *signification,* in language: "To determine what a five-franc piece is worth one must therefore know: (1) that it can be exchanged for a fixed quantity of a different thing, e.g. bread; and (2) that it can be compared with a similar value of the same system, e.g. a one-franc piece, or with coins of another system (a dollar, etc.). In the same way, a word can be exchanged for something dissimilar, an idea; besides, it can be compared with something of the same nature, another word. Its value is therefore not fixed so long as one simply states that it can be 'exchanged' for a given concept, i.e. that it has this or that signification: one must also compare it with similar values, with other words that stand in opposition to it. Its content is really fixed only by the concurrence of everything that exists outside it. Being part of a system, it is endowed not only with a signification but also and especially with a value, and this is something quite different" (accurate translation by Wade Baskin, Internet Archive). The question is whether signification and value can be separated totally. In the case of money, the quantitative value of coins is dependent on their being carriers of protective force; in the case of words, their interdependent "value" depends on their significance as carriers of meaning that can support the communication of thoughts. If the understanding of things protects us from dangers, we have here an analogous function of money and language in terms of signification, rather than of meaning.

41 Fontanille (1998).

42 To speak is to give a part of oneself to someone who listens and takes what is being offered in good faith. Hence speaking in "bad faith" is reprehensible per se. I call this the inherent ethics in language use.

43 As the French ecologist, formerly minister, Nicolas Hulot writes on the web page of his association: "In 2050, two hundred fifty millions of people will be forced to leave their habitat by extreme meteorological events (cyclones, typhoons, floods...). The rising waters may swallow between ten thousand and twenty thousand islands, many of them inhabited. One out of six animal species may definitively disappear."

44 See Jacques Lacan (1966, 1975), and passim. Lacan proposed to see the three orders as intertwined by a Borromean knot of three rings, each of which holds together the two others. Lacan is a difficult read, compared to Freud, but his three orders, developed in the discussion around the structuralist turn of psychoanalysis and the humanities in the 1960s, may be one of his lasting contributions to social psychology.

45 In "Elements in Poetic Space" (this volume), we have seen a similar tripartition of experiential and emotional meaning: the bio-imaginary (I), the socio-imaginary (II), and the phantasmatic imaginary (III). According to Larsen's (ibid.) groundbreaking analysis, madness occurs when (I) and (III) merge, which happens in psychosis and other critical mental states; the phoric values share orientation in these zones of bodily feeling: euphoric proximity, dysphoric distality. The subject wishes to be "near to God," for example.
46 Whereas the inclusive *we* expresses ordinary social subjectivity, the exclusive *we* (= *we, but not you*) may be in the same game as the royal *we*, an expression of power. In fact, power is essentially exclusion.
47 In fact, the affective triad—Symbolic moods, Imaginary emotions, Real passions—even corresponds to a basic semiotic triad distinguishing symbolic signs, diagrammatic signs, and iconic signs. Ecology is pervasive.
48 Psychoanalysis as a paid cure—a moneto-therapy—is itself a symptom of monetary submission.

References

Agamben, G., 1995. *Homo sacer. Il potere sovrano e la nuda vita*. Torino: Einaudi.
Antonelli, E., 2018. "Del denaro, ovvero di un supplemento di presenza." *Studi di estetica*, anno XLVI, IV serie, 2.
Bataille, G., 1949. *La part maudite* (The cursed share). Paris: Minuit. In: *Œuvres Complètes*, Vol. 7. Paris: Gallimard.
Bataille, G., 1944. *Le coupable*. Paris: Gallimard. In *Œ. C.* Vol. 5.
Baudrillard, J., 1972. *Pour une critique de l'économie politique du signe*. Paris: Gallimard.
Brandt, P. A., 2015a. "La construction sémio-cognitive de la valeur économique." In: (Ed.) A. Biglari. *Valeurs. Aux fondements de la sémiotique*. Paris: L'Harmattan.
Brandt, P. A., 2015b. "On the Origin and Ontology of Money. A Brief Note." ResearchGate.
Diamond, J., 1994. "Ecological Collapses of Past Civilizations." *Proceedings of the American Philosophical Society*, 138 (3).
Fontanille, J., 1998. *Sémiotique du discours*. Limoges: Presses Universitaires de Limoges.
Foucault, M., 1971. *L'ordre du discours. Leçon inaugurale au Collège de France prononcée le 2 décembre 1970*. Paris: Gallimard.
Graeber, D., 2011. *Debt. The First 5,000 Years*. New York: Melville House.
Jaspers, K., 1949. *Vom Ursprung und Ziel der Geschichte* [The Origin and Goal of History]. München: Piper.
Kelly, P. H. (Ed.), 1991. *Locke on Money*. Oxford: Clarendon Press.
Keynes, J. M., 1919. *The Economic Consequences of the Peace*. New York: Harcourt, Brace, and Howe.
Lacan, J., 1966. *Écrits*. Paris: Éditions du Seuil. Le champ freudien.
Lacan, J., 1975. *Encore (1972–1973). Livre XX du Séminaire*. Texte établi par Jacques-Alain Miller. Paris: Éditions du Seuil.
Minsky, H., 1986. *Stabilizing an Unstable Economy*. New Haven: Yale University Press.
Monsaingeon, B., 2017. *Homo detritus. Critique de la société du déchet*. Paris: Le Seuil.
Rossi-Landi, F., 1975. *Linguistics and Economics*. The Hague: Mouton.
de Saussure, F., 1962. *Cours de linguistique générale*. Fifth ed. Paris: Payot.

Schmandt-Besserat, D., 1996. *How Writing Came About*. Austin, Texas: University of Texas Press.

Tonkonoff, S., 2012. "Homo Violens. El Criminal Monstruoso según Georges Bataille." *Gramma*, XXIII, 49.1. Buenos Aires.

Weber, M., 1905, 2016. *Die protestantische Ethik und der Geist des Kapitalismus*. Berlin: Holzinger.

Wray, L. R., 1990. *Money and Credit in Capitalist Economies: The Endogenous Money Approach*. Aldershot: Edward Elgar.

15

Postscript

In this postscript, I will shortly summarize and integrate some of the apparently wildly diverse perspectives unfolded in this book. The widest horizon will be that of the semio-cognitive framework of the sociohistorical world and its conditions in nature; the most restricted perspective would be that of the individual psychological mind and its conditions in brain and body. In between, we can situate the realms of cognitive-semiotic displays, from language and discourse to art. As we have seen, social semiotics may be grounded in a general ecology of human societies. The cycles of extraction and expulsion that characterize the interaction between nature and "culture" in the fundamental sense of human habitat essentially form three ecological layers: a basic *organic* layer, an organizational, *political* layer, and finally an overarching symbolic, *identitary* layer (terms are arbitrary and will be allowed to vary until consensus be reached). Firstly, we need to eat and breed; secondly, we need to organize and produce for stabilization, protection, and improvement of life; and ultimately, we need community, order, and authority to be signified in such a way that the population can orient itself as a society, a "people," defined by a sense of unity (order) and identity (authority).

Meaning unfolds differently on each level. "Organic" meaning is intimate, existential, and predominantly iconic; we remember our personal life in a format close to the sensory register and react affectively to images and other perceptive traces of our past or sensations in the present. We could semiotically speak of an iconic anchoring of our life.

"Political" meaning, by contrast, is conceptual, epistemic, constructive, strategic, imaginative, and representative of what we call thinking proper. Semiotically, we may fundamentally be thinking constructively, "rationally," schematically by topologies, that is, in mental or expressed diagrams that allow us to unfold our ideational and encyclopedic spiderwebs of ever-changing concepts. Finally, symbolic "identitary" meaning is, tautologically speaking, clearly marked by symbols, giving privilege to performative, imperative, ritual acts and feelings of sacredness.[1] The unity of the collective being, symbolized by the (armed) ruler, and the identity of the same collective being, symbolized by the (wealthy) authority of a ceremonial priest of some religion (not necessarily well defined), constitute the transcendent heterology of societies and now of the entire planetary sociosphere.

So, I have distinguished the performative (symbolic), the informative (imaginary), and the formative (existential) meaning as the three constitutive modes and levels of meaning in society, in communication, and in the mind.

This correspondence between social-ecological categories and meaning modes means that semiotics may be shaped by the semiotic evolution of our species that stratified all human social formations and simultaneously stratified the human minds that they implied. Social feelings are natural; in a sense, we "are" our society. We are mentally shaped by our social evolution in such a way that our intimate existential and affective imagery is connected to our epistemic conceptual cognition and to our performative dynamics by what I have discussed as our stratified mental architecture. Language testifies to the latter, and language no doubt developed in the mental interstice separating the "lower somatic" level of sensory perception from the "higher somatic" level of our semanticized affectivity. Language may have contributed to the categorical stabilization of this mental interstice in our soma that makes it both a mental architecture and a scaffolding of the basic properties of language.

I would like to elaborate a bit more on the ecological view of social meaning. On the "identitary" or symbolic level, I placed rulers and priests. They are not exactly the same, though; rulers provide unitary order, and priests provide authority (sacredness of principles). Their alliance provides so-called *sovereignty*; however, sacred principles are mostly disruptive, unorderly, often belligerent, anti-legalist. The alliance covers a conflict within the realm of sovereign power and on all social levels depending on it. As money and capitals illustrate, the order of monetary exchange is also a disorder of ill- or undistributed wealth, systematic "egalitarian unequality," so to speak. Semiotically, and as Georges Bataille observed, sovereignty relies on a constitutive grounding in Death. Social power emanating from this sovereign level in fact builds on performativity in the two conflicting modes corresponding to the *two ways in which we die*: there is a *formal* power based on nominal rituals and divine oversight, represented by the priests and of course referring to dying by chance, or destiny, decided by fate, that is, the divinities; and there is a *substantial* power based on the exertion of concrete violence and brute force, required for physical punishment, the origin of law.[2] Both modes, and their alliance, are grounded in the most "spiritual" motive of human beings, the absolute reality of *Death*. That is the absolute from where all power emanates and to where it returns (e.g., in civil wars).

So, if I am right about this, the model I once (Brandt 2004) proposed for the analysis of urban semiotics[3] may now be generalized to cover the social formation as such. There is a dynamic conflict opposing the (origin of) *Law* and the (origin of) *Name*, the substantial and the formal power, the armed ruler and the magical priest, and it runs all the way down through the institutional and political complexity to the concrete, organic opposition of work (Law) and family (Name) in the scope of every living person. On the political or civil level, we get an opposition between what is common (order, institutions, more or less violent; *laws* of all kinds) and what is proprietary (in modern states: goods, real estate, markets, brands and chaotic competition, chance, arbitrariness; *names* of all kinds). As subjects of the (unitary) law we are "same," equal, and as subjects of the (identitary) name, different, unequal—our feelings want both to be *unified* as same and to be *identified* as different, however contradictory this double desire may be.

The topology of the Thomian catastrophe called a cusp opposes in a suitable interpretation two attractors and shows how they locally merge or locally diverge along an axis that I now suggest to articulate following the ecological stratification—which also allows us to illustrate the continuity of the social transitions from level to level in the perspective of the experienced social reality. The result is the following topological graph representing the instances that a society must comprise.

The basic attractors of the topology, here just short-termed Law and Name, are evidently represented in the schematisms of the individual human mind, namely, by the dynamic opposition of two standard concepts of personal identity, the "legalistic" and *numerical identity* (I am just anyone, a civil person, in the eyes of the law) and the *qualitative identity* (I am someone belonging to a very special group equipped with highly valuable cultural and natural qualities and thus deserving general respect in the Olympian eyes of a God or History). In this sense, the topology also accounts for certain conflicting semiotic properties of human subjectivity. Our styles of thinking and the typology of signs reflect this isomorphism, which as mentioned is likely to be grounded in human evolution.

Individually, we think and speak in the symbolic style when we impose obligations on ourselves and others or when we grant permissions, give advice, make declarations, or otherwise perform the *modal* repertoire of "speech" acts of monitoring and control, which by the way should rather be termed symbolic acts.[4] Here, we are our own or each other's rulers and priests, so to speak.

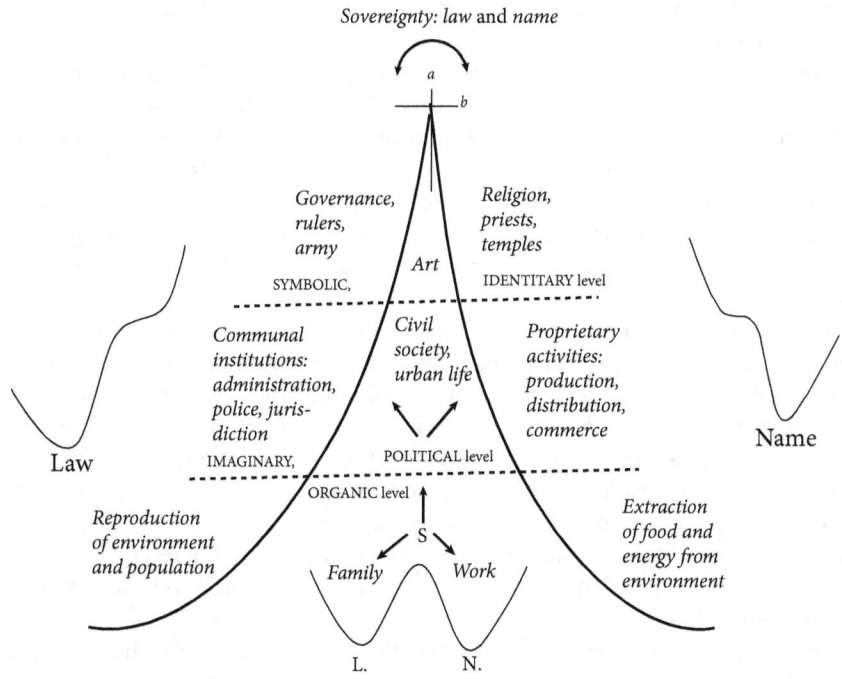

The cusp topology equation: $y = x^4 + ax^2 + bx$

Figure 15.1 A socio-ecological topology.

We individually switch to the organic and affective style of intimacy when we find ourselves in markedly aesthetic and existential situations, such as making love, enjoying art, or being in immediate sensory contact with the natural world. By contrast to the symbolic style, we may describe this mode of meaning as *demodalized*; the only modality that persists is of course basic "root" *possibility*—since *what is* belongs to what is possible or impossible (miraculous).

We think in the imaginary style when we try to understand and develop problems of all kinds, imagine solutions and "strategies," "policies," or simply imagine causal connections between things. *Imagination* in this sense is epistemic, basically hypothetic, and creative, and in this capacity, it feeds both (upward) the symbolic and (downward) the intimate registers of passionate "reasoning." This style and mode of meaning is particularly often shared; we collaborate in epistemic and critical thinking, such as science, education, politics, social planning of all kinds. This is also the mode of poetic imagination, as we have seen, where a phenomenology of elements opens us to the conceptual representation of all registers of affectivity, from the intimate (bio-imaginary) to the sovereign (phantasmatic).

Semiotically speaking, the signs we call *symbols* are the forms of semiosis that pertain to the symbolic levels of meaning-making. The symbolic force of the deixis that binds its signifiers, mostly conventional, to its signifieds, often related to acts and attitudes, is what defines the performative mode. Symbols are always some kind of powerful instructions. Some are monumental, others more discreet, but all eventually express modalized programs for agents.

By contrast, the signs that carry the communication we unfold in the intimate and affective register are those properly called *icons*. Here, the semiosis is assured by a deixis that presents the signifiers as framed images of experienced or experienceable contents. Our intimate episodic memory is entirely iconic in this sense. Emotions carry images of what they mean, and images carry potential emotions corresponding to what they show. Therefore, icons function as the mind's affective markers of what we remember, even when it is epistemic and abstractly "semantic" in Endel Tulving's sense (1972).

Icons are regularly confused with the *diagrams* our mind uses for its imaginary endeavors. From our daily weather reports to our theoretical representations, from maps and charts to our models and mathematical or musical explorations, diagrams are the spontaneous, core semiotic expressions of constructive imagination. A diagram does not present an experienceable content but an immaterial, hypothetical space, an imagined topology of variable dimensions and variable plasticity, that allows us to synthesize and analyze an idea by rotation, zooming, projection, mereological change, conceptual investment (letting labeled concepts be positioned within its critical points and zones), and comparison to other topologies (i.e., analogy) and conceptually blending with them.

The problem of the origin of the remarkably stable inventory of human sign types, which Peirce tried to solve by introducing his phaneroscopic concepts of firstness, secondness, and thirdness, may in fact be compared to the ecological model presented here. His signs of firstness are indeed *iconic* and, unsurprisingly, in exactly the same perception-based sense as the above notion. His secondness signs, however, would correspond to our *symbolic* signs because of the dynamics of the modal determinations involved. Traffic signs, for example, are symbolic instructions, indicators of urban secondness. Peirce's thirdness, where his semeiotics is supposed to become a logic, is what I have described as the (second ecological level) meaning mode of imagination, characterized by diagrams and mental topologies—which is what purely "logical," truth-oriented, epistemic thinking is made of. The semiotic model of mental spaces and conceptual blending, discussed in Chapters 6–8, is a way to describe meaning production in the imaginary mode; diagrams appear in the relevance component of all blending networks. Peirce's three "nesses," and his one-two-three progression, however, do not really offer an answer to the question of the origin of sign classes; it is not the "firstness" of the icons that constitutes them but rather the function of perception in the affective mind and the function of emotional images in memory; these are interrelated cognitive functions that dwell far from Peirce's concerns. Similarly, it is not the triangular "thirdness" in symbols (Representamen, Object, Interpretant) that constitutes them as symbols but rather their intersubjective performativity based on the dynamics of modality, a totally different story. As to the intermediate "secondness" of the Peircean index, it may be one of the most stubborn misunderstandings in the history of semiotics. Not seeing the difference between icons and diagrams prevented the American philosopher and his followers from grasping the topological originality of diagrammatic signs and the primordial role of this sign type in expressed reasoning, though he indeed saw the importance of diagrams in reasoning. Diagrams are expressed mental topologies that may *contain* icons and symbols, but it is their particular *nonfigurative*, abstract, geometrical forms, so to speak, that makes them serve human, nonfigurative thinking.[5]

Indices, understood as natural signs, whether causal or mereological, have to be mentally *diagrammed*, that is, schematized, in order to make sense. They are only "signs" in a metaphorical sense, since nature does not communicate in the intentional human and animal sense. The additional confusion between index and deixis makes the disaster complete, except for historians of philosophy. Deixis is the calling, "phatic" function (Jakobson 1960) of all signs, a calling function that precedes their cognitive specification into icon, symbol or diagram, and more complex signs.

What happens to the semiotics of language, linguistics, in this framework? Linguistic structure may in fact be somewhat more accessible to modeling here than in current linguistic theory. Theories of language must be usage-based, since there is no coherent system in language, although there are components and an architecture. Linguistic deixis is a basic communicative function organized in the component we have called *enunciation*. This component specifies the subject-to-subject (I/you) relation presupposed in dialogue and discourse; and in language use, it is superimposed on all other components of linguistic structure. *Words* (lexemes and morphemes) and *sentences* (syntax and semantics) are the two essential parts of linguistic structure, and both are marked by enunciation, when we speak or write, when choices of expression are made, and texts emerge. I have argued that apart from being what sentences are made of, words have a privileged connection to the internal patterns of thought (whether affective, epistemic, or performative), because as labels, they primarily refer to instances in topologies. Therefore, words form paradigmatic groups within the encyclopedic cultural memory of speakers.

When words integrate into sentences that follow the principles of sentential semantics, propositional contents arise, and these contents again refer to the internal patterns of thought; we often correct ourselves while speaking, because our monitoring of the way sentence meanings *simulate* parts of our thinking is variable, both in granularity and in exactitude. As Alice (in Wonderland) explains to the Mad Hatter, to say that I say what I mean and to say that I mean what I say are certainly not the same, and meaning and saying are always in a potentially conflicting relation, since saying, signing, showing come with enunciative structure, while thinking ("meaning" as such) does not.

Phonetics, writing, and gesture all together structure the lexical signifier, often in complicated ways, and they also determine the significant melo-rhythmic phrasing of sentences and larger rhetorical sequences. The identity of each word is a matter of alliances between a panorama of sounds, gestures, written traits, and a panorama of meanings; how this all-important complex phenomenon works is still not well understood, but it is likely that an intentional and potentially shared reference to an activated *concept* is implied. Words are always ambiguous in themselves. Sentence semantics is never unambiguous for a similar reason: we have to go back to internally activated *concepts* in order to "understand" what is "meant." Thought does not need language nearly as much as language needs thought in order to function. Maybe the same can be said, ontologically, about cognition and semiotics: the latter needs the former more than the inverse. However, methodologically, the *study* of cognition is literally impossible without some (implied or conceptualized) form of semiotic approach.

And the *study* of meaning, which most often stays intuitive and entirely, exclusively historical, as in the current academic disciplines of the humanities, arts, and social sciences, would gain substantial insights from including the concern for the very conditions of *possibility* of meaning that a cognitive semiotics offers. I hope to have argued for this idea in this book about signs, mind, and meaning. Those technical terms in fact refer to basic aspects of the human world; if I could argue less technically, I would not hesitate to do that. But the problem of understanding meaning may really be one of the hardest in the world. That is because in a sense, meaning, immaterial reality, is *us*, our precious selves, who do not necessarily wish to be known. We resist but need to resist to that resistance. Our species must *understand*; without understanding we would not be here and will not be here for long.

***

Notes

1   When the political level of a society collapses, which happens regularly, the identitary and the organic tend to merge, creating what we know as the modern mob-identitary phenomenon of fascisms, ethnicisms, racisms, populisms, and militant nationalisms.

2   This argument, or observation, was made by Jacques Derrida, *Donner la mort*, 1999. I remember having contested its cynicism, but I admit his point. Legality must be and is based on substantial power, that is, unidirectional violence; this is the well-known problem for international law.
3   I originally presented the Thomian dynamic model of urban spatial meaning, opposing the strata of formal and substantial power, in the last chapter of *Spaces, Domains, and Meaning* (Brandt 2004) "What's New?—50,000 Years of Modernism."
4   This is what I meant by *La charpente modale du sens* (*The Modal Timberwork of Meaning*) 1992. In this book, I introduced catastrophe-topological models of various forms of modality in order to describe these symbolic phenomena in narrative, argumentative, and simply grammatical contexts.
5   The cusp figure shown above is an example of such nonfigurative representations in thinking.

Index

absurdity
  in metaphor 92
  in narrativity 117–121
actants 49, 153–155
agency 20, 95, 214
  agency in puns 149
art 35–36, 47–48, 78, 206, 209

Barthes, Roland 2, 39, 140
Benveniste, Emile 6, 54, 138
blending 65, 72–79, 89–97
  in exchange 195–196
  in songs 103–110
  in the imaginary 235
Borges, Jorge Luis 127–131

catastrophe theory 84–85, 96
  in narratives 124–132, 140
  in social topology 232–233, 237
causation 94–95, 99, 119, 134, 136, 139, 143
change 84, 94–96, 119
  agentive 133–136, 139, 142–143
Cohen, Leonard 5, 103–115
comparisons 72, 86, 95
conditionals 59–60, 84, 98
  counterfactual 86, 89
connotation 36, 39, 53, 194
consciousness 12, 16, 22, 27, 31–38, 41–48
  animal 143
  architecture of 86–89
  disembodied 50
  ecological 204
  embodied 51
  five levels of 51
  linguistic 49
  situational 97, 194
Copeland, Brooklyn 156–159
counterfactuals 19, 54, 63, 84, 124, 127

deixis 52, 83, 88, 109, 114, 118, 184, 188, 234, 235
  enunciation as deixis 178
Derrida, Jacques 27, 158, 237
Descartes, René 3, 11, 15–29, 51, 70, 157
diagrams 21, 28, 39, 99, 228, 231, 234–235
  actantial 155
  blending 79, 83, 113
  force-barrier 135–136
  mental 195
  narrative 133
  semiotic square 143
dialogue 4, 33, 57, 68, 95, 148, 175
  arguments in 59–60, 74
  deixis in dialogue 235
  in poetry 62–63
  in prayer 61
  rhythm in dialogue 195
diegesis 5, 117, 122–132
discourse 2, 4–12, 33, 51, 57
  base spaces and discourse 68
  construction model of discourse 59
  discourse as semiosis 151
  discourse linguistics 65
  discourse meaning 63, 80
  discourse *quanta* 63
  discourse semantics 175–177, 181–183
  narrative, descriptive, argumentative 117–118
  public sphere of discourse 211–218
Donald, Merlin 22, 40, 194, 200
dualism 3, 11
  causal dualism 18, 25
  methodological 16
  substance dualism 17, 25

Eco, Umberto 2, 39, 159
écriture 63, 78, 150
enunciation 6, 49, 54, 59, 84, 86, 103, 150, 175–178, 183–185, 221, 226, 235

as deixis 178
ethics of enunciation 218
hyperbolic 127
Nietzschean 157
as semiosis 151
in songs (melic) 103
ethics 4, 8, 21, 27, 45–48, 51, 125
versus money 213, 215, 218–220
of translation 151–153
exchange 2, 4, 7–8, 42–43, 52, 195–196
of bullets 179–180
of goods 207, 223
imaginary 57
intertextual 159
intimate 107
in Mauss 53
monetary 232
in Saussure 227
unstable 181

Fénéon, Félix 7, 179, 181–184
Fauconnier, Gilles 1, 23, 27, 28, 65–81, 83, 90, 98, 99, 113, 195
Foucault, Michel 185, 218
Freud, Sigmund 22, 26, 143, 227

Gestalts 7, 52, 87, 97, 111, 158
rhythmic 190
tonal, verbal 103
God 4, 11, 17, 26, 68, 126, 128, 130–131, 228
Aztec 54
in Cohen 105, 109–110
gods and money 224
gods and numbers 191
or Nature 18–19, 25
in the calendar 191
Greimas, Algirdas-Julien 1, 53, 80, 113, 135, 138, 141, 143, 152, 153–154, 159, 162, 172, 181

Hemingway, Ernest 131–132
Hjelmslev, Louis 1, 147, 150, 175, 185, 203
hypothesis 4, 26, 93–95, 99

iconicity 3, 35–38, 40
agonistic 48
antagonistic 43

imaginary 6, 8, 18, 20, 23–24, 32, 88, 161, 195, 219–221, 231, 233–235
bio-, socio-, phantasmatic 161–172
blend 76
emotions 228
experimental 27, 131
in music 190
space delegation 75
spaces 67–68, 80, 88, 99
present 109
property of money 209

Jakobson, Roman 5, 22, 26, 46, 121, 138, 147–148, 158, 235

Lacan, Jacques 22, 219–221, 227
Lakoff, George 7, 23, 27, 28, 98, 143, 187, 199
Langacker, Ronald 1, 58
Larsen, Hans-Erik 6, 161–163, 172, 228
love 4, 5, 8, 10, 28, 31, 38, 47–48, 51, 62, 63, 78–79, 87, 92, 105, 108, 110, 164, 168–169, 192, 194, 199, 220, 221
of God 61, 108
making 234
in metaphor 9, 143
in song 109
in story 131–133, 142
in translation 158

Marx, Karl 7, 195–196, 200, 207, 208, 210, 223
Matisse, Henri 4, 77–79
Maupassant, Guy de 5, 122–127, 141, 144, 224
metaphor 4, 6, 7, 23, 33, 70, 73, 91–93, 98–99, 106, 149, 162
arithmetic 187, 199
conceptual 23, 26–27, 73–74, 143, 158, 187
de-metaphorized 149
macro-metaphor 109
political 172, 210
structural 86
synesthesic 39
metonymy 47–53, 78
mimesis 53, 56, 78, 79, 194, 200

money 2, 7–8, 181, 196, 200, 203, 207–227, 232
  fiat, bona fide 223
  madness of 212, 218
  meaning of 213
  ontology of 223
  semantics of 209
  speculative 216, 218
  in stories 122, 126, 127–128, 142
monism 3, 18, 20
  causal monism 17, 25
  substance monism 17, 25, 27
music 5, 7, 13, 24, 31, 34, 36, 39, 40, 50, 76, 87, 96, 105, 148, 151, 176, 186, 190, 192, 194, 219, 234
  god of 114
  intersubjective musicking 190
  jazz music 90–91
  music in blending 108–110
  musical cognition 51
  musical imagination 162, 171
  in poetry 159
  sung music 103–104
  in synesthesia 197–199

narrativity 3–6, 9, 24, 31–35, 37, 45–46, 51, 52, 54, 87, 94, 117–133, 148, 194
  event spaces 122, 124
  micro-, macro-narrative 183
  narrative forces 119
  narrative genres, worlds 120
  narrative semantics 153–154, 175
  phenomenology 134
  in songs 103, 110

Peirce, Charles S. 1, 4, 11, 15, 21, 39, 99, 217, 226, 234, 235
Petitot, Jean 1, 96, 100

real 17
  symbolic, imaginary, real 219–221, 228
relevance 39, 52, 60, 64, 76, 78, 80, 89, 113, 195, 220, 235
  in enunciation 178
  relevance schema 76, 77, 79, 90, 91, 92, 94, 95, 98, 106, 107, 108, 110, 196
  relevance space 81, 98
rhythm 7, 44, 50, 63, 154, 159, 167, 190–195, 198, 200, 221, 236

Saussure, Ferdinand de 1, 19, 24, 26, 58, 147, 150, 175, 176, 199, 227
semiosis 4, 6, 9, 13, 16, 24, 34, 44, 76, 88, 122, 151, 198, 234
Södergran, Edith 6, 156–157
Spinoza, Baruch 3, 4, 11, 15, 16–23, 25–27, 65, 67, 68, 69, 70, 80, 158
stemmatic 6, 159, 179, 180, 185
structuralism 2, 12, 22
style 16, 17, 36, 39, 48, 63, 65, 68, 69, 71, 77, 78, 79, 233
  affective 234
  aspectual 178
  behavioral 215
  discursive 212
  dynamic 120
  enunciation 154
  imaginary 234
  intentional 200
  management 226
  narrator 139
  symbolic 233, 234
symbolic 4, 7, 8, 22, 27, 28, 34–36, 38, 39, 44, 46, 51, 53, 88, 128, 132, 142, 190–192, 194, 198, 221, 222, 223, 235, 237
  acts 220
  affect 228
  aspect of sign 221
  instructions 235
  loop, level 205–209, 225, 232–233
  style 233, 234
synesthesia 39, 88, 197–200
Sweetser, Eve 1, 96, 97, 134, 139, 143

Talmy, Leonard 1, 96, 134, 139, 143, 184
Tesnière, Lucien 6, 159
Thymic 6, 9, 161–164, 172
translation 5–6, 21, 33, 147–159
  dynamics of 155
  ethics of 151, 152
  genres of 153
  poetic 156
  semiotic formula 147
Tu Fu, 6, 171
Turner, Mark 1, 23, 27, 28, 54, 69, 72, 75, 76, 80, 81, 90, 97, 98, 99, 113, 138, 195

Waldrop, Rosmarie 4, 62, 64
Wildgen, Wolfgang 1, 96, 171
word 6, 7, 8, 26, 33, 98, 151, 175, 176–185, 187, 200, 220, 222, 223, 227, 235, 236
    deictic 109
    meanings 59
    password 124, 141
    in poem 62, 63, 104
    rewording 155
    wording of song 104, 107
Wordsworth, William 6, 161, 164–171, 200

Yeats, William Butler 6, 161, 165–171, 172

www.ingramcontent.com/pod-product-compliance
Lightning Source LLC
Chambersburg PA
CBHW052113010526
44111CB00036B/1984